Emperor Titus

Emperor Titus
The Right Hand of Vespasian

MARC HYDEN

McFarland & Company, Inc., Publishers
Jefferson, North Carolina

All maps and photographs are by the author.

ISBN (print) 978-1-4766-9747-5
ISBN (ebook) 978-1-4766-5623-6

LIBRARY OF CONGRESS CATALOGING DATA ARE AVAILABLE

Library of Congress Control Number 2025017041

© 2025 Marc Hyden. All rights reserved

No part of this book may be reproduced or transmitted in any form or by any means, electronic or mechanical, including photocopying or recording, or by any information storage and retrieval system, without permission in writing from the publisher.

Front cover image: "Scene from the Arch of Titus," Jean-Guillaume Moitte (France, Paris, 1746–1810, active Italy, Rome) circa 1791, Sculpture Earthenware 14 × 24 × 2.5 in., (Gift of Camilla Chandler Frost [M.86.322.1] Los Angeles County Museum of Art).

Printed in the United States of America

*McFarland & Company, Inc., Publishers
Box 611, Jefferson, North Carolina 28640
www.mcfarlandpub.com*

To my beautiful and supportive wife
and our perfect little child.

You hold my heart.

Table of Contents

Preface 1

I	Flavians	3
II	Titus	12
III	Boudica	22
IV	Judaea	32
V	Jotapata	43
VI	Tarichaea	54
VII	Gischala	62
VIII	Vindex	70
IX	Antonius Primus	80
X	Kidron	88
XI	Jerusalem	96
XII	Nikon	105
XIII	Crucifixions	113
XIV	Antonia	122
XV	Temple	128
XVI	John and Simon	137
XVII	Triumph	144
XVIII	Caesar	153
XIX	Praetorian Prefect	165
XX	Princeps	172
XXI	Vesuvius	180
XXII	Amphitheatrum	187
XXIII	Domitian	197

Chapter Notes 207
Bibliography 225
Index 227

Preface

For over two millennia, people have marveled at ancient Rome's military and architectural accomplishments and the storied individuals behind them. Julius Caesar, Augustus, Trajan, Hadrian, Constantine and many others have received the attention of historians, and for good reason. Their triumphs far surpassed those of their contemporaries. These figures have since enjoyed myriad historical volumes dedicated to their lives and achievements, but many other Romans have been sadly neglected, including one of ancient Rome's most celebrated—but enigmatic and polarizing—emperors: Titus.

As I write this, there has only been one long-form biography about Titus ever published in English. Esteemed historian Brian W. Jones wrote the book over 40 years ago, and it is no longer in print. Despite it being an impressive piece of scholarship, it was far from comprehensive. Between Jones' limited account of Titus' life and other historians' disregard for the emperor, there are significant gaps in the modern historical record. This is a tragic disservice to one of Rome's more recognizable names.

Titus lived a life of adventure and is inextricably linked to more decisive events and calamities in Roman history than most others. At an early age, he survived imperial turnover and even the assassination of his friend Britannicus (Emperor Claudius' son)—an act that nearly also ensnared Titus. Not terribly long after, he served in Britannia after the Boudica rebellion, and he lived through the Great Fire of Rome in 64 CE, as Emperor Nero purportedly fiddled.

Following Nero's death, Titus played a contributing role in the tumultuous Year of the Four Emperors that ultimately led to Vespasian's coronation. This permitted Titus to take command of the ongoing Judaean campaign in which he eventually sacked Jerusalem and mostly brought the First Jewish Revolt to a close. Then he shared the burden of ruling Rome with his father until Vespasian passed away.

Titus subsequently became emperor and presided over the empire as disasters ravaged it. During his reign, Vesuvius destroyed numerous cities and fire and plague gripped Rome, but the ever-capable Titus responded with great aplomb. He also helped build Rome's greatest and most well-known construction, the Colosseum, where he hosted much of the inaugural hundred days of games. All the while, he witnessed early Christianity slowly spreading across the empire. Love him or hate him, there are few pivotal figures like Titus who straddled more momentous history.

Given all of this, it is easy to understand why he is such a fascinating character and why it is important to raise his profile once again. To end his long-term neglect, I pieced together a comprehensive biography—drawing on the scant ancient sources (primarily Suetonius, Cassius Dio, Josephus and Tacitus), modern academic commentary and archaeological findings. Together, they provide the fullest known account of his life, but doing so was no easy feat.

There are numerous problems with the ancient sources. Suetonius' *Life of Titus* is brief, and Suetonius often presents events thematically instead of chronologically. Moreover, some of Suetonius' writings are suspect, considering that he had a penchant for presenting salacious rumors as veritable history. While Cassius Dio was a more serious historian, his narrative covering Titus' life is similarly limited in scope. Meanwhile, Tacitus' *The Histories* offers some clues that contribute to Titus' biography. However, it is important to remember that the Flavians were Tacitus' benefactors, and Tacitus was hostile to the Jewish people who played a large role in Titus' ascent—meaning his account may not be entirely fair and balanced. What's more, the volume of *The Histories* that presumably outlined the latter part of Titus' life is no longer extant.

Josephus' *The Jewish War* is markedly different from the previously mentioned literary works. It provides the most detailed account of Titus' time in Judaea, but it is also hardly objective and unbiased. Josephus was a general in the Jewish revolt who fought against the Romans. So he had reason to overstate his importance and impact on the war, and he bore grudges against some of his countrymen, which may explain why he denigrated certain rebel leaders. Likewise, he was quick to criticize the insurgents as a whole and called some of them terrorists while largely praising the Romans, including Vespasian and especially Titus.

Josephus even strove to exculpate the Flavians from some of the more unfortunate events in the Jewish War, including the holy Temple's needless destruction, and he had good reason to do so. The Flavians spoiled Josephus—even sparing his life upon capturing him in Jotapata—and provided him an apartment in Vespasian's home and land in Judaea. Because of this, it is clear why Josephus—despite being a Jewish Pharisee—drafted an account of the war that largely sided with the Romans and presented Titus in glowing fashion.

Many of the ancient writers who chronicled the era fawned over Vespasian and Titus were decidedly pro-Roman and some were overtly anti-Jewish, which results in a largely one-sided historical record. While the ancient works contain biases, some suspect accounts and other limitations, they are still essential works that help build a broader picture of who Titus was. Parsing through them is challenging, but when combined with archaeological findings and modern commentary, an amazing story comes into focus. Thanks to the diligent work of ancient and modern historians, this manuscript is possible, and it represents the most complete biography of Titus ever undertaken—one that will hopefully end his long-term neglect.

I

Flavians

> *"This house was, it is true, obscure and without family portraits, yet it was one of which our country had no reason [whatsoever] to be ashamed."*
> —Suetonius[1]

In 71 CE, Titus Flavius Vespasianus—better known as Titus—entered the city of Rome alongside his father Vespasian, the recently christened Roman emperor and progenitor of what became the Flavian dynasty. Accompanied by musicians, loyal legionaries adorned with laurel and the spoils of their recent military victories, the father-son duo leisurely rode through Rome's narrow streets in a jubilant triumph. Romans rich and poor lined the sinuous avenues and climbed atop roofs to capture a glimpse of the euphoric, gaudy parade as they applauded and shouted in support of their emperor and his heir-apparent, Titus.

The two Flavians received the plaudits with the dignified decorum expected of men of their status, but they still must have enjoyed the attention and their popularity, which was beyond anything they could have reasonably imagined only a year before. The people viewed them as the empire's saviors, and they were the recipients of the public's seemingly endless love and adulation, and for good reason.

They were renowned military heroes—heralded for bringing peace and stability to the troubled empire. They ended Rome's internecine civil war that had dogged the empire and the concomitant, uncertain times that saw four different emperors preside over Rome in the span of a single year; stamped out a deadly revolt in the East; and Titus had earned acclaim on his own accord by sacking the resplendent and powerfully defended ancient city of Jerusalem.

While Titus was only around 31 years old at the time, he had enjoyed a successful—albeit relatively short—military career, but he had many future successes to look forward to. The youthful Flavian would share the burden of ruling Rome with Vespasian, serve a term as one of Rome's censors, hold the consulship eight times and assume the role of Praetorian Guard prefect in order to protect his father's well-being. What's more, the two men would strive to put Rome on more stable footing, ensure peace reigned supreme during their time in power and redesign the city of Rome for the people—commissioning the construction of architectural wonders.

In time, Titus would succeed Vespasian and become Rome's emperor, host lavish games lasting 100 days and be loved by the masses, but as Titus learned, ruling Rome was not always an easy task. He would guide the massive empire as it was beset by disasters. During his emperorship, Mount Vesuvius erupted—burying once-thriving cities and killing thousands in one fell swoop; the colossal city of Rome caught fire, which destroyed temples, homes and livelihoods; and the empire faced a plague of epic proportions. Titus was well-prepared for his future, but in 71 CE, it seems impossible that he and his father could forget their past and rise to power, which was so unlikely that only the gods and most talented prophets could have predicted it.

Unlike the Julio-Claudian imperial dynasty that ruled Rome from 27 BCE to 68 CE, the Flavians were not of noble stock.[2] They were plebeians, although more recent generations had become equestrians—members of a well-to-do business class. The Flavians were not even from the city of Rome. They hailed from the provinces where life was simpler and slower, and Latin was even spoken differently.[3] Vespasian and his ancestors probably had thick provincial accents that blue-blooded Romans simply could not ignore.[4] Yet with Vespasian's meteoric ascension, they were forced to accept his unmistakable country accent, humility and endearing provincial ways. Meanwhile, the Flavians had to learn how to navigate their newfound positions of influence, which was a stark change for the ascendant family.

The Flavian household sprang from obscurity years prior. There is little record of them before 48 BCE—scarcely a handful of generations before Titus' birth—but it is obvious that the Flavians of the late Roman Republic and early empire had experienced a mixture of embarrassment, adversity, privilege and triumphs.[5] They additionally had witnessed Rome at its best and very worst—during civil wars, despotic imperial reigns, and even the extended period of internal peace and prosperity within the empire, the celebrated *Pax Romana* or "Roman peace."

The Flavian family had reason to be proud of their ability to tenaciously claw their way to the pinnacle of Roman power because their beginnings were so rustic. The first direct ancestor of Titus to receive any real attention in the ancient records was his great-grandfather, Titus Flavius Petro whose background is unclear. Some unsubstantiated allegations suggested that Petro's father had been little more than a temporary farmhand—a lowly pauper possibly of Gallic descent—but it is not apparent whether there is any truth to Petro's rumored ancestry. Regardless of his background, Petro far exceeded his station, despite living in the Roman Republic during a time of great danger and transition.[6]

The Republic traced its roots to 509 BCE when the Romans deposed their tyrannical king, known as Tarquinius Superbus. Afterward, they instituted a republican form of government with various checks and balances and also granted the Romans additional rights and liberties.[7] Eventually, popular assemblies voted on various legislative proposals, declarations of war and to elect candidates for a host of offices, including the Republic's top regularly elected posts, the consuls. Two were elected, served concurrently and could veto each other's actions, and they relied heavily on the Roman Senate. It was largely composed of noble and wealthy politicians, and while the Senate technically only existed as an advisory board, it wielded incredible power. It often served as a counterbalance to the popular assemblies' whims, which frequently voted to appoint candidates and enact legislation that undermined the nobility's agendas.[8]

The Roman Republic thrived for centuries, but suffered from recurring internal disputes, especially in its waning days. Rome's ancient aristocracy—the patricians—routinely joined with the equestrians and clashed with the poorer plebeians as each party pursued reforms that benefited themselves at the expense of their opposition. This greatly influenced and destabilized Rome's political landscape, and even though Rome did not have political parties like we envision today, they did have two primary political factions.

The patricians and many equestrians frequently coalesced around the *optimates*, which translates to "best men." They represented a more conservative wing that sought to preserve Rome's traditions, crowed about adhering to an idealized set of norms called *mos maiorum,* or "ancestral custom," and they generally served the aristocrats' interests. In contrast, the *populares*—or "supporters of the people"—regularly promoted populist ideologies, including providing people with debt forgiveness, free grain and complimentary land tracts, and they aimed to place more power and wealth into the plebeians' hands.[9]

Despite different political and social classes being dominant themes in the Roman Republic, its unwritten constitution had long held the growing state together, but the constitution was only as strong as the Romans' desire to retain it. Their adherence and devotion to it began to wane in due time. Following centuries of existence, political violence and civil wars replaced mostly peaceful public discourse as many Romans switched their loyalties from the rule of law to self-interested political and military leaders who promised to reward them—a change that brought disastrous results. Unfortunately for the Romans, politicians then regularly circumvented the constitution and seemed to look at the Republic as little more than a means to great wealth and puissance. The *populares* politician and vaunted general, Julius Caesar, even once quipped, "the [Republic] is nothing, a mere name without body or form."[10] When a critical mass of leaders and voters no longer believed that the constitution and individual liberty were worth safeguarding, the Republic was doomed.

Titus' great-grandfather, Petro, lived during this time and witnessed the destruction and pettiness firsthand—thanks to men like Caesar. In the 50s BCE, the legendary general led campaigns against numerous tribes in Gaul and met with great success, which provided him vast riches and popularity. After spending years in Gaul, the Senate ultimately ordered him to relinquish his command and return to Rome a private citizen. If he obeyed, Caesar feared that he would be prosecuted for some of his questionable behavior and might be convicted and publicly disgraced. Instead of complying with the Senate's decree and risking ignominy, he mustered his battle-hardened troops, crossed the Rubicon River in northern Italy and marched on Rome as an invading enemy army. Caesar's selfish decision ignited a civil war that altered the course of history, but many Romans refused to passively observe Caesar's conspicuous power grab. Pompey the Great, who sided with the *optimates*, marshaled the Republic's defense, and he looked to restore order and discipline the recalcitrant Caesar on the battlefield.[11]

Petro participated in this civil war, but the circumstances of his involvement are uncertain. Either he was an officer known as a centurion, who commanded 80 legionaries, or simply a volunteer veteran. What is known is that he sided with Pompey and fought for him, which was a regrettable choice. The bloody conflict between Caesar and Pompey culminated in a massive battle at the Greek site of Pharsulus in 48 BCE. Standing in formation with his comrades and staring across the field at Caesar's grizzled veterans, Petro readied for battle. The troops adjusted their grips on their shields and javelins (called pilums) and secured their *gladii*—the Roman short swords—in their sheaths. After their generals sounded the charge, the massive armies collided and hacked and stabbed relentlessly at their opponents, but Caesar gained the upper hand. In the process, Pompey's lines disintegrated, and Pompey and Petro fled the battlefield.[12]

Defeated but unwilling to surrender, Pompey retreated to Egypt in hopes of continuing his war against Caesar, but Pharaoh Ptolemy XIII had other plans. The young pharaoh had Pompey stabbed to death and decapitated, and then he presented the decaying head to Caesar as a gift—a gesture that was not well received.[13] Meanwhile, Petro journeyed toward his home in Reate, around 50 miles northeast of Rome, but unlike Pompey, Petro did not suffer a disgraceful end. Caesar pardoned the Flavian, and he enjoyed a life of peace and prosperity. He fostered a budding banking business, which was a lucrative undertaking that might have helped him reach equestrian status. He simultaneously cared for his well-to-do wife Tertulla and raised his son Titus Flavius Sabinus.[14]

With Caesar now enjoying nearly unchallenged power, he assumed the title of dictator in perpetuity—blatantly disregarding constitutional forms and precedent—but the Senate quickly tired of his rule and planned to assassinate him.[15] As their plot unfolded in 44 BCE, disgruntled senators exposed their knives and stabbed wildly at the bewildered dictator. The old general tried to defend himself with a stylus, but he was outnumbered and unprepared. The senators struck him 23 times. Most of the wounds were superficial, but one proved fatal. Caesar subsequently collapsed at the foot of Pompey the Great's statue and perished.[16]

With the dictator dead, Roman leaders reinstituted republican rule, but civil wars continued to nag the ailing state. Caesar's allies, including his heir and great-nephew Octavius (later called Augustus) and Mark Antony, waged war against the dictator's primary assassins—Marcus Junius Brutus and Gaius Cassius Longinus. In 42 BCE, they handily defeated them in the Battle of Philippi at the northern end of modern-day Greece.[17] Years later, Antony and Augustus turned on each

The Roman world in Titus' lifetime.

other—sparking another civil war—in which Augustus came out on top after his resounding naval victory over Antony and his Egyptian lover Cleopatra in 31 BCE at Actium.[18] Defeated, Antony ultimately killed himself—leaving Augustus without a serious challenger and holding supreme power. In 27 BCE, Augustus announced that he was giving the people back their Republic, but it was a dishonest gesture. The Republic would exist largely in name only. He effectively replaced the Republic with a new form of government that modern historians call the principate, and Augustus became *princeps*—or first citizen—and emperor of a Roman empire.[19]

Despite the era's tumult, Titus' grandfather, Sabinus, may not have participated in any of these military conflicts. In fact, the famous Roman historian Suetonius asserted that he "took no part in military life," but not every ancient writer agreed. Some sources claimed that Sabinus had served honorably as a centurion, while others asserted that he was the commander of a cohort but retired due to failing health.[20] Whatever the case, he earned a living and renown as a tax-collector and—had his father not already accomplished the feat—he ensured the Flavians' place as an equestrian family thanks to his business acumen.[21]

Tax-collecting was necessary to keep the empire's finances on stable footing, but it was a cut-throat and oftentimes disreputable business. It frequently led to rapacious behavior as taxmen stripped people of their wealth for their own benefit. Sabinus, on the other hand, was a conscientious tax-collector who served in the Roman province of Asia, which corresponds to part of modern-day Türkiye. While there were many ways the Roman state raised taxes, officials tasked Sabinus with levying and collecting import/export duties. The tax stood at around 2.5 percent, but that could change with various emperors' impulses.[22] There was rarely any love for tax collectors. They were generally a loathsome bunch, which can be clearly observed in ancient Roman and Greek writings and even in the Bible's New Testament. Within the Gospel of Matthew, the Pharisees expressed outrage that Jesus Christ would dare share meals with tax collectors and sinners—as if the two were the same.[23]

Sabinus was far different from your typical tax-collector. He was held in such high esteem that cities in Roman Asia erected statues in his honor, and at least one read, "To an honest tax-gatherer." Honest or not, Sabinus eventually retired from his posting, and he later engaged in banking, like his father, Petro, but in Gaul. Throughout his life, Sabinus must have amassed a small fortune from his business dealings because at some point he married Vespasia Polla, who was part of a family with some notable political success. Her brother was a Roman senator, and her father had held various senior military posts. Between their union and accumulating wealth and influence, they almost certainly managed to forge some important connections to the royal court, which would serve as a springboard to propel the Flavians to great heights.[24]

Together, Sabinus and Polla sired two boys who became some of Rome's leading men—Titus Flavius Sabinus and the younger Titus Flavius Vespasianus, better known as the future emperor Vespasian.[25] The brothers were born in the outskirts of Reate, in a village known as Falacrina during the waning years of Emperor Augustus' reign (27 BCE–14 CE). For whatever reason, the brothers' paternal grandmother Tertulla helped raise the boys and often did so from her home in Cosa near the Tyrrhenian Sea, and she earned Vespasian's everlasting love and affection.[26]

Most of Vespasian's childhood occurred during the tenure of the tightfisted, uncharismatic and sometimes cruel Emperor Tiberius (14–37 CE) who was Augustus' adopted son. While he had been a successful general, he was not Augustus' top choice as heir, but he turned out to be a highly capable imperial administrator who presided over a mostly peaceful period in foreign affairs. However, he is remembered for wantonly ordering the executions of a host of Romans, banishing a number of Jews and Isis worshippers from the city of Rome, and withdrawing to Capri where he reportedly engaged in all forms of depravity. While there, he supposedly sexually abused children, even a boy named Vitellius who later became emperor, although this might be a form of postmortem character assassination spuriously recorded by his political enemies.[27]

This aside, during Tiberius' reign, Vespasian decided to seek a public career. He only did so after being overshadowed by his brother, Sabinus. He was more ambitious than Vespasian at the time and had taken the preliminary steps toward hopefully becoming a Roman senator. Observing Sabinus' success and Vespasian's complacency, his dissatisfied mother hounded the young man. "She constantly taunted him with being his brother's footman," reported Suetonius. Feeling family pressure, Vespasian acquiesced. Thanks to some hard work and likely also wealth and family connections to the royal court, Vespasian tasted some moderate early success.[28]

Pursuing a seat in the Senate was no easy feat. For aspiring young men who were of the senatorial rank—meaning their fathers were members of the Senate—they faced fewer obstacles in their quest for a series of public offices. Yet they were mostly held in a particular order. This political ladder was known as the *cursus honorum*—or "course of honors." It included the quaestorship, which led to senatorial admission and then even higher offices, but the democratic forms of the defunct Roman Republic were long gone. The noblest offices in the *cursus honorum* were no longer truly elected by the people, but rather the Senate. Furthermore, in many cases, the emperor nominated his chosen candidates, and if the senators knew what was good for them, then they appointed the emperor's picks.[29]

Recent upstart non-senatorial, equestrian families, like the Flavians, faced an even more daunting path to the Senate. They needed to obtain imperial approval by applying to wear the *latus clavus*, which was the broad purple stripe of the senatorial order. Doing so announced their intention to seek a seat in the Roman Senate, and receiving permission to wear it was critically important. Only then could such equestrians hope to begin climbing the Roman political ladder by holding the prescribed offices of the *cursus honorum*.[30]

To begin his charted path toward the Senate, Vespasian successfully applied to wear the *latus clavus* and plotted his ascent on the *cursus honorum*. However, he was certainly aided by his family's contacts within the imperial court and one key advocate in particular—namely his maternal uncle who was a senator. He may have counseled the young Flavian, spoke highly of him to his colleagues and introduced him to influential power brokers, and his efforts were successful. Around 27 CE or a little later, Vespasian assumed one of Rome's military tribuneships, which was a high-ranking position within the legions, and reached his provincial posting. He was deployed to a region of Southeastern Europe called Thrace.[31] Virtually nothing else is known of his tenure as a military tribune, but he likely would have been busy overseeing and drilling troops, assisting in the army's administration and possibly engaging in fierce combat. Thrace laid on the fringes of the sprawling Roman Empire and close to barbarian-held territory. Unsurprisingly, violent disturbances erupted in Thrace around this time, which must have demanded Vespasian's attention.[32]

Once Vespasian finished his term as military tribune and plotted his continued advance toward senatorial admission, he probably pursued and obtained membership in the Vigintivirate, which was a college of lower-level magistrates. Vespasian's family was relatively unremarkable compared to incredibly wealthy and influential senatorial clans whose sons likewise vied for membership in the Vigintivirate. This meant that when Vespasian secured a position in the college sometime in the early 30s CE, his posting was underwhelming. He could have been charged with overseeing executions or book burnings. These roles were considered vital to the empire, but they were hardly the Vigintivirate's most coveted posts.[33]

After successfully fulfilling his duties, Vespasian decided to run for one of Rome's 20 quaestorships—essentially assistants for higher level magistrates. Becoming a quaestor represented the culmination of years of work, which, if his toils were successful, would provide Vespasian a permanent seat in the Senate. It would also mean that his offspring would be able to more easily seek senatorial admission.

Vespasian had reason to be cautiously optimistic, thanks to his family's connections. In whatever manner they aided him, the Roman Senate elected Vespasian, and he was subsequently tasked with serving in Crete and Cyrene. The latter being in modern-day Libya. His one-year term seems to have fallen around 35 CE but would not have been particularly thrilling. He presumably spent his tenure poring over accounting ledgers and ensuring that all the state's local financial obligations were met. As his term expired, Vespasian relinquished his post—perhaps eagerly—and looked to continue furthering his nascent career.[34]

At this point, Vespasian must have been fairly confident in his abilities. While he was far from a household name and was not part of one of Rome's great families, he had already achieved senatorial admission. Further, he had served as a military tribune, in the Vigintivirate and as a quaestor, and he prepared for another step along the *cursus honorum*. In 36 CE, he stood for one of Rome's six aedileships—a public position of decreasing importance that oversaw some public works and wielded minor regulatory powers. Once an influential role during the Roman Republic, aediles were now relegated to pedestrian activities.

Regardless of their humble duties, it was the next logical step in the *cursus honorum* that garnered competition from ambitious Romans, and in fact, Vespasian's campaign for the position was a failure. He was defeated, which was an embarrassing public reversal. This implies that Emperor Tiberius either had not endorsed his candidacy or simply left the matter up to the Senate, which was not inclined to support Vespasian for whatever reason. Undeterred, Vespasian returned to run for one of the aedileships of 38 CE and just barely clinched victory. It appears that he was rewarded by being assigned to oversee street-cleaning—a menial and ignoble role—in what was a time of great upheaval in Rome and Vespasian's personal life.[35]

In 37 CE, Emperor Tiberius died, probably of natural causes—although some rumors circulated that he was murdered—and Augustus' youthful great-grandchild succeeded him. He was named Gaius Caesar Augustus Germanicus, but today he is remembered as Caligula. It was a nickname essentially translating to "little boots," which legionaries gave him as a child because of his legionary costume provided by his parents. When the 24-year-old assumed the imperial throne, the Romans were ecstatic. They believed that he was full of promise and his rule would be a welcome departure from Tiberius' surly and sometimes cruel tenure. While Caligula could be generous, he ultimately proved to be a mercurial tyrant who may have also suffered from mental illness—something modern historians still debate.

Salacious stories—some true and some very likely exaggerated or fabricated—of the mad emperor persist even today. They include vignettes about him inviting married couples to dinner, only to sleep with his guests' wives and then openly critique their sexual skills; stealing a man's bride on his wedding night; his alleged incestuous relationships with his sisters; bringing his favorite horse to dinner and threatening to make it consul; feeding condemned criminals to wild beasts after discovering how expensive their feed was; berating men of status; and exhibiting murderous tendencies. He even demanded to be viewed and treated as a living deity.[36]

Caligula was so determined to be recognized as a god meriting worship and unquestioned obedience that he ordered one of his subordinates to prepare a large, dazzling statue of the emperor and place it in the hallowed Jewish Temple. The notion of erecting a statue of the emperor as a god and placing it there would have been an unbelievable affront. Fortunately, it never came to fruition. Nevertheless, in a meeting with a Jewish embassy, he complained, "Are you the god-haters who do not believe me to be a god, a god acknowledged among all the other nations but not to be named by you?" Rome's misunderstanding and disdain for the Jews became a recurring theme that Vespasian and Titus personally witnessed.[37]

Sometime earlier in Caligula's reign, during Vespasian's aedileship, the emperor humiliated the Flavian. Apparently, the young ruler was displeased with Vespasian's work as an aedile, possibly due to the streets remaining filthy, and as a result, ordered Romans to pelt him with mud.[38] They obeyed and left Vespasian covered in detritus. This embarrassment aside, it was not an altogether terrible time for Vespasian. Sometime around 37–39 CE, Vespasian married a woman named Flavia Domitilla. Marriages at this time, especially among ambitious families, were not always formed in love. They were often business and political transactions that were sealed by marriages and linked families together. This helped them pool influence and wealth, and it solidified their stature in Roman society.

If Vespasian's marriage was one such union, then it is evident that he was not a particularly impressive or promising individual yet—despite being a senator—because Domitilla did not hail from a consequential family. Her father had been an unassuming quaestor's clerk, and he had to sue in order for his daughter to be recognized as a freeborn Roman citizen. From the Romans' point of view, this was not a marriage that should produce greatness. Luckily, Vespasian would far surpass all expectations. In a turn of events that the Flavians never could have imagined, Vespasian and his son Titus would rule the Roman world, be remembered as some of Rome's most revered emperors and even be deified, but that would come much later.[39]

II

Titus

> *"Titus, of the same surname as his father, was the delight and darling of the human race; such surpassing ability had he, by nature, art, or good fortune, to win the affections of all men."*
> —Suetonius[1]

Details surrounding Vespasian's tenure as a military tribune, quaestor and aedile are unfortunately scarce, but some conclusions can be gleaned from the ancient sources. While Caligula publicly humiliated Vespasian, he fulfilled his duties well enough to continue climbing the political ladder. Following his most recent electoral success—that of securing the aedileship—Vespasian announced his candidacy for the next step in the *cursus honorum*: one of the 16 praetorships of either 39 or 40 CE.

There were different kinds of praetors, but their duties largely consisted of administrative and magisterial functions. Possibly after garnering the emperor's nomination or permission to run, the Senate duly elected him to one of the praetorships. Sadly, it is unknown which praetorship he acquired. Whatever one it was, he enjoyed a relatively quiet one-year term.[2]

It was around this time, on December 30, 39 CE, that Vespasian and Domitilla welcomed their first child—a boy—whom Domitilla birthed in an unassuming house in Rome, which must have been a time of great anxiety.[3] Maternal mortality rates were high, and newborns' survival was hardly a given. Fortunately, Domitilla survived, but if the couple held fast to tradition, then they may not have named their baby immediately, in part, because the infant mortality rate was so high. Perhaps around 30 percent or more of children died before they turned one, and about half perished before the age of 15.[4] Given this reality, boys might not be named for upward of nine days post-birth, but simply surviving the birthing process was not always enough. An ancient and unforgiving law supposedly dating back to Rome's first king, Romulus, gave Roman parents the right to discard their infants for death if they were deformed in some way. It is not clear how many parents executed the privilege in this era. Regardless of this matter, if the babes during the *Pax Romana* survived these nine vulnerable early days and did not suffer from malformities, then they would certainly be named.[5]

In Vespasian and Domitilla's case, their child was a healthy boy. They named him after Vespasian—Titus Flavius Vespasianus—and he became known as Titus. When he was old enough—if he was like other Roman youths—his parents hung a protective amulet, known as a *bulla*, around his neck, which supposedly warded off evil spirits. On special occasions and with the help of his parents, Titus also wore the *toga praetexta*. It was a woolen garment with a purple stripe that denoted youths' importance and protections under the law. On most days, however, Titus presumably donned a wool tunic. Trousers were, of course, considered only fit for barbarians.[6]

Vespasian was probably thrilled to have a healthy child, but he was busy with other affairs, including navigating Rome's complex political landscape. During Vespasian's term as praetor, he tried to ingratiate himself with the unpredictable and violent Caligula, but his efforts ended up being wholly unnecessary. In 41 CE, Caligula's Praetorian Guard—or personal bodyguards—assassinated the emperor, which initially left Rome leaderless. For a short period of time, the Senate mulled abolishing the principate altogether and giving the people back their Republic, but there was little appetite for that. Instead, Roman power brokers—at the strenuous urging of the Praetorian Guard—replaced Caligula with his uncle Claudius, who then became emperor.[7]

Originally a black sheep of the imperial family, Claudius had studied to be a historian but was considered a man of low intellect. This could have stemmed from some perceived physical disabilities, including his tendency to drool, stutter, limp and exhibit head tremors. Despite these traits and his quick temper, Claudius was no dolt and ultimately became a largely competent and conscientious ruler, aside from some notable chapters in his reign. These include some violent episodes and banishing the Jews and possibly also early Christians from the city of Rome, possibly as late as 49 CE, via the Edict of Claudius.

The Christian population of Rome in this era was exceptionally tiny, which is understandable. Christianity may have only existed for around two decades at this juncture, according to Biblical accounts. It was so new that it is improbable that many Romans could distinguish Christianity from Judaism. Indeed, some of these early Christians may not have fully understood their religion either. Paul's ministry to the gentiles was likely in its initial stages, and the earliest written gospel to be canonized—the Gospel of Mark—had not even been drafted yet.[8]

The precise reason Claudius expelled the Jews and maybe Christians too is not evident. Suetonius merely claimed that Claudius banished them because they "constantly made disturbances at the instigation of Chrestus." This has led plenty of ancient and modern scholars to postulate that Chrestus is a reference to Jesus Christ, although it could be the name of an unknown Jewish rebel. Ancient historian Orosius recorded a slightly different version of Suetonius' statement, writing, "Claudius expelled the Jews from Rome because in their resentment against Christ they were continually creating disturbances." In the end, even Orosius admits historical ignorance over the Edict of Claudius, and wrote, "No one can say whether the emperor ordered the Jews to be restrained and repressed because they were creating disturbances against Christ or whether he wished the Christians to be expelled at the same time on the ground that they were members of an allied religion." One way or another it seems Claudius ejected numerous Jews and perhaps early Christians from Rome.[9]

This was a dismaying turn of events for the expelled, but Rome was a place of opportunity and wealth for others. While it had not reached its full potential yet, Titus entered a Roman world that was in the golden age of the *Pax Romana*. Gone were the days of frequent civil wars waged by men, like Lucius Cornelius Sulla, Julius Caesar and Augustus, that had ravaged Rome. Yet the *Pax Romana* is a bit of a misnomer. Rome had been spared major internal armed conflicts during this time, but the legions remained active. They put down revolts, engaged in serious military operations on the frontiers and expanded Rome's reach.

By Titus' childhood, Rome was the undisputed master of the Mediterranean world. The regions that Roman leaders did not officially incorporate into their empire were often led by client-kings, like the Jewish monarchs, who suppliantly bowed to emperors' wills and ruled at their pleasure. They were far from independent, but client-kings learned that Rome could be generous, which helped enrich loyal vassals and kept some complacent.

Rome's internal peace and outward expansion also padded the pockets of well-connected and industrious Romans. Wealth flowed in from the provinces, foreign conquests, trade and the empire's silver mines, but there were many other opportunities for wealth generation within Rome. Like any complex economy, there were different businesses in which entrepreneurs could earn a small fortune, including engaging in the service industry, construction, banking, shipping and the production of various goods.

Throughout Rome, there were jewelers, couturiers, pottery-makers and bakers. Rome even had ancient forms of fast-food restaurants, which offered Romans on-the-go with quick options. Lawyers abounded, thugs were willing to protect or hurt you for the right price, salesmen offered quickly-spoiling produce and meat, and fullers washed Rome's dirty laundry at laundromats—using foul-smelling urine as a cleaning agent. For highly ambitious free Romans, there was a path to riches, but it would not come easy in a city that was growing rapidly.

Augustus boasted that he had "found [Rome] built of brick and left it in marble," but that was only partially true.[10] As Titus saw, Rome of this era was studded with ornate temples, administrative buildings, towering monuments, bath houses, theaters and works of impressive art. He observed Rome's Circus Maximus, where upward of 150,000 Romans could watch dramatic chariot races and games, and he was well-aware of the complex system of aqueducts that rushed fresh water into the city and fed the bath houses and fountains. However, Titus only had to wander outside of Rome's affluent districts to see how most of Rome's citizens truly lived.

Rome was a confused maze of narrow, winding streets filled with Romans, noisy

Remains of the Circus Maximus, Rome, 2016.

carts, human and animal excrement and even the occasional corpse. This filth aside, the avenues themselves were a feat of engineering, which the Romans formed using a kind of multi-layered pavement; many of these roads survive to this day. Lining the avenues were shops and tightly packed tenement housing that reached multiple stories. As Rome built upward toward the sky, the population density surged—possibly reaching around 55,000–70,000 people per square kilometer according to some estimates—but this came with risks.[11] The wooden, several-story buildings periodically collapsed, killing their inhabitants, and were prone to deadly fires. The Romans had a fire brigade for such scenarios—the *vigiles*—but they were better at containing conflagrations than extinguishing them.[12]

Rome would have overwhelmed the senses and offended modern moral sensibilities. While some Roman leaders strove to instill some semblance of morality in the Romans, their efforts came up well short. Romans engaged in a fair amount of drunken debauchery and gluttonous overeating, particularly on certain Roman holidays. The wealthy gravitated toward strange, exotic dishes that make modern readers recoil, including stuffed dormice, flamingo tongue, various kinds of animal brains and the favorite Roman condiment, garum. It was a salty fermented sauce made, in part, from rotting fish intestines, and it reeked terribly.[13]

The Romans' eating habits were not the biggest concerns among those who wished to reinstitute some form of idealized behavior associated with *mos maiorum*. They saw corruption in the Romans' characters elsewhere, too, and groused about their many vices. The Romans were not sticklers for marriage fidelity, they enjoyed gambling, read scandalous and perverted poetry, left lewd graffiti throughout the city, and prostitution was rampant in old Rome. If the ruins of Pompeii are any indicator, evidence of prostitution was conspicuous. Erect phallic symbols—strategically placed throughout Rome— either served as good luck charms or pointed the way to the ubiquitous brothels, which the state regulated.[14]

The Rome of Titus' childhood would have been a fascinating and impressive sight to behold, but it is fair to assume that much of his upbringing would have been centered around his family's provincial values. Vespasian and Domitilla had witnessed Rome's immorality and the consequences of such behavior. As such, they clearly placed a premium on ingraining good character in Titus. Vespasian was his son's central role model, but it was likely his mother who established Titus' moral and intellectual foundation. If his youth was like many other Romans, then his mother took primary responsibility for providing Titus rudimentary lessons and caring for him during his infancy and early youth. This was especially necessary considering that Vespasian was busy nursing a budding military and political career, which appeared increasingly promising.[15]

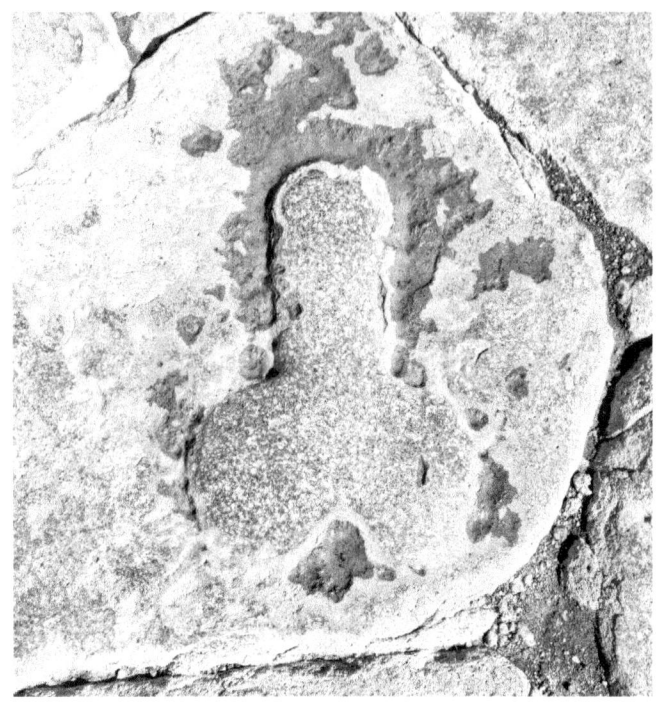

Phallus, Pompeii, 2022.

Claudius' ascension to the purple presented Vespasian a valuable opportunity. Gone was the mad emperor Caligula who had a fraught relationship with him, and Vespasian enjoyed some special connections in Claudius' court. Vespasian's former mistress, Caenis, had long been a servant to Claudius' mother, which worked to Vespasian's benefit, and he grew close to Claudius' freedman—a manumitted slave— and adviser Narcissus who worked to promote Vespasian's career. Thanks to his prior military and political service and well-placed allies, Claudius appointed Vespasian to lead one of Rome's legions—roughly 5,000 foot soldiers and cavalrymen— near the wild and treacherous frontier of Germany. Vespasian eagerly accepted the position and may have even brought Domitilla and Titus with him to Germany, although the ancient sources are silent on their whereabouts at this time.[16]

While this was an immense opportunity, it came with dangers. During Augustus' reign, Germanic tribes had ambushed three legions—led by Quinctilius

Varus—in Teutoburg Forest and killed the lot of them. The defeat was so absolute and shocking that Augustus suffered from a kind of nervous breakdown. During his fits, he would bang his head against the door and cry out, "Quinctilius Varus, give me back my legions!"[17] The Romans returned to Teutoburg Forest to punish their enemies years later. Thanks to Germanicus—Caligula's father—they regained their honor and buried their fallen comrades who had been shamefully left strewn on the forest floor—a fate that the Romans believed could haunt the souls of the deceased.[18]

Vespasian's time in Germany was much less eventful and did not last long. He and his legion were chosen to participate in one of Rome's greatest military campaigns in decades—the planned conquest of Britannia, at least part of it. While Domitilla and Titus might have accompanied Vespasian to the Germanic front, they certainly did not travel to Britannia. It was too dangerous, and they would have been a burden on the army. After all, the Romans had engaged the Britons before and understood the threats they posed. Julius Caesar had invaded Britannia in 55 and 54 BCE, but his forays were short-lived and did not leave a significant Roman presence there.[19]

Looking for enduring glory, Caligula had concocted a plan to conquer Britannia beginning in 40 CE, but with his troops standing on the coast, he instead ordered them to collect seashells and return to Rome. The reason for his curious volte-face is not entirely clear, but it could have stemmed from his legionaries' fear of crossing the treacherous British channel and engaging a mysterious enemy. If they refused the emperor's demands, then he would humiliate them and force them to march back to Rome with their embarrassing spoils—humble seashells.[20]

Whatever Caligula's reasons, Vespasian's appointment by Claudius provided him a chance to prove his mettle and make a name for himself, but it kept him busy and away from his family. During these formative years in the early-to-mid 40s CE, little Titus lived a relatively carefree life. He played with other children, remained especially close to his mother and helped her with chores and spent the majority of his time with family until he was old enough for formal education.[21]

The Roman state did not fund schooling—meaning all education was private—nor was it mandatory. It was left entirely up to parents, who wielded a great deal of power over child-rearing, to decide whether or not to educate them. Practically all Romans understood the critically important value of schooling, and they would have done their best to send their kids to a private institution or hire a teacher to instruct them in the comfort of their homes. The latter must have been prohibitively expensive for most Romans.[22]

Like many Roman parents, Vespasian held education in particularly high esteem and ensured that Titus learned everything needed to succeed in the Roman world. By around the age of seven—in 47 CE—Titus likely began his schooling, but it was a strict and grueling regimen. School days began early in the morning and lasted for many hours, and the children sat in uncomfortable chairs and held their implements in their laps. Teachers were unforgiving and known to cane or whip misbehaving children on their hands or backs, but this is not the extent of the differences between today's education and ancient Rome's. Even the method of learning seems backward to modern educators. Instructors required Roman children, for instance, to learn the names of letters before they could see the actual letters. Fortunately for the youths, there were breaks in the demanding school calendars. Children enjoyed several weeks off in the summer, time off for holidays like the Saturnalia Festival in December and could look forward to about a day off per week.[23]

If Titus was anything like other privileged Roman youths, then from around the age of 7 to 12 he studied under a *litterator* who instructed the boy on basic reading, writing and arithmetic. The ancient sources failed to disclose whether Titus received this education at one of the many available schools or from a private tutor. Considering that Vespasian was not an excessively wealthy man by senatorial standards and group education was preferred for socializing youths, Titus probably learned with other children. He could have even done so alongside young girls, given that co-education was permitted.[24]

Armed with a wax tablet, some papyrus to scratch notes on and an abacus, little Titus went to school each morning, but he might have had a companion. Some Roman children were accompanied by a slave, whose duties were to carry the child's school supplies and perhaps ensure the youth's good behavior and safety. There is no mention of whether Titus enjoyed one, but it is very possible. Slaves were prevalent in old Rome. Some estimates suggest that as many as one in three people in the Italian peninsula were enslaved, and Vespasian had been well-placed—in Germany and Britannia—to obtain cheap slaves.[25]

While Titus had been busy learning, his father earned a great amount of acclaim in Britannia. Suetonius mentions that he impressively led his legion into 30 battles, captured 20 cities and an island, and pacified two barbarian nations. Ultimately, the Roman invasion was a success. Much of modern-day Great Britain remained outside of the empire's grip, but it expanded its reach far into southern Britannia—thanks in part to Vespasian's endeavors. Almost certainly because of his friendship with Narcissus, his mistress' connections and his exceptional service in Britannia, Vespasian formed an even tighter bond with Claudius and his imperial court.

Claudius subsequently awarded him military honors, appointed him to two priesthoods and nominated him to serve as consul for 51 CE—virtually guaranteeing his election. Vespasian leaped at the chance and received the Senate's support, but the consulship of this era was a mere shadow of what it had once been. Originally one of the Roman state's chief executive officers, military commanders and judges who held one-year terms, the consulships of the 50s CE were reduced to lesser importance. To begin with, emperors limited their terms to a matter of months, and they spent their time presiding over the Senate, overseeing games and serving as judges in certain cases. Despite the office's waning influence, this was a proud moment and crowning achievement for Vespasian. While his career was taking off, his private life was busy too. When Titus was nearly 12 years old, Vespasian and Domitilla bore another son, Domitian, who would later gain infamy, and at some point in Titus' youth, he welcomed a sister, named Domitilla.[26]

Probably around the age of 12—in 52 CE—Titus started the next stage of his education. He studied with a *grammaticus* who built upon the foundation laid by the *litterator*. Under the *grammaticus'* tutelage, Titus learned to speak and write correctly. He studied Greek authors as well as Latin poets, including Virgil, Horace and Ovid. Titus may have additionally practiced drafting poetry and persuasive essays that he recited during the school days. The study of history, philosophy and advanced math would have been conspicuously underwhelming to modern eyes. Many Romans did not place a high priority on these subjects, and most Romans would have learned only what was needed to get by.[27]

Around this point, if not earlier, it seems that Titus became close intimates with Claudius' son—Britannicus—and the two grew ever closer to one another. They even received their education from the same tutors and learned the same topics, which demonstrates Vespasian's strong relationship with the imperial family. A court education for someone unrelated to the royal family was something of a rarity, but it was an honor. In addition to providing the Roman world's best education, it presumably came with military training from none other than the praetorian guards, which served Titus well, but this opportunity could be a blessing and a curse.[28] Claudius' wife Agrippina was suspicious of Narcissus and those who were close to him, like Vespasian, and maybe for good reason.[29]

Britannicus was not her biological son; Lucius Domitius Ahenobarbus—better known today as Nero—was. She naturally promoted her son's interests with zeal, but a physiognomist hired by Narcissus made a curious prediction. While he did not mention anything about Nero's future, the clairvoyant claimed that Britannicus would never ascend to the purple, but Titus would rule Rome—a prophecy that eventually came true. If Agrippina heard this, then that would have ensured lasting enmity between her and the Flavian household because it is plausible that she worried Titus would somehow rise to power at Nero's expense.[30]

So long as Claudius and Narcissus remained the Flavians' benefactors, they were relatively safe from Agrippina, but Claudius would not rule in perpetuity. By the time that Titus was nearly old enough to begin the subsequent phase of his education—that of studying under a *rhetor* who would teach him how to speak and write eloquently—tragedy struck. In 54 CE, Claudius died, likely poisoned by his meddling wife Agrippina. Ancient historians claim that she murdered Claudius with poisoned mushrooms, which led to a slow, painful death, and he even required a second dose of the poison to finally succumb to it. After his demise, her son Nero succeeded Claudius, instead of Britannicus. This was a major setback to the Flavians, who had lost their benefactor, and they quickly faced a hostile imperial court.[31]

Matters quickly became dangerous for Britannicus, Vespasian and even the youthful Titus. One day in 55 CE while lounging with Britannicus, Titus shared a drink with the boy. Titus sipped from his cup to quench his thirst, as did

Britannicus. Unfortunately, it had been laced with poison to remove Britannicus as a threat to Nero's rule. The young emperor had plotted with a renowned expert in poisons—known as Locusta—who mixed a potion sure to strike Britannicus down. The ancient historians failed to disclose the specific poison she used, but the Romans had access to many dangerous elements, including poisonous mushrooms, hemlock, arsenic, atropa belladonna—a kind of nightshade—and so on.

Whatever comprised Locusta's deadly concoction, both of the youths ingested it. Britannicus almost immediately collapsed, but to avoid suspicion, Nero falsely claimed that the boy must be suffering from an epileptic seizure and nothing more, which was a malady Britannicus had long battled. Britannicus died shortly thereafter, and while Nero took pains to conceal the poisoning, the people saw through the emperor's treacherous ruse.

Like Britannicus, Titus had imbibed some of the poison, but he somehow survived—perhaps because he had ingested less of it. Nevertheless, he suffered from an undisclosed, long-term ailment because of the poison, and was distraught by his close friend's death.[32] From Vespasian's perspective, matters had become too hazardous. To guarantee his safety and his family's, he voluntarily went into temporary retirement from public life, at least according to ancient accounts. It is possible that he subsequently focused on private enterprises to avoid Nero and Agrippina's suspicious gaze and murderous plotting. Vespasian may have even retreated from Rome to the countryside until matters were safe again. If he did withdraw, then he was not gone long. He must have returned to Rome and carried out his duties as a priest and a senator but remained on his best behavior to avoid Nero and Agrippina's wraths. The new imperial court's animosity toward the Flavians cost Vespasian access to the emperor and his favor, but Vespasian retained his previously obtained positions.[33]

Titus probably studied under a *rhetor* during this unsure time of his life. The adolescent surely practiced writing and speaking in preparation for a political and legal career. However, skilled public speaking was increasingly becoming less important in Rome. During the Republic, politicians relied on their oratory to win over the masses, but under the empire, emperors ruled as autocrats. Thus oratory for a political career's sake was largely unnecessary, and could turn fatal if one was viewed as a rival to the imperial throne. Rather, the only real need of public speaking skills was in the legal field where ambitious Romans could still make a name for themselves, but even the need for silver-tongued lawyers might have been waning under the principate. With emperors increasingly wielding more power over the judicial system than juries who could be swayed by colorful oratory, well-spoken attorneys were no longer held in the same regard.[34]

Regardless of the Flavians' falling out with the imperial family, Titus still enjoyed some of the same rites and rituals that most youths did. Sometime after he turned 16 or 17, Titus entered what was broadly considered adulthood, and to celebrate it, he removed his protective *bulla*, was likely shaved for the first time and given a more mature haircut and the toga of adulthood—the *toga virilis*. It was a plain, white semi-circular woolen garment that was absolutely stifling to wear in the summer months, and it was draped over the wearer and folded in a very particular way. It was so cumbersome that some adult Romans employed slaves to help dress them in it. Once donning his toga and a more adult style, Titus and his family marched into the city center and offered a sacrifice to the goddess of youth—Juventus—probably during the Liberalia festival on March 17 of 56 or 57 CE. Titus was now officially a man and could begin to put his talents to work.[35]

Titus' education and upbringing served him well. He mastered the Greek language, could skillfully compose poetry and knew how to deliver tantalizing and persuasive speeches with little to no preparation. He boasted other strengths as well. He was proficient with the harp and could even sing, and he ultimately demonstrated his mastery of horsemanship and with military arms. While he was relatively short and had a potbelly later in life, he was physically strong and considered handsome by Roman standards. Beyond these talents, he also developed another skill: forgery. He apparently had a knack for replicating virtually anyone's handwriting with ease, and he enjoyed exhibiting this talent, which may have landed him in trouble on more than one occasion. As the young man's schooling drew to a close and he matured, he plotted his rise in Roman society and had ample aptitudes on which to rely.[36]

III

BOUDICA

> *"The person who was chiefly instrumental in rousing the natives and persuading them to fight the Romans, the person who was thought worthy to be their leader and who directed the conduct of the entire war, was [Boudica], a Briton woman of the royal family."*
> —Cassius Dio[1]

LIKE MUCH OF TITUS' EARLY LIFE, there is little record attesting to his whereabouts and activities, but enough is known about him and ancient Roman society to draw some probable conclusions. After finishing his education, like most other Roman adolescents, he looked to begin a career and eventually start a family. Despite the Flavians' poor relationship with Nero's mother, Agrippina, Titus wanted to pursue public life and follow in his father's footsteps by gaining admission into the Senate. However, the Flavian household understood that doing so would be challenging without assistance, and they received some in the form of court intrigue.[2]

In the mid–50s CE, Nero was already distancing himself from his overbearing mother—a familial conflict that had nasty consequences. First, Nero forced his mother out of the imperial household, but even that was not enough. Nero so tired of his mother's interference and plotting that he decided she must die. There are some confusing ancient accounts surrounding his attempts to kill Agrippina. Yet it seems that Nero first tried to poison her three different times. Yet the wily Agrippina stymied Nero and inoculated herself by taking the antidote. Following these foiled attempts, he gave up on poison and decided to engineer a ceiling collapse to kill her, but this overly complicated plan did not succeed either.

Frustrated by these failures, Nero adopted a different approach. He had a boat specifically designed that would lead to her death. After building the faulty craft, attendants helped her aboard. Then according to plan, the vessel began to succumb to its flaws, but she again survived and safely made it ashore. With these creative plots foiled, Nero's men decided that they ought to bludgeon her to death—a fate she could not escape. Seeing her would-be killers, she presented her stomach and instructed them, "Smite my womb," where she had once carried Nero. They were happy to oblige and subsequently struck her down. With her finally dead in 59 CE, the unhinged Nero viewed and critiqued her corpse. Her assassination did not bring him peace, though. Legends state that her memory and perhaps ghost haunted him.[3]

This period was tortuous for Nero, but things were looking up for Titus from what little historians can tell. Titus undoubtedly took his first step toward senatorial admission and served a one-year term in the Vigintivirate possibly in 60 CE, although it is not clear what his specific position was or what he accomplished. While Vespasian probably served in one of the humbler roles in the Vigintivirate, the Flavians' fortunes had changed. Agrippina was dead and Vespasian was a senator, and he was able to foster Titus' political rise. So it is very likely that Titus attained a prouder capacity within the Vigintivirate than Vespasian had held. Whatever the case, Titus continued to climb the *cursus honorum*. He next became military tribune for a term not to exceed three years, which may have begun around 61 CE, but considering the ambiguity in the ancient records, this is educated guesswork.[4]

While there were different kinds of tribunes in old Rome, it seems that Titus was specifically a *tribunus laticlavius*, which was a position reserved for senators' sons who had no prior military experience. These fortunate scions often served in the provinces under a family friend who watched over the youngsters and mentored them, which indicates that Vespasian had been gaining important contacts across Rome. This was an immense opportunity for Titus too, because the *tribunus laticlavius* acted as a legion's second in command whereupon Titus gained firsthand knowledge of the ins and outs of military leadership. Titus certainly learned how to organize and build a camp, manage complex logistics to supply the legions, formulate and lead offensive and defensive maneuvers, and so forth.[5]

During his tenure as military tribune, he was first stationed in Germany, just like his father, but this was a relatively quiet period on the Germanic front. While there, aside from learning the basics of being a Roman officer, Titus presumably stayed busy training and drilling his subordinates, guarding the border, taking part in minor skirmishes against nearby barbarian tribes, participating in building operations and leading diplomatic missions. In whatever manner he occupied his time, he earned his fellow legionaries' and the locals' admiration, but he did not remain in Germany for long.[6]

Titus and his troops were eventually transferred to Britannia, again like Vespasian. While Suetonius offers no justification for this re-assignment, modern historians have pinpointed a plausible reason. The Romans had subdued vast swaths of Britannia during Claudius' reign, and Vespasian had played a central role in the invasion's success. However, the Romans' hold on many British tribes was tenuous at best. People do not appreciate being conquered and especially loath being mistreated, like the Romans sometimes did to those whom they subjugated. Moreover, the Romans were imposing a painful financial burden on the Britons by calling in massive loans for repayment and confiscating wealth. For all of these reasons, Britannia was a tinderbox waiting for a spark.[7]

Even though Rome was a conquering alien force in Britannia, it enjoyed alliances with some locals, including King Prasutagus of the Iceni tribe. It was centered in eastern Britannia—an area largely corresponding to modern-day Norfolk,

England. In his will, he even bequeathed his kingdom to the Romans and his two daughters. He had intended for the girls to rule jointly along with the Roman emperor, which was a clever ploy to ensure that his kingdom and relatives would remain in the Romans' good graces, but matters did not go quite as he had planned. After his death, the Romans gleefully exhibited their willingness to disregard his last will and testament and how cruel they could be.[8]

Rather than respecting the spirit of Prasutagus' will, the Romans assumed complete control over his land and people. They plundered his kingdom and household, and maybe after Prasutagus' wife Boudica objected, the Romans decided to make an example of her and the royal family. The Romans restrained Queen Boudica, likely in public view, and whipped her mercilessly—leaving her clothes in tatters and skin bloodied and bruised—but this torture and humiliation was nothing compared to the next disgrace. With Boudica restrained and quite possibly watching in horror, the Romans savagely raped her two young daughters—a wanton and outrageous offense. The Romans' message was clear: They were the world's superpower and expected passive obedience. For the time being, the Romans were finished making their brutal and heartless statement, but their greatest mistake was allowing Boudica to remain alive after committing these terrible atrocities.[9]

She planned to repay them for their savagery, and her subsequent endeavors and even her appearance would strike fear into the hearts of the Romans. The Roman historian and senator Cassius Dio described Boudica as "very tall, in appearance most terrifying, in the glance of her eye most fierce, and her voice was harsh; a great mass of the tawniest hair fell to her hips; around her neck was a large golden necklace; and she wore a tunic of diverse colours over which a thick mantle was fastened with a brooch. This was her invariable attire." This was the woman who would shake the empire to its core.[10]

Dishonored and motivated to seek vengeance, Boudica roused the Iceni to turn against the Romans. Then she recruited others into the fold as she cobbled together a foreboding coalition of forces with one shared goal in mind: achieving freedom from the Romans. Barbarian revolts and uprisings were not particularly unusual in old Rome, but this one was different. Within a short span of time, Boudica raised a formidable army allegedly numbering 230,000 men and led many of them into battle beginning in 60 CE.[11]

With relative ease, she captured and razed cities that stood in her way, including Camulodunum (modern Colchester), Londinium (London) and Verulamium (near St. Albans). Boudica and her supporters responded to Roman cruelty with their own form of barbarism. They took no prisoners. Instead, they remorselessly slew the Roman men but had unconscionable plans for the captured women. "The worst and most bestial atrocity committed by their captors was the following," wrote Cassius Dio. "They hung up naked the noblest and most distinguished women and then cut off their breasts and sewed them to their mouths, in order to make the victims appear to be eating them; afterwards they impaled the women on sharp skewers run lengthwise through the entire body."[12]

Boudica did not just kill defenseless farmers, merchants and women. She also defeated experienced Roman veterans on the battlefield. The Romans in Britannia were in full retreat in the face of Boudica's relentless, deadly onslaught. During the conflict, the Britons massacred around 70,000–80,000 Romans and Roman allies—numbers that should be treated with skepticism.[13] Matters were so dire that Nero at some point even considered abandoning the island altogether, but the Romans reconsidered and resolved to try to re-pacify the region, which would not be easy.[14]

In response to the uprising, Rome mounted a competent, but unlikely, defense of their interests in Britannia—thanks in large part to the commander Gaius Suetonius Paulinus. He was Britannia's provincial governor, and at the onset of the Boudica rebellion, he was in Wales subduing the region. After learning of the uprising, he gathered the 14th legion, part of the 20th and other troops from nearby. All told, he mustered around 10,000 men, which paled in comparison to Boudica's enormous army, and he readied for a set-piece battle with the fearsome queen.[15]

The two met on an open plain, but its location is unknown. Some modern researchers have suggested that it was near High Cross in Leicestershire or Mancetter in Warwickshire. Regardless of the setting, with Boudica standing proudly on a horse-drawn chariot along with her daughters, she flew across the field, exhorting her troops to defeat the Romans, eject the invaders from their island and help her repay the Romans for their savagery. According to Tacitus, she exclaimed,

> But now it is not as a woman descended from noble ancestry, but as one of the people that I am avenging lost freedom, my scourged body, the outraged chastity of my daughters. Roman lust has gone so far that not our very persons, nor even age or virginity, are left unpolluted. But heaven is on the side of a righteous vengeance; a legion which dared to fight has perished; the rest are hiding themselves in their camp, or are thinking anxiously of flight. They will not sustain even the din and the shout of so many thousands, much less our charge and our blows. If you weigh [...] the strength of the armies, and the causes of the war, you will see that in this battle you must conquer or die. This is a woman's resolve; as for men, they may live and be slaves.

It is easy to imagine her speech generating a chorus of supportive shouts as her army was eager to engage the Romans. Presumably after making some tactical adjustments, Boudica sounded the charge. Even without much battle armor, her trouser-wearing followers rushed headlong with their swords, spears and shields toward the Roman lines, while her charioteers aimed to throw the Romans into chaos.[16]

Despite the Romans being grossly undermanned, Paulinus ordered his heavily armored legionaries to respond in kind. As a result, the two factions collided sometime in 61 CE, but Roman tenacity, discipline, training and organization ultimately won the day. Paulinus' legionaries broke Boudica's lines and methodically cut down the enemy—killing around 80,000 Britons. Supposedly, only 400 Romans died in the battle, but these casualty estimates should be taken with a grain of salt, given the ancients' propensity for exaggerating them. Regardless of the widespread carnage, Boudica managed to survive the battle, but she realized that the war was largely lost.

Rather than allowing herself to become a spectacle in a Roman triumph, as some accounts go, she drank poison—killing herself. Cassius Dio contended otherwise and stated that she fell ill to some malady and perished. There is no record of what became of her daughters, but they either escaped to the countryside to live in obscurity, consumed poison or the Romans killed them.[17]

Even with the queen dead, the campaign was not over. Some Britons were still in revolt, and Roman interests were not entirely secure in Britannia. In an effort to shore up the Romans' defenses and provide reinforcements, Nero transferred troops from Germany to Britannia. They included two thousand legionaries, eight auxiliary cohorts and one thousand cavalrymen—nearly 7,000 men in total. This is possibly when Titus found himself in Britannia, although he could have been deployed later, and if he did arrive at this time, then he must have taken part in reasserting Roman control over much of the region. It is unclear what role he might have played in the conflict, but he may have gained valuable war-time experience and witnessed extreme Roman brutality. After all, in order to neutralize the British tribes, the Romans took a ruthless approach.[18]

There is some scholarly debate over whether Titus' time in Britannia was particularly notable. The Roman historian Tacitus relayed a speech supposedly produced by an influential Roman named Gaius Licinius Mucianus. Within it, Mucianus extolled Titus' early successes, but failed to mention anything about his time in Britannia. Considering this, Titus might have been relegated to remaining encamped and managing logistical duties, instead of leading expeditions, but that is purely speculative.[19]

If Titus was tasked with leading troops, it is plausible that he and other Romans flew across Britannia and attacked locals who had warred with Rome and even those whose loyalties were simply in question. The Romans planned to make a devastating statement. They massacred an untold number of men from these tribes and destroyed their villages. As the consummate soldier, Titus would have obeyed his officers' commands even if they seemed unnecessarily severe, but as a military tribune, Titus could have played an even more important role.

It is possible that he also served as a conduit between tribal leaders and Rome's commander in order to achieve peaceful terms, but not all tribes were prepared to lay down their arms. While the barbarian cause was largely futile at this juncture, some Britons were steadfastly married to the notion of fighting Rome to the last, but they committed a grievous error that hastened their demise. They had assigned far too many men to their armies during the Boudica revolt, and far too few to farm the fields—resulting in a famine. In time, the rebellious Britons were starving, and they accepted their fates as the Romans subdued them.[20]

According to Suetonius, Titus appears to have assumed an important function in Britannia—whether that was related to the Boudica revolt or something else—and he earned great acclaim for his bravado, vigor and leadership. Proof of this could be seen during Suetonius' lifetime. The ancient author mentioned an inordinate number of busts and statues dedicated to Titus existing in both Germany and Britannia with glowing inscriptions—attesting to Titus' renown. Yet they could have been erected during or after Titus' ultimate ascent to the height of Roman power.[21]

Following Titus' apparent success, his military tribuneship ended, and maybe around 63 CE, he returned to Rome to foster his budding public career, promote his private business interests, including a legal practice, and build a family, but first, he needed a wife. Before long, he found one. Whether established in love or, more likely, because his family had organized the union, Titus married a woman named Arrecina Tertulla. Once the prenuptial relationship began, Titus probably courted her similarly to the way that people date today. They spent much of their free time together, shared meals, took strolls through the town center and gardens, and talked about their interests and aspirations. The two grew closer to one another even though this was almost certainly an arranged marriage, but the union revealed much about Vespasian's standing. It seems that Vespasian and Titus' status had improved since Vespasian's marriage because Titus' bride hailed from a family of some notable recent success, although their origins were more obscure.[22]

They had achieved equestrian status and undoubtedly enjoyed some wealth, which the Flavians needed since Agrippina had stymied the public career of Vespasian, who could have experienced some financial setbacks in the process. Titus' marriage could help change all of that. Arrecina's father, Marcus Arrecinus Clemens, was well-to-do and influential. He had served as one of the Praetorian Guard's prefects under Emperor Caligula, which was a prestigious and powerful role in which he co-commanded the emperor's private guard. Despite being charged to protect the emperor, he may very well have participated in Caligula's assassination or at least had knowledge of it.[23]

When the time came sometime in the early-to-mid 60s CE for Titus to wed Arrecina, if they held fast to tradition, then she excitedly readied herself at her father's home. Surrounded by her female relatives and friends, she prepared for the occasion. Using a spearhead to style Arrecina's hair, her helpers parted it into six locks—denoting the inextricable relationship between Rome's foundation, earliest weddings and warfare. They dressed her in the *tunica recta*, which was essentially a white robe with fringed edges, and tied a special belt around her that Titus would later untie. Finally, Arrecina draped a bright yellow veil over her head and slipped her feet into yellow shoes made for the day's festivities.[24]

Titus presumably waited at his home during much of Arrecina's preparation, dressed himself in his finest toga or tunic and styled his hair, and after some time, he slowly, albeit anxiously, traveled to his bride. When they met, they may have grasped each other's hands excitedly and made their way to see a priest who would oversee their wedding. Upon arriving, a sheep was sacrificed and its skin was then stretched over two chairs. Titus and Arrecina subsequently sat on these seats with their heads covered as a priest recited the marriage prayer. Then the two were wed, and another sacrifice was offered.[25]

This probably elicited applause from the spectators, but the festivities had just begun. At some point, Titus might have feigned pulling his supposedly reluctant bride from her mother's arms, which was done in fun. The genesis of this tradition supposedly traced back to the early Romans' forceful abduction of a host of virgins. Regardless of whether there's truth to this legend, the wedding cortege marched to Titus' house with his bride carrying a distaff and spindle for spinning wool. As they proceeded, they were flanked by family and friends who carried torches and made lewd jokes at the groom's expense. They also ceremonially shouted "Talassius!," which allegedly harked back to when Romulus' associates kidnapped a virgin for a well-liked man named Talassius. Eventually, Titus and Arrecina arrived at their destination, but halted outside of Titus' home.[26]

Before entering, Arrecina placed wool on the door and anointed it with either wolf's fat or some other kind of lard. Then Titus presented her with fire and water, which she ritually and very briefly touched. This being completed, Titus asked her what her name was, and she responded, "Wherever you are Gaius, I will be Gaia," Gaius being the generic male praenomen and Gaia being the feminine form of it. Afterward, Titus picked Arrecina up and carried her inside. This was generally done very carefully because if he tripped or her foot knocked on the door, then that was considered an ill omen.[27]

Once inside, Arrecina laid down her wool-spinning tools, and Titus handed her the keys to his home, which she eagerly accepted. With most of the rituals completed, both families enjoyed a sumptuous feast, perhaps including delicacies of the era, like stuffed dormice, and drank prodigious amounts of wine as they lounged on couches, conversed and enjoyed music. Some time later though, Titus and Arrecina's drunken guests needed to be off. The newlyweds had private business of their own to conduct. After drinking a fair amount of wine himself, Titus might have felt the impulsive urge to remove Arrecina's special matrimonial belt, and if anyone lingered when he untied it, then this served as a sign that they needed to quickly be on their way.[28]

So far as modern academics can tell, the two newlyweds wasted little time building a family. Titus very quickly impregnated Arrecina, who gave birth to a girl. She became known as Julia Flavia, although there is some scholarly debate over whether Julia belongs to Titus' first or second marriage and how many children he sired—one or two. This aside, little Julia certainly garnered Titus' love and affection, but this was not a time for celebration because tragedy struck. Arrecina died.[29] The ancient accounts do not offer a cause for her death, but she could have perished as a result of childbirth, which was a hazardous enterprise in antiquity. Very conservative estimates suggest that ancient Rome's maternal mortality rate was around 2.5 percent.[30] Even if childbirth did not cause Arrecina's death, there were still a host of ways to die young in old Rome thanks to regular bacterial outbreaks, various plagues, mosquito-borne diseases and consuming untreated water.

However she perished, Titus was left to provide her a funeral befitting the woman. Roman historians recorded no information whatsoever about her funeral, but propertied Romans often followed similar funerary practices. If Titus adhered to funerary norms of the day, then once she passed, the widower or one of Arrecina's other loved ones respectfully closed her eyes, and slaves washed her body with oils and perfumes and clothed her in some of her best attire. She was then placed on a couch within Titus' home and a coin was placed in her mouth—to enable her to pay the mythical ferryman to transport her across the River Styx and into Hades. The Romans believed that if this was not done, then it could result in the soul being left in a kind of metaphysical limbo, which could be tortuous on the soul.

After Arrecina's body laid on the couch for around eight days and received distraught visitors who gave her their last respects, the funeral began. Funerals generally occurred at night, and thus, one evening, loved ones carried Arrecina out. Mourning family members and musicians playing sorrowful music trailed along and passed Rome's *pomerium*, or sacred boundary. They did so because cremations and burials within the city were expressly forbidden for fear of contaminating Rome. Once the cavalcade reached its destination, Titus saw a funeral pyre—built of wood and appearing as an altar.

They placed Arrecina upon the pyre, and Titus or her father likely provided the young lady a glowing eulogy and recounted her and her family's successes. With this completed, everyone bade her goodbye, and the pyre was set ablaze. It took time for the conflagration to reduce her to ashes, but after the fire lit up the dark night, it slowly extinguished. At this point, the embers were doused with wine, and her remains were carefully collected and placed in an urn. With this step completed, a priest subsequently purified the people tasked with collecting the remains using water from either a laurel or olive branch. They were then free to finalize the funerary ceremony and inter Arrecina's ashes in the family mausoleum.[31]

Regardless of whether Titus' union with Arrecina was forged in love or arranged by his parents, the loss was shocking, but Titus may have been forced to grieve without the love and support of his father. With Agrippina no longer an obstacle ever since Nero had her killed, Vespasian had felt safe enough to once again promote his political career and managed to re-forge a relationship with Nero, and his endeavors paid off. The emperor appointed him governor of the Roman province of Africa where he became Nero's representative, served as the region's administrator, ruled in some judicial disputes and commanded the legionaries stationed there. Unfortunately, nobody can say with certainty when Vespasian held this one-year posting, but it would have taken place sometime around 63 CE. This was an immense opportunity. Provincial governors often enriched themselves at the expense of their subjects and sometimes waged lucrative wars against Rome's enemies, but glory did not await Vespasian in Africa.[32]

Vespasian appears to have governed the province conscientiously for the most part. He earned a name for being an effective and just administrator while there, but a riot in the ancient city of Hadrumetum, which now rests in the Sousse governorate of Tunisia, marred his tenure. Little detail remains of the uprising, but one thing seems clear: The locals were not pleased with Vespasian, possibly due to food shortages thanks to imperial public policy. He attempted to quell the riot, but the people of Hadrumetum responded to his entreaties by hurling turnips at the man—the second time Rome's subjects had pelted him publicly in anger. This dishonor aside, the violence subsided in time. He was subsequently free to focus on the normal business of governing the province, but he did not unfairly enrich himself. In fact, when he departed Africa for Rome, he was in worse financial shape than before he left. Upon his return to the Italian peninsula, he even resorted to either selling mules or running a transportation company that relied on mules to earn a living and received the embarrassing sobriquet "the muleteer" as a result. This was not the limit of his humiliation. His credit and level of debt was so disturbing that he mortgaged his estates to his brother.[33]

Perhaps while Titus' father was away governing Africa or—more likely—shortly thereafter, the young widower mustered his strength to raise his infant child and continue his career. He presumably tended to the family business—maybe overseeing some farmland—and began practicing law thanks to his education. Grieving or not over Arrecina's recent death, Titus remarried. While it is not evident if he made the decision to do so or Vespasian did in order to link the Flavians with another influential family, Titus resolved to remarry and took Marcia Furnilla's hand in marriage.[34] Marcia was part of a noble family that traced its lineage to Rome's fabled fourth king, known as Ancus Marcius. Even in Titus' time, they had enjoyed political success and boasted considerable wealth—something that could benefit Vespasian following his financial troubles.[35]

As before, Titus and his bride probably organized a wedding with the usual pomp and pageantry normal for the time to the delight of their guests, but the marriage was short-lived. For an undisclosed reason, the two quickly divorced one another, but as modern historians have suggested, it seems that the divorce was a political necessity. Marcia's family had been accused of conspiring against Nero. Marcia's uncle, Barea Soranus, had allegedly incited Romans to rise up against Nero. What's more, Marcia's cousin, Marcia Servilia Sorana, was married to Gaius Annius Pollio—a man whom Nero had exiled for conspiring against him. Considering all of this, the Flavians subsequently must have worried that if Titus remained married to Marcia, then they would lose favor with Nero. While Vespasian and Titus would not be executed, they would be guilty by association and each would become *persona non grata*. Nero would ensure that they would receive no further appointments, and their influence would wane. In order to spare the family from this undue punishment, Titus severed ties with Marcia, who was likely innocent of any wrongdoing.[36]

Divorce was not altogether uncommon. It was easy in ancient Rome and widely practiced. In order to obtain a divorce, state and religious authorities did not need to be involved. The general practice involved delivering a written notice of the intent to divorce and a justification to the opposing party. In order to be well-attested and accepted, there ought to be seven witnesses to the dissolution, and the husband should restore all his wife's property to her, unless she faced a penalty for misbehavior. In some cases, a religious ritual accompanied divorces, but this was not necessary for most people.

Titus and Marcia went through the relatively painless divorce process, which kept the Flavians in Nero's good graces, but some anguish remained. At some point, Marcia had provided Titus with a child, another girl also named Flavia. Unfortunately, like the aforementioned marriage, this child appears to have died young, given that there is no record of her other than her birth—leaving him with only Julia Flavia. This was not the only tragedy facing the Flavians. Sometime very possibly in the mid–60s CE, Titus' mother and sister—both named Domitilla—passed away from unknown causes.

The late 50s and very early 60s CE seemed to provide the Flavians with many opportunities, but they were beset with misfortunes shortly thereafter. Between Vespasian's financial difficulties, Titus' failed marriage, and the deaths of his first wife, second child, mother and sister, much of the later 60s CE presented the family with tragedy, adversity and challenges. This suffering aside, an incredible sequence of events, including a fire of epic proportions, domestic unrest and foreign war would thrust the Flavians to the forefront of Roman society and turn Titus into a veritable national hero.[37]

IV

Judaea

> *"So the time when we should have done everything possible to keep out the Romans was when Pompey was invading our country. But our forefathers and their kings, despite financial, physical, and moral resources far greater than yours, failed to resist a small fraction of the Roman army."*
> —King Agrippa II[1]

AFTER NERO ORDERED HIS MOTHER'S MURDER, matters began to deteriorate for him in ways that turned many of his subjects against him. Titus and Vespasian were well-aware of his many faults, scandals, rumors of his debauchery and external events that shaped his imperial tenure for the worse. For starters, Nero seemed as though he was more interested in the arts and athletic contests than he was in the day-to-day administration of Rome, which was initially a dismaying revelation to his subjects. The Romans considered actors, musicians and athletes as disreputable people—even though the Romans loved watching them perform—but Nero was determined to excel in these industries even if they eroded imperial dignity.[2]

Nero was known for traveling the empire and giving prolonged, boring performances that exposed his lack of talent, but no matter how desperately his audience members wanted to leave his shows early, they knew doing so would risk the emperor's ire and might prove dangerous to their well-being. In some cases, pregnant women gave birth during his recitals and men feigned death in order to exit the theater.[3] Others simply stared off into space or fell asleep. Some accounts even claim that Vespasian either quietly left or dozed off during one of Nero's recitals in Greece around 66 CE, which drove a wedge between the two.[4]

Nero was no better in his other endeavors. While he enjoyed competing in chariot races, he apparently lacked the necessary skill. During one such race, he fell from his carriage, had to be helped back on and apparently did not even finish the race. Despite this, the judges awarded him the crown of victory, and how could they not when he was the sitting emperor?[5]

Nero's theatrical and athletic obsessions were not the least of his scandals from the Romans' perspectives. Ancient authors related stories of Nero dressing as a bride and celebrating a wedding ceremony with a freedman—Pythagoras.[6] While homosexuality was entirely acceptable in old Rome, there were some caveats, particularly including that men of status should never take the subservient, passive role in copulation with lower-class males. Nero apparently violated this social norm and flaunted it before his subjects. In another incident, Nero married a boy named Sporus whom he had castrated. Over the course of his life, Nero also married three different women, but he supposedly killed one of his wives, Poppaea Sabina, who was pregnant at the time, by brutally and repeatedly kicking her.[7] For men with provincial values, like Vespasian and Titus, Nero's proclivities were nothing short of appalling.

Before some of these controversies supposedly came to pass, tragedy struck Rome. On a mid-July night in 64 CE, fire broke out either in or near the Circus Maximus. How it began is anyone's guess. It could have sprung from an unattended cooking fire, misplaced oil lamp or even arson. The dried timber supporting many Roman buildings quickly caught fire, which spread from house to house and shop to shop. Even opulent villas, temples and administrative buildings were not immune. The fires roared day and night, and fanned by the wind, it consumed Rome. The *vigiles* worked their hardest to tame the great fire. While they maintained impressive numbers—supposedly seven cohorts of 1,000 men each—and were armed with water buckets, axes and ladders, their implements were insufficient. Realizing this, they began to topple buildings to contain the fire, but they faced a blaze unlike anything they had seen before. In the end, after six days and seven nights, more than two-thirds of Rome's districts were impacted, and while most Romans survived, it left many thousands of people homeless and uncontrolled looting became rampant in Rome's ruins.[8]

Some blamed Nero for starting the fire and spread rumors about his alleged involvement, and these unsubstantiated reports persist today. A few claimed that he sent men into the city to start the blaze because he found the city disorganized and ugly. As another account goes, watching from a safe distance, he performed—singing the Capture of Troy—but this is unlikely. These stories were probably created or at least disseminated by his enemies. After all, there is little evidence supporting these accusations, and it seems as though he was not even in Rome when the city burst into flames. Tacitus claimed that Nero was at one of his villas at Antium—dozens of miles away from Rome—preparing for a singing contest when the conflagration broke out. Yet, once the fire began, he hastened to Rome's assistance. He provided food and temporary housing to the recently displaced refugees from his own purse. To ensure a disaster of this magnitude never again transpired, he instituted anti-fire regulations and began to remove the city's rubble, but he soon considered how to rebuild Rome and saw a personal opportunity.[9]

He planned to annex vast swaths of the recently vacated space and build himself a luxurious estate unequaled in the ancient world. It would be adorned with gold, precious stones and ivory; have therapeutic baths and a circular dining room that could rotate to the delight of guests; have a colossal 120-foot statue of himself towering over the villa; workmen would create a personal lake on the property for

Nero and undoubtedly ornate gardens; and the estate would cover around 200 acres of Rome. Nero's zeal for building a grand estate—called the *domus aurea*—in the charred city center doubtless added to the rumors that he was behind the fire. To pay for the lavish palace, Nero levied burdensome taxes on the provinces and debased Roman money by minting more coinage and reducing the silver content and weight of the link coin known as the denarius. This was a recipe for economic instability.[10]

It is possible that Titus and Vespasian did not witness the great fire of Rome firsthand, given that they could have been elsewhere at the time furthering their careers. Titus had already served as military tribune in Germany and Britannia, and he certainly eyed his entrance into the Senate. Like his father, he sought the quaestorship. With his father's help, the Senate presumably elected him—providing him a seat in the Senate. His quaestorship may have fallen in 64 CE or later. While it is plausible that he was stationed in Rome, he could have been deployed to any one of a host of provincial postings.[11] Meanwhile, Vespasian had been Africa's governor sometime around 63 CE. He may not have returned in time to witness the fire or if he had, he might have been safely lodged in Sabine country selling mules.

Regardless of their whereabouts, Nero sought to insulate himself from accusations that he was behind the fire, and according to Tacitus, he found a scapegoat, a newly formed cult: Christianity.[12] To the pagan Romans, Christians were bizarre and seemed like little more than a strange sect of Judaism, which they also scarcely understood. They looked at Judaism as less of a religion and more of a superstition. Yet both Christianity and Judaism posed some problems to the Romans. To begin with, the monotheistic adherents were reluctant to worship Caesars as gods and did not recognize the pantheon of pagan deities. From the Roman perspective, all subjects needed to show the proper respect to the gods in order to avert their wrath, and the Caesars demanded obedience. What better way to do this than to require their worship?

The Romans tolerated the practice of Judaism, in part, because it was an ancient, established religion and wanted to keep peace in the tumultuous regions of Judaea and Galilee. However, the Romans increasingly looked at Christianity with skepticism and contempt.[13] Given all of this, Nero decided to accuse them of starting Rome's great fire, and he initiated Rome's first known Christian persecution.

"Mockery of every sort was added to their deaths," wrote Tacitus, who was no friend of the Christians. "Covered with the skins of beasts, they were torn by dogs and perished, or were nailed to crosses, or were doomed to the flames and burnt, to serve as a nightly illumination, when daylight had expired."[14] Nero's cruel and heavy-handed persecution did not just affect new converts and anonymous congregants. Some of those who have become household names reportedly perished in this pogrom. Saints Peter and Paul also died around 64 CE, per some accounts. In the end, an untold number of early Christians met their end in the Neronian persecution, but not all modern historians agree that it actually occurred. A more recent theory suggests that Nero instead targeted members of the cult of Isis, an Egyptian goddess.[15]

Whatever the case, not long after, Titus may have looked to promote his career further and obtained an even more prestigious public office—possibly serving as an aedile in 66 CE, although this is purely conjecture. Nevertheless, around the same time, Nero faced a threat in the East that would make Vespasian and Titus famous—a revolt in Judaea, which fell under the empire's purview. The Biblical story of the Jews is known the world over. The Jewish people had been slaves in Egypt, secured their freedom and settled in what is largely known as Israel today, according to the Biblical narrative. Their existence, on the other hand, was anything but peaceful.[16]

After establishing themselves there, the Jewish tribes were frequently mired in conflict with various enemies, including the Canaanites and Philistines. In time, the Jewish people formed a unified kingdom called Israel, which later split into two, Israel and Judah, that in many ways thrived before falling under the dominion of other ancient superpowers, including the Babylonians, Persians and then Hellenistic kingdoms. Following centuries of oppression, the Jewish people achieved greater autonomy and formed an independent state in the second century BCE. The Hasmonean dynasty of kings led it, but the Jewish independence did not last long.[17]

By around 67 BCE, the mother of two Hasmonean princes, Hyrcanus and Aristobulus, died. Her name was Salome Alexandra, and she had effectively ruled Judaea. Upon her death, her sons sparked a civil war to determine who would ascend to the purple and govern the kingdom. The brothers desperately jockeyed for a decisive advantage and looked for foreign aid from the Roman Republic. They both courted Pompey the Great who eventually sided with Hyrcanus. The Romans subsequently marched into Judaea and easily defeated the opposition. Upon doing so in 63 BCE, Pompey entered the Holy of Holies, which was the Jewish tabernacle's inner sanctuary and where the Ark of the Covenant would have been placed, had the Jews still been in possession of it. He did so out of curiosity, but in the process, he desecrated the sacred Temple.

Pompey also solidified Hyrcanus' claim with some stipulations. He would become high priest, but not king, of Judaea; Rome would take possession of parts of the kingdom; the remaining Jewish nation would become a Roman client-state; and its people would be required to pay hefty taxes to Rome. Put simply, the brother's feud cost the Jews their independence, and the results embittered and impoverished them. Decades of Roman involvement in Judaea followed, which provided Vespasian and Titus lasting glory.[18]

By Titus' lifetime, Jews lived throughout the Roman empire and interacted with the pagan Romans regularly. However, the Romans' relationship with the Jewish people was always strained—leading to protests, revolts and various scandals. The Romans' views on Jews ranged from indifference to contempt, while the Greeks in the Roman empire tended to be even less accepting of the Jews. To begin with, the empire's majority pagan population simply could not understand why the Jews rested once a week, refused to eat delicacies like pork, circumcised their penises and only recognized one God. To keep the peace, Roman officials permitted the Jews to worship as they wished—with one particular requirement. Roman emperors wanted those living in the East to make regular sacrifices to them. The Jews steadfastly refused to do this, but the Romans struck a deal with them. They only had to make recurring sacrifices on behalf of the emperor, instead of to the emperor.[19]

This worked for some time, but during Nero's reign, factions within the Jewish population were quickly tiring of Rome's brutal oppression and complained of myriad affronts. The Romans were not especially sympathetic to the Jewish protests and often operated with a heavy hand. At times, they were dismissive of their traditions and observances, and they assigned flawed administrators to oversee matters in the region, which was not a particularly desirable posting. Yet there were other issues bubbling below the surface. Local socioeconomic difficulties troubled the Jews, and widespread brigandage was on the rise as gangs roamed the countryside. This presented a challenging set of factors on its own, but matters quickly came to a head starting around 66 CE.[20]

First, some Greeks in Caesarea Maritima—on the Mediterranean coast northwest of Jerusalem—mockingly sacrificed birds near a synagogue's entrance, which angered the Jews and led to a riot. The Jews looked to Gessius Florus, the Roman procurator—or administrator—of Judaea for help, but he sided with the Greeks. Sadly, the offenses did not end there. Already tired of Rome's oppressive taxes and currently in arrears, Roman troops entered the Jewish treasury and removed 17 talents—an immense fortune—of wealth for the emperor. While this covered some of the Jews' back-taxes, this may have been intended to go toward relieving the financial pain of rebuilding Rome.

Whatever its planned use, the seizure did not go over well. The Jews were understandably outraged, and they insulted Florus. To taunt him, they began a grassroots fundraising campaign for the Roman procurator—passing around a donation basket—as if he was a beggar stricken with poverty. This offended the easily roused and thin-skinned Florus who, in turn, marched into Jerusalem and demanded that the Jewish nobility surrender those who had ridiculed him. When they failed to acquiesce, he released his troops on the city with orders to wreak havoc. They plundered part of Jerusalem and tortured and slaughtered a host of Jews. All told, the Romans massacred around 3,600 people, including newborns.[21]

The Jews tried to reason with Florus and suppliantly asked for his mercy as well as applied for his superior's support—a man named Cestius Gallus—who was the governor of Roman Syria, but their efforts failed. Many Jews began to conclude that a holy war of independence was their only option, but some cooler heads attempted to quell these revolutionary ideas. Even the pro–Roman, Jewish client-king Herod Agrippa II and his sister Berenice tried—but failed—to forestall the looming revolt because many Jews wanted freedom and Roman blood. To his credit, the client-king tried to convince the instigators to adopt a more rational approach. In a long speech,

Agrippa called for patience and restraint and warned his subjects of the futility and dangers of provoking the Roman Empire.[22]

Agrippa exclaimed, "Granted that the Roman ministers are intolerably harsh, it does not follow that all the Romans are unjust to you any more than Caesar; Yet it is against them, against him, that you are going to war." Agrippa asserted matters would likely change for the better soon. "The same procurator will not remain forever, and it is probable that the successors will show greater moderation on taking office," the King said. "But war once [begun] cannot be lightly [...] broken off or carried through without risk of disaster."[23]

He then recounted the innumerable foes that the Romans had vanquished—leaving much of the known world squarely in the empire's control. Challenging the Romans would simply risk Jewish lives, livelihoods and their holiest relics and buildings. "Take pity, then, if not on your children and your wives, at least on your mother city and its sacred precincts," Agrippa urged. "Spare the Temple and preserve for yourselves the sanctuary with its holy places; for the Romans, once masters of these, will refrain their hands no more, seeing that their forbearance in the past [has been] met only with ingratitude."[24]

If the Jews truly wanted independence, then given the current state of affairs, they had missed their opportunity thanks to their forebears' machinations, according to Agrippa. "So the time when we should have done everything possible to keep out the Romans was when Pompey was invading our country. But our forefathers and their kings, despite financial, physical, and moral resources far greater than yours, failed to resist a small fraction of the Roman army."[25]

Agrippa spoke some sense—as did many others within Jerusalem who opposed war with Rome—and in fact, a host of Jews had no desire for the conflict. The moderates understood that there were some benefits to being in the empire. It certainly boosted trade, provided some kind of protection from external threats and made many Jews rich and powerful. Others were likewise sympathetic to Agrippa's concerns that war against a hulking empire would devastate the Jewish homeland and result in defeat. None of this is to say that the vast majority of the Jews did not want to be free of the Roman shackles, but they understood that their quest for independence would fail and the effort would not be worth the cost.

Some of the other Jewish factions were not willing to wait for Rome to address its misdeeds, and many called for Agrippa's banishment and even attempted to stone him. They did not stop there, though. An insurgency rose up and revolted against the Romans. As it did, the Jews forbade sacrifices for the Roman people and emperor, which was a veritable declaration of war; a Jewish militia attacked the desert fortress of Masada and massacred the Roman defenders; and the Jews turned on one another—even waging a kind of civil war within Jerusalem whereupon the insurgents ultimately overpowered Agrippa and his pro-peace faction. As a result, the rebels seized much of the city and its Antonia Fortress. It was a citadel built by Herod the Great and named for Mark Antony that protected the northwestern corner of the Temple Mount. With revolutionaries asserting their control, King Agrippa II was forced to flee.[26]

The Jewish rebellion gradually took form, but it was not a neat, well-organized, centrally orchestrated affair. There were competing warlords who acted independently; it appeared like an improvised uprising early in the revolt; and it afflicted different parts of the Jewish world at different times. Yet the Jews were not in agreement over the need to rebel. Some Jewish cities refused to side with their countrymen. Nevertheless, the Jewish combatants managed to obtain weapons on a large scale and demonstrated that they could be just as cruel as the Romans.[27]

What followed was pandemonium. Jewish insurgents swept across the region—capturing forts and cities and massacring an untold number of those who stood in their way, even if they were Jewish. They seized the Cypros fort near Jericho, slaughtered the legionaries stationed there, and ejected the Romans from Machaerus, a fortress near the Dead Sea. Meanwhile, many Romans turned on Jewish populations and slaughtered tens of thousands of them across the empire. During the early days of the revolt, they reportedly killed 20,000 defenseless Jews in Caesarea Maritima, 50,000 in Alexandria, 2,500 in Ascalon, 2,000 in Ptolemais and eventually 10,500 in Damascus.[28]

Matters were quickly spiraling out of control, and Cestius Gallus decided to march into Judaea and end the revolt. Supported by thousands of locals, including King Agrippa II and his loyalists, the Roman troops invaded Judaea and initially tasted a fair amount of success—killing thousands of enemy combatants and beginning an abortive siege of Jerusalem. Likely due to dangerously overextended supply lines, Cestius retreated, but the Jewish rebels harassed him and his legions. As the Romans withdrew, the Jews ambushed Cestius' army and inflicted serious losses—killing nearly 6,000 Romans and capturing supplies and weapons. What must have initially seemed like just another minor revolt on the fringes of the empire quickly proved otherwise, which shocked imperial officials.[29]

With the Romans gone, leaders in Jerusalem formed a provisional government in the power vacuum, but it never exerted complete control over the Jews or even Jerusalem, at least for long. This aside, it was led by Joseph ben Gurion and Ananus ben Ananus—who is perhaps best remembered for ordering the stoning of Jesus Christ's brother James, according to Jewish historian Flavius Josephus. There is plenty of academic debate over what the provisional government's goals truly were, especially considering that it was largely administered by a more moderate Jewish faction.[30]

Some have suggested that the new government was not particularly married to the notion of an all-out war with Rome, although they knew a conflict of some form would invariably transpire. Rather they wanted to consolidate power, unify the Jews' ancestral homeland and elbow radicals out of positions of power. Then, so the theory goes, they could more adequately defend themselves from Roman attacks if necessary and—most importantly—be in a position to negotiate a more favorable peace settlement with the Romans. This is plausible, but it is the stuff for academics to argue over.

One thing is certain: Jewish leaders made serious preparations for war, including completing and raising some of Jerusalem's unfinished walls, fortifying other cities and recruiting troops. They also appointed military captains over different districts, including sending a man who later became the aforementioned historian known as Josephus, to Galilee. He was an interesting choice for the job. He hailed from a priestly family, claimed noble descent, was a Pharisee and, as his autobiography claims, he had tried to prevent the revolt, but peace turned out to be elusive.[31]

The more bellicose elements within Judaea were steadfastly intent on waging a war of independence. This was an unfortunate reality for the Romans. Responding to the threat would require the empire's attention and resources. Meanwhile, Jerusalem was in turmoil, and many people understandably fled the holy city. Among those quitting Jerusalem were members of the fledgling Christian community. According to an ecclesiastical tradition first recorded by early church leader Eusebius, the Christians deserted the holy city and marched for Pella, which now lies in Jordan, possibly just before the war started. Yet the specific date and even year that they left is up to debate. Regardless of their departure, some pro-Roman Jews remained in Jerusalem and hoped to persuade their countrymen to abandon their futile war with Rome. Meanwhile, the rebels understood that the Romans would ultimately return. So one of the revolution's chief and most capable generals—Josephus—began reinforcing strongholds across Galilee.

He naturally predicted that the Romans would invade from the north. As such, he focused on fortifying positions in Galilee first, while the Jews raised walls and bulwarks across their ancestral homeland. Josephus and his fellow Jews supposedly erected defenses in the cities of Jotapata, Bersabe, Selame, Caphareccho, Japha, Sigo, Mount Tabor, Tarichaea, Tiberias, Seleucia, Sogane, Gamala, Sepphoris, Gischala and Achabari. He even fortified the caves near the Sea of Galilee, and raised a massive army that he hoped would be capable of countering the well-trained and professional Roman legionaries.

Josephus reportedly levied an army of 100,000 men at arms—drawing from various sources including mercenary bands—but this is almost certainly an exaggeration. Modern estimates have suggested that Josephus only had 8,000–10,000 under his control, including allied troops. However, this was supposedly no "rag tag" army. While they were not professional soldiers—more likely peasants and bandits—Josephus organized them meticulously by creating a chain of command with officers, much like the Romans did. They were likewise well-provisioned and felt ready to take on the Roman juggernaut. Despite these impressive preparations, internal disputes—sometimes violent and always self-defeating—between different Jewish factions continually hampered their cause.[32]

News traveled slowly in the ancient world, but before long, reports of the disastrous events in Judaea reached Nero who was nothing short of stunned, which added

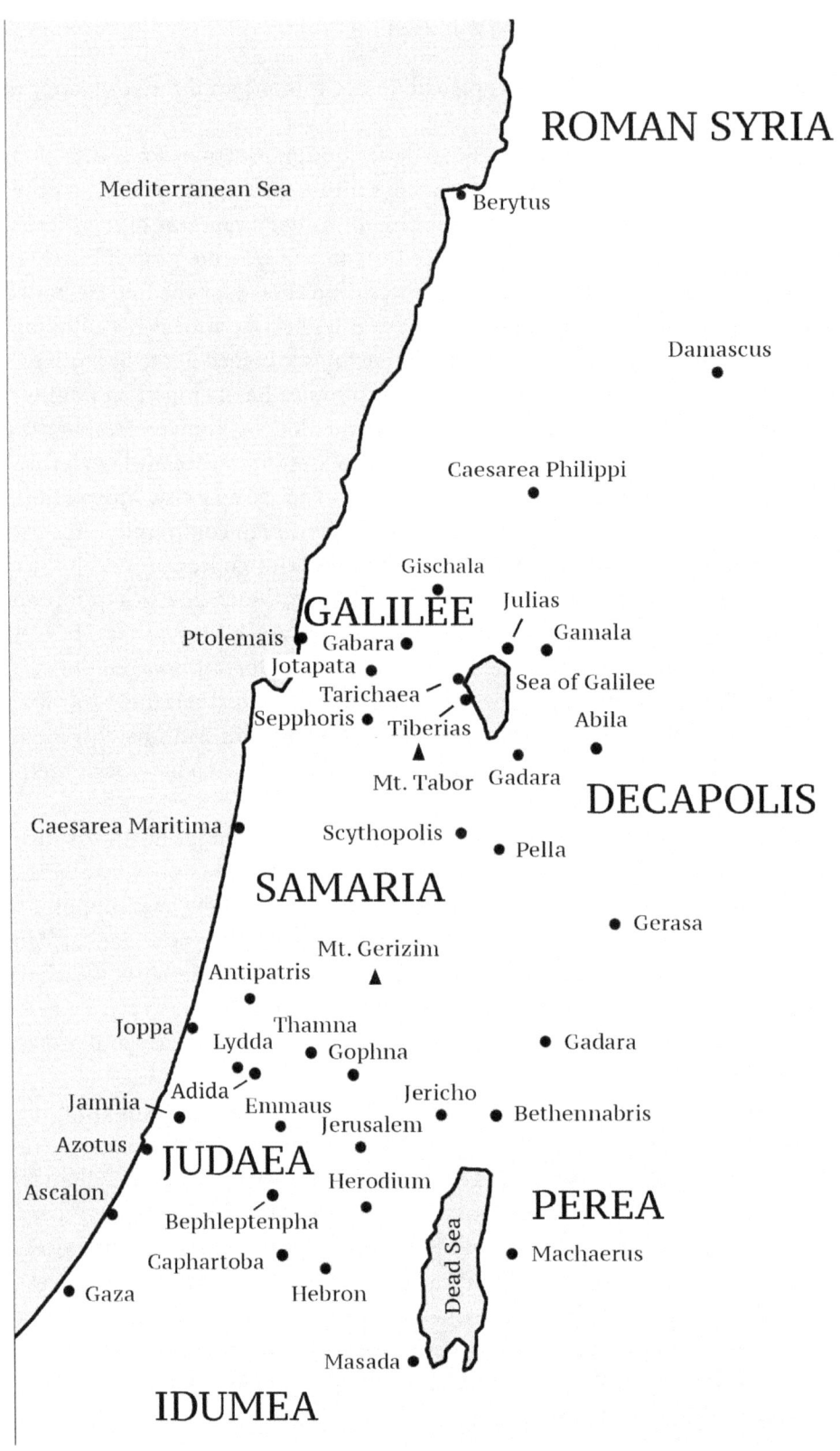

Judaea and its environs in the time of Titus.

to his already-existing anxiety. After all, two years prior, much of Rome had burned to the ground, and he was growing increasingly unpopular among the aristocracy and around the empire. In fact, conspiracies had formed to assassinate Nero, but they had failed. Regardless, they were chilling reminders to Nero that his grip on power was tenuous and unassured. What's more, this appeared to be more than a simple uprising. The Jews had already shown remarkable strength and the ability to capably challenge Rome. This could not be tolerated anywhere in the empire, especially in this region. Instability in the eastern reaches of the Roman Empire could present the Parthian Empire—Rome's rival in the East—a tempting opportunity to destabilize the geopolitical landscape. The Judaean news was the last thing he needed, and he probably feared that it could prevent him from focusing entirely on what he deemed critically important: the arts and athletic contests.[33]

Even though this reportedly sent a fearful shiver down Nero's spine, he sought to project confidence and downplay the seriousness of the revolt, which makes sense. He understood that telegraphing an air of superiority and dignity was required of the emperor of the ancient world's greatest empire at the time. He also did not want to give his enemies fodder to use against him. Privately, he must have revealed his feelings to his confidants and trusted lieutenants, but he had little time to wallow in terror; he needed to solve the crisis.[34]

Unlike Julius Caesar, who was a storied military commander, and even emperors Augustus and Tiberius, who had some legitimate battlefield experience, Nero had virtually none. He was an inexperienced, pampered young man who largely relied on others to ensure the mechanics of the empire continued to function. Dealing with the Judaean uprising was no different. Given his ignorance of warfare's intricacies, he needed to appoint someone to reassert Rome's dominance and quell further disturbances.

Nero had plenty of viable options as there was no shortage of promising military men in the empire who had successfully led legionaries into serious battles. However, Nero needed someone who met specific criteria: His prospective commander needed to be a loyalist and have a strong military record; must be able to take command of troops as quickly as possible; and perhaps most importantly, he could not be expected to challenge the emperor's position as ruler of the empire or become more popular than him. So Nero looked around for a battle-tested veteran of humble origins who was relatively close to the Judaean front and not particularly charismatic. There was just one man for the job: Vespasian who was—evidently along with Titus—currently in Greece because they had traveled there with Nero as the emperor strove to demonstrate his artistic abilities.[35]

Vespasian was originally an equestrian from an uninspiring family, and he was not a particularly charismatic character. He had struggled to climb the *cursus honorum*. His record was marked by at least one electoral loss and being pelted with turnips and mud. He was apparently also a poor businessman and resorted to selling mules—meaning he did not seem like someone who could become a rival claimant to the throne or even outshine Nero. Even so, he had enjoyed a successful career as a military man—serving in the invasion of Britannia and elsewhere. Beyond this, he had an energetic son—Titus—who showed promise, had military experience and would certainly serve as a benefit to Vespasian in the East.

Despite recently falling asleep during one of Nero's performances, the emperor approached Vespasian, flattered him with sundry compliments and offered him the power to prosecute the Jewish War. Seeing this as a massive opportunity—not just for him, but for his son Titus too—Vespasian eagerly accepted. Thus Vespasian was tasked with taking command of legions in the Roman province of Syria and one legion stationed in Alexandria, Egypt. Together, Vespasian and Titus prepared for their roles in the coming war. Little did they or anyone realize, the path to Jerusalem would eventually lead to unrivaled power in Rome.[36]

V

Jotapata

> *"And now at one and the same time the trumpets of all the legions blared their signal, the whole army raised a terrific war cry, and at the given sign volleys of arrows from all positions darkened the sky."*
> —Josephus[1]

VESPASIAN WASTED LITTLE TIME UPON RECEIVING his charge from Nero. One of his first acts as chief commander of the Jewish War was to appoint his son—Titus—leadership over the 15th Legion, and dispatched him to collect it. The 15th Legion was not the most experienced or renowned, but it was not terribly far from the front. It was stationed in the port city of Alexandria, Egypt. This assignment was a bit unusual for a commander's son to receive, especially given Titus' youthfulness, level of experience and that he had not even held the praetorship yet. Nevertheless, Titus excitedly accepted the posting, and he knew that it could provide him with riches, fame and political power. Being ambitious and steadfastly loyal to his father, he obeyed Vespasian's directives, and armed with official decrees, he boarded a vessel in Greece, set sail for Egypt and crossed the treacherous Mediterranean Sea, which the Romans called "*Mare Nostrum*," or "Our Sea."

The Roman sea was notoriously dangerous to traverse during the winter. To this day, the Mediterranean Sea floor is littered with the remains of ships—both ancient and modern—that could not withstand its infamous rough seas and tempestuous weather. These risks did not stop Titus. Perhaps in late 66 or early 67 CE, he pressed on toward Alexandria, and he arrived without reported incident and much more quickly than anticipated. Once there, he presumably met with the local Roman officials—maybe including the governor Tiberius Julius Alexander—to discuss his new posting and upcoming operation.[2]

If he had not heard already, Titus learned of the mass killing of some 50,000 Jews in Alexandria—a tragic and lamentable turn of events—but Titus was not tasked with meting out justice or instituting order in Alexandria. Rather, he and the 15th Legion needed to depart from Egypt as soon as practicable to assist his father and quell the Jewish rebellion. After speaking with his troops, cobbling together plans with his lieutenants and ensuring the legionaries would be well-provisioned on their expedition, they began their long march from Egypt to Judaea—a trek of hundreds of miles.[3]

As Titus labored to fulfill his father's commands, Vespasian traveled from Greece to the Roman province of Syria overland to take command of the war effort, prepare the 5th and 10th Legions for an extended conflict and raise additional troops. Soon enough, he arrived in Antioch, Syria and solicited aid from allied client-kings, including King Agrippa II, Antiochus of Commagene, Soaemus of Emesa and Malchus of Nabatea. Very quickly, it became clear that this was not a simple war pitting Rome against the Jewish people. It was now a complex international affair and an untold number of Jews opposed one another. Many of them fought for Rome's client-kings, and considering Rome's history, there were doubtless many with Jewish ancestry serving in Rome's legions.

Before long, Vespasian sat at the head of a growing multinational army capable of accomplishing both great and terrible things. Pleased with his groundwork, he began to march toward the coastal city of Ptolemais—modern-day Acre, Israel—with a simple plan in mind: first neutralize Galilee and then Judaea, while slowly tightening the noose around Jerusalem, which would be the last major obstacle in the war. In spite of these lofty goals and Vespasian and Titus' war preparations, the Jewish combatants were not ready to passively surrender nor were they idle in the interim.[4]

A large band of Jews—led by Niger of Perea, Silas the Babylonian and John the Essene—decided to attack the city of Ascalon in the southern Levant. A relatively small detachment of Romans, including an infantry cohort and a squadron of cavalry, held the town. This only amounted to 500 or so Romans, but the rebels quickly learned that not all Romans were as ineffective as the ones they had routed earlier in their revolt. The Jewish insurgents launched their assault on Ascalon with optimism, but the Romans fought admirably and killed 18,000 Jewish besiegers in the city's defense, including two of their generals, John and Silas. In the end, Ascalon remained in Roman hands, and the devastating defeat dismayed the Jews to such a degree that they reoriented their strategy, as they largely avoided this kind of direct contact with the Romans going forward. The failure at Ascalon was understandably demoralizing. Many Jews must have subsequently realized that victory would be difficult—if not impossible—without divine intervention, and the Jews were forced to cope with other disheartening news.[5]

When Vespasian and his men arrived at Ptolemais, a deputation from the Galilean city of Sepphoris—about four miles northwest of Nazareth—met him. Despite being Jewish and Josephus allegedly helping them fortify against Rome, they pledged their unwavering support for Rome and peace. Furthermore, they asked Vespasian to dispatch Roman troops to guarantee their city's safety—fearing that their countrymen might strike them because of their perceived disloyalty. Vespasian was happy to comply. With Sepphoris under his control, he would hold an important toehold in Galilee. Sepphoris was the second largest Jewish city after Jerusalem, and it was strategically situated and strongly defended. As such, he ordered a military tribune named Placidus to take 6,000 infantry and 1,000 cavalry to see to the town's defenses—help that Sepphoris' citizens joyfully accepted.[6]

Placidus and his men garrisoned the town and used it as a springboard to raid parts of Galilee while stationed there. In the process, they ravaged the surroundings, and the combination of their scorched earth campaigns and Sepphoris' defection made Josephus feel as though he had to act—thereby forcing his hand. Thereupon, he mobilized his men and attacked Sepphoris, but its defenses and the Romans' determination were too much. He failed to capture it, and the Romans continued to devastate the portions of Galilee not safely ensconced behind Josephus' fortifications. At this point, Josephus wrote, "The whole of Galilee was a welter of fire and blood, put to every form of suffering and tragedy." Indeed, the Romans acted cruelly—plundering the countryside mercilessly and remorselessly killing males old enough to bear arms.[7]

Around this time, Titus and his 15th Legion reached Ptolemais—presumably exhausted from the forced rapid marches—and united with Vespasian. Once Titus arrived, it is probable that Vespasian and local client-kings, including Agrippa and his entourage, greeted him. While there is no definitive date for when it transpired, it seems very possible at this point, if not a little later, that Titus noticed Agrippa's sister, the powerful Queen Berenice. Whether it was her beauty or charisma, he was quickly smitten with her, and the two began a romantic relationship that ultimately spanned years. She may have welcomed or even pursued this development. She had been married previously on more than one occasion, but she now lived with her brother—prompting rumors of incest—and thought a liaison with a powerful Roman might improve her reputation and prospects. Whatever the case, it was an enjoyable diversion from the rigors of war for Titus, but military matters took precedence.

After auditing their troop strength from their allies and the three legions, Vespasian and Titus boasted roughly 60,000 soldiers, who were eager for combat, and they would soon experience it. They were already in Ptolemais, which was within striking distance of the heart of Galilee, and Placidus had been actively weakening the region with his raids. Vespasian and Titus' plans were swiftly coming together, and they were finally ready to begin their invasion in earnest and affixed their sites on Galilee.[8]

Vespasian—possibly along with Titus—exited Ptolemais with his troops and advanced east toward the Galilean city of Gabara. Before long, Vespasian and Titus neared the town, but two things must have stuck out to them: No Jewish army dared to confront them, and Gabara was lightly defended, which made it simple to sack. This was wonderful news for the Roman commanders who evidently wanted to give their troops an easy victory to begin the campaign. After receiving their orders, the legionaries assaulted the Jewish city and effortlessly captured it on their first attempt. Once within it, they were anything but merciful. Vespasian gave orders to slay every person in the town, and then the Romans burned it to the ground, along with nearby villages.[9]

The Romans were not in a forgiving mood, and they were tired of the Jewish people's perceived treachery and sought to make a devastating statement early in the campaign, which would be punctuated with bloodshed and destruction. From the perspective of the rebels, the path forward seemed clear. While surrender was always an option, the insurgent leaders refused to consider it. Rather, they believed that they had to defeat the Romans or else they would experience the Gabarans' fate. With the town a smoldering heap of ashes, Vespasian and Titus turned their attention to an even greater prize: the city of Jotapata, which was one of the primary centers of the Jewish revolt.[10]

It was another Galilean city, but unlike Gabara, a large number of enemy combatants had congregated there and it was highly defensible, according to Josephus. Yet modern estimates suggest that during peacetime, the city only had 1,500–2,000 inhabitants, but with refugees and revolutionaries funneling into the city, its population might have surged to 7,000 people. Regardless of the population, Jotapata benefited from an especially defensible location. The town rested on an imposing hill and was protected by steep cliff faces on three sides. Only the northern end offered enemies an approach to the city, but even that would be difficult thanks to the terrain and the town's walls, which modern excavations have shown were nearly six-feet thick in some locations.

Upon learning that Vespasian and Titus were preparing to besiege Jotapata, the Jewish leader of the Galilean war effort, Josephus, rushed there to lead its defense and improve the city's flagging morale. This may have made seizing Jotapata even more enticing to the Romans because they realized that if they could sack the city, they could greatly hinder the rebellion in Galilee and capture the regional commander. After sending advance troops to prepare for the Roman army's arrival, Vespasian and Titus eventually reached the city with tens of thousands of their men.[11]

Prior to any armed hostilities, Vespasian and Titus decided to first engage in some psychological warfare. So they initially parked the bulk of their troops in a conspicuous location just north of the city. The Galileans looked on with fear as the Roman troops carpeted their land, while they cowered inside the town's walls. They were outnumbered and targeted by the known world's foremost military machine, but the Romans were not satisfied with simply frightening the Jotapatans. They wanted to neutralize them entirely, and they began to tighten their stranglehold on the city by surrounding and sealing it off from the outside world. Before long, the soldiers formed a tight, virtually impervious perimeter around Jotapata, and the Jews realized that they could not escape—if it became necessary—or import vital goods. They were on their own to face Vespasian, Titus and their troops.[12]

Before long, the Romans were ready to confront the enemy. Seeing a body of Jewish rebels situated just outside of the walls and in battle array, Vespasian and Titus' troops unleashed a devastating salvo of projectiles on their enemies as the legionaries marched up the hill to meet them. A hail of arrows, bolts and stones rained down on the Jews, which must have been terrifying. Archaeological excavations at the site have uncovered iron arrowheads ranging in size. Many were unspectacular, but some were ballista arrowheads that stretched nearly 6 inches long. Meanwhile, discovered ballista stones also vary, but are up to 9 inches in diameter and weigh almost 4.5 pounds, although the Romans were capable of firing much larger projectiles. Despite this artillery barrage, the Jewish revolutionaries bravely and stubbornly awaited the Roman infantry's arrival, which soon came. This resulted in tough hand-to-hand combat that lasted for days, but the contest was essentially a draw.[13]

Vespasian watched as the Jews repeatedly repelled the Romans' attempts to gain the advantage and breach the town, and he called his son and lieutenants together to change their plans. After some discussion, they resolved to build a siege ramp on the northern end of the town. The Romans employed such ramps for different purposes. They were often used to create a kind of embankment to permit legionaries to more easily climb over enemy walls, which appears to be the first type of ramp the Romans used in Jotapata. In other cases, siege ramps provided an approach to cities by which the Romans could use hulking siege engines, like battering rams. With their new strategy in place, Roman legionaries and auxiliaries—non-regular locals enlisted to fight on the Roman side—began stripping the countryside of trees and stones and transported them toward the front. Then armed with wicker screens to protect the soldiers from enemy darts and other projectiles, they began using the material to build a ramp up to the city, but the Jews continually harassed them. Therefore Vespasian and Titus placed 160 pieces of artillery around much of the city and rained down stones, fireballs and arrows on the Jotapatans.[14]

The Romans made great progress—while simultaneously grappling with the unrelenting enemy fusillades and tactics—and built a ramp that nearly reached the requisite height, but the Jews responded in a surprising way. Protected by their own kind of defensive screen, they increased the height of their wall and built additional defensive towers. The Romans had completed hard and deadly work, but it seemed as though it was for nothing. They would not be able to easily scale the walls at this rate. Perceiving this, Vespasian once again changed tactics. If the Jews planned to frustrate his current strategy, then he knew how to respond. He postponed work on the ramp and most offensive engagements with the enemy, and he instead relied on a blockade to use hunger and thirst to bring the Jews to their knees.[15]

Adequate provisioning was one of the Achilles' heels of Jotapata. The city had a large supply of food stored for such a scenario, but no natural access to water. They simply relied on a dwindling supply in their cisterns, which they rationed daily, and the Romans used this to their advantage. As the people within Jotapata assembled to obtain their daily water allowance within the town, the Romans would launch aerial barrages from their artillery engines—killing many of the parched Jews. Josephus worried about the Romans' new approach because he knew that a blockade would doom the town. The Jotapatans only chance of survival was to fight the Romans hard enough that they would give up on taking the town and leave, but that was highly unlikely. Why would they risk fighting when they believed the Jews were dying of thirst? Josephus recognized this and engaged in some psychological warfare as well to frustrate Vespasian, Titus and their soldiers and encourage them to fight or suspend their siege. He told his subjects to soak their clothes and hang them over the walls. This would give the impression that they had so much water that they could afford to waste it on washing laundry, and that they could survive an extended siege, which might force the Romans to risk fighting a losing battle or leave the city to its devices. The plan struck fear in the weary Jews who were distressed over wasting what little water they possessed, but they followed Josephus' directives anyway.[16]

Astonished by the sight of the Jews appearing to have excess water, the Romans felt stymied once more, and Vespasian and Titus decided to return to their earlier strategy of direct military engagement with the enemy and building the ramp. Regardless of their tactics, the Jews were faced with the reality that they could not withstand the Roman siege for much longer. They were weak and low on water, and they needed to make some difficult decisions. They desperately attempted to break the blockade and obtain supplies from their allies, but the Romans were diligent and prevented this. Their lines held firm. In a last-ditch effort, Josephus began planning his own escape to supposedly raise a force and draw the Romans away from Jotapata, but the plan to abandon the Jotapatans offended them, and understandably. To them, it seemed like he was trying to save his own life from a hopeless situation.[17]

Josephus ultimately resolved to stay and fight with the rebels and seek a glorious death. He announced to his frail countrymen, "All right, now we start fighting when we have no hope for survival: it is a fine thing to exchange life for glory, and before we fall to do some noble deed which future generations will remember." Thereupon, the Jews regularly launched lightning-fast sorties on the Roman lines, which wore on the legionaries, but perhaps not as much as they exhausted the Jews. Vespasian eventually told his infantrymen to stop engaging with the enemy in these skirmishes. There was no point. The Jews were wearing themselves out. Consequently, Vespasian commanded archers and artillerymen to respond to the sallies.[18]

In time, the siege ramp neared completion, and impatient with the drawn-out blockade, Vespasian and Titus determined it was time to take the next step in their strategy. They moved their ballistas closer to the city and launched volleys of devastating fire on the town. They simultaneously inched a massive battering ram up the ramp. It was capped with an iron ram's head and suspended by ropes from a wooden enclosure. Once the Romans reached the town's walls, they repeatedly swung the ram against Jotapata's defenses. Terrified, the Jews deployed countermeasures, including lowering sacks of hay before the ram to blunt its blows, but the most effective action stemmed from dropping a stone on the ram, which snapped the head off. This probably elicited cheers from the Jews, but this was little more than an annoyance to the Romans. It only halted the battering temporarily.[19]

Undaunted, the Romans repaired the ram and renewed their efforts, and Vespasian and Titus managed them from the front. While monitoring the legionaries' progress, an enemy arrow shot from the walls struck Vespasian's foot. The wound was minor but still drew blood and distressed the soldiery. With fear in his eyes, Titus rushed to his father's side, but Vespasian's poise calmed the anxious Titus and their troops and demonstrated that he was not seriously hurt. Nevertheless, the legionaries pined to avenge him, and the Roman battering operations continued into the night as they slowly undermined the integrity of the Jewish defenses.[20]

By the early morning, the Roman battering ram finally breached the town. Without time to rebuild the wall or fill the gap with debris, the city's defenders hurried to block it with their bodies. Vespasian, Titus and Josephus knew that the next engagement might decide the town's fate. Vespasian ordered troops to engage the defenders and lay ramps over the rubble to make it easier to infiltrate the city, while archers provided covering fire. They complied, and the opposing forces fought valiantly and exhausted each other. However, the Romans could replace their ranks with fresh soldiers, but the Jews did not enjoy this luxury. Slowly, the Romans leveled the approach into Jotapata and pushed the parched Jews back, but every inch of Jotapata cost valuable lives.[21]

Josephus was not prepared to surrender and still had some surprises for the Romans. So he next commanded his men to boil oil and pour it on the invading Romans. With their limited strength, they did as he instructed and dumped cauldrons and buckets of bubbling oil down on the unsuspecting legionaries, which caused terror and agony in the front lines. The Romans screamed in anguish as the oil burned through their skin—leaving them disfigured. Moreover, the Jews doused the Roman ramps with oil—rendering them slippery and nearly useless—which greatly hampered the legionaries' advance. The Romans were taking serious casualties in the face of a determined counterattack. Instead of permitting the melee to continue, Vespasian called off the offensive until he could devise an appropriate response, but his troops were not demoralized; they were furious and wanted further action. After mulling over his next steps, Vespasian decided to raise the siege ramp to hasten Jotapata's fall and build three fireproof 50-foot siege towers to provide covering fire and keep the Jews at bay. Before long, the Romans completed these projects. The legionaries stationed on the towers subsequently devastated the wall's defenders who then focused on periodic sorties against the Romans, but their counterattacks failed.[22]

Whether Josephus knew it or not at the time, another city near Nazareth—called Japha—also revolted, but it was not large enough to save Jotapata. Rather, Vespasian dispatched Marcus Ulpius Traianus—commander of the 10th legion and father of the future Emperor Trajan—and 3,000 soldiers to deal with it. Traianus reached his destination in short order, but even though it was a double-walled city, Japha's defenses were woefully deficient. Traianus' troops fought the enemy before the walls—forcing them to retreat in panic—and captured the first wall and killed 12,000 enemy combatants. Traianus, however, halted his operations. He believed that Japha was essentially finished, but he wanted to reserve the glory of sacking the town for Vespasian.[23]

Appreciating the gesture but suspecting that capturing Japha still would not be easy, Vespasian instructed his son to travel to Japha and take 1,500 additional troops with him. With his orders in hand, Titus quickly gathered a fighting force and rapidly advanced for the beset town. When they arrived, they united with their comrades and pieced together a plan to storm Japha's defenses. Armed with ladders and weapons, Titus and Traianus' men rushed for the city's inner wall, and the Romans managed to climb over and infiltrate Japha's fortifications where they met a determined Jewish force. They fought the Romans for six long hours as the legionaries faced ambushes in the narrow streets, rooftop assaults and were forced to clear the city house-by-house. Eventually, the Romans neutralized the town sometime in June of 67 CE, but Titus and Traianus were not gracious victors on this occasion. The legionaries killed every male they found—save for infants. All told, the Romans slew 15,000 people from Japha and enslaved 2,130 others. Their message was unmistakable: Opposition to Rome would not be tolerated. With these matters settled sometime in late June, Titus wasted little time and turned back to Jotapata.[24]

Meanwhile, Vespasian worried that a fresh rebellion might erupt among the Samaritans and gain momentum. After all, they were mobilizing on a holy mountain called Gerizim, although it is not evident that the Samaritans claimed a common cause with those at Jotapata. That aside, Vespasian sent Sextus Vettulenus Cerialis—who commanded the 5th Legion—600 cavalry and 3,000 legionaries to quash any possible revolt among the Samaritans. He fulfilled his duty with zeal and slaughtered a total of 11,600 of them, and Cerialis presumably returned to Jotapata to assist Vespasian in his endeavor to take the stubborn town.[25]

Before long, the earthworks in Jotapata reached an appropriate height to allow the legionaries to overcome Josephus' defenses, and Vespasian was ready to re-attempt to take the city. Before doing so, he received some welcome news. One of the defenders defected from the town and offered the Romans valuable advice. He described a scene in Jotapata as one of the Jews barely holding on. The Romans had greatly reduced their numbers, and the Jotapatans were parched, exhausted and demoralized. Most importantly to Vespasian, they were not diligently guarding the walls. The deserter said that the sentries slept during much of their duty, especially around the time just before sunrise. He advised the Romans to attack then, but Vespasian was skeptical of the man, given that he viewed the Jews as fiercely loyal to their own people. Not long before, the Romans had captured someone from Jotapata who refused to aid the Romans even when they tortured the poor man in search of information. Disgusted by their lack of progress during the interrogation, the Romans crucified him, but he died with a smile.[26]

While crucifixion is today mostly associated with the Christian gospels, crucifixion on an industrial scale had a long history in ancient Rome and in the Near East. It was a terrible method of public execution generally reserved for non–Roman citizens or slaves, and it was intended to be humiliating. For those unfortunate enough to receive this ghastly punishment, their executioners affixed them to wooden poles—often with accompanying crossbeams—by nailing them to the structures, using ropes or a combination thereof. Then the crosses were erected, and the condemned were left to hang for an inordinate period of time.

There is plenty of scholarly debate over crucifixions and the actual cause of death of crucified victims, but much of it depends on the manner of crucifixion and how the condemned bodies were arranged. If their feet had been nailed in place, then they had a means to push themselves up and down, which permitted them to continue breathing, but pain, exhaustion, blood loss and dehydration took its toll. This eventually led to death hours or days later either by asphyxiation or hypovolemic shock, which occurs when the heart can no longer pump enough blood throughout the body.[27]

While Vespasian was evidently no stranger to inhumane crucifixions, he treated the aforementioned Jewish defector who offered to aid the Romans differently. Even though he worried that the deserter's intelligence could be a trap, he was willing to take his advice to capture the town. As a result, he tasked his trusted son—Titus—with gathering a few other Romans, following the traitor's advice and taking on the dangerous mission. Under the cover of darkness, Titus and his comrades silently ascended the ramp, stepped over onto the city wall and located the sentries who were in fact sleeping. Titus and his comrades subsequently slit the guards' throats. After giving a signal to Vespasian, a host of other Romans silently entered the city and quietly captured the citadel unbeknownst to most of Jotapata's defenders. Thanks to Titus' efforts and the defector's valuable intelligence, the Romans had secured part of the town, and then much of the army marched into the city, which alerted the Jews.[28]

The legionaries next methodically funneled the enemy onto terrain within the city where making a defensive stand would be difficult and then attacked the unnerved Jews who knew that they stood little chance of surviving. Following a long, hard-fought siege, the Romans were bent on obtaining revenge, and they killed the Jotapatans with impunity. Other Jews within the town took matters into their own hands and killed themselves, and some hid—and for good reason. Wherever the Romans found them, they struck almost all of the Jews down, except infants, women and perhaps a small number of men. Throughout the siege, an estimated 40,000 Jews reportedly lost their lives, and after 47 days, in early July, Vespasian and Titus finally gained complete mastery of Jotapata, which they destroyed and leveled to the ground. They would not suffer it to stand against Rome ever again. While the Romans were thrilled to have sacked Jotapata, the war was far from over, though this represented an important test. The battle for Jotapata turned out to be the Jewish War's second bloodiest and third longest siege.[29]

While the Romans were victorious, they had not found the wily Josephus. He had hidden himself with 40 others, but the Romans soon learned of his secret refuge. Vespasian sent Josephus messages and assured him that he would receive fair treatment if he would just surrender. Upon hearing the Roman entreaties, Josephus and his friends debated their next steps. Josephus wanted to accept Vespasian's offer, but this angered his comrades. They preferred a so-called honorable death to this even if it was by their own hands. Despite Josephus' pleas, the group decided to slay each other, and they drew lots to determine which man would dispatch who. The killings began, and then with only Josephus and one other person alive, the Jewish leader persuaded his friend to end the string of deaths. They subsequently handed themselves over to the legionaries.[30]

Shortly thereafter, the Romans brought a dispirited Josephus before Vespasian and Titus. Vespasian must have looked on with a mixture of curiosity and admiration. Josephus had fought with honor, tenacity and defiance against Rome for some time. Various other Romans reacted differently. Some cursed Josephus, others stared at him with hate and more than a few called for his execution. Nothing short of his crucifixion would satisfy them. However, one man in particular—Titus—greatly pitied Josephus and pleaded for restraint. Vespasian acquiesced to Titus' petitions and kept Josephus under guard with plans to transfer the vanquished general to Nero to determine his fate. In the meantime, Vespasian treated him extremely well—thanks to Titus' influence.[31]

Josephus learned that he would eventually be handed over to Nero, and he understood what that meant. He could expect to be used as a humiliating spectacle in Rome, tortured and then ingloriously executed. He naturally wanted to live. So at this point, Josephus asked for a private conference with Vespasian who accepted the invitation, but insisted on Titus being present. Once the trio was alone, Josephus delivered an astonishing prophecy to the Flavians. He exclaimed:

> Vespasian, you may think that in Josephus you have simply won yourself a prisoner of war: but I [have] come to tell you of your greater destiny. If I were not God's chosen emissary, I would have followed the Jewish tradition—I know it well, and how a defeated general should meet his death. Are you sending me to Nero? Why to him? Do you think Nero and his successors will last long before your hour [comes]? You, Vespasian, will be Caesar and emperor, both you and your son here with us. So chain me tighter now and keep me for yourself, as you, Caesar, are master not only of me but of all land and sea and the whole human race. Punish me, please, with yet harsher confinement if I am taking the name of God in vain.[32]

This was a curious response from Josephus, but Vespasian and Titus may have believed that the man was simply trying to ingratiate himself with them to avoid Nero's wrath. Soon enough, Vespasian learned that this was not Josephus' first prophecy. He had allegedly predicted that Jotapata would fall to the Romans after 47 days and the Romans would capture him. Vespasian investigated the veracity of this rumor and found prisoners who verified it, which piqued Vespasian and Titus' interest. From then on, they showed Josephus compassion and kindness, deciding to keep the Jewish commander in their custody indefinitely.[33]

With Jotapata now a ruined ghost town, sometime around July 67 CE, Vespasian and Titus marched their troops away from the scene of their latest victory. Vespasian and two legions headed to Caesarea Maritima and Titus and the 15th Legion to the less-than-desirable Scythopolis (modern-day Beth-Shean) where they would camp,

Hippodrome, Caesarea Maritima, 2019.

import provisions, see to the wounded and provide their soldiers some rest. They needed it too. The fall of Jotapata was a critical step toward ending the rebellion, but complete victory was still years away. As Titus enjoyed some down time in Scythopolis, he might have sent for his paramour, Berenice, who comforted him until he needed to turn his attention to war again. Meanwhile, Vespasian and his soldiers could enjoy Caesarea Maritima, which was filled with the usual splendor and entertainment of a Greco-Roman town. Even today, among its ruins are a temple, theater, and an exceptional sea-side hippodrome.[34]

VI

Tarichaea

> *"I shall be the first to charge the enemy. So do not fail me. Trust that God is with me and supporting this drive, and have it clearly in your minds that this battle outside the walls is just the beginning of our further success."*
> —Titus[1]

As Vespasian and Titus' men recuperated from the long, exhausting siege of Jotapata, their enemies were trying to mobilize. Jews who had been exiled from pro-Roman cities and those who had been displaced by the nascent Roman war effort began to consolidate their forces near the ruined coastal town of Joppa, modern-day Jaffa. They even rebuilt much of it, and cobbled together a kind of pirate armada—made up of fishing boats and merchant vessels—bent on harrying naval traffic on the Roman Empire's eastern end. For some time, the pirates successfully interrupted shipping lanes, which placed pressure on Roman communication lines and supply chains, but the pirates' plans were flawed from the beginning.[2]

Upon hearing of the mayhem they were inflicting, Vespasian dispatched a small company of troops to Joppa. They entered it without incident because the Jewish revolutionaries had fearfully fled for their boats once they learned of the approaching Romans, but matters worsened for these Jews. They had picked Joppa as their naval base of operations, but its so-called port was treacherous. Cliffs overlooked its foreboding coast, which was lined with sharp, jagged rocks. The waves were rough, and the wind seemed constant in the area. A simple storm was all that was needed to turn this port into a graveyard.[3]

With the Romans watching, a "Black Northerly"—what the locals called a gale—erupted and battered the Jewish ships into the deadly rocks and each other. They rolled and listed as the wind and waves slammed into them, but escape was not an option. The storm sealed many of them into the dangerous port where they sank, while others, in a desperate attempt, made it to deeper water but succumbed nonetheless. In the end, the tempest utterly destroyed the fleet. Myriad men drowned, but some decided to take matters into their own hands; they killed themselves. It is unknown how many Jews perished in total, but 4,200 decaying and putrid corpses washed ashore sometime after.[4]

As Vespasian had previously ordered, his troops razed most of Joppa to prevent it from serving as a Jewish base again, and he garrisoned the ruins. This permitted the Romans to maintain constant guard, keep Joppa out of enemy hands, defend the area and use it as a staging area to harass Jewish insurgents. From there, Roman legionaries traveled to nearby cities, villages and farmsteads where they laid waste to the countryside and left a path of death and destruction in their wake. Vespasian and Titus had now secured Sepphoris and sacked four notable cities, including Jotapata, and a host of smaller towns and villages. Meanwhile, they raided the surroundings—all to great effect.[5]

Unfortunately for the Romans, turmoil bubbled up elsewhere in the region. Within certain corners of King Agrippa II's client-kingdom, there were fresh outbursts of unrest. As such, Agrippa invited Vespasian to visit one of his sumptuous palaces in hopes that he would see the disturbances and help put them down. Vespasian answered the call, and with some legionaries accompanying him, he traveled from Caesarea Maritima to Caesarea Philippi, which was at the base of Mount Hermon, about 30 miles north of the Sea of Galilee. While there, he enjoyed the king's generosity and the luxurious quarters, but he eventually learned that cities in Agrippa's titular realm were in danger. Tiberias was on the verge of revolting and Tarichaea, which bordered the Sea of Galilee, had already done so.[6]

Additional Jewish uprisings anywhere in the region were a threat to Vespasian's plans, and he apparently felt some loyalty to Agrippa. Vespasian accordingly tasked his son Titus with collecting the troops at Caesarea Maritima and marching them to Scythopolis. Titus followed his father's commands and then presumably worked with the army's lieutenants to organize the legionaries and their baggage train to enable them to quell disturbances in Agrippa's kingdom. Vespasian and many of his troops simultaneously traveled to Scythopolis to rendezvous with the other Roman forces and take command of the army. Upon doing so, they marched for Tiberias, which was not far.[7]

When the Roman army arrived, they made camp, but Vespasian's first instinct was not to besiege the city. Rather, he sought peaceful negotiations and sent a Roman named Valerianus and 50 cavalrymen to confer with the city's elders. Yet they never reached them because Tiberias' combatants marched out to fight the Romans. Unprepared for battle, Valerianus withdrew from the enemy, and the rebel faction captured some of his company's horses. Despite the overt provocation, this incident was not representative of the people of Tiberias. In fact, some of its leaders escaped the city and rushed to meet with Vespasian to plead for mercy and help with ejecting their captors—the insurgents.[8]

They apparently learned of this and decided that their best chance at survival was to flee before the Romans seized the town or the locals turned on them. So they bolted for safety and managed to somehow dodge the Romans. With the revolutionaries gone, the people of Tiberias subsequently flung open its gates and welcomed the Romans into the city with open arms. They even hailed Vespasian as their "savior and benefactor." With little effort, Vespasian and Titus had restored order in Tiberias, and they next turned their attention to another wayward city, Tarichaea, and began their advance toward it.[9]

Tarichaea promised to be a much more challenging situation than Tiberias because rebels had been flooding into the city, stoking discontentment and encouraging action against Rome. Beyond this, the city was well-fortified and sat on a major waterway—the Sea of Galilee—which made a blockade difficult. Given their proximity to water, the people in Tarichaea had also raised a fleet—comprised of fishing boats and rafts—to import provisions, provide for their escape or, if occasion called for it, battle the Romans on water.[10]

Soon enough, the Romans reached Tarichaea and started building their defensive camp, but a gang of revolutionaries attacked them. The legionaries quickly brandished their weapons and turned on the Jews who withdrew to the safety of their boats, shoved off into the lake and dropped anchor once they were beyond the Romans' reach. Meanwhile, another rebel faction poured out of Tarichaea and drew up for battle. Vespasian issued orders to Titus to take 600 cavalrymen and drive the combatants back. Without hesitating, Titus gathered together some trusted associates and rode posthaste toward Tarichaea, but when he arrived, he realized that he was vastly outnumbered. He subsequently forwarded a message to Vespasian requesting reinforcements, although he recognized how glorious it would be to win the battle without this aid. Outnumbered or not, many of Titus' men were ready to follow him into battle if need be, but more than a few of his soldiers were crippled with fear before the enemy horde. They needed encouragement, and Titus perceived this. In response, he delivered a lengthy motivational speech to his men, but Josephus almost certainly recreated it and did so in a manner incorrectly suggesting that the pagan Titus was monotheistic[11]:

> Romans, I cannot begin better than by reminding you of the name you bear, that you may realize how different we are from the men we are going to fight. From our hands nothing in the wide world has [...] escaped, though the Jews, we must admit, have not yet shown any sign of lying down under defeat. It would be a shocking thing if, when they stand unbowed in the midst of disaster, we should flag in the midst of success. The enthusiasm you outwardly display I am delighted to see, but I fear that the enemy's advantage in numbers may produce [secret apprehension] in a few of you.
>
> If so, they should again ponder the difference between their opponents and themselves, and the fact that the Jews, though extremely bold and contemptuous of death, have neither discipline nor experience of war, and are nothing but a rabble, not fit to be called an army. Of our own experience and discipline nothing [needs to] be said. But our object in being the one people to undergo military training in peacetime is that in war we may not have to compare our numbers with those of our opponents. What should we gain by being constantly on active service, if we needed equal numbers to oppose a mob of raw recruits?
>
> Remember again that you are fighting in full armour against men who have none, that you are horse and they are foot, that you have leaders and they are leaderless. These advantages make you in effect far more numerous than you are, while the enemy's disadvantages make their numbers count for very little. Wars are won, not by the size of an army however [skillful], but by courage, however tiny the forces available. Small forces can be quickly deployed and can readily support each other, while swollen armies do themselves more damage than the enemy can do.
>
> The Jews are inspired by reckless audacity and desperation, emotions that invigorate while things go well but are extinguished by the smallest setback. We are inspired by disciplined courage

and fortitude, which in prosperity reaches its greatest heights and in adversity endures to the end. And you will be fighting for a greater prize than the Jews; for though they face the dangers of war to defend the liberty of their country, what greater prize could you win than glory and the assurance that, after mastering the whole world, we do not acknowledge the Jews as rivals? Observe too that there is no fear of our suffering any irretrievable disaster. Ample reinforcements are at hand; but we can snatch the victory ourselves, and we must not wait for the men my father is sending to support us: if no one shares it, our triumph will be [even] greater.

My own feeling is that at this moment my father is on trial, so am I, and so are you. Does he deserve his past triumphs? Do I deserve to be his son, and you to be my soldiers? With him victory is a habit; I could not bear to return to him if you abandoned me; would you not be ashamed if your commander led the way into danger and you failed to follow? I shall lead the way, you may be sure, and shall be the first to charge the enemy. So don't you fail me, or doubt for a moment that with God at my side my efforts are bound to succeed. I tell you plainly in advance that infighting here outside the walls we shall win a far-reaching triumph.[12]

It is not difficult to imagine Titus' off-the-cuff inspirational message eliciting a chorus of supportive shouts, applause and clamor from his troops who were now invigorated and ready for battle. Before charging for the enemy, however, reinforcements arrived, including 400 cavalrymen led by Traianus and 2,000 archers whom Vespasian stationed on a nearby hill. Even though Titus had requested the assistance, the reinforcements upset his men who felt that they might rob them of a glorious victory against a larger enemy. Nevertheless, once prepared, Titus sounded the charge and led from the front.[13]

Galloping at full speed, Titus and his comrades reached the Jewish combatants and fought relentlessly, but at first, the Jews managed to repel the constant assaults. It may have been at this point that a Jewish insurgent struck Titus' horse—killing it—as Titus tumbled to the ground. Facing a constant enemy onslaught, he surveyed the situation and noticed that one of his comrades had fallen prey to the Jewish attacks, but his horse was unharmed. Titus mounted the steed and courageously continued his offensive, according to Suetonius who recorded this vignette. Considering the ancient historian's propensity toward thematic, rather than chronological, storytelling, it is impossible to determine with certainty in which battle this occurred, but it could very well have been at this moment.

Whatever the case, Roman dedication and determination proved too much for the Jewish rebels in this battle. Titus began to wear down the enemy, and an unmitigated slaughter began. Trying to save their lives, the Jews scattered and fled for cover, but the Roman cavalry followed in hot pursuit—easily outstripping a number of them. Titus' soldiers killed a host of the insurgents as they desperately sought refuge, but many others scampered into the perceived safety of Tarichaea.[14]

Once inside the walls, a new danger confronted the rebels. Much of the city's citizenry did not want to take part in the war, see their property destroyed or be abused by the Jewish revolutionaries. As a result, a conflict within the walls came to a head as the Jewish moderates and insurgents clashed. It was so loud that Titus could hear the commotion from outside of Tarichaea's defenses, and understanding that this was a great opportunity, he announced to his fellow Romans:

> Now is the time. Why do you tarry, comrades, when God himself delivers the Jews into our hands? Hail the victory that is given [to] you. Do you not hear that clamour? They are at strife with each other—those men who have just slipped through our hands. The town is ours if we are quick. But besides haste we need effort and resolution; great successes never come without risks. We must not wait till concord is re-established among our enemies: necessity will reconcile them all too soon. But neither let us wait for assistance from our friends: after defeating such a multitude with our small force, let us have the further honor of taking the city unaided.[15]

Eager to sack the town and attain further glory, Titus led his troops on what could have been a hazardous mission. He guided them around the city and into the lake's shallows. Mounted on their horses, they trudged through the water and entered Tarichaea seemingly unopposed, and the sight terrified the rebels. Some retreated to the countryside, but others sprinted toward the lake. They did so not to fight, but to flee. As they labored to swim away or make their way to their boats, Titus and his men struck many down en masse. Death and confusion reigned on the Sea of Galilee's shores and within Tarichaea. Once the Romans marched into the city, they began to slaughter those inside, regardless of guilt or innocence. Jew after Jew fell to the Roman short swords, but Titus felt great sorrow and compassion for the locals. Unlike many of his contemporaries, he bore some admiration and pity for the Jewish people, at least according to Josephus, and often advocated that they receive mercy. Thus he quickly halted the butchery once he believed that many of the combatants had been slain or at least restrained and the city was fully under Roman control.[16]

Now with Tarichaea largely secured, Titus ordered a missive be sent to Vespasian informing him of the great success, which thrilled the weathered old general, but they had not entirely pacified the area. Some revolutionaries had escaped Titus' reach and were biding their time on boats in the Sea of Galilee, but they had limited places to withdraw with the Romans spread across the region. Even so, the Romans wanted to subdue the rebels sooner rather than later. As such, Vespasian and Titus oversaw the rapid construction of a fleet to confront the Jewish flotilla. Before long, they boasted enough vessels to challenge the Jews, and the legionaries climbed onto their rafts and paddled across the lake.[17]

The Romans located the enemy boats without much difficulty, and a naval battle of sorts broke out. The Jews hurled stones at the Romans with little effect, while the Romans battered them with arrows as they approached their vessels. When neared them, the Romans sank some and boarded others whereupon the Romans put their *gladii* to use—stabbing the Jewish sailors who fell ingloriously dead. Some Jews jumped overboard to escape, but once they rose to the surface, the Romans fired arrows at them or cut their heads or hands off. Some of the Jews managed to make landfall, but death stalked them there too. The Romans patiently waited for them to reach the shore and massacred them when they did.[18]

In time, the carnage ceased, but the scene was appalling. The lake was littered with floating corpses, the water polluted with gore and the beaches covered with bloated, decomposing bodies. Between the battles of Tarichaea and the Sea of Galilee, 6,700 Jews lost their lives, but even with Tarichaea's fall sometime around early September 67 CE, the killing had not ended. Vespasian formed a tribunal to determine guilt and innocence of all those within Tarichaea and mete out justice.[19]

The Romans summarily found myriad guilty and needed to determine their fates. Yet Vespasian concluded that he could not spare and release the captured rebels because they would simply join forces with their allies and wage war on the Romans again. Conversely, he could not immediately execute them either because it could turn the moderates within Tarichaea against him and the Roman cause. So the Romans misled the Jews. Heralds announced that the guilty would be granted safe passage, but only by one road, which led to Tiberias. Thinking they had been granted mercy, tens of thousands obliviously marched out of the city on the approved thoroughfare, which armed Romans lined. Then they entered Tiberias only to realize the Romans' treachery. Vespasian ordered 1,200 of them to be executed, 6,000 to be shipped to Nero to do with as he pleased and more than 30,000 were enslaved.[20]

By September 67 CE, Vespasian and Titus had successfully reasserted Roman control over many trouble spots, and the fall of Tarichaea specifically induced many Galileans to determine that war with Rome was utterly futile. Many of them then laid down their arms, surrendered their cities and handed over their forts to the Romans. This progress aside, there were still three notable holdouts in the immediate vicinity that demanded Vespasian and Titus' attention: Gischala, Mount Tabor and the stronghold at Gamala.[21]

Gamala—now called Tell es Salam—was the highest priority of the three aforementioned rebel enclaves, and the more difficult proposition. It was the preeminent insurgent-held stronghold in the Golan district. The town was situated on a mountain's summit that resembled the back of a kneeling camel, and it was guarded by steep cliffs and ravines. The challenging terrain made it hard to live there, but the locals managed to build homes virtually on top of one another as they precipitously meandered up the peak. If this was not daunting enough, Josephus had previously augmented the towns' fortifications, and it boasted a citadel, defensive walls as thick as 6.5 feet, trenches and underground passages. While this description mainly comes from Josephus, more recent excavations have confirmed the veracity of his report and Gamala's imposing nature. It was so well defended that King Agrippa II had previously besieged the town, but after seven months failed to capture it.[22]

Vespasian decided to march on Gamala and succeed where Agrippa had failed, but evidently before setting out, Vespasian sent Titus on a mission to the Roman province of Syria to meet with Gaius Licinius Mucianus who was the incoming Syrian provincial governor. Unfortunately, the ancient writers did not record the reason for this visit or what occurred during the conference. However, one thing is beyond doubt: It must have been critically important for Vespasian to send his omni-capable and loyal son during the war. In all likelihood, Titus welcomed Mucianus to his new posting on behalf of Vespasian, and the two delineated their spheres of influence. Titus assured Mucianus that Vespasian had no intention of inappropriately interfering in his realm and that they could be partners rather than competitors. It is plausible that the silver-tongued Titus also provided a high-level update on the Jewish revolt, worked to warm relations with Mucianus and sought certain provisions for the war effort. Whatever topics were discussed, Titus made an unmistakable impression on Mucianus, and the two became fast friends—a relationship that would eventually prove indispensable to the Flavians.[23]

Regardless of what Titus' mission entailed, Vespasian and his army advanced for Gamala, but could not surround the city due to the topography. The Romans were, on the other hand, able to post guards at various points around it to hopefully ensure that nobody entered or exited the fortified city without their permission. While being unable to fully encircle the settlement served a small disadvantage for the Romans, they enjoyed a massive benefit in Josephus. With him in their custody, Vespasian boasted inside knowledge of the town and surely employed it. Thereupon, he ordered his troops to build siege ramps to Gamala and fill the defensive trenches protecting the town. They accomplished both feats in rapid time and soon reached the city's walls, and the Romans carted up their siege engines. With bolt and stone throwers providing covering fire, the battering rams swung into action and ravaged the walls—causing a portion to collapse.[24]

The Romans instantly saw their opportunity and charged headlong into the gap, but the city's defenders met them there. Intense hand-to-hand fighting ensued, and the Romans ultimately forced their way through the shattered wall. The rebels withdrew to a higher part of the inner city but were unwilling to lay down their arms. Rather, they organized a devastating counterattack that took the Romans by surprise. They took heavy casualties in the process, and even Vespasian at one point had a close brush with death. During the melee, homes built high on the peak collapsed and slid down onto other homes—creating a kind of avalanche. Facing a looming disaster, the Romans retreated in disorder from the city. Meanwhile, Gamala's defenders re-took possession of the walls and stationed troops in the gap—or gaps since archaeologists have discovered three of them—and many of the town's inhabitants escaped through its underground tunnels.

Recent discoveries have demonstrated the fierceness of the battle for Gamala. Modern archaeologists have found ample weapons near Gamala's walls and within the city. A large number of them were found in a relatively small area—suggesting an excessively violent battle occurred there—but the sheer number found throughout the site is astounding. In addition to 1,600 arrowheads, some 2,000 ballista balls have been collected to date.[25]

The recent setback disappointed Vespasian, but he continued his siege and even opened a new front. He dispatched Placidus and 600 cavalrymen to confront the combatants at Mount Tabor. While he was almost certainly outnumbered, Placidus led his troops into battle and defeated the enemy there—forcing the survivors to flee for the safety of Jerusalem. With Mount Tabor now in Roman hands, only Gamala and Gischala stood in their way of pacifying Galilee.²⁶

This was welcome news for Vespasian who had tasted little success at Gamala since first breaching its walls, but some of his men had been busy with a special operation. Roman soldiers quietly and very carefully had been working to undermine one of the enemy towers. Eventually, they pried stones supporting the structure out of place. Then the tower collapsed in on itself—causing terror and death within Gamala. Unlike the last time they demolished part of Gamala's defenses, the Romans chose not to immediately invade the town. Instead, they wisely decided to bide their time and wait for an opportune moment.²⁷

As this was underway, Titus returned from his mission to Syria and learned of the Romans' failures at Gamala. Eager to avenge his comrades and redeem the legions, Titus and his father pieced together a strategy to take the city. Quite possibly under the cover of darkness, Titus, 200 cavalrymen and some infantry surreptitiously entered Gamala without being detected. When the Jewish sentries finally noticed the Romans' unwanted appearance, chaos and pandemonium gripped the Gamalans. Some fled for the citadel, others tried to escape the city but ran into Roman guards, and an inordinate number decided to challenge Titus and his men. That turned out to be a grievous mistake as the legionaries massacred them. "The groans of those that were killed were prodigiously great everywhere, and blood ran down over all the lower parts of the city," Josephus reported.²⁸

Vespasian witnessed his son's valiant success and gave orders for a larger portion of the army to enter Gamala and rush toward the city's high point—the citadel. In a last-ditch effort, the besieged Jews in the citadel shot projectiles and flung stones at the Romans who were vulnerable, but then a violent storm developed over Gamala. A strong wind blew against the defenders—forcing them to relent—while simultaneously giving the Romans' arrows more distance, which battered the Jews, according to Josephus.

This may seem like hyperbole on behalf of ancient historians, but there seems to be truth rooted in this account. As modern researchers have discovered, the region's topography is conducive to high-speed gusts of wind—probably intensified by storms. This tempest was all the Romans needed to secure victory. The change in weather allowed the Romans to capture the citadel, but after their failed attempts to seize Gamala, the legionaries thirsted for revenge. The Gamalans understood this. So, instead of giving the Romans the satisfaction of controlling their fates, 5,000 of them reportedly leaped from the precipice to their deaths. Modern scholars, however, doubt the scope of this supposed mass suicide, but the Jews in Gamala faced an almost certain death one way or another. The Romans slaughtered 4,000 other Gamalans, even including infants whom they barbarously and remorselessly tossed from the cliff. Only two women survived the melee, and they likely became slaves. By October 67 CE, the Romans had finally taken Gamala, but at a terrible cost. Now only Gischala stood in their way of obtaining mastery over Galilee.²⁹

VII

Gischala

> *"[Titus] knew that if he stormed [Gischala] there would follow a wholesale massacre of the population by his troops, and he was now sick of the slaughter and moved by compassion for the innocent majority."*
> —Josephus[1]

With nearly all of Galilee pacified and his troops in need of a respite, Vespasian gave orders for the 5th and 15th legions to march to Caesarea Maritima and the 10th to encamp at Scythopolis. Upon arriving, the legionaries were able to briefly relax, re-provision and get the wounded necessary medical assistance. While there, Titus may have reunited with Berenice, but he and his fellow legionaries could not rest for long. Vespasian began training his troops for the largest test that they would face—the siege of Jerusalem—a confrontation that would likely determine the outcome of the Jewish War, and he also aimed to subdue Galilee's remaining holdouts.

At this point, only one Galilean town was still defying Rome and remained a haven for Jewish combatants: Gischala. It is in northern Galilee at the foot of Mount Meron, and today, the town is called Jish. To bring the city back into the fold, Vespasian gave orders to send one of his chief lieutenants—Titus—and 1,000 cavalry to Gischala. This was a great honor and opportunity. To date, Titus had played critical roles in dangerous battles, but perhaps his greatest contribution was wielding his diplomatic prowess by negotiating with Mucianus and possibly also drawing King Agrippa II and Berenice even closer to Rome. Militarily, Titus was relatively inexperienced and youthful, but Vespasian awarded him this task anyway, which was the first siege that became Titus' sole responsibility.[2]

Despite certainly being weary from travel, extended sieges and bloody warfare, Titus rose to the occasion. He obediently called up 1,000 men to help him sack the town, and together, they advanced toward Gischala, which they had reason to believe would fall relatively easily. Most of the town's inhabitants were farmers who opposed the war, but a violent element had taken root there. A certain instigator—John of Gischala, the son of Levi—and his troop of bandits had seized control of Gischala where they recruited young men to their cause and fostered a revolutionary environment.[3]

Titus and his fellow cavalrymen quickly reached Gischala. After surveying the city, Titus knew with certainty that the Romans could sack it with relative ease—thanks to its humble defenses and lack of professional soldiers. Yet doing so would pose serious risks to the innocent moderates within Gischala. If Titus' men stormed the city, then an indiscriminate slaughter would inevitably occur that might especially impact the noncombatants. Laboring to avoid this lamentable outcome, Titus offered John and his gang the opportunity to surrender peacefully—an offer the Romans thought John could not refuse. After all, as Titus noted, Gischala had no chance of defeating his legionaries. Its defenses were practically laughable by Roman standards and every other rebellious Galilean city had fallen to the Romans—sometimes with devastatingly bloody consequences.[4]

John contemplated Titus' generous offer—and without giving a voice to the moderates within Gischala—he hatched a dishonest plan. He claimed that he supported Titus' terms, but that he needed to persuade others within the town to accept them. The problem was that this was transpiring on the Sabbath. John asserted that religious obligations mandate that he must wait a day to convince his countrymen to embrace the peace agreement. Titus considered John's response plausible, given Jewish tradition, and thought that granting the Gischalans another day would be a harmless proposition. So Titus granted John an extra day, and possibly as a sign of good faith and to be protected from any potential counter-attacks, the Romans made camp at the nearby village of Kadasa. It was a sizable settlement of people who were hostile toward the Jewish Galileans, and it boasted significant fortifications. While it was a modest distance from Gischala, it was safest place within the vicinity for Titus and his men.[5]

With Titus elsewhere, John, his gang members and many innocent Jewish bystanders crept out of Gischala during the night and dashed full speed toward Jerusalem where they hoped to continue their stand against Rome. The women and children in John's cavalcade failed to keep up with him and the other men in his party. In response, he instructed his male comrades to abandon their sluggish wives and children, instructing them "save yourselves first." John was happy to leave the women, children and the weak behind if that meant he could ensure his well-being. Many Jewish refugees became separated in the process. Some lost their way, but others maintained their path toward Jerusalem. After the sun rose the next morning, Titus returned to Gischala to hopefully accept the city's surrender, and he observed the locals opening the gates for him. Noncombatants flooded out and shouted praise in support of Titus for securing their freedom from John's reign. They also described John's treachery and how he had scurried off into the night.[6]

Titus must have been furious that John had exploited Jewish law to mislead him and fled justice. Hoping to capture John and his agitators, Titus dispatched some cavalrymen to hunt them down. They mounted their horses and galloped toward Jerusalem, and they easily discovered many people from John's party. Outraged by John's duplicity, the Romans began striking the Jews down. In the end, the legionaries killed 6,000 of them and seized 3,000 women and children, but John and many of his associates reached the safety of Jerusalem. This was a disappointing end to Titus' mission, but he could at least boast about extinguishing the final embers of the Galilean revolt.[7]

At some point, Titus entered Gischala where the people continued to obsequiously heap praise upon him, but he was sure that some rebellious elements remained hidden quietly in Gischala. Yet Titus refused to seek them out and discipline them. He worried that prosecuting the guilty might also ensnare the innocent as the locals would turn on each other and take advantage of the legal proceedings to settle personal scores. He supposedly believed that it was better to spare the guilty than to kill an innocent person. Even so, he did not entirely trust the Gischalans, and he installed a Roman garrison in Gischala to ensure its loyalty. He additionally pulled down a small part of the city wall as a symbolic gesture denoting the Gischalans' defeat, and then he and many of his men returned to Caesarea Maritima for the winter where he provided a detailed report of the brief campaign to Vespasian and resumed his role as one of his senior advisers.[8]

As Titus remained encamped, Vespasian and some troops moved to pacify the cities of Jamnia and Azotus—both of which are just south of modern-day Tel Aviv—presumably to give the Romans free rein along the coast and to begin encircling Jerusalem. Vespasian quickly reached Jamnia and Azotus and easily dispatched his enemies there. Afterward, Vespasian garrisoned the towns with Roman troops. However, he observed that Judaea was gripped by anarchy and rebellions. Factional strife plagued the region as insurgents plundered the countryside and clashed with their countrymen who advocated for peace. This alone did not satisfy the bandits. Once they got their fill of Jewish booty, they began to consolidate their forces and marched toward Jerusalem to join with other revolutionaries, continue fighting Rome and take advantage of defenseless Jews in the process.[9]

Meanwhile, John had already entered Jerusalem with some of his followers, and what he saw must have reminded him of where he hailed. Jerusalem was filled with a host of moderate, peace-loving Jews who had little desire to get entangled in a conflict with Rome. There was also a considerable population eager for a war of independence—no matter the consequences. This provided John a fertile recruiting ground to fuel his revolutionary designs. While there, it seems that John's behavior changed. He had already been a rebel leader, but as Josephus' account goes, he may not have necessarily been a fanatical insurgent. Sometime after his arrival in the holy city, John was radicalized.

He wanted to lead Jerusalem against the Romans and may have seen this change as a way to bring his aspirations to fruition, considering that there was a revolutionary climate in Jerusalem, but this posed challenges. There were plenty of other insurgent leaders in and around Jerusalem vying to lead the Jewish revolt. Further, there was still a provisional government in Jerusalem—albeit a weak one—and much of the Jewish uprising was not centrally organized. Instead, there were various disparate factions. They were not natural allies or necessarily loyal to the Jewish population as a whole. In time, the Jews in Jerusalem discovered that the varying factions within their holy city could be as cruel and dangerous as the Romans, if not worse, and John learned a hard lesson. Uniting the Jewish factions and keeping them united against the Romans was a herculean task.

Without delay, John traveled across Jerusalem urging people to join his cause. He exaggerated the Jewish people's military strength, disparaged the Romans' prowess and spoke of Jerusalem's imposing defenses. While Jerusalem's walls and towers were formidable, the city was not impregnable. Nevertheless, John overstated the virtues of Jerusalem's fortifications, which he claimed the Romans would never be able to breach. He even falsely reported that the Roman siege engines had struggled mightily against the Galilean villages. These were bold claims for a man who had absconded from the Romans in the dead of night. Perhaps when pressed to answer why he deserted Gischala, John said that he had not fearfully retreated from the Romans but came to Jerusalem to fight from a position of strength for the good of the Jews.[10]

He was not the only newcomer to Jerusalem. Criminals from across the region, including much of John's horde, filed into Jerusalem as the holy city quickly became the setting for factional strife and wanton violence. Gang members robbed unsuspecting Jews with impunity, murdered men of low status and even of royal blood and kidnapped well-connected people. Often when rumors of an uprising against them spread, they simply killed those whom they assumed were their adversaries, and they also seized extraordinary powers. They decided to elect their own priests, some insurgents—led by Eleazar ben Simon—took up residence in the holy city's Temple compound and violently oppressed the locals along with a new ally. While John initially acted as though he was allied with Ananus and the more moderate faction, he and his followers were up to no good. They formed an alliance with Eleazar as they shared vital intelligence with them and engaged in violence. Terrorism and other abominable activities subsequently became rampant in Jerusalem as the people were paralyzed with fear.[11]

A handful of influential Jews who led the more moderate provisional government, including Ananus, Joseph ben Gurion and Simeon son of Gamaliel, delivered impassioned speeches to the masses. Within them, they tried to goad the people into rising up against their oppressors and ejecting them from Jerusalem. These were primarily known as the Zealots and followed Eleazar's leadership. Their name stemmed from the word "zeal." Josephus did not mince words in describing the Zealots. "This was what the terrorists called themselves, as if their zeal was for the promotion of virtuous practice, rather than for the worst of vices taken to the extremes."

In one of his orations, Ananus castigated the Zealots for their crimes against the Jews and how they had desecrated the Temple and violated Jewish law. He exclaimed, "They have mastered the strongest point in the city—for henceforth the Temple must be spoken of as a mere citadel or fortress—but with such a tyrants' stronghold entrenched in your midst, with the spectacle of your foes above your heads, what plans have you, what further cherished hopes console your minds?" Ananus urged the Jews to take matters into their own hands and secure their freedom from the Zealots' tyranny.

"Their numbers are growing daily," Ananus added, "as every villain deserts to [those that are like to themselves]; their audacity is fired by meeting so far with no obstruction; and they will doubtless avail themselves of their superior position, with the added benefit of preparation, if we give them time. But, believe me, if we mount to the attack, conscience will humble them and the advantage of superior height will be neutralized by reflection. Maybe, the Deity, whom they have outraged, will turn their missiles back upon them, and their own weapons will bring destruction upon the impious wretches. Only let us face them and their doom is sealed."

"If the venture has its attendant risks, it [would be] a noble end to die at the sacred [gates] and to sacrifice our lives, if not for wives and children, […] for God and for the sanctuary. But I will support you both with head and hand: there shall be no lack on my part of thought to ensure your safety, nor shall you see me spare [myself]," Ananus exclaimed. Despite the pervading terror and failed prior attempts to remove the revolutionaries from Jerusalem, Ananus and other leading Jews successfully persuaded many of those in Jerusalem to fight to eject the rabble from their city.[12]

Ananus began mobilizing a citizen militia, but Eleazar's Zealots learned of his activities—possibly thanks to John's treachery—and kept applying pressure on the moderates. The Zealots periodically poured out of the Temple and killed everyone they saw. Eventually, Ananus and his men confronted the Zealots, and a deadly brawl transpired. A host of men from both factions suffered serious wounds. Thereupon, Ananus' men temporarily retreated to their homes and the Zealots to the safety of the Temple compound, which they defiled with their blood. Undaunted, both groups resumed their struggle and kept harassing each other until Ananus' men broke into the Temple complex and the Zealots withdrew to the inner court. With the Zealots hemmed in and moderate Jews keeping watch from the heights of the towering colonnades, the Zealots—with the help of John and his followers—took a new approach. They somehow solicited the support of a host of Idumeans, who were a Semitic people living in the mountainous regions south of the Dead Sea. The Idumeans answered the Zealots' call, sent 20,000 men to Jerusalem and entered one of Jerusalem's gates unscathed thanks to the Zealots' help.[13]

The Idumeans wasted little time and joined the Zealots in an attack against Ananus' militia and overpowered them, which permitted the Zealots to escape Ananus' blockade and exit the Temple compound. When the battle ended, thousands of moderate Jews were imprisoned and 8,500 were dead, but the killings had only just begun. The rebels then joined with the Idumeans as they swept through Jerusalem and murdered at least another 12,000 Jews—particularly from the upper classes, including Ananus—and plundered the city. John's men, Eleazar's Zealots and the Idumeans had toppled the provisional government and did so in violent form, but it did not take the Idumeans long to realize their mistake. They saw firsthand that it was the Zealots, not the broader population of Jerusalem, who were the wrongdoers. As such, the Idumeans released some 2,000 Jews from their custody, most decided to quit the city and washed their hands of the destruction. Sadly for the Jews, this left Jerusalem firmly in the rebels' hands.[14]

Jerusalem ripped itself apart, but the Romans were not moved to take any swift action. Rather, Vespasian decided to give the Jews time to wear themselves out. It would simply make it easier for him to take Jerusalem, and they had plenty of intelligence coming from the holy city, given that refugees regularly quit Jerusalem and made for the Roman camps. Yet it was challenging to escape the Zealots. As Josephus pointed out,

> Flight was difficult, because guards were posted at all the outlets and anyone caught there, on whatever business, was slain, on the assumption that he was going off to the Romans. If, however, he paid [a ransom to the Zealots], he was allowed to go, and only he who offered nothing was [punished as] a traitor; the result being that the wealthy purchased their escape and the poor alone were slaughtered. Along all the highways the dead were piled in heaps; and many [who started] to desert changed their minds and chose to die within the walls, since the hope of burial made death in their native city appear more tolerable. The Zealots, however, carried barbarity so far as to grant interment to none, whether slain within the city or on the roads.

Even so, the Zealots' control was not absolute. In fact, John and Eleazar began distancing themselves from one another—as their alliance showed fractures. Before long, John recruited a corps of supporters from Eleazar's Zealots to follow him, and they continued engaging in violent behavior.[15]

Meanwhile, Judaea fell further into anarchy as insurgents emerged in previously peaceful cities and turned against their countrymen—even launching assaults on defenseless synagogues. Just as concerning, an organized group called the *Sicarii* was growing in power, terrorizing their fellow Jews, and eventually, seized the fortress of Masada from their countrymen, which served as their protective base of operations. The *Sicarii* were a terrifying militant group. According to Josephus, they "slew men in the day time, and in the midst of the city: this they did chiefly at the festivals, when they mingled themselves among the multitude, and concealed daggers under their garments, with which they stabbed those that were their enemies; and when any fell down dead, the murderers became a part of those that had indignation against them, by which means they appeared [to be] persons of such reputation, that they could by no means be discovered."[16]

Seeing Judaea and Jerusalem falling deeper into mayhem, Vespasian and Titus decided that they could no longer sit by. They evidently felt great sorrow for the innocent Jews who were essentially held captive to the combatants. Vespasian and Titus consequently mobilized their troops with plans to march south, eliminate remaining pockets of resistance around Jerusalem and then besiege the holy city. While sacking it would help bring the war to a close sooner, Vespasian's main objective was to reportedly free the innocent bystanders from the rebels' tyranny and violence. Put simply, he intended for Jerusalem's sacking to be a kind of rescue mission, or so Josephus suggested.[17]

Possibly along with Titus, Vespasian and his massive army broke camp and united. They planned to stamp out any opposition that could potentially threaten their planned siege of Jerusalem, and their first target was Gadara. Its location is the subject of some modern debate, since there were at least two ancient Jewish cities named Gadara. Yet Josephus asserts that it was the capital city of the region known as Perea and that many of its people were not enthusiastic about the war, even though combatants had overrun their city. Thus, without alerting the insurgents, its leading men secretly forwarded an embassy to Vespasian to negotiate the town's surrender, which thrilled the general. When Vespasian neared, the rebels learned of the plan to hand Gadara over to the Romans, lost heart and fled for their lives.[18]

In an act of overt supplication in March 68 CE, the people of Gadara voluntarily toppled their walls, invited the Romans into the city and showered them with their sincere gratitude. Vespasian appreciated the gestures and understood that the Gadarans had sought peace with Rome, not war. So he took no drastic measures. Instead, he exhibited mercy and even installed a Roman garrison there to protect them from reprisals and secure local Roman interests. However, Vespasian wanted to prevent the rebels who withdrew from finding another haven and undermining Rome's standing. As a result, he charged one of his capable lieutenants, Placidus, 500 cavalrymen and 3,000 infantrymen with tracking the fugitives down. Unlike the Gadarans, these men would receive no compassion.[19]

While Placidus pursued the insurgents, Vespasian returned again to Caesarea Maritima, likely to wait until Placidus finished matters, but he would not have to wait long. Placidus pursued the fugitives to the village of Bethennabris, which was less than 10 miles north of the Dead Sea, where the opposing factions collided. Placidus' men gained the upper hand and took the village, but he did not share Titus' merciful inclinations. The Romans plundered the town, razed it to the ground and massacred the entire population, regardless of whether they were combatants or not—save for a considerable body of men that escaped.

Trying to evade Placidus' terrible wrath, many of the Jewish insurgents hastened toward the city of Jericho. Today Jericho lies in the region known as the West Bank. It is best remembered from the Biblical account in the Book of Joshua in which the Israelites marched around the city, blew their horns and the walls tumbled down. Afterward, they eradicated the local Canaanite population without mercy, but by the Roman era, glory did not wait for the Jews there. Unfortunately for the fleeing Jews, Placidus caught up with them before they could find safety. They tried to form an ordered retreat, but they stood little chance. Placidus struck down many as they fled, and he outmaneuvered the others—pinning the bulk of them against the Jordan River. They were trapped and practically defenseless against the Roman war machine, and Placidus showed little compassion. He unleashed his legionaries on them. The Romans killed 15,000 and captured 2,200, and an unknown number of others fearfully leaped into the river and drowned.[20]

These engagements had a particularly demoralizing effect on the Jews.

Reminders of wholesale death were everywhere. The path from Bethennabris to the Jordan River was littered with deceased insurgents, and the Dead Sea and Jordan River were overwhelmed with decaying bodies floating in the water. Parts of the Jordan even became impassable by boat because of the staggering number of corpses that blocked the river, like a macabre human dam.[21]

Displeased with returning to camp just yet, Placidus continued his assaults on nearby villages. He captured Abila, Julias, Besimoth and others close to the Dead Sea, and he garrisoned them—hoping to guarantee that they would remain loyal to Rome. Some fugitives apparently looked for safety elsewhere and paddled out on the Dead Sea, but they did not find sanctuary. Placidus shipped his men out on boats in order to locate any of those who had tried to escape by water. They found these men and put them to the sword. Placidus' campaign was nothing short of brutal, but from the Roman perspective, he fought with distinction and neutralized much of the region.[22]

Vespasian and Titus were undoubtedly pleased by Placidus' overwhelming successes to date, which Placidus or messengers told them about, but around this time, they received incredibly distressing news from another messenger. A fresh revolt was underway, but not in Judaea or Galilee. Rather, this one was far closer to Rome and would drastically change the political landscape and play a pivotal role in Vespasian and Titus' lives.[23]

VIII

Vindex

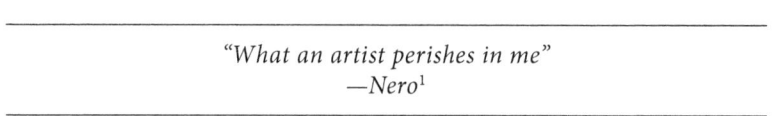

"What an artist perishes in me"
—Nero[1]

Just as Vespasian and Titus were re-securing the empire's eastern reaches, a shocking uprising rocked the entire Roman world. Sometime in the Spring of 68 CE, Gaius Julius Vindex—the governor of the Roman province of Gallia Lugdunensis, which encompasses much of modern-day France—openly revolted against Nero. As he roused many of those in Gaul to rise up against the emperor, he said in a speech:

> [Nero] has despoiled the whole Roman world, because he has destroyed all the flower of the senate, because he debauched and then killed his mother, and does not preserve even the semblance of sovereignty. Many murders, robberies and outrages, it is true, have often been committed by others; but as for the other deeds committed by Nero, how could one find words fittingly to describe them? I have seen him, my friends and allies—believe me—I have seen that man (if man he is who has married Sporus and been given in marriage to Pythagoras), in the circle of the theatre, that is, in the orchestra, sometimes holding the lyre and dressed in loose tunic and buskins, and again wearing [...] general-soled shoes and [a] mask.
>
> I have often heard him sing, play the herald, and act in tragedies. I have seen him in chains, hustled about as a miscreant, heavy with child, aye, in the travail of childbirth—in short, imitating all the situations of mythology by what he said and what was said to him, by what he submitted to and by what he did. Will anyone, then, style such a person [as] Caesar and emperor and Augustus? Never! Let no one abuse those sacred titles. They were held by Augustus and by Claudius, whereas this fellow might most properly be termed Thyestes, Oedipus, Alcmeon, or Orestes; for these are the characters that he represents on the stage and it is these titles that he has assumed in place of the others. Therefore rise now at length against him; succour yourselves and succour the Romans; liberate the entire world![2]

Some of the Gallic Romans might not have needed much cajoling to turn against Nero because he burdened them with oppressive taxes and mismanagement—much like Nero had treated the Jews. Yet Vindex wanted to build a larger coalition, including Romans from across the empire. He even tried to obtain the support of nearby provincial governors to join him in his bid to depose Nero, but he did not seek to become emperor himself. He certainly understood that he would never receive enough support to attain the imperial purple, given his family's non–Roman, Aquitanian origins. So it seems Vindex's primary goals were to remove Nero from power and install a more competent ruler—someone other than himself.[3]

At first, many of Vindex's peers rebuffed his requests to join forces with him, and they forwarded reports of his machinations to Nero. Soon enough, news of Vindex's revolt reached the emperor just after lunchtime one day, while he was in Naples watching a gymnastic event. However, he did little to quell the rebellion in the early days and essentially wallowed in complacence. Rather than taking it seriously, he was more interested in the physical contest that he was viewing, and he continued training for future musical recitals. This simply let the uprising take root and gain momentum, and he soon faced a growing coalition. One person affirmatively answered Vindex's call—Servius Sulpicius Galba—who governed Hispania Tarraconensis, which accounts for most of modern-day Spain, and he had a sizable corps of troops at his disposal.

He was an older man, but he had enjoyed a long, successful military and priestly career. He hailed from a distinguished lineage and was even once close friends with Emperor Claudius. Yet he was known to be miserly with money, required strict discipline among the soldiery and doggedly adhered to the justice system. Like many others, he may have had reason to be sympathetic to Vindex's call, including being disgusted with Nero who was draining Hispania Tarraconensis of its wealth and acting beneath his station. One offense in particular was doubtless the deciding factor for Galba. Suetonius claimed that Galba supposedly intercepted an official letter from Nero ordering his death, which could account for Galba's betrayal. It surely also helped that Vindex offered Galba the imperial throne, but he initially did not accept the title of Caesar; he was content with being called "General of the Roman Senate and People." Upon learning of Galba's defection, Nero reportedly fainted. When he regained consciousness, he finally accepted that the situation was dire and demanded decisive action.[4]

Despite the expanding revolt, Nero still held the stronger hand. He was largely popular with the Roman commoners in the Italian peninsula, and he had massive armies ready to do his bidding and resources at his disposal. In fact, Lucius Verginius Rufus who governed the province of Upper Germany marched his legionaries to confront Vindex. He did so successfully and killed 20,000 of Vindex's soldiers sometime in 68 CE, and Vindex killed himself afterward. Following Vindex's fall, Galba initially contemplated suicide, but opted against it. Biding his time in Spain, Galba survived and so did his legionaries and the growing disdain for Nero. Even with Vindex's defeat, the revolt had already begun and was not easily extinguishable. Others flocked to Galba's standard.[5]

The reports that Vespasian and Titus had been receiving from Rome were unfathomable. Since Emperor Augustus assumed power, the Julio-Claudian dynasty had not faced any serious internal threats from their own armies, and the Romans had enjoyed the peace and prosperity of the extended *Pax Romana*. Sure, there had been imperial assassinations and many more failed attempts, but the legions mostly stayed true to the emperor. With Vindex and Galba's revolt, all of that changed. This must have also felt deeply personal to Vespasian and Titus too. The Flavians benefited from Nero's favor, and Vespasian almost certainly knew the major players in the revolt personally. Titus might have as well or at least grown up with some of their sons or grandsons as they were educated, played together as children and climbed the political ladder.

Throughout the early days of the revolt, Vespasian and Titus understandably remained steadfastly loyal to the current emperor, in spite of his critical flaws. He was the legal ruler by every definition, but Vespasian and Titus understood that the rebellion might spread—requiring their legions to participate in a deadly civil war, like the ones that had ravaged the late Roman Republic. So they thought it best to try to resolve the Jewish War as quickly as possible to free themselves and their legionaries for another war.[6]

Both Vespasian and Titus knew that sacking Jerusalem was key to concluding the Jewish revolt, but they were not ready to besiege it yet. They first wanted to secure vulnerable cities and villages and root out insurgents around Jerusalem. Doing this would enable the Romans to control vital paths in and out of the holy city and ultimately help them protect their flanks and rear when they decided to commence their siege.

To achieve these goals, Vespasian—maybe along with Titus—marched his army to subjugate numerous Jewish towns. To deter future uprisings, he placed garrisons in them and even rebuilt some of the war-torn settlements that deserved or needed Rome's assistance. In what appears to be a quick campaign beginning in 68 CE, Vespasian pacified the city of Antipatris, which was northeast of Joppa, and raided the countryside of its wealth. The legions subsequently moved on to Thamna where they launched attacks. Then Vespasian turned toward the already-conquered towns of Lydda and Jamnia, and he relocated Jews there who were loyal to the Roman cause to keep the peace.[7]

With these issues settled, Vespasian marched his men into the Emmaus district northwest of Jerusalem, neutralized all notable opposition and raised a defensive camp. He decided to station the 5th Legion here—to secure his army's rear—for his upcoming campaign to capture Jerusalem. Then Vespasian took the remainder of his army to the southerly region of Bephleptenpha and even into Idumea. Vespasian ravaged the countryside and sacked two Idumean villages, called Betabris and Caphartoba. The Idumean campaign was swift, and left around 10,000 Idumeans dead and 1,000 captured who were probably destined to become slaves.[8]

Vespasian was now prepared to tackle a larger prize—the city of Jericho. The Roman general advanced his troops toward his objective and ordered his lieutenant Traianus to meet him there with his soldiers, and the two united near the important town. However, the Jewish population of Jericho got wind of the Romans' rapid advance, and most deserted the city—leaving it a ghost town for the legionaries to do with as they pleased. Despite their flight, the Romans discovered many from Jericho in the nearby hills and slaughtered them.[9]

In preparation for the extended siege of Jerusalem, Vespasian left troops in Jericho and Adida—a town northwest of Jerusalem. Meanwhile, one of his deputies—Lucius Annius—sacked Gerasa, which was an obscure settlement near Jerusalem. Annius captured and destroyed other nearby villages too. At the end of this campaign, Vespasian had pacified large swaths of land and secured critical paths in and out of Jerusalem. Vespasian and many of his legionaries then marched back to Caesarea Maritima to finalize plans for Jerusalem's sacking. While there, he received more distressing news from Rome.[10]

As much of these activities were underway, matters were deteriorating even further in and around Rome. The Roman Senate had declared Galba a public enemy, but other than that, he had not been reprimanded. Rather he remained free and safely encamped in Spain, and a mutinous environment continued growing against Nero. The troops serving Verginius—who defeated Vindex—even begged him to seize the imperial throne—something he refused to do—but it was proof that the emperor's soldiers were abandoning him. At some point during the revolt, Nero finally took action and charged a senator named Publius Petronius Turpilianus and a massive army with ending the rebellion, but he defected from Nero to Galba. The emperor now felt alone and vulnerable. After gathering together some poison that Locusta had mixed for him, he planned to flee Rome with a retinue of attendants, but he soon learned that even the Praetorian Guard had deserted him. This left the emperor even more defenseless. So he removed his royal clothing, donned the garb of a commoner and went into hiding with three of his intimates, including his lover Sporus and secretary Epaphroditus. Even at this juncture, Nero still held hope that he might be permitted to survive and live the life of a full-time artist.[11]

With Nero missing, the Senate entirely reversed its prior decision on Galba. They subsequently proclaimed him emperor in June 68 CE and declared Nero a public enemy—news that reached Nero. The Romans then began searching for the deposed emperor, who eventually took refuge in a cave, to execute him. When his would-be executioners approached his hiding place, he begged his associates to strike him down. With the help of Epaphroditus, Nero stabbed himself in the throat with a dagger—leading to his demise. Sometime before he perished, Nero declared, "What an artist perishes in me." With these acts on June 9, 68 CE, the celebrated Julio-Claudian dynasty that traced its roots to Julius Caesar fell out of power for good, which elated many of the Romans who tired of Nero's rule. It did not take long for the reports of Nero's demise to reach Galba and that he had been appointed emperor. He consequently adopted the title of Caesar, mobilized his troops and marched toward Rome.[12]

News of Nero's untimely death and Galba's ascension reached Vespasian at Caesarea Maritima, which must have come as a disappointing surprise. First of all, Nero had largely helped promote the Flavians' careers. Second, this was a seismic shock to the Roman state. The Julio-Claudians had fallen from power, and a usurper now ruled the empire. If anything, this demonstrated that emperors' grasps on power were insecure, and rivals—even those with no real claims to the imperial purple—could replace them. No doubt this caused uncertainty and disquiet among the Flavians and many Romans.

Anxiety aside, Vespasian and Titus both accepted Galba as the new emperor, given that the Senate had confirmed his candidacy, and were happy to serve him. Other than some flaws, he seemed like a qualified and worthy claimant. With a new emperor entering office during these turbulent times, Vespasian thought it wise to postpone his assault on Jerusalem and wait for direction from Galba. Vespasian consequently tasked Titus with sailing to Rome to meet with the emperor, express their unwavering loyalty to him and determine his preference for handling the Judaean revolt. One questionable account suggests that Titus' journey was for a different reason because he planned to stand for higher office in Rome, but this makes little sense. He would have remained at his father's side—serving as his legate instead of pursuing an elected office in Rome.[13]

Accompanied by King Agrippa II and a cortege of officials and soldiers, Titus and his friends boarded warships and set sail for Rome, and his trip sparked some rumors. A number of Romans evidently believed that Galba intended on adopting Titus as his son and heir, but that was not the case, nor would Titus' expedition be easy or productive. To begin with, travel by sea was the fastest mode of transportation, but it was hardly quick and was always treacherous in the Mediterranean Sea. To better ensure their safety, Titus and his comrades took a coastal route, but by the time Titus reached the Greek city of Corinth, he learned that Galba was dead after a reign of only seven months. Titus' voyage was an utter waste.[14]

The Senate may have extended the imperial throne to Galba, but he had not consolidated his power or kept his allies happy. While Galba showed flashes hinting that he could have been a decent ruler, he made enemies across Rome, and there were plenty who did not accept him as emperor. It did not help that he exhibited his inclination toward harshness. He had previously ordered the random killing of one in ten soldiers in a particular company for their misbehavior in a punishment known as decimation, but not every killing was unwarranted. He ordered the execution of the poisoner Locusta—probably with the people' support—but he faced problems still. His troops expected a generous donative, but the old parsimonious Galba refused and exclaimed, "I am accustomed to levy soldiers, not to buy them."

What's more, the legions of Upper and Lower Germany did not accept Galba as emperor in large part because they wanted to be lavished with wealth and benefits. According to Suetonius, these soldiers sent a message to the Roman Senate stating, "The emperor created in Spain did not suit them and the Guard must choose one who would be acceptable to all the armies." They took matters into their own hands and nominated the general and governor of Lower Germany—the corpulent Aulus Vitellius—as emperor whom Vespasian and Titus likely knew personally.

Vitellius' meteoric ascent was surprising even to himself, but he accepted the role and grew his base of support. The legions of Germany now recognized him as Rome's ruler. While this was an astonishing turn of events, he was a particularly well-connected individual—having been personal friends with Caligula, Claudius and Nero. He also had an extensive *curriculum vitae*—serving in many official political and religious postings—but he was a troubled individual and leader. He did whatever was needed to keep his soldiers pleased and was cruel to others. He was apparently fond of gambling, struggled with his finances and had a historic eating disorder—reportedly eating prodigious amounts of food, only to vomit between meals and then continue eating.[15]

In what seemed like a stinging betrayal, Galba had been the one to appoint Vitellius to the governorship, and now the Germanic legions refused to support Galba. Yet he wrongly believed that they rejected his claim to the throne because he was an elderly man without offspring to serve as his successor—although he had a male relative named Dolabella—and this could set the empire up for chaos upon his death. Hoping to calm matters by picking a relatively popular and well-deserving heir to the throne, Galba chose Lucius Calpurnius Piso Licinianus, which offended Galba's ally Marcus Otho who wanted to be Galba's heir.

He was one of Galba's earliest supporters, and he might have had cause to rebel against Nero. While they had once been close friends, they had a falling out over a love interest. Nero consequently appointed him to a posting outside of the city of Rome—in Lusitania in modern-day Spain and Portugal—as an alternative to formally banishing him. He was also a military man who generally had a good reputation—boasting some instances of integrity—but many individuals criticized him for his vanity. He apparently wore a specially made wig to cover his balding head, had his body hair depilated and would regularly hold wet bread to his face as a skincare routine.

In response to Galba's adoption of Piso, Otho orchestrated the assassination of both men by relying on Galba's own Praetorian Guard. In mid–January 69 CE when Galba was in his early 70s, his would-be assassins caught up with him in the Roman Forum. Astounded, Galba asked, "Why, what harm have I done?" There was no reasoning with these men. So the emperor exposed his neck, and instructed them, "Do your work, if this is better for the Roman people." Thereupon, they butchered him, cleaved his head from his torso and placed it atop a pike. They subsequently slew some of Galba's allies, including Piso—leaving their bloodied, headless corpses laying in the Forum and their heads impaled on poles.[16]

Following Galba's death, the Senate acted quickly and decisively—especially after witnessing the spate of brutal public murders—and named Otho emperor of Rome. In a manner that became customary among Roman leaders, he claimed that his ascension was against his will. Realizing Galba's fatal flaw, he resolved to pamper the soldiers with donatives, but he labored to show deference to Nero. His grip on power was unsure as well, since there was another rival claimant to the throne—Vitellius—setting up a hazardous confrontation between the two supposed emperors. Indeed, Vitellius wasted little time and began the march to war with Otho.[17]

Otho was either hoping to spare Rome from a devastating civil war or simply feared Vitellius' troops. Either way, he dispatched emissaries to Vitellius offering him a compromise: They would both share imperial authority and Otho would marry Vitellius' daughter to seal the deal. Vitellius was not interested in this division of power with Otho and continued on a trajectory for civil war. Meanwhile, Otho seems to have been working to raise support in the provinces, which must not have been too difficult since he was the only person the Senate had named emperor. In fact, legions from Dalmatia, Pannonia and Moesia sided with Otho, but their assistance would take time to materialize, given their distance from Rome.[18]

Titus was still in Greece on his abortive mission to meet with Galba when he learned of this. As he contemplated his next steps, he must have been at a loss over what to do. He mulled his options, including continuing his journey and accepting one of the two claimants, but he worried about being held hostage by one party to ensure the Flavians' support. He also did not know which, if any, of the parties he should back, and he began considering his family's future. If flawed men like Otho and Vitellius could claim the empire, then upright gentlemen like Vespasian could too, and Titus evidently believed that his father was worthier of the honor than the current usurpers. Thus Titus seems to have been the first Flavian to seriously ponder advocating that Vespasian seize the throne.

After some consideration, Titus wisely decided to return to Caesarea Maritima to take counsel with Vespasian, and he charted a course back to his father and once again set sail. From Greece, his vessel hugged the coastline and passed by modern-day Türkiye, Rhodes and Cyprus, but he decided to make an unplanned stop to visit the famous Temple of the Paphian Venus where priests maintained a cult. After Titus explored the resplendent temple, he asked the oracle about the last leg of his trip to Caesarea Maritima—wishing to avert any possible catastrophe—and the oracle responded that the seas and signs were favorable. Titus sacrificed numerous beasts and then posed some ambiguous questions to the temple priest. Titus was clearly inquiring about his nascent plan to make the Flavians Rome's ruling family but without openly stating that. The priest inspected the sacrificial animals' entrails, and reported to Titus that everything appeared propitious, which must have come as a great relief to Titus.

He subsequently shoved off for Caesarea Maritima where Vespasian had already learned of Otho's ascent. The commander even required that his troops proclaim their loyalty via an oath to the new emperor. Sometime later, Titus arrived without incident. Once there, he may have reunited with his love Berenice, but he had much bigger issues to tend to. He surely told his father about Galba's death and Otho and Vitellius' rise, and also his grand plans to seize power from those deemed unfit to govern the empire. This was difficult for Vespasian to digest, and perhaps sensing this, Titus disclosed his visit to the Temple of the Paphian Venus and the priest's findings. It is not clear whether Vespasian and Titus immediately—but very quietly—began laying the groundwork to claim the imperial purple or if they first determined that it was best for them to simply wait and see how matters played out.

One way or another, they eventually agreed to take Rome by force. In the meantime, they temporarily ceased major activities in the Jewish War and impatiently lingered for news from Rome.[19]

Vespasian's decision did not help the situation in Jerusalem, which was devolving even further, and its people would soon have to contend with another tyrant. Simon, the son of Gioras, from Gerasa, was another revolutionary with plans to seize vast power over his fellow Jews. While initially banished from Jerusalem by Ananus, he chose to join the *Sicarii* at Masada and led raids in the neighboring districts, but he was not content with local plundering operations. He wanted to prosecute a grand war and set himself up as the Jewish people's leader. When the Idumeans and Zealots murdered Ananus, Simon left Masada and recruited a body of men with plans to head toward Jerusalem.[20]

Simon ultimately mustered a veritable army of combatants and began overrunning villages, which alarmed the rebels in Jerusalem. They realized his aims were to march on their city in due time, and in fact, Simon's men clashed with them outside of Jerusalem. Simon drove them back into the city but opted against entering it just yet. In the interim, he and about 20,000 of his militiamen invaded parts of Idumea and overran it—capturing cities, like Hebron, and valuable provisions—and he grew his army's size in the process.[21]

The insurgents in Jerusalem were beyond worried about Simon's enterprises, and they laid ambuscades to hinder his success, although they were mostly ineffective. At one point, they captured his wife and planned to hold her hostage to force Simon to relent. Instead, it just angered him, and he went on a killing spree of Jews whom he found near Jerusalem. Soon thereafter, he turned to another form of brutality and began severing captives' hands and forcing them to march into Jerusalem. Upon entering, they told Jerusalem's captors that Simon had sworn an oath to God to do the same to everyone in Jerusalem unless they gave his wife back to him. Fearing this ghastly fate, they meekly sent Simon's wife to be with her husband. Even so, John's rabble, Eleazar's Zealots and Simon's men were not inclined toward peace with one another, and their struggle continued to beleaguer Jerusalem.[22]

Similarly, Rome was in the midst of a civil war. Otho and Vitellius both wished to be Rome's solitary emperor and were willing to throw the empire into chaos to obtain mastery over it. Their conflict came to a head in Cisapline Gaul—even though Otho's Danubian legions had not arrived yet—where the two enormous armies collided and fought a bloody engagement. While Otho did not participate in any of the battles—leaving matters up to his generals—his soldiers charged the enemy and seemed to initially seize the advantage, but their gains quickly disintegrated. Vitellius' legions overwhelmed them and claimed victory, and Otho decided to kill himself after being emperor for scarcely three months.

According to Suetonius, some of his last acts included burning "all his letters, to prevent them from bringing danger or harm to anyone at the hands of the victor. He also distributed what money he had with him among his servants." Sometime later, Otho inspected two of his knives, and when he believed the time was right, he drew one of the daggers and plunged it into his heart—leading to his death in mid–April 69 CE. Yet before his demise, he worried that his enemies might abuse his corpse. Therefore, in one of his last directives, he instructed his allies to hastily organize a funeral and cremate his body. With Otho dead and his remains disposed of, Vitellius was now the lone claimant to the throne. Once many of Otho's soldiers switched their loyalties to Vitellius, he and his formidable army advanced toward Rome to take what he believed was his—the emperorship—and they reached it in the summer of 69 CE.[23]

As much of this was underway, Vespasian and Titus likely understood that they could not sit by and let the Jewish revolutionaries undo all of their progress in Judaea, nor leave the unpacified regions to their own devices. Similarly, they could not let John, Eleazar and Simon continue their reigns of terror over Jerusalem and the Jewish people. As a result, Vespasian departed from Caesarea Maritima with his legionaries, and they captured two small settlements called Bethel and Ephraim—both in the hill country north of Jerusalem. With these towns pacified, Vespasian marched toward Jerusalem where the Romans killed a host of Jews who were not behind the city's protective walls.

Meanwhile, one of Vespasian's deputies invaded part of Idumea where he captured the cities of Caphethra and Charabis. Next he besieged Hebron, which Simon had sacked, and showed no mercy. He seized the city, slaughtered everyone regardless of age and razed it to the ground. After a couple years of fighting, only Herodium, Masada, Machaerus and Jerusalem stood in Vespasian's way of achieving total victory, but they would not fall quickly. As he prepared for what he hoped would be the final steps in the Jewish War, Vespasian and his men returned to Caesarea Maritima for a brief respite.[24]

When the Romans were preoccupied with other issues in Judaea, Simon returned to Jerusalem and surrounded it, which left the moderate faction of the Jewish population facing a dilemma. They feared Simon more than the Romans and loathed John and Eleazar more than either. Ever since John had entered Jerusalem, the insurgents had intensified their crimes and also dabbled in what Josephus called depravity. They looted Jerusalem mercilessly, murdered men, raped the female population, violated other Jewish sexual mores and spent the rest of their days in a drunken stupor.[25]

They terrified the broader Jewish population, which caused dissension in John's ranks. One of his contingents revolted against him, and in their short-sightedness, they and the moderate Jewish population invited Simon into Jerusalem to free them of the rebels' treachery, which was a deadly blunder. Simon was no friend of the moderate Jews, but he was excited to be master of Jerusalem. So Simon and his militia entered the holy city, while John and his gang huddled in the vicinity of the Temple complex. Caring less about freeing Jerusalem from oppression and more about obtaining tyranny for himself, Simon launched an assault on their position, but the outnumbered defenders repelled his attempts. They were at a bloody stalemate. Around the same time, Rome was experiencing its own set of harrowing issues.[26]

IX

Antonius Primus

> *"The very best security for peace lies in a legitimate succession to the throne. If, then, sovereignty calls for the experience of years, we have Vespasian, if for the vigour of youth, there is Titus; the pair of them will combine the advantages of their respective ages."*
> —Roman legionaries[1]

After churning through several emperors in short succession—Nero, Galba, Otho, and now Vitellius—many Romans must have been confused and in a paralyzed state of disbelief. Never had this occurred in the Roman Empire's short lifetime, and the Romans had reason to be apprehensive of the newest regime. Vitellius relied on the advice of incompetent associates, acted with unrestrained cruelty and made a mockery of Rome's constitution, laws and justice system. Moreover, the Romans were eventually dismayed by the conduct of Vitellius' men.

His army was too large for the local barracks, but they marched for Rome anyway where they would need to billet in the city. Given that Vitellius' troops had engaged in many forms of degeneracy and violence, the Romans could expect the same in their capital. Indeed, these legionaries busied themselves with revelry, plundered towns and villages, harassed the residents and murdered many of the centurions loyal to Otho. In many ways, their behavior was similar to that of John, Eleazar and Simon's insurgents in Jerusalem.

Vespasian was well-aware of these unfolding events, and did not take them well. The normally even-tempered and good-humored commander was beside himself. He was incensed and considered Vitellius unfit for the office he had seized. Vespasian's mind obsessed over Rome's predicament, and this fixation and agony made it difficult for him to prosecute the Judaean war. He wanted to somehow come to his countrymen's rescue and had thousands of troops at his disposal to do so. While marching on Rome and deposing Vitellius may have seemed like a romantic notion, he knew that doing so would be fraught with danger.[2]

As Vespasian and Titus lamented Rome's fate under Vitellius, their soldiers began pondering Rome's future and advocated revolutionary ideas of their own. They were disgusted with the new Roman emperor and his legionaries who felt that they were empowered to decide who should rule over the empire. Some of Vespasian's soldiers complained,

Those soldiers in Rome, now living in luxury, who cannot bear to hear even a rumour of war, are electing whom they choose [for our governors] and in hope of [making them] emperors. [While] we, who have undergone such numerous toils and are growing gray beneath our helmets, are giving up this privilege to others, when all the time we have among us one [worthier] of the government. What juster return can we ever render him for his kindness to us, if we fling away the present opportunity?

Vespasian's claim to the empire is as far superior to that of Vitellius, as are we to the electors of that emperor; for, surely, we have waged wars no less arduous than the legions of Germany, nor are we inferior in arms to the troops who have thence brought back this tyrant. Besides, there will be no need for a contest; for neither Senate nor Roman people would tolerate the lewdness of Vitellius in place of the temperance of Vespasian, nor prefer [...] a most brutal tyrant to a virtuous ruler, a childless prince to a father, since the very best security for peace lies in a legitimate succession to the throne. If, then, sovereignty calls for the experience of years, we have Vespasian, if for the vigour of youth, there is Titus; the pair of them will combine the advantages of their respective ages.

Nor will the persons of our choice be dependent solely on the strength which we can supply, mustering as we can three legions and the auxiliaries furnished by the kings; they will have the further support of the whole eastern world and of all in Europe too remote to be intimidated by Vitellius, as also of our allies in Italy, a brother and another son of Vespasian. Of these, one will gain many recruits from the young men of rank, while the other has actually been entrusted with the charge of the city—a fact of no small importance for any designs upon the empire. In short, if there is any delay on our part, the senate will probably elect the very man whom his own soldiers, who have grown gray in his service, have disgracefully neglected.[3]

Inchoate, wishful thinking must have prompted much of the aforementioned talk. It is hard to imagine that they had any inkling over whether other legions and Vespasian's brother—who was the prefect of Rome—would join them in their counter-coup. They also had no reason to believe that Vespasian would be interested in this intrigue. Either way, the legionaries' discussions over revolting against Vitellius and proclaiming Vespasian emperor allegedly started quietly and was secluded to certain circles, but before long, the barracks were filled with such chatter.[4]

It is implausible that Vespasian and Titus were wholly ignorant of their soldiers' plotting—especially after it had spread throughout the officers' camps. Yet this purportedly did not immediately move Vespasian to seek the imperial office. Nevertheless, he could only ignore his legionaries' scheming for so long because one day his troops did the unthinkable. The army unanimously declared Vespasian emperor of Rome and requested that he save their country from the tyrants, injustice and uncertainty that stalked it.[5]

The proclamation and his troops' faith in him doubtless humbled the old commander, but he supposedly was not interested in seizing control of Rome at this juncture. Being emperor had become a dangerous proposition. Nero, Galba and Otho had all died recently either by suicide or assassination, but the violent precedent was not entirely new. Claudius and Caligula had both been murdered too. Why would Vespasian want to risk this fate? He allegedly did not, and preferred the quiet solitude of a private life as opposed to the risky, high-profile nature of being emperor. Besides, he could serve the Romans in an untold number of other capacities. At the same time, he could still retain his freedom and privacy, while safeguarding his life and the lives of his family members in a way that emperors cannot. Further, Vespasian did not consider himself of imperial quality. He hailed from a family with humble and obscure origins, and it was not long before that people had called him the muleteer and he was forced to mortgage his estates.[6]

With his legionaries standing before him, Vespasian offered his gratitude for their trust in him, but he politely declined the offer and explained his reasoning. His deputies were not willing to take no for an answer and consequently badgered the commander and urged him to reconsider. The lower-level soldiers were far less subtle in their manner of persuasion. They surrounded Vespasian, drew their *gladii* and demanded that he assume the title of emperor or die. Faced with this choice on July 3, 69 CE, Vespasian relented and accepted their nomination with great hesitation, or at least that is the suspect account that Josephus recorded.[7]

The truth is that it seems virtually unbelievable that Vespasian had not already seriously considered taking the steps and initiated a complex plan to become emperor, especially after Titus had previously received favorable omens from the Paphian Venus. It is likewise preposterous that Vespasian only agreed to seize Rome because he had been threatened at the point of a gladius. Put simply, this would not have happened and his imperial bid was not some half-baked impromptu decision. As later events showed, Vespasian and Titus appear to have meticulously pieced together a coalition and campaign to dethrone Vitellius. What's more, Vespasian's legionaries were steadfastly loyal to him. They would not have suddenly abandoned their blind fidelity to Vespasian and instead threatened his life if he did not accept their nomination.

Rather, this story was likely a piece of fiction invented after Vespasian sought the imperial throne. However, if the account bears any factual elements, then it doubtless transpired at Vespasian's bidding and upon carefully designing what would have been little more than political theater. Refusing the imperial purple until his troops demanded it under threat of violence would have demonstrated his great humility and reluctance toward accepting the emperorship, which the Romans appreciated.

However matters developed, it is clear that Vespasian and Titus mulled revolting against the most recent regime much earlier and began piecing together their coup weeks or months prior—sometime after Titus returned from Corinth. As Vespasian considered it, his senior officials, including Mucianus—during the preliminary planning stage—urged him to take quick and decisive action. Luckily, the Flavians were adept military leaders. Vespasian and Titus had drafted their plan to topple Vitellius, and they ultimately executed it flawlessly. The Flavians believed that victory over the ruling regime in Rome could hinge on Alexandria, Egypt, and they needed to address this portion of their plan as soon as possible. They wagered that if the coming civil war was prolonged, then the only way to ensure Vitellius fell would be to cut off Rome's grain supply, much of which came from the empire's breadbasket: Egypt. When/if this came to fruition, the people would turn on Vitellius and welcome Vespasian.[8]

There were two Roman legions stationed in Alexandria, and it was a well-defended city. If Vespasian could encourage them to join his standard, then Vitellius would have little hope of reopening the grain trade in the short-term, but the Flavians needed a friend in Egypt. To this end according to Josephus' questionable account, Vespasian penned a letter to the governor of Egypt in Alexandria, known as Tiberius Julius Alexander. He was a staunchly pro-Roman administrator who happened to be Jewish, and his brother had once been married to Berenice. Within the message, Vespasian supposedly explained that his troops had declared him emperor against his will, and that he hesitatingly accepted in hopes of alleviating Rome's plight. He respectfully asked Alexander to ally with him. It does not seem that it took much convincing. Alexander quickly sided with Vespasian, and he read the missive publicly and required his legions and the locals to swear an oath to Vespasian. Yet they evidently acted prematurely—giving credence to the theory that Vespasian's bid was meticulously pre-planned—and declared him emperor on July 1, 69 CE, which was two days prior to Vespasian's own troops' acclamation. Sometime later, Mucianus—whose friendship Titus had carefully cultivated—and his troops also hailed Vespasian emperor, as did others.[9]

The Romans legions of Dalmatia, Moesia and Pannonia learned of Vespasian's endeavors, and they too swore allegiance to him, although this might have been out of necessity. They had earlier supported Otho's candidacy and began their march toward Rome to defend his claim, but before they could play a role in Otho's civil war, he perished. So they naturally were not well-disposed toward Vitellius. Beyond these matters, nearby provinces without armies contributed aid to Vespasian in other ways, including manufacturing arms and providing monetary support.[10]

News of Vespasian's imperial bid and the legions in Alexandria defecting to Vespasian swiftly spread across the empire. Within a matter of days, much of the fighting force—14 legions plus auxiliary units—in the eastern half of the Roman Empire had sworn loyalty to Vespasian. Upon hearing this, Roman cities celebrated and offered sacrifices for Vespasian's success and well-being. With the legions in Egypt, Dalmatia, Moesia, Pannonia, Syria and Judaea aligned with Vespasian, his brother Sabinus, who was the powerful prefect of Rome, likewise plotted Vitellius' demise. After learning that so many legions had rejected him, Vitellius worked to supplement his Germanic legions, and he resorted to levying commoners within the city of Rome. He was desperate to do so because he understood that Vespasian's coalition forces could soon converge on him.[11]

Leaving from Caesarea Maritima possibly in July 69 CE, Vespasian and many of his legionaries marched north to the Roman colony of Berytus—modern-day Beirut—to prepare for the coming campaign. Despite everything that was happening, he remembered that, while Nero was still in power, Josephus had predicted that he—Vespasian—would become emperor. Vespasian had originally dismissed the prophecy before learning that Josephus had a knack for making accurate predictions. Pitying Josephus, regretting his confinement and acknowledging his prophetic powers, Vespasian exclaimed, "It is disgraceful that one who foretold my elevation to power and was a minister of the voice of God should still rank as a captive and endure a prisoner's fate," and he ordered his release.[12]

Titus responded to the newly proclaimed emperor, "Justice demands, father, that Josephus should lose his disgrace along with his fetters. If instead of [loosening,] we sever his chains, he will be as though he had never been in bonds at all." Cutting a prisoner's chain in such a manner was a symbolic gesture done to those who had been wrongly accused or convicted. With Vespasian and Titus' blessing, a subordinate walked forward and broke Josephus' chains with an axe. He was now a free man without the blemish of a legitimate conviction.[13]

Even without overthrowing Vitellius, Vespasian began carrying out imperial duties, including speaking with foreign envoys and appointing Romans to various postings in the empire—ensuring that competent, loyal administrators were installed in his realm. While these were critical actions, Vespasian could not dawdle. Therefore the Flavians continued their march northward—coming to Antioch where Vespasian reassessed the situation. Even though he believed that Alexandria was in capable hands with Alexander, Vespasian and Titus agreed that they should travel there to ensure matters were in order before continuing to Rome. Given that it was mired into chaos, they could not leave it in such a state for long. As such, he ordered Mucianus to head to Rome at the head of an army. Mucianus trembled at the thought of a winter sea voyage, and as a result, he decided to march his troops overland to Rome. Vespasian and Titus subsequently made their way to Alexandria.[14]

While this was underway, Antonius Primus—a Roman military commander and Vespasian's ally or at least Vitellius' enemy—decided to lead thousands of legionaries, including those tasked with guarding Pannonia, to confront Vitellius without permission and swiftly neared Vitellius' sphere of influence. For some reason, Vitellius decided against personally defending his claim to the throne, and he forwarded one of his subordinates—named Aulus Caecina Alienus—to take an army north to Cisalpine Gaul for a showdown with Primus. Regrettably for Vitellius, Caecina had second thoughts, and he believed that Vespasian was destined to claim victory. So he entreated his troops to switch their loyalties to Vespasian, but they vacillated—ultimately opting to fight for Vitellius and turning against Caecina whom they imprisoned.[15]

Primus got wind of the widespread dissension and disarray in Caecina's ranks and decided that he could not waste this opportunity. After each side vainly strove to induce the other to defect, battle became inevitable. Primus drew his men up in battle formation and attacked Caecina's troops near the northern Italian city of Cremona. A bloody battle erupted in October 69 CE, and each side took heavy casualties. Eventually, Caecina's men broke ranks and retreated, but Primus cut off their retreat by dispatching his cavalry to block their escape route. They were now trapped, and Primus methodically slaughtered the army—leaving 30,000–50,000 men dead, possibly including some local noncombatants and foreign traders who were caught in the melee. Primus fared much better but still lost 4,500 men. It was a painful victory, but the deed was done. Afterward, Primus released Caecina from the custody of Vitellius' allies and sent him to Vespasian who treated him like a valued friend.[16]

Rumors of the crushing defeat and Primus marching toward Rome swirled throughout the eternal city, and Vespasian's brother—Sabinus—believed that it was time for him to act. He held numerous conferences with Vitellius in the fall and encouraged him to surrender peacefully. In time, Vitellius agreed, and the two men formed a pact in which Vitellius would hand over imperial power to Vespasian and likely be permitted to live a life of luxury outside of Rome. Sadly, many of Vitellius' men refused to accept the deal, and they decided to confront Sabinus. As prefect of the city, he was considerably powerful and had many armed men at his disposal. Thus he recruited their support, but Vitellius' soldiers gained the upper hand. Outflanked, Sabinus and his comrades then retreated and seized the Capitol where they hoped to hold out.

Numerous men of rank and even Vespasian's youngest son—Domitian—then joined with Sabinus, but they risked great peril. Vitellius' partisans were infuriated and desperately wanted to stamp out Sabinus' uprising. Consequently, Vitellius' deputies unleashed their remaining troops on the Capitol. Sabinus and his allies presumably fought with honor, but they could not match the numbers, training and arms of Vitellius' troops who won the day. In the process, the Capitol and Temple of Jupiter were burned to the ground. Domitian managed to escape Vitellius' wrath by going into hiding, but many others, including Sabinus, did not. Vitellius' troops captured and summarily executed them, although Sabinus' treatment was particularly abhorrent. Vitellius' men beheaded Sabinus and punctured his torso with a hook so that they could drag his corpse around the city as they abused it further, but this brutality would not go unpunished.[17]

Shortly thereafter, on December 20, 69 CE, Primus and his troops arrived at Rome's walls and entered the city where they realized they would face the remnants of Vitellius' army, but Roman legions were not made for urban warfare. They performed much better on open plains, but Primus did his due diligence and prepared his men accordingly. They took up position in three different locations within the city, and Vitellius' men pursued them there and tried to drive them from Rome. However, Primus' soldiers were victorious on every front and massacred Vitellius' troops.[18]

Vitellius apparently understood that his imperial bid was over, and it did not take long for his enemies to locate him even though he had gone into hiding. At first, he begged for mercy, but their vengeance was unrestrained. They plucked him from his refuge and put him in a holding cell. Following a short span of time, they bound his hands, placed a noose around his neck, drug him around the city and hurled insults and manure at him. When they got their fill of that, they tortured and then killed him after he had been in power for about eight months. They subsequently pierced his body with a large hook, pulled his body around town and tossed it into the Tiber River as if it was meaningless refuse. Primus' men were not finished with their butchery. They combed through the city slaughtering any pro-Vitellius troops and partisans, including Vitellius' brother. Primus' men must have thought this fitting since Vitellius' partisans had killed Vespasian's brother Sabinus, which the Romans lamented. In the end, around 50,000 people laid dead within the eternal city.[19]

Mucianus reached Rome with his soldiers not long after and largely ended the killing spree, but the counter-coup against Vitellius required more than just military might. Mucianus needed to solidify Vespasian's grip on power and install a temporary regent to act on Vespasian's behalf. With Sabinus dead and Titus in Africa, Domitian was the natural choice. Thereupon he began to serve in the role, but he was more of a Flavian figurehead than anything else. The skilled and experienced Mucianus effectively administered the state in Vespasian's stead and enjoyed vast power given to him by Vespasian. Domitian, meanwhile, was little more than his mouthpiece. Regardless of this arrangement, the people joyfully declared Vespasian princeps and emperor of Rome, and the Senate formally confirmed his appointment and celebrated his ascension heartily.[20]

They hoped to be done with the spate of tyrants and living under the threat of constant civil war and mass murder. Vespasian represented a new beginning for Rome and a new kind of leader with whom the Romans identified. He rejected decadence, embraced provincial values and understood the plight of Romans. After all, his family had humble origins and Vespasian seemed like a man of honor.

Around this time, Vespasian and Titus were still in the midst of planning their long voyage to Rome from Alexandria. While in Egypt, they helped secure the province, collected money and resources and prepared for their invasion of the Italian peninsula when they received reports that Vitellius had been overthrown. What's more, Vespasian had been officially proclaimed emperor, and there were fortunately no other serious claimants to the throne. This was thrilling news, and before long, Alexandria was overwhelmed with embassies, well-wishers and imperial deputations whom Vespasian and Titus entertained. Vespasian lingered in Alexandria for months, and his reason for doing so may be due to his agents needing to remove those hostile to his reign and taking some heavy-handed approaches to right the state. With Vespasian in Alexandria during this, the new emperor could remain blameless.[21]

Suetonius and Tacitus offered some unique tales about Vespasian's time in Alexandria. The ancient historians claimed that two men—one blind and one with a lame hand or leg—came to visit Vespasian. They asserted that the Greco-Egyptian god Serapis had come to them in a dream—stating that Vespasian could heal them if he were to spit upon the blind and touch the handicapped limb with his heel. Sitting before a large crowd and being encouraged to entertain the request, Vespasian bowed to their petitions, and the men were healed. While this may seem miraculous, Tacitus provided rational, medical explanations for their recovery.[22]

Miraculous healer or not, with Vitellius' fall, the Romans could reasonably hope for peace within most of the empire. The immediate threat of massive civil wars dissipated; aside from some minor trouble spots, only the Jewish War remained. Yet Vespasian was needed in Rome. The heart of the empire had languished during the latter part of Nero's reign and during the imperial turnover of 69 CE, which historians call the Year of the Four Emperors. Vespasian needed to see to the empire's well-being, consolidate support in Rome and work to restore the city to its potential. Given these realities, Vespasian promoted his son Titus, gave him control over Judaea and Syria, including a host of legionaries, and Tiberius Julius Alexander would serve as his chief of staff. Then Vespasian charged Titus with sacking Jerusalem and concluding the nagging Jewish War. He would be more than just a commander, though. Upon Vespasian's elevation, Titus received the title of Caesar, and Vespasian held the upcoming consulship of 70 CE with Titus, although the latter's role as consul was nominal, considering his absence from Rome. Nevertheless, Titus must have been thrilled with his social promotion and opportunities, but he had little time to revel in the news; the war in Judaea awaited him.

Before departing, Titus thought it wise to convey some advice to his father who was apparently disquieted by some of Domitian's concerning activities in Rome. It appears that his younger son was beginning to believe that he was in power and acted accordingly. So Titus pleaded with his father to be forgiving and patient. "Neither armies nor fleets are so strong a defense of the imperial power as a number of children," Titus told Vespasian. "For friends are chilled, changed, and lost by time, fortune, and sometimes by inordinate desires or by mistakes: the ties of blood cannot be severed by any man, least of all by princes, whose success others also enjoy, but whose misfortunes touch only their nearest kin. Not even brothers will always agree unless the father sets the example." Upon delivering these remarks, the two parted to fulfill their new roles.[23]

X

KIDRON

> *"Without any flattering addition or carping detraction, [Titus] was personally responsible for twice rescuing the entire legion from a perilous situation, and enabling them to build their camp defenses in safety."*
> —*Josephus*[1]

WHILE ROME WAS MIRED IN A POWER-STRUGGLE for control of the imperial throne, Jerusalem had been plunging into further chaos. John and Simon's destructive conflict within the holy city had continued largely unabated—leaving death and destruction throughout Jerusalem. Yet the internal conflict became more complex. Eleazar ben Simon and his supporters formally splintered from those whom John led and abrogated their alliance that had already been fraying. Their official complaint was that John had become too bloodthirsty, which is nothing short of the truth, but Eleazar and his adherents were likewise violent. Nevertheless, Josephus avers there may have been more to Eleazar's reasoning. It is likely that Eleazar broke away from John because he wanted to be chief tyrant, not some lieutenant to a relative newcomer like John.[2]

Among Eleazar's allies were notable Jews who boasted a considerable following, and they were well-positioned to obstruct John's activities too. Upon marshaling his forces, Eleazar and his comrades solidified their control of the Holy Temple's inner court and stationed men overlooking the holy gates. Within this precinct, there were ample provisions, and it provided a strong defensible position. While this rebel band was smaller in number than John's gang, they posed a serious threat because of their superior position.[3]

John was doubtless furious. One of his erstwhile allies had deserted his cause, turned against him, recruited a body of men to counter his goals and secured the Temple's inner court and some surroundings. Worst of all, this opened a new front against John. He was now sandwiched between Eleazar and Simon's men. Put simply, he was practically surrounded and needed to change the dynamic fast. John wasted little time and attacked Eleazar's position relentlessly, but John fought from a weaker position and took heavy casualties, compared to Eleazar, as they polluted and desecrated the venerated Temple complex with blood.[4]

This seemed like a gift to Simon who controlled the Upper City and much of the Lower City. With his enemy John under duress, Simon also decided to strike. Similar to Eleazar, John enjoyed a more defensible position than Simon held, despite the latter boasting more men at arms. Undeterred, Simon urged his revolutionaries to march on John's position and launch their assault. They executed Simon's plan and began harassing John's men as he engaged in a two-front battle. As a result, Jerusalem was filled with hand-to-hand fighting and aerial barrages as the different factions fired projectiles across the rooflines. Thanks to these tactics, an untold number of Jews—both combatants and noncombatants—fell prey to the bombardment. However, neither Eleazar, John nor Simon could declare victory. The three independent enemies were largely at a bloody stalemate and needed to alter their strategy.[5]

Before long, the three parties adopted alternative—but devastating—tactics. While they still engaged in deadly skirmishes and artillery bombardments, they also launched firebrands into various buildings, including those serving as food stores. As they put them to the torch, they destroyed critical provisions that the Jews would desperately need, and the fires spread among the dried timber within the city. Josephus noted the extent of the destruction: "The result was that all the environs of the Temple were reduced to ashes, the city was converted into a desolate no man's land for their domestic warfare, and almost all the [grain], which might have sufficed them for many years of siege, was burnt up." The insurgents' short-sighted endeavors would eventually cost them and the rest of those in Jerusalem greatly.[6]

The tripartite conflict weighed heavily on the noncombatant population of Jerusalem too. Aside from dodging catapult fire and conflagrations and dealing with starvation, the Jewish civilians endured the tyrannical rules of John, Simon and Eleazar. They were more interested in securing their hold over Jerusalem and negating their rivals' power than aiding many of the civilian Jews, which was unfortunate. The latter felt helplessly trapped, watching the internecine conflict or worse—facing the insurgent leaders' violent wraths. The three competing rebel factions slaughtered defenseless Jews who spoke out in favor of peace. Due to the ongoing partisan battles and wanton attacks on the civilian population, Jerusalem was very quickly littered with unburied corpses rotting in the streets, which the three warring factions trampled during their sallies. For many Jews, they only saw one viable solution: They prayed that the Romans would deliver them from John, Simon and Eleazar's profane barbarity.[7]

Fortunately for them, Vespasian, Titus and their allies had mostly settled the direst matters in and around Rome, defeated Vitellius' faction and seized the throne. In time, Vespasian sailed for Rome to begin his imperial rule, and he empowered his son Titus to prosecute the Jewish War and bring it to a swift end. With these orders, the youthful commander collected legionaries in Egypt who had been earmarked for the sack of Jerusalem. They included 2,000 men stationed in Alexandria, and Titus would also add 3,000 legionaries from the forts near the Euphrates River. From Nicopolis—scarcely a couple miles from Alexandria, Egypt—Titus and his legionaries climbed aboard ships and sailed across the Nile Delta to the city of Thmuis where they disembarked and readied for a long, rapid march across unforgiving terrain.

This was nothing short of an impressive feat of logistics, given that successfully marching armies through deserts requires meticulous planning and ample access to food and water, which can be hard to come by in these regions.[8]

From there, Titus advanced to and made camps at Tanis, Heracleopolis, Pelusium, and into the northwestern Sinai Peninsula close to the Casian Zeus Temple. Titus and his legionaries must have already been exhausted and tired of the dry desert after this leg of the journey alone, but they had days of marching still ahead of them. From the Temple of the Casian Zeus, they marched to Ostracine, Rhinocorura, Raphia, Gaza, Ascalon, Jamnia, Joppa, and finally to Caesarea Maritima, which was a welcome sight for the weary soldiers. At Caesarea Maritima, Titus gave his soldiers a brief rest after their rapid marches through deserts and difficult terrain. He may have also reunited with Berenice as he re-provisioned his army and consolidated his forces with some of the other Roman legionaries who had already been engaged in the Jewish War.[9]

Very quickly, Titus began recalling soldiers to—and assembling his armies in—Caesarea Maritima. Meeting him there were auxiliaries, troops from nearby client-kingdoms and legions who had loyally served his father in the ongoing Jewish War. However, not all of the Roman legionaries were in Caesarea Maritima. Two other legions were dispersed elsewhere in Judaea, but Titus felt that he needed their support to end the Jewish revolt. After taking counsel with his deputies and advisers, Titus resolved to march toward Jerusalem with the troops currently at his disposal and dispatched orders to the others, including the 5th and 10th legions, to meet him near Jerusalem. They received their orders and began making their way to unite with Titus. Including these troops, Titus had four legions under his command plus his allies, which totaled anywhere from 65,000–80,000 soldiers bent on Jerusalem's sacking.[10]

Marching in a seemingly interminable column, Titus' army exited Caesarea Maritima for Jerusalem, which was bloated with more than just insurgents. With Passover approaching, a steady stream of pilgrims had flocked to the holy city to celebrate the venerated Jewish holiday. Others had also rushed to Jerusalem previously—hoping to escape the anarchy and war plaguing the countryside. As they filed in, Jerusalem's population surged to over 600,000 according to Tacitus or more than 1,100,000 per Josephus, but the latter probably exaggerated the numbers in Jerusalem. Nevertheless, a host of Jews journeyed to Jerusalem to celebrate, but unbeknownst to them, they had inadvertently marched to their doom.[11]

Titus was advancing directly for them. Leading the cavalcade were troops from allied kingdoms and auxiliaries, army engineers, surveyors and the Roman leadership's baggage train, which was heavily guarded by legionaries. Behind this vanguard was Titus—now the war's chief commander and son of Rome's newly appointed emperor. Armed cavalrymen and highly trained bodyguards flanked the general to ensure his safety and anxiously scanned the field for possible danger. Some of the army's broader cavalry, artillerymen and their engines, including ballistas, slowly trailed behind.[12]

Onlookers next saw the Roman army's tribunes and prefects who were likewise protected by a select corps of legionaries, and then the soldiers escorting the venerated legionary standards—poles topped with silver eagles that served to identify legions and could be used to communicate during battle—and trumpeters marched by. Following these displays were the common legionaries marching in unison and in formation of six men across. Then came the legionaries' baggage train, legionary servants and a defensive contingent of mercenaries intended to protect the column's rear from surprise attacks. The procession was incredibly long, and even though the Romans marched six men abreast and maintained a reasonable speed, with such a massive army, it took an inordinate amount of time for it to pass by curious onlookers.[13]

Advancing in order, the troops first reached Gophna, stopped for the night and then advanced to the Valley of the Thorns where they made camp, which rested only around three miles from Jerusalem. Eager to survey it, assess the Jews' morale and finalize his battleplan, Titus and 600 of his battle-tested elite cavalrymen galloped posthaste for the holy city. Riding in an elongated column, they neared Jerusalem via one of the main roads and detected no signs of resistance, which was an interesting development that provided a false sense of security.[14]

Seeing no imminent danger and wanting to reconnoiter the area, Titus turned his horse westward off the path, but around the time he did, Jewish rebels crept out of a nearby city gate and adroitly severed the cavalry column in two. The Jewish contingent formed a wall between the bulk of the cavalry company and Titus as well as a small number of his comrades, which reduced the Romans' ability to capably respond. In a shocking turn of events, Titus found himself and some fellow cavalrymen isolated and trapped. He needed to extricate himself to avoid a looming disaster, but the insurgents ensured that escaping would be challenging. Titus could not urge his horse forward because trenches, walls and fences blocked his path, and he could not easily retreat because there was a body of Jewish rebels obstructing the route. Even worse news, the Roman horsemen who had separated from him decided to retreat—believing that he was safe and had likewise withdrawn. They were woefully wrong, and now Titus and some of the other Romans were abandoned and in serious peril.[15]

In what was a terrifying reality, Titus understood that his only chance of survival rested with his own singular martial abilities and whether he could fight his way through the wall of Jewish revolutionaries or not. Even though he was without a helmet or protective cuirass, Titus bravely rode directly for the enemy who fired darts and launched spears in his direction, but they all miraculously missed the commander who was brazenly undeterred by their tactics. Brandishing his cavalry sword, he swung left and right wildly to keep the enemy from wounding him or plucking him from his horse. Rather than prevailing over Titus, he struck many down and urged his steed to trample over their dead or dying bodies.[16]

Titus' bravado caused terror in the attacking Jews who fearfully raced to escape his horse's path—likely colliding into their friends and allies in the process—and Titus' fellow cavalrymen endeavored to follow their leader. Two were not successful. The enemy cut them down. While this was dismaying, Titus and his other cavalrymen needed to first look to their own survival, given the hazardous situation. In time, Titus and a small number of other Romans fought their way through the Jewish ranks, galloped away from Jerusalem and safely made it to their camp.

There is no record of what Titus said or did when he arrived, but it seems that he must have delivered some stinging remarks to the bulk of the cavalry that had obliviously left him behind. Moreover, he probably made some somber remarks in remembrance of the two fallen cavalrymen. Regardless of Titus' disappointment, he had survived, and the Romans learned that the Jewish rebels were full of vigor. Meanwhile, they celebrated their supposed victory over the Roman cavalry company, which raised their hopes that they could survive a war with Rome.[17]

The Jews initially reveled in unfounded confidence, but their spirit presumably began to flag when they witnessed Titus and his next operation. That night the 5th Legion arrived in Titus' camp. By morning, Titus rallied his troops and ordered them to march closer to Jerusalem—to a hill called Scopus. It stood about three-quarters of a mile north of Jerusalem and provided the Romans a good vantage point. At that position, Titus tasked his engineers with raising a defensive, joint camp large enough to house two Roman legions and another camp 600 yards behind this. As the Romans broke ground, Rome's 10th Legion also arrived. They began to make camp on the nearby Mount of Olives, east of Jerusalem.[18]

Titus' force was now at full strength and in position. Whatever confidence had existed among the Jewish combatants began dissipating as they saw thousands of Romans swarming the area and realized that they were facing a much different scenario than they had just months ago. Rome was no longer plagued by civil wars; Vespasian and Titus had already pacified most of the Jewish countryside; Titus commanded four Roman legions and a host of allies and auxiliaries; and he focused all of his energies on Jerusalem. This was such a terrifying prospect for the Jewish revolutionaries in Jerusalem that they reconsidered their internal squabbles. They complained, "Is [...] our valour to be displayed only against ourselves, while the Romans, through our party strife, make a bloodless conquest of the city?" After realizing the gravity of the situation, they decided to join forces—at least temporarily. Once enemies, Simon, John and Eleazar's men now formed an alliance, although they surely remained distrustful of one another.[19]

Unified by a common enemy at their doorstep, the Jewish militants seized their weaponry and rushed out of Jerusalem toward the 10th Legion stationed on the Mount of Olives. Normally, untrained fighters such as these would have been no match for a Roman legion of professional soldiers, but the legionaries were not expecting an offensive. They held a position of strength and believed the Jews were crippled by internal strife. Given these assumptions, the Romans spread out across the Mount in smaller parties, busied themselves with erecting a camp and lacked easy access to their arms. It was the best-case scenario for the Jewish rebels who crossed the Kidron Valley unchallenged and ascended the Mount of Olives.[20]

The spectacle stunned the unprepared and overconfident Romans who cast their tools aside in the face of the onslaught. Some retreated for safety, while others ran for their weapons to defend their partially constructed camp, but the Jewish insurgents slew many of these legionaries before they could make an adequate stand. The Jewish combatants who were still in Jerusalem were heartened by what they saw, and this encouraged more rebels to pour out of the holy city and join the fight against the 10th Legion. Its legionaries were in a frenzy, and those who had not fled or perished, desperately tried to form an orderly defense. It was for naught. The Jews overwhelmed the disorganized Romans who ultimately withdrew wholesale from the onslaught—deserting their camp site.[21]

The Romans ran for their lives as the Jews pursued them and hoped to make it to the safety of the Roman camps near Scopus. However, they risked being slaughtered as they withdrew, but someone alerted Titus to their peril. Likely mobilizing his elite cavalry contingent, Titus hurried to the 10th Legion's defense and quickly saw a disaster in the making. Titus wheeled his horse around and chastised the retreating legionaries for their failure and cravenness. They were Roman soldiers, not cowards, he probably exclaimed. Titus' remarks particularly stung. As shame spread throughout the 10th Legion, Titus was able to reorganize enough legionaries—along with his cavalry contingent—to mount a counterattack.[22]

Once ready, Titus led the advance against the Jewish company harrying his legionaries and wisely targeted their exposed flank. During the course of his relentless counter-offensive, the Jewish revolutionaries began taking heavy casualties, as Titus and his men methodically pushed the rebels back down into the Kidron Valley. Despite this reversal, as they neared the Kidron brook, the Jews discovered newfound courage and even reorganized their ranks to deal with Titus' painful flanking maneuvers. With the two factions facing one another, they locked in a deadly stalemate. The Jews dug-in and refused to give ground, while the Romans steadfastly held their position. The battle had begun as a Roman embarrassment, but Titus had prevented a complete rout, stalled the Jewish advance and apparently believed it was time to focus on other matters. He left reinforcements to keep the Jews fighting near the Kidron stream in check and directed the 10th Legion to finish the construction of their camp, which seemed even more important now. The recent attack confirmed that they needed the defensive fortifications.[23]

After promulgating his orders, Titus and his bodyguard began riding away from the battlefront to take care of other business, but the Jews misinterpreted the turn of events as a Roman reverse that presented a valuable opportunity. So a fresh body of Jews poured out of Jerusalem to join their comrades and hopefully defeat the Romans, and Titus' reinforcements witnessed the horde approaching them with dread. Instead of standing their ground, they turned and ran for the Mount of Olives—the second time in a single day that the Romans had retreated before the Jews.[24]

This was a discouraging response, but it was also potentially detrimental to Titus who had only recently left the front. He and some of his faithful soldiers were alone and wedged between the fleeing Roman reinforcements and those on the Mount of Olives. Fortunately for Titus, he learned of his troops' withdrawal and the Jewish offensive. As he often did, he planned to ignore imminent dangers to himself and thought about saving his men and achieving his mission. His loyal bodyguards remained by his side, but they pleaded with him to form a hasty retreat to ensure his well-being. Why, they asked, should he risk his life to come to the defense of those who had neglected their posts? Despite their best efforts, Titus could not be persuaded to withdraw.[25]

Jewish insurgents were sprinting toward Titus' position, and he and his comrades prepared to meet the enemy who quickly clashed with them. Risking life and limb and overwhelmingly outnumbered, Titus and his guard fought gallantly and engaged in fierce hand-to-hand combat. Titus subsequently managed to form another orderly counterattack. Exposed and leading from the front, he and his fellow Romans systematically thrust the Jews back down the hill. Yet the Jews still pined for victory, and they pivoted and took a circuitous path back up the hill in hopes of striking Titus' flanks and outstripping the other Romans who were still in retreat. Titus recognized their plans and harassed their flanks first—causing death and destruction in their ranks.[26]

Titus' brave exploits saved Roman lives, but the reinforcements were still in flight. When the 10th Legion saw them in disarray, they assumed that the Jews had routed them and that defeat was imminent. Fear spread throughout the 10th Legion, and courage in its ranks began to falter. They considered withdrawing once again and believed that Titus must have also retreated. Fortunately for the Romans, someone in the 10th noticed Titus bravely fighting the enemy, and shared his findings with his fellow legionaries. Members of the 10th could not bear the thought of losing their commander as they mulled abandoning their posts out of timidity.[27]

The 10th Legion's men resisted the impulse to retreat and were emboldened to come to Titus' defense and regain their honor. As a result, they marched against the Jews and forced them back down into the Kidron Valley. Meanwhile, Titus continued his assault on the enemy. As time passed, the Romans unmistakably seized the upper hand, and the rebels returned to the relative safety of Jerusalem. Titus subsequently gave orders for the 10th Legion to finish raising their camp. Rather than allowing the Jews to repeat their recent near-success, Titus personally stood guard along with his elite cavalry, likely supplemented with auxiliaries, until members of the 10th finished their encampment.[28]

It is hard to overestimate Titus' contribution in the battle of the Mount of Olives and Kidron Valley. As Josephus noted, "Without any flattering addition or carping detraction, [Titus] was personally responsible for twice rescuing the entire legion from a perilous situation, and enabling them to build their camp defenses in safety." Titus also demonstrated that he was unlike many other commanders. He was not satisfied with giving orders while watching battles from a safe distance, nor did he entirely rely on his deputies. He was resolutely loyal to his men and mission, and he was more than willing to personally engage the enemy, regardless of the dangers. On this day, the Romans prevailed, but they were far from sacking the well-defended Jerusalem. To hasten its demise, the Romans would need determination, irresistible force and Titus' steady leadership.[29]

XI

JERUSALEM

> *"Oh, my poor city, what did you ever suffer from the Romans compared to this? They invaded to purge with fire the pollution among your own people. You were no longer God's place. You could not survive once you had become a cemetery filled with your own dead, and your internecine warfare had turned the sanctuary into a mass grave. Yet even now you could recover, if only you would make atonement to the God who brought you to ruin!"*
> —*Josephus*[1]

FOLLOWING THE JEWISH REBELS' ROUT, Titus and his men evidently focused less on direct engagement with the enemy and more on preparing for a prolonged siege of Jerusalem. Titus certainly oversaw the construction of camp fortifications, the assembling of siege engines and importing of food, medical supplies, weapons and water. The latter was in particularly short supply, and the Romans needed enormous quantities of it. Leading four legions, plus allies, into less-than-hospitable terrain required exceptional logistical planning, as did confronting a city as large and well defended as Jerusalem. While Titus wanted to sack Jerusalem as swiftly as possible, he needed to ensure that everything was in place first, and he did not plan on attacking a moment before he was confident in victory.[2]

With Titus and the Romans busy with other issues, the tenuous alliance among the Jewish combatants began to fray. John had no desire to respect the tripartite agreement and eyed Eleazar and his band of Zealots ensconced in the Temple. As the Jewish Holiday of Passover approached—in April 70 CE—John recognized an opportunity to bolster his efforts and topple Eleazar. As the holy period arrived, Eleazar permitted Jews to enter the Temple compound to worship as was customary in peacetime. Thus Jewish noncombatants flooded into the sanctuary to make the necessary religious offerings, but so did many of John's armed men. John commanded a corps of his fighters to don attire appropriate for Passover and hide their weapons under their clothing. They followed his directives and slipped into the Temple complex with plans to wreak havoc.[3]

Once inside, John's men removed their cloaks and brandished their weapons—causing terror among Eleazar's Zealots and innocent worshippers alike. Eleazar's revolutionaries quickly surrendered their positions without attempting to counter John's ruffians, and they huddled in the Temple's underground storage rooms.

Meanwhile, Jewish pilgrims were exposed and received the ire of John's faction. They mercilessly beat and killed an untold number of them. This was not only cruel and unnecessary, but it was also bizarre, given that John's party eventually pardoned Eleazar's men. What happened to Eleazar, on the other hand, is a mystery. One translation of Tacitus claims that John assassinated him, but Josephus suggests that John welcomed him back into the fold as an ally. Whatever the case, John's rebels seized the Temple and overpowered Eleazar's bandits in one fell swoop. With Eleazar neutralized, his supplies confiscated and contingent enrolled into John's, the rebel leader now felt increasingly confident in his chances of smiting Simon.[4]

With the Jews engaged in internecine conflicts, Titus was preparing to mount an offensive on Jerusalem. To do so, Titus relocated his camp at Scopus to a location much closer to the holy city. A sizable corps of cavalry and infantrymen kept guard, while they built the new camp, and then Titus directed the bulk of his troops to begin a painstaking objective: To make it easier to transport matériel to Jerusalem, maneuver siege engines and pummel the holy city's walls, Titus wanted the ground to be level and free of impediments. As such, he ordered his men to clear much of the land approaching Jerusalem's walls. Without demur, the legionaries destroyed orchards, removed fences, relocated obstructive stones and filled gullies with debris. It was backbreaking work, but the Romans completed it and created a flat path to Jerusalem.[5]

Around this time, Titus deputized Josephus to serve as an intermediary and invite the Jews to open peace discussions. Titus took this step even though it seemed that the insurgents had no desire to lay down their arms and agree to terms that the Romans would have deemed acceptable. Indeed, the revolutionaries refused to consider Titus' offers. However, the next day, the Jews expelled a party of rebels from the city—appearing as though the more moderate Jews had taken control of Jerusalem. From the city walls, the Jews yelled "Peace!" as they pelted the exiled band with projectiles, and they even offered to open their gates to the legionaries.[6]

This looked like an unmistakable opportunity for the Romans to end the conflict, but it was a dishonest ruse intended to kill as many as possible. Titus was suspicious of the turn of events and commanded the legionaries near him to remain in position, but a segment of the Roman army believed that the Jewish spectacle was genuine. Without receiving orders to do so, those nearest to the city walls naively ran toward Jerusalem to seize it, but when they approached, the Jewish combatants sprung their trap and surrounded the Roman contingent. Attacked from every angle and beset by missiles fired from the walls, the Romans realized that they would have to overpower the Jews and break the encirclement to survive. Fighting feverishly, they slew myriad Jews and escaped the trap, but they were humiliated and ashamed of their naivete.[7]

The Jewish insurgents made matters worse by loudly mocking them for their ignorant misadventure, and Titus likewise had strong words for the impetuous legionaries. He castigated them for rushing headlong into an obvious ambush without orders, and he reminded them that martial success depends on discipline and meticulous planning and execution. Acting rashly, on the other hand, guaranteed disaster. Even more concerning than Titus' harangue was the fact that disobedience in the legions was punishable by death, which terrified the guilty soldiers and upset their comrades. Many legionaries entreated Titus to spare the guilty troops. Upon weighing his options, Titus announced his plans for clemency. Titus decided that the legionaries in question would be forgiven, but he instructed them to act sensibly and within the Roman army's accepted rules.[8]

With these matters settled, Titus looked to further safeguard his army, and there was plenty to protect too. Within a matter of days, the Roman legionaries had reshaped the landscape to enable the Roman baggage train and siege engines to reach Jerusalem more easily. To avoid a repeat of the Jewish sally that encircled a Roman company, Titus positioned seven lines of troops—beginning with three infantry lines, one line of archers and three lines of cavalry—in front of the northern and western portions of Jerusalem's walls. The different Roman lines prevented the Jews from seriously considering any sorties, while the rest of the Roman army lumbered into position thanks to the earth-flattening project.[9]

Once the Romans completed all of these operations, Titus and part of his army encamped 400 yards from Jerusalem's Psephinus Tower. Another large segment of Titus' soldiery also camped about 400 yards from the city's wall, but across from the Hippicus Tower. Both bivouacs rested on the western side of the city. Meanwhile, the 10th Legion remained on the Mount of Olives, likely serving as a reserve force that protected the army's rear and critical supply lines. At long last, Titus was nearly ready to finally begin besieging Jerusalem.[10]

From the Roman camps, he and his army could closely see firsthand just how well-protected the city was from outside attacks. Three walls comprised much of Jerusalem's defenses, but these were not concentric barriers. Rather, as the city had expanded over the centuries, the Jews had raised additional walls to protect newer neighborhoods that sprung up to accommodate its growing population. The most ancient of the walls was the Old Wall, which supposedly traced its roots back to kings David, Solomon and subsequent monarchs who gradually fortified it. After enemies had pulled down much of the walls, as the Biblical account goes, Nehemiah restored them during the Persian occupation of the Jews' ancestral homeland. The Old Wall was considered the most formidable of the walls. It was tall, thick and was aided by the natural topography, and the Jews had integrated 60 defensive towers into it. King Herod the Great had built at least three of them—the Hippicus, Phasael and Mariamme towers, which stood 120 feet, 135 feet and 83 feet tall, respectively. These were largely considered impregnable by conventional means, and from the Romans' perspective, they towered ominously over the city. The Old Wall encircled the southern half of Jerusalem—encompassing what was known as the Upper and Lower city—and it was built into the Temple complex.[11]

Jerusalem's Second Wall extended north of the original Old Wall's circuit to protect a new district—the Northern Quarter. Fourteen towers were built into the Second Wall, and it terminated at the Antonia Fortress on the eastern side of the city, which adjoined the Temple compound. The Antonia Fortress was an imposing structure on its own. It sat atop a 75-foot-tall plateau, and its walls stood another 60 feet high. Four towers offered further protection to the Antonia Fortress. Three of them rose 75 feet and the fourth towered 105 feet.[12]

The Third Wall was by far the newest. It jutted out even further north than the Second Wall and surrounded Bezetha, a newer part of the city. King Agrippa I (reigned 41–44 CE) had begun the wall's construction to protect Bezetha's inhabitants, but he feared that the Romans would take offense to the structure and believe the Jews were preparing to revolt. Indeed, it seems that Emperor Claudius at the time was displeased by the defensive construction. Therefore Agrippa I halted the building projects, which were only later completed by the rebels, although not with the same care or skill that Agrippa I had started. All told, these walls stood almost 38 feet tall, and the base was 15 feet wide. Strengthening the already imposing defenses were 90 towers built into the wall spaced out every 100 yards. One particular tower in this circuit was the Psephinus—near where Titus and much of his army had camped—and it rose to a height of 105 feet.[13]

Between Jerusalem's natural topography and commanding towers and walls, it was highly defensible. While the Jewish revolutionaries were embroiled in self-defeating infighting, they boasted enough combatants in Jerusalem to create further headaches for the Romans. Simon had 10,000 Jews at arms and 5,000 Idumeans to do his bidding, and they maintained control over most—but not all—of Jerusalem. Following Eleazar's defeat, John had around 8,400 men under his command. They held the Temple compound, some surrounding areas and exerted nominal control over the Kidron Valley.[14]

Had the Jewish people been united against the Romans or at least had John and Simon remained allied with one another at the onset, sacking Jerusalem could have posed an even taller task than the already daunting mission. However, after briefly putting aside their differences, the Jewish factions again turned against each other. John had already ambushed Eleazar's gang and defeated them, but that was not enough. Simon and John turned their ire on one another and reopened hostilities even though thousands of Romans remained encamped 400 yards beyond Jerusalem's walls and tens of thousands of Jewish noncombatants were mostly trapped between them.[15]

Spies or escapees from Jerusalem must have risked their lives to bring news of discord in Jerusalem to Titus who was pleased by the reports. Continued factional strife would benefit his efforts greatly. With his plans coming together, the Roman decided to gather a small party of cavalrymen and explore Jerusalem's defenses more closely to locate a weak point where the Romans would eventually begin their siege operations with unforgiving ferocity.[16]

Setting out from his camp, Titus and his comrades galloped closer to Jerusalem

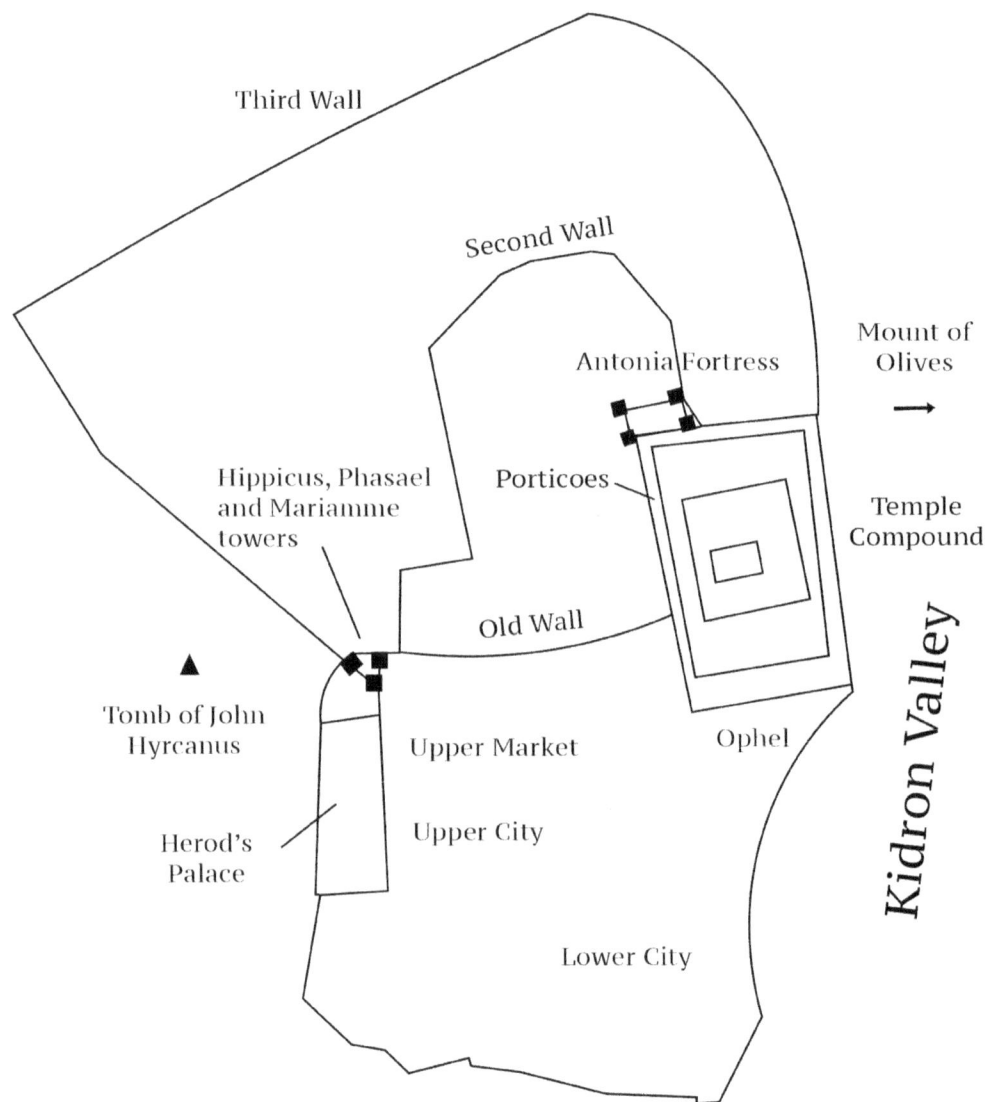

Valley of Hinnom

Jerusalem, circa 70 CE.

and reconnoitered the city. Initially what they observed was disheartening. As they made their way around the city, while likely dodging missiles fired from the walls, they lamentably observed that the natural topography made certain sections of the walls far too difficult to consider as a tenable point of attack. Meanwhile, other walled sections were too thick for the Roman siege engines to contend with in a timely fashion. Undaunted, Titus continued scanning the city's defenses and finally observed an opportune location on the western side of Jerusalem. The walls near the Tomb of John Hyrcanus were weaker. If Titus could breach these defenses, then he felt confident that it would give him a viable toehold in the city—leading to its doom.[17]

While Titus' reconnaissance mission was underway, Josephus and one of Titus' lieutenants, known as Nicanor, approached Jerusalem to attempt to come to peaceable terms. Instead of resolving the conflict, a Jewish revolutionary fired an arrow that struck Nicanor. This sent the Romans a clear message. Despite facing overwhelming odds, the Jewish combatants had rejected any form of surrender; they would rather fight until the bitter end than come to an agreement with Rome. Seeing that even peaceful embassies protected by venerated diplomatic codes of conduct were met with violence, Titus resolved to open direct hostilities with the rebels as soon as practicable.[18]

Titus relayed orders to his men to begin denuding the countryside of trees, which they would later use to build earthworks near the vulnerable section of the wall he had identified. Without demur, thousands of Titus' legionaries spread across the region, felled trees and transported them just beyond Jerusalem's walls, but Titus ensured that these laborers were protected from enemy assaults. The Roman commander placed archers, javelinmen and artillery engines, including ballistas, near the Jewish defenses. If the Jewish insurgents wanted to impede Titus' enterprises, then they would need to contend with walls of armed Romans and their deadly weapons. The Romans probably also employed the use of screens to shield workers from Jewish archers and slingers to great effect.[19]

In time, myriad legionaries lugged the lumber from various groves toward the Tomb of John Hyrcanus. From that area, Titus' engineers and laborers began the difficult process of creating three massive ramps approaching the city walls, while their comrades stood ready to repel any Jewish sorties. Hour by hour, the Romans raised and elongated the ramps at a pace that surely surprised the Jews, including the non-combatants. Many of them wanted nothing to do with the war and opposed John and Simon's reigns of terror. When they observed the Romans inching closer and closer, they grew ever hopeful that the legionaries would free them from the tyranny that gripped the holy city or that they would at least keep the rebels preoccupied with other matters.[20]

The speed at which the Romans worked must have simultaneously alarmed John and Simon. Yet John did not do enough to prepare for the Romans' inevitable arrival in the city. Rather he seemed keener on keeping a close eye on Simon's exploits in order to maintain his control over a relatively small patch of land. Simon, on the other hand, would almost certainly face the Romans first. He busily began redirecting his energies toward combating the Romans, and had some technologically advanced weapons at his disposal. During the rebels' adventures, they had captured many Roman artillery pieces prior to Vespasian and Titus' arrival in Judaea and they had seized other long-range weapons from the Antonia Fortress.[21]

With these in their possession, Simon ordered his insurgents to place them within range of the Romans, but they had little inkling over how to competently use the machines. They lacked the professional training and experience of the Roman legionaries. As a result, they fired them wildly and inaccurately, which failed to seriously imperil the Romans, but the Jewish revolutionaries pressed on with other tactics. They tried showering the Romans with stones and sallied out from Jerusalem to prevent the completion of the ramps. They managed to harry the Romans to a degree, but it was not enough. Titus had thoroughly prepared for these counterattacks, arranged screens to protect his workmen and placed artillery and archers in strategic locations. The artillery proved particularly devastating and was more powerful than those the Jews had seized. The Roman equipment launched enormous bolts and stones incredible distances—some heavy projectiles could be fired 400 yards or more away.[22]

Titus unleashed the ferocity of his many weapons, and as the projectiles flew rapidly across the sky, the Jews heard them whizzing by before they collided with their targets—leaving buildings critically damaged and Jews dead or severely injured. Likewise, when Simon's men attempted suicidal sorties from the city, the Roman archers and legionaries checked their advances and demonstrated that they were no match for the Romans' might. Nevertheless, Simon's gang tried desperately to impede Titus' workings. While their relentless tactics were inconvenient and left an untold number of legionaries dead, the Romans managed to build three large siege ramps that led to the city's walls anyway, and Titus' men constructed three siege towers to use on those ramps that loomed ominously.[23]

These were no common towers either. They were each 75 feet tall and mobile, so that troops could move them closer to Jerusalem's walls and reposition them when needed. At the base of these towers were probably battering rams sturdy enough to destroy fortified cities, although it is possible that the rams stood independently of the towers. Whatever the case, these towers were also capable of holding legionaries at numerous levels where they could fire arrows and javelins and even heavy artillery equipment, which provided covering fire for the other siege activities. The troops within the towers were protected too. The Romans built them in such a way to shield their timber skeletons from firebrands, but they were not entirely impervious to fire.[24]

Despite enduring nearly constant assaults from Simon's men, Titus was ready to initiate the next stage in his plan. He gave commands for his troops to relocate their artillery closer to Jerusalem to provide greater suppressive fire if need be. Then his soldiers moved three battering rams up the newly constructed ramps, and while taking fire from above, they inched the colossal structures forward until they reached the walls. As the artillerymen and archers scanned Jerusalem for signs of resistance and located combatants, they fired their weapons with deadly accuracy. Meanwhile, with the rams in position, the legionaries began swinging them into the sturdy walls. The heavy prows smashed into the stone in a terrifying rhythm that vibrated throughout the beleaguered city and inspired widespread terror. The sound to the

Romans, on the other hand, was welcome and reminded them that Jerusalem was presumably one step closer to falling.[25]

As this was underway, Simon realized that his squabble with John was counterproductive and that he needed the Zealots' help. Thus he offered John a truce and asked his rebels to join them in a fight against the Romans. John was clearly suspicious of the offer, given that they were bitter enemies, but he realized that the Romans were the greater foe. So he relented and allowed his men to unite with Simon. Now a consolidated force, the erstwhile enemies stood shoulder-to-shoulder on the walls and maintained a near constant pressure on the Romans. The Jews conducted sorties, hurled firebrands on the battering rams and launched a steady stream of missiles on the legionaries.[26]

The incessant harassment slowed the battering rams' progress, but the Romans responded with counterattacks and artillery fire. Titus also stationed cavalry and archers alongside the rams to provide further protection from the enemy. Combined, they temporarily suspended the Jewish attempts to overwhelm the battering operations as the rams continued hammering Jerusalem's walls, although with little effect at first.[27]

As the fighting subsided one day, many legionaries began making their way back to their camp to have dinner and rest for the night, and witnessing this, Jewish insurgents burst out of the city from a gate near the Hippicus Tower and assaulted the Romans. Those nearest to the Jews attempted to form an orderly defense, but the Jews overwhelmed them. Then the Jews noticed another body of Romans marching in formation for them. In time, they clashed in a deadly encounter as the Jews desperately tried to keep the Romans at bay so that they could destroy the earthworks. As fierce fighting raged, the revolutionaries managed to catch the Roman works on fire, but hope was not lost for the Romans.[28]

The Roman legionaries struggled to stand firm against the Jewish onslaught, and Titus collected his cavalry and galloped posthaste to save his army and siege works. He reached the enemy very quickly, and throwing caution to the wind, Titus once again inserted himself into a deadly battle. The accomplished military man demonstrated his martial prowess and killed 12 Jews by his own hand. The combined efforts of Titus' cavalry and his legionaries who countered the Jews was enough, but it may have come at a cost. Cassius Dio wrote that at some point in the siege of Jerusalem—maybe at this juncture—Jewish rebels fired a stone that struck Titus in the shoulder. The wound was not life-threatening, but it was serious. It even permanently weakened one of his arms. This aside, the legionaries eventually routed the Jews who fled for Jerusalem and re-entered the city, which allowed the Romans to extinguish the fires and save the siege works, but not every Jewish combatant made it back. The legionaries slaughtered a host of them, including the Idumeans' leader.[29]

The Jews' recent tactics were not Titus' only concerns. Maintaining an army tens of thousands strong in Judaea without ample access to water created a logistic nightmare. Titus worked with his lieutenants to constantly import the necessity to the front, but the Jews had an answer for this. Sometime during the siege, they either dug mines or used previously existing ones from inside Jerusalem to the outer districts to ambush unsuspecting Romans transporting water to the legions at Jerusalem. Titus understood that no matter the strength of an army, thirst and hunger can abruptly end any campaign, and the brazen Jewish strategy jeopardized Titus' plans. Unwilling to let this continue, Titus' troops found these tunnels and destroyed them. This safeguarded the legions' supply lines, but the Jews continued their attempts to hamper Roman logistics and supply trains.[30]

Frustrated with the Jews' refusal to surrender and their constant attacks, Titus decided to make a terrible example of a Jewish prisoner of war. In view of the city, Titus' subordinates erected a cross and crucified the man—letting him slowly die in anguish before his beset countrymen. They almost certainly heard the man's screams and moans and watched as he labored to catch his breath while hanging from the cross. He undoubtedly struggled, but it was all in vain. He ultimately perished. Titus presumably wanted the demonstration to instill further fear in the Jews and encourage them to consider submitting to Rome, but they were stubbornly married to defending Jerusalem and their claims to the city. From the insurgents' perspective, they were waging a just holy war against an empire that often acted with unrestrained cruelty. This crucifixion probably seemed like the latest example. Nevertheless, the cruel and macabre spectacle was proof that Titus' patience was wearing dangerously thin. It was also an ominous warning to the rebels. Perhaps they too could look forward to similar torment. They had plenty of time to ponder their fate because night soon approached, and most hostilities came to a halt as the Romans and Jews prepared for renewed violence the following morning.[31]

XII

Nikon

> *"The time came when the wall began to succumb to 'the Conqueror'*
> *... and by now the Jews were exhausted after days of fighting*
> *and nights spent on guard duty."*
> —Josephus[1]

THE ROMAN LEGIONARIES HAD RETURNED to their camps after a long, tiring day of battering Jerusalem's walls and engaging in hand-to-hand combat with the relentless insurgents. While they had successfully repelled the recent Jewish offensives and yearned for a respite, terror eventually emanated throughout the camps. Titus had previously ordered the construction of 75-foot towers that the Romans placed on each of the three ramps. Despite the towers' strengths, in the middle of the night, one collapsed—causing a terrible crash—and awoke the sleeping legionaries.[2]

Unsure over what exactly had transpired, the legionaries leaped from their slumber, hurriedly grabbed their weapons and ran throughout the bivouac in confusion. They assumed that a Jewish contingent had infiltrated their camp and somehow undermined the tower. Fearing that they were under attack, they frantically searched for the enemy but repeatedly bumped into their own men in the night, which frightened them and could have led to friendly casualties. Titus' planning prevented this potential disaster by mandating the use of watchwords. So whenever the legionaries crossed one another, they demanded the watchword as evidence that they were not Jewish combatants. After some time and plenty of chaos, Titus realized what had happened. The tower had fallen under its own weight due to some defect, and there were no Jewish saboteurs in the camp. He relayed his findings to his associates and managed to calm his soldiers, but following this fright, getting any additional sleep seemed unlikely.[3]

The next day, the exhausted Romans were left to deal with the realization that they had lost one of their super weapons—a 75-foot-tall tower—but they still had two others. This offered them some consolation and the ability to continue their battering operations. Once they had prepared for another grueling day of pummeling Jerusalem's walls, the legionaries took their positions. From the two towers, the Romans unleashed a constant barrage of projectiles on the city—driving the Jews back. Meanwhile, the battering rams rhythmically pounded the stone walls, and after each ram swing, the Romans were incrementally closer to breaching the city, although progress was slow. Being driven back from the walls, the Jewish combatants could do little to frustrate the Romans as the walls slowly cracked and chipped into shards. Eventually, the hulking siege engine the Jews called *Nikon*, or "the Conqueror," broke through the wall. The Romans now had a means of entering Jerusalem. Understanding their situation's dire reality, the Jewish revolutionaries conceded their nearby posts and took refuge behind Jerusalem's other walls.[4]

The Romans, their towers and the ramps had accomplished a major feat. In May 70 CE, only 15 days after Jerusalem's siege began, the Romans flooded into the breach. Evidently without facing much—if any—opposition, they flung open one of Jerusalem's gates to grant the rest of their comrades entry into this section of the holy city. A host of legionaries marched in and presumably protected a larger portion of the army as they disassembled part of Jerusalem's crumbling outer wall. This provided effortless egress and ingress for themselves and their siege equipment, but this was only one step of many toward sacking the city.[5]

With one wall compromised, Titus established a camp within Jerusalem but only stationed a fraction of his army there. Josephus asserted that the bivouac was near the so-called Camp of the Assyrians, but its precise location has been lost to time. Notwithstanding its whereabouts, Titus moved his artillery and siege engines into place to begin hammering the second wall, and the Jews responded to the Roman tactics. The revolutionaries still had not resigned hope of success, and they continued fighting valiantly. John and Simon split their men into two primary parties. John's gang fought from the north and Simon and his rebels from the west. They kept constant pressure on the Romans, showered them with missiles and launched sorties against their position. Regardless of the Jews' indomitable courage, the professional legionaries managed to push them back toward their defensive positions time and time again.[6]

As the conflict raged on, Titus' men were eager to prove their mettle to the Roman commander, even if that meant putting themselves in perilous situations, like engaging in foolish fights. Titus swiftly criticized this behavior and urged his men to think rationally. They should not act boldly for brief individual glory—no matter the possible rewards—but instead strive for self-preservation and toward their mission's ultimate goal. Titus truly seemed to care about his soldiers' well-being, and his orders mirrored that concern as well as focused on the broader war effort.[7]

Within the second wall was a tower that Titus believed was vulnerable—one of the central towers of this walled section. Sensing an opportunity, he ordered his troops to move one of his battering rams—perhaps *Nikon*—into position to hopefully topple the stronghold. His subordinates obeyed and relocated the mammoth siege engine in front of the fortification. Before long, the Romans began the arduous and repetitive process of swinging the ram into the stone tower—causing loud booms to reverberate throughout Jerusalem and shaking the tower to its foundations.[8]

Titus' archers had forced most of the tower's defenders to flee, with the exception of a Jewish combatant named Castor and ten of his comrades who hid atop the tower. As the Romans worked to bring it down, Castor sprung up and pleaded for Titus' mercy. In response, Titus halted all battering operations and instructed his archers to hold their fire until he could ascertain what Castor was seeking. Castor shouted to the Romans that he wished to give himself up to Titus, if he gave assurances that he would be spared from any reprisals. Titus was pleased with Castor's apparent good sense, and the Roman commander explained that he would be happy to offer Castor fair, merciful terms.[9]

Five of Castor's countrymen appeared to side with him, but the other five argued loudly against surrendering themselves to the Romans. Unbeknownst to the Romans, this was all a ruse. As the faux argument was underway, Castor sent word to Simon letting him know that he was delaying the Romans' progress, which would provide Simon more time to counter the Romans. Castor and his ten colleagues then created a dramatic show for the Romans below. Five of them asserted that they would rather die than submit to the Romans, and they acted as though they committed suicide. With only Castor and his five other friends appearing alive, Titus planned to send a Jewish ally to negotiate with them. Josephus refused to go, believing that this was a charade. Unpersuaded, Titus sent a man named Aeneas to confer with Castor, but before he could arrive, Castor hurled a stone at the man. While it missed Aeneas, it demonstrated that Castor and his men were acting dishonorably.[10]

Titus was absolutely furious and came to a terrible conclusion. In his opinion, "mercy in war is a pernicious thing; because such cunning tricks have less place under the exercise of greater severity," wrote Josephus. In short, amnesty seemed like liability, while savagery was a more dependable tool in war. Given this latest example of treachery, Titus decided to refocus Rome's efforts on destroying the tower, and he intensified the ramming operations. Before long, the once-sturdy stronghold began showing signs of stress and its collapse became imminent, but Castor and his men stole the satisfaction of razing the tower from the Romans. Seeing the tower's precarious state, Castor and his rebels set the fortification ablaze, and the conflagration consumed it. Meanwhile, Castor and his comrades appeared to leap into the flames, ostensibly choosing an honorable—but painful—death over capture, but in reality, they safely hid themselves in a lower chamber.[11]

Castor may have robbed the Romans of being solely responsible for the tower's fall, but it mattered little. The fortification was now unsuitable as a defensive structure. Many of the Jewish insurgents realized at this point that holding this portion of the second wall was futile, and they abandoned it. Between their retreat and the tower's destruction, Titus and his legionaries could more easily breach the wall, which they did and placed Roman sentries on it. Titus, his loyal guard and 1,000 legionaries entered the gap to secure the area. A mere four days after poking through the first wall, Titus had captured another wall or so it seemed, and the rebels watched the Romans who methodically tightened the noose around Jerusalem.[12]

As Titus and his select men marched through the second wall and hoped to secure the area so that they could press further into Jerusalem, they certainly marveled at the city. Titus' men pined to exact their vengeance and plunder the district. While the intra-Jewish conflict and gang warfare within Jerusalem had likely left this area devoid of highly valuable goods, there were still plenty of enticing products. Among the winding, narrow streets were numerous shops selling textiles and metals, but Titus gave specific orders to his troops: They were forbidden from looting this district, unnecessarily destroying any of the property or killing any peaceful Jews.[13]

Despite concluding that mercy was not a winning strategy in this war, Titus continued to exhibit his willingness to spare the Jews and their city, and he made a show of it. First, he did not order his men to pull down a larger section of the second wall, which would have made retreating and attacking easier for the Romans. Second, he offered to restore the property of the Jews who laid down their arms. Last, in an attempt to spare the noncombatant Jewish population, he offered to provide the insurgents safe passage to depart from Jerusalem and continue waging their war beyond the city's walls. The broader Jewish population was eager to accept Titus' terms, but the revolutionaries swiftly rejected the offer and clearly understood that they would not stand a chance against the Roman legions without the protection of Jerusalem's fortifications. What's more, they believed that Titus' conditions revealed a lack of confidence among the Romans. Nevertheless, some of the Jewish civilians spoke in support of surrender. To quell any further talk of submitting to the Romans, the rebels started murdering those who advocated for accepting Titus' proposal.[14]

Believing that Titus had admitted weakness by offering peace and detecting Titus' tactical errors—entering with too few troops and not widening the wall's breach—the Jewish revolutionaries launched an attack. They charged toward Titus and his legionaries from dark alleys, out of unsuspecting homes and from the farther reaches of the second wall. This terrified the Roman guards stationed on the walls, and they fled from their posts—leaving Titus and his men virtually surrounded and in unfamiliar surroundings. The Romans knew nothing about the streets or where they led, nor were they prepared for an urban fight.[15]

Titus and his soldiers were cut off from their comrades and knew that they only had one chance of survival. They needed to battle the Jews and slowly make their way to the wall's breach, which was too narrow to permit them to escape in formation. Successfully conducting a tactical retreat under these circumstances presented many challenges, but the Romans had little choice and decided to fight their way to safety. Fierce combat erupted, and Titus acted quickly. He stationed archers at critical points on the streets to keep the enemy at bay, and then Titus and some of his loyal troops rushed toward the thick of the fighting and constantly battered the enemy as his legionaries slowly squeezed through the wall's breach until it was finally time for Titus to do the same. With the enemy under duress from Titus' personal efforts and a barrage of arrows, the Roman commander and the rest of his company ultimately withdrew from this district after suffering an unknown number of casualties. Thanks to Titus, the Romans averted what could have resulted in the complete slaughter of the Roman contingent, and most of them evidently managed to escape.[16]

The Jewish combatants probably felt vindicated for assuming that the Romans were too weak to seize the rest of Jerusalem. After all, they ejected them from this district after they had captured part of the second wall, and an irrational air of invincibility pervaded the rebel camps. Their supposed victory blinded them to the realities facing Jerusalem. They had driven out only a tiny portion of Titus' massive army, which was well-provisioned, well-fed and invigorated, and Titus looked at the recent engagement as a minor setback and nothing more. Meanwhile, in their internal fighting, the Jews had destroyed much of their food stores, reduced their fighting power and exhausted many of their supplies. In the extended war, the Romans were not their only enemy. Factional strife and hunger proved to be equally deadly foes. Many Jews were already starving, but the revolutionaries were not particularly worried about the untimely deaths of civilians. Rather, each one's demise represented one less impediment and one less hungry mouth competing for dwindling rations.[17]

While the Jewish combatants had been filled with undeserved confidence, they quickly understood that Titus and his legionaries refused to abandon their efforts. They had already knocked a hole in the second wall and planned to exploit it. With the Romans obviously preparing to seize a toehold within the second wall, the Jewish defenders stood near the breach ready for any Roman attempts to break through and establish a considerable presence within the wall. For three straight days, Titus launched sorties against these Jews. He likely tried various tactics, including unleashing missile barrages and ordering men to hurtle into the gap and force the Jews backward, and for three days, the revolutionaries held their ground against all odds. On the fourth, the Romans' determination, training, numbers and discipline turned out to be too much for the Jews guarding the void. The legionaries marched through and secured a foothold, which forced the Jews to withdraw.[18]

For the second time in less than a week, Titus entered the gap and labored to establish control over this district, but he adopted a different approach on this occasion. First, he suspended siege operations and sorties, and he almost certainly established a controlled and well-defended perimeter where he placed guards and lookouts at key locations. Then he ordered many of his troops to pull down large sections of this wall. In this way, Titus and his men could more easily attack and retreat at will, and the Jews would not be able to use the fortifications for their benefit. Yet it appears that Titus did not topple a number of the towers connected to this wall. He preferred to use them for his own purposes, and within each of them, he placed sentinels who watched for enemy troop movement and were ready to bombard their foes.[19]

With these matters complete, Titus still did not restart hostilities. There was little reason to do so with haste. The Jewish defenders were slowly starving and growing weaker. As they did, Titus hoped to create a spectacle that would demonstrate Rome's might and wealth and damage the Jews' morale. Perhaps then they would consider surrendering, Titus hoped. As such, when the legionaries' payday arrived, Titus gave orders to his men to use it to their advantage. The Roman soldiery dressed in their full panoply, and while donning their glimmering armor and weapons, they marched to receive their wages. However, Titus wisely instructed this to all be done within view of the Jews huddling behind the inner wall. With the Roman officers holding vast sums of wealth, the soldiers slowly strode up, accepted their wages and flaunted it before the Jews. This process repeated itself for four long days as Roman morale increased and the Jews sank in despair.[20]

This theatrical performance made a psychological impact on both warring parties, but it failed to bring the revolutionaries to the bargaining table. As each day passed without receiving a peace delegation, Titus' hopes for a speedy end to the war diminished. Finally, five days after beginning the payroll operation, Titus understood that the Jewish rebels were not prepared to quit. So he once again turned his attention toward taking Jerusalem by force. He split a portion of his soldiery into two massive groups and charged each contingent with constructing earthworks to enable them to break further into Jerusalem. One company began laboring to raise two earthworks near the Antonia Fortress and the other started erecting two not far from the Tomb of John Hyrcanus.[21]

As they had done before, they collected timber and stones to create the earthworks, but this was a dangerous undertaking. Simon, his men and allies harassed the Romans working near the Tomb of John Hyrcanus, and John and his Zealots targeted the Romans near the Antonia Fortress. They were relentless in their assaults and gained new skills. While they had initially employed the use of ballistas incompetently, they now had learned to use them with some skill, which led to the injuries and deaths of an untold number of Romans. Titus doubtless helped protect his soldiers with screens, walls of heavy infantry and archers. He also fired his long-range weapons at the Jewish insurgents, and the construction continued.[22]

As the Roman ramps inched higher and closer to their targets, Titus pleaded with the Jews to consider surrendering. They could come to terms and avoid the looming death and destruction that lurked before Jerusalem. He even empowered and dispatched Josephus to reason with the Jews. Standing out of range of any Jewish weapons but close enough to speak to the Jewish fighters, Josephus stated his case in the Jewish language. He declared that the Romans were far too powerful for them to counter. They had already seized much of their homeland, toppled many of their fortifications and were slowly nearing the point of subjugating their chief city. They had no hope of overpowering Rome, Josephus asserted.[23]

The Jews within Jerusalem were also grappling with another enemy, as Josephus pointed out. The Romans could halt all siege efforts and maintain a blockade, and without firing a missile could defeat the Jews because famine was rampant within the holy city. There was no escape, and Josephus begged them to consider peace and saving their city and Temple. He promised that the Romans would act with restraint and offer fair terms, but he warned that the Romans would slaughter them wholesale if they were forced to take the city by storm.

Despite speaking sensibly, the Jewish rebels mocked Josephus, shouted at him and attempted to strike him with their longer-range weapons. Standing a safe distance from them, their projectiles had no effect other than to encourage him to change his tone. Enraged with their intransigence, he claimed that the Jews had never been victorious solely on their own accord; they had only tasted success when God sided with them; but the Jews were waging war against their God, failing to follow His laws and reveling in corruption and sin. Josephus rhetorically asked them, "After all this do you expect the God you have offended to be your ally?"[24]

In closing, Josephus offered the Jewish revolutionaries a way out:

> There is a place left for your preservation, if [you are] willing to accept [...] it: and God is easily reconciled to those that confess their faults, and repent of them. Oh! iron-hearted men, fling away your weapons, take compassion on your country even now tottering to its fall, turn round and behold the beauty of what you are betraying: what a city! what a temple! what countless nations' gifts! Against these would any man direct the flames? Is there any who wishes that these should be no more? What could be [worthier] of preservation than these—[you] relentless creatures, more insensible than stone! Yet if you [do not] look on these with the eyes of genuine affection, at least have pity on your families, and let each set before his eyes his children, wife and parents, [soon] to be the victims either of famine or of war. I know that I have a mother, a wife, a not ignoble family, and an ancient and illustrious house involved in these perils; and maybe you think that it is on their account that my advice is offered. Slay them, take my blood as the price of your own salvation! I too am prepared to die, if my death will lead to [you] learning wisdom.[25]

Emotional and convincing as his oration was, Josephus failed to persuade the rebels to surrender and avert the impending destruction. However, it weighed on the noncombatants wedged between the Jewish revolutionaries and the Roman legionaries. In increasing numbers, they sold their valuables or swallowed coins of worth so that they could smuggle them out of the city. Then they attempted to sneak out of Jerusalem as they carefully avoided detection and the attention of Simon and John's men. Not all were successful. While the insurgents largely did not care about the noncombatant Jews' well-being, they sought to prevent them from escaping, under pain of violence or death. Even so, a number of them managed to slip out of Jerusalem where they came face-to-face with the Romans, and Titus was happy to let most of them be on their way.[26]

Those who willfully remained in Jerusalem were not safe, though. Jerusalem was dangerously low on food, and the wealthy spent prodigious amounts of money to purchase the smallest morsels and cooked them in secret. Others fought over tiny portions. "Wives would snatch the food from [their] husbands, children from fathers, and—most pitiable sight of all—mothers from the very mouths of their infants, and while their dearest ones were pining in their arms they [had no scruples over robbing] them of the life-giving drops," Josephus wrote. John and Simon's men conducted raids in Jewish houses in search of provisions and employed terrible violence on the frail people of Jerusalem. The rich were at the greatest risk, but any house with a closed door was suspected of possessing provisions.

When observing barred doors or supposing that a family had secreted away food by some means, the Jewish combatants would break into these homes and threaten and abuse the Jews within. If they found anyone with food in their mouth, the revolutionaries would force them to spit it out for their own consumption. In the process, they wantonly beat men, drug women by their hair and even violently cast children with food down to the floor. As they searched for increasingly rare provisions, John and Simon's men began painfully torturing the Jews—hoping to find hidden stores of food—by molesting their rectums. The Jews were malnourished, had lost much of their dignity and many yearned for the Romans to seize the city and end their torture. With construction on Titus' earthworks underway, they would not have to wait terribly long.[27]

XIII

Crucifixions

> *"I believe that if the Romans had been slow to move against these sinners, either the earth would have opened up and swallowed the city, or it would have been swept away by a flood, or thunderbolts which destroyed Sodom would have struck again. The city had produced a generation far more godless than those afflicted by such catastrophes in the past."*
> —Josephus[1]

WHILE JOSEPHUS HAD FAILED TO INDUCE the revolutionaries to lay down their arms and end their war with Rome, some civilians had either bribed insurgents to allow them to escape Jerusalem or managed to escape undetected through other means. How they did so is not apparent, but the nights may have provided enough cover to evade their captors' watchful eyes, as the Jewish civilians quietly slipped out of various passageways. They subsequently sprinted for the safety of Rome's legionaries and begged for mercy. Titus pardoned most of these starving wretches and released them because they were not part of John or Simon's gangs—just unfortunate civilians caught in the melee. Yet the Romans were forced to cope with others who crept beyond the holy city's walls but were not attempting to escape Jerusalem.

In a desperate search for food scraps, seeds or anything remotely edible, some Jews began sneaking out of their fortifications and combing the ravines between them and the Romans. Some of these Jews included combatants who were willing to risk danger for the chance of finding food, but the majority of these foragers were civilians. Unlike the aforementioned deserters, they had no intention of surrendering to the Romans. They believed that they would not be able to successfully elude John and Simon's men, and if the rebels seized them while escaping, then they would surely meet their end. Even if they managed to quit Jerusalem, they would have to leave their families behind, which would result in a terrible fate. The insurgents would likely torture and murder their loved ones in response.[2]

The legionaries stood guard and regularly patrolled Jerusalem's perimeter. When they observed Jews beyond the safety of their walls, they were naturally concerned that they were plotting against the Romans—possibly to impede their ramp-building operations. Given that the noncombatant foragers feared the combatants more than the Romans and there were revolutionaries within the foraging parties, submitting to the Romans was never a first option. Thus, when the Romans detected their activities and confronted them, the Jews either hurried back to their homes or assaulted the Romans—ensuring the legionaries assumed that these Jews were all dangerous. The two parties inevitably clashed with regularity—resulting in terrible violence—but the Jews were no match for the professional, battle-hardened Romans. An untold number of Jews died in these senseless skirmishes, and the Romans captured around 500 of them per day for some time.[3]

Titus had released many Jews who willfully surrendered and demonstrated that they were not engaged in any fighting against the Romans. The captives whom the Romans seized as they foraged were different, since they had resisted the Romans, although many did so out of fear of the tyrants who controlled parts of Jerusalem. Regardless of their reasoning, the Romans considered them all combatants and treated them as such. Titus was reportedly inclined to show mercy, but maintaining a prisoner of war camp for the increasing number of captives was untenable. Doing so would force him to redirect many of his soldiers away from building earthworks to building jails and serving as prison guards. Alternatively, he could not risk releasing Rome's enemies, or at least presumed enemies. They might return and kill his men. Understanding this reality, the Romans opted for unrestrained cruelty.[4]

The legionaries first mercilessly flogged the Jewish captives—leaving their clothes in tatters, skin ripped and bruised, and bodies battered—but this was the least of their torture. Next the legionaries nailed the Jews to crosses of various forms and arranged the tormented bodies in different poses. Finally, they erected the crosses all along Jerusalem's wall for all of their countrymen to see. For days, the Romans repeated this process as the Jewish people hiding in their city witnessed the slow agony of many hundreds of Jews and their loud wails, prayers for a quick death and stench of their corpses' decay. A number of the Roman legionaries were bitter and filled with rage. So they gleefully entertained themselves by inflicting this terrible punishment, and they methodically continued until they ran out of crosses and space before the wall. The breadth of the crucifixions boggles the mind and shocks the conscience. They supposedly disgusted Titus, but he allowed them—hoping that it would destroy the Jews' morale and persuade them to sue for peace.[5]

At some point during the war, perhaps as this rash of crucifixions was underway, Josephus decided to explore the Romans' barbaric handiwork, and he noticed three Jews whom he personally knew hanging from crosses. This moved Josephus to tears, and he located Titus and begged him to save his acquaintances. Upon hearing his earnest pleas, Titus delivered orders for the three men to be removed from their crosses and have their wounds treated. Rome's physicians did what they could to aid the men, but two of the Jews perished, while the third recovered from the terrible wounds.[6]

From the Romans' perspectives, crucifixions were not particularly cruel or outlandish. They were well-versed in crucifixions and prolonging agony. One estimate suggests that between 200 BCE and 337 CE, upwards of 150,000 people died by crucifixion in Roman controlled territories, but for years, there had only been limited physical evidence of Roman crucifixions for modern researchers to consider. This is probably because the Romans removed and repurposed the nails, reused crosses and the bodies of the condemned were disposed of in a manner that did not preserve them. However, in the late 1960s, the remains of a first-century Jew with a crucifixion nail still lodged in his heel was uncovered—providing conclusive evidence of ancient crucifixions—and evidence has since surfaced elsewhere too. Was this one of Titus' victims? Maybe, but unfortunately, it is impossible to know.[7]

This finding aside, one particular incident shows how the Romans sometimes scaled up their executions. Following the Spartacus revolt in the 70s BCE, Roman general Marcus Licinius Crassus ordered 6,000 slaves to be crucified along the Appian Way from Capua to Rome, and the suspended corpses lingered there for weeks or even months to make a point: Don't rebel against Rome; resistance is futile. With his ongoing crucifixions, Titus made a similar point.[8]

Instead of allowing Titus' crucifixions to give them cause to surrender, the rebels used the spectacle to their advantage. They told those in Jerusalem that the Jews hanging from the crosses were noncombatants who had not fought against the Romans; they asserted that they were innocent deserters, which laid bare the Romans' barbarity. The insurgents drug those related to the condemned and those who were inclined to call for peace to the city walls and showed them the slowly dying Jews nailed to crosses to make their dishonest point. While these were not the willful deserters whom Titus had released, the revolutionaries hoped that their dishonesty would keep the people of Jerusalem under their control. For the time being, this was enough to convince the Jews that the Romans were worse than John and Simon.[9]

Somehow Titus caught wind of the falsehoods swirling in Jerusalem, and he decided to prove that those in his custody were not deserters, but rather combatants from his perspective. The Romans quickly concocted a brutal method of doing so. Without enough room to conduct more crucifixions, the Romans had apparently begun confining newer captives, and now Titus knew what to do with them. He ordered his subordinates to sever their hands, and one by one, the Romans cleaved them from their bodies in what was a horribly excruciating experience. Then Titus sent the handless Jews back to Jerusalem where the locals were able to note that none of these people were deserters. This could have served some other Roman purposes too. It guaranteed that these poor mutilated Jews would not be able to wield arms against the Romans again, and the spectacle—while ostensibly demonstrating Titus had not mistreated deserters—might intimidate the enemy. Upon sending these rebels back, he also implored the Jews to give up their cause and save themselves. In the end, Titus' point was as clear as it was barbaric, but the Jews rebuffed his pleas for peace.[10]

As all of this was transpiring and Titus and his men were busy raising siege ramps, Titus received a royal guest. Antiochus Epiphanes, the son of Antiochus Epiphanes IV of Commagene, a Roman client-kingdom, arrived in the Roman camp.

Antiochus brought with him a body of well-trained fighters, but they were haughty and overconfident. They were baffled that the Romans had not taken Jerusalem yet and believed that a simple frontal assault would lead to the city's fall. Titus must have been annoyed at their implications, but he gave Antiochus his blessing to try to seize the city, saying, "Well, many hands make light work!"[11]

Antiochus consequently gathered his loyal soldiers and arranged them in battle formation. Then they marched directly for Jerusalem's wall, which was a peculiar sight for the Jews who pummeled them with missiles. Antiochus and his men responded with their own volley of arrows, but with little impact. Ultimately, the Jews easily overwhelmed them. They enjoyed the protection of their fortifications, and Antiochus was comparatively exposed. After taking heavy casualties, Antiochus sounded the retreat. He and his surviving men returned to the Roman camp humbled, and the legionaries refocused their attention on the siege works at strategic points about the city.[12]

Two of the massive Roman ramps were near the Antonia Fortress—one close to the Struthion Pool and the other about 30 feet away. The final two were not far from the Amygdalon Pool and the Tomb of John Hyrcanus, respectively. After 17 days of grueling labor, sometime in late May 70 CE, the four ramps were finally complete. Without wasting time, Titus commanded his troops to begin inching siege engines up the ramps and toward Jerusalem's enemy-held fortifications, and they very quickly and carefully moved them into position.[13]

For a brief moment, the Romans had reason to believe that they would soon breach Jerusalem's final major defenses and conclude the siege. Unbeknownst to them, the Jewish insurgents had been feverishly working to counter their tedious operations. John had instructed his men to dig mines under the Antonia Fortress and toward the ramps. In what was surely terrifying and difficult work, they obeyed. In the process, the sappers risked deadly mine collapses, choked on the dank, stale air and struggled to see their workings in the dark tunnels. In time, their mines reached underneath both ramps near the Antonia Fortress, and they reinforced the tunnels with beams and filled it with wood coated in highly flammable materials, including pitch and bitumen.[14]

When the Jews believed that the time was right, they set the mines alight. A fire quickly consumed the wooden structures supporting the tunnels—causing them to collapse under the ramps, which caved in next. The Romans watched the demoralizing sequence of events as the Jews destroyed the fruits of their toils. More than two weeks of their hard work crumbled before them as the flames from the mines reached higher and likely claimed some of the siege engines trapped on the once-impressive earthworks.[15]

The two ramps on the other side of Jerusalem were untouched, and after being dealt a stinging reversal, the Romans redirected their efforts there. Battering rams rolled up the earthworks and began pounding the thick stone walls, but Simon had plans for these rams. Two days after destroying the ramps near the Antonia Fortress, three combatants brandishing torches darted out from the city and ran full speed for the other siege works. Despite the Romans' best attempts to thwart them, they reached the siege engines and set them alight. The legionaries strove to smother the flames, but the Jewish rebels flooded out of their fortifications and attempted to slay anyone laboring to extinguish the fires. Eventually, the flames leaped from the engines and to the ramps—leaving them utterly destroyed.[16]

Seeing that the earthworks and battering rams were lost, the Romans retreated in the face of the Jewish attacks. The revolutionaries followed in quick pursuit, reached the Roman camp near the recently destroyed ramps and launched an assault against the Romans. Joined by more insurgents who rushed to aid their comrades, Simon's men confronted the legionaries attempting to defend their camp. Meanwhile, Titus was inspecting the destroyed ramps near the Antonia Fortress when he learned of his army's peril and was ashamed that his men had permitted such tragedy to unfold.[17]

Disappointed or not, Titus gathered his elite cavalry, and they galloped posthaste for the beset Romans. In short order, he reached their position and then threw himself into the melee. During the battle, confusion spread throughout the Roman and Jewish factions. The noise of war, dust and smoke from the battle polluted the air—making it difficult to effectively discern friend from foe and wage battle. Nevertheless, Titus employed a flanking maneuver, but the Jews pivoted and put up a stout defense. Titus fought valiantly and put himself at great risk. His soldiers were heartened by his example and pressed hard against the Jews who withdrew to the fortified sectors of Jerusalem. After the fires died out and the fog of war settled, the Romans knew for certain that they had lost their ramps and siege engines. Their arduous work had been for naught, and the Jewish combatants had embarrassed them. Morale reached new lows in the Roman camps, and Titus was furious and desperate to find a way to sack Jerusalem.[18]

Not long after, Titus assembled his senior deputies to discuss their next steps. Even though they were closer to taking Jerusalem than when they had started, the Romans had suffered numerous setbacks thanks to the insurgents' activities, which ruined weeks of hard work. Considering these difficulties, Titus wanted to confer with his most trusted lieutenants and consider alternative strategies for taking Jerusalem and resolving the war.[19]

During their conference, they debated their options. A sizable corps of officers believed that the Romans could overwhelm Jerusalem with their massive army. Since the beginning of the siege, Titus had never unleashed his legionaries in full force on Jerusalem's walls. Rather he relied on smaller numbers to accomplish his goals. In light of this, these deputies suggested ordering the entire army to storm Jerusalem, which they believed would overcome the insurgents' defenses, and sack the city. Such a plan may have worked, but Titus vetoed the idea. It would simply risk too many Roman lives when there were other available options.[20]

Others suggested maintaining the current plan of building earthworks and battering the walls, but Titus was skeptical. The status quo had failed to produce his intended results in a timely fashion, and they had wasted precious timber in the failed projects. What's more, they would remain vulnerable to hit-and-run and mining tactics.

A considerable number of officers preferred another strategy. They wanted to slowly starve the city into submission by placing troops around the city. This faction of Roman officers believed that they could seize the city by simply maintaining a blockade, since the Jews were already succumbing to hunger. Jerusalem's fall would not happen immediately, but it would be inevitable. Yet Titus again vetoed the notion of relying only on a blockade. He declared that it would be difficult to maintain a tightly sealed blockade without exposing themselves to enemy offensives. Moreover, it would be a waste to leave an army of this size idle—especially when the legionaries yearned to exact vengeance on the Jewish combatants. Further, defeating the Jews in this manner would discredit Titus' military abilities. His detractors would suggest that he won, not through his martial prowess, but by passively starving his enemies.[21]

After weighing his options, he decided to incorporate different components that his officers had offered into an overall plan. Instead of blockading Jerusalem with his legionaries and exposing them to attacks, he wanted them to build a wall around the city. Once completed, the Jews would not be able to import anything into the city—even in small amounts—or escape, and the wall would help protect the legionaries. Following this, Titus would give the Jews time to grow hungrier and contemplate surrender. Then he would command his troops to rebuild earthworks and take the city by force, but that would be challenging. Given that there was already a shortage of available timber and they were building a wall around the holy city, the legionaries needed to expand logging operations even further away from Jerusalem.[22]

After Titus presented his plan, his lieutenants wholly endorsed it, and immediately put the soldiery to work on the wall. The labor invigorated the legionaries, and they even competed against one another—hoping to be the first to complete their section of the wall. Titus regularly inspected their workings and judged their success. Within three short days, the Romans completed a wall that encircled Jerusalem, and it formed a circuit of 4.25 miles and had 13 forts built into it. Titus stationed guards at key locations, and always willing to engage in the common soldiers' drudgery, Titus took first watch and made his rounds to ensure all was in order the first night, which passed quietly.[23]

The Jews had already been in dire straits and facing starvation. After Titus raised his wall, it became virtually impossible to escape or smuggle even limited provisions into Jerusalem, and the noncombatant Jews increasingly lost whatever slivers of hope that remained. The Jewish civilians were reduced to bones, and it did not take long for the rampant malnutrition to take its toll. Youths and the elderly meandered the narrow streets displaying their empty—but distended—stomachs. Without warning, many collapsed dead on Jerusalem's avenues. At first, the Jews certainly tried to bury their fallen countrymen, but it was an immense burden for the weakened Jews. Some fell dead as they buried their family members, while others marched to their graves before they perished—only to lay down in them as they awaited the inevitable.[24]

It eventually became too difficult for the slowly dying Jews to bury the masses of deceased friends and family members, but there was little crying or mourning. The emaciated Jews had been drained of human emotion and sat in their city in eerie silence. The insurgents also dealt with sharp hunger pangs, but they exploited their positions of power to ensure that they were better situated than their civilian counterparts. They ate enough to keep up their energy, which they sometimes used against the deceased. The rebels rummaged through the homes of the recently perished, despoiled them of their clothing and callously tested their swords on the corpses. However, when the living pleaded with them to end their suffering, they refused to kill them.[25]

Initially, it seems that the combatants helped bury some of the dead when the families of the deceased could not do so, but this was not done out of altruism. Rather the smell within the city was insufferable. At one point, the burials swiftly ended, presumably because the revolutionaries did not have space or interest in burying the dead. Instead of entombing them, they treated the corpses as meaningless refuse and either dumped them just beyond their gates or tossed them over the city's walls where they quickly piled up. The sight was nothing short of abhorrent. "When Titus, [making] his rounds along those valleys, saw them full of dead bodies, and the thick [matter oozing from] them, he [groaned]; and spreading out his hands to heaven, [he] called God to witness that this was not his doing," Josephus reported.[26]

Matters were beyond bleak in Jerusalem, but unfortunately for the Jewish people, they would get much worse. As their health deteriorated, Titus' men received more than adequate amounts of food. Nearby port cities and Roman provinces, including Syria, had served as critical links in Rome's supply chain that brought in grain, water, wine and other necessities to the legionaries. Myriad Roman troops carried their food near the Jewish walls and displayed their veritable cornucopias to the enfeebled Jews. Even this was not enough to persuade the rebels to consider peace. As time passed, the Roman soldiers' strength increased with their toils and thanks to a brief respite because the insurgents had reduced their attacks on the Romans ever since they had completed the wall. Wanting to finish the siege quickly and supposedly save the innocent civilians within Jerusalem, Titus resolved to begin his next building project.[27]

In order to gain easier access to the city, Titus once more ordered his men to erect earthworks and settled on raising four different ramps. However, the legionaries would not raise them in different corners of the city. Titus wanted them all near the Antonia Fortress—thereby concentrating their efforts and forces in one district. Constructing these earthworks was no easy feat, given that the Romans had already felled nearby trees for their prior building projects. So the legionaries were forced to raid groves up to 10 miles away in order to find the necessary lumber, and then they labored to transport it to Jerusalem. The engineers put it to good use as the Romans slowly built ramps larger than before. As the process continued, Titus moved from legion to legion encouraging his troops and urging them to finish their work quickly as the insurgents stoically looked on from their fortifications.[28]

While they seemed bereft of emotion and even fear of the Romans, they still terrorized the civilian population in Jerusalem. Simon went on a brutal killing spree of notable Jews, and he forbade civilians from congregating in groups—concerned that they might be conspiring against his tyranny. In time, his oppression and murderous behavior sparked a minor revolt within his own ranks. A small number of Jewish partisans planned to orchestrate some form of surrender to the Romans and sent word of their intent to Titus. As he approached the wall to learn more, Simon discovered the plot. He slaughtered his erstwhile allies and flung their corpses over the wall. Both Simon and John were unyieldingly opposed coming to terms with the Romans.[29]

Despite this—as the ramps moved higher and closer to the Antonia—Josephus continued pleading with the revolutionaries. He visited different portions of the city's walls and attempted to persuade the Jews to use reason and abandon their faulty plans. This clearly angered some of the Jewish combatants, and when Josephus was speaking close to the wall, one fired a missile that struck him on the head. Stunned, Josephus fell to the ground in a painful daze. This seemed like a coup for the insurgents who rushed out of their walls to seize Josephus' body, which they wanted to mutilate mercilessly.[30]

Titus learned of Josephus' peril, and he sent a cavalry unit to rescue him from the rebels' clutches. The horsemen galloped with haste and arrived in time to prevent his capture, but the Jews wrongly believed that he was dead. Rumors of his death spread throughout Jerusalem—even to his incarcerated mother. Some, including her, bewailed his supposed demise, while others cheered it. After briefly recovering from the blow, Josephus returned to the city walls and proved that he was still alive. His arrival dismayed John and Simon's men but gave some solace to the civilian population whose cause he diligently espoused. Standing before the wall, he promised Rome's enemies that they would be punished for harming him and that the Romans could be lenient victors to the innocent.[31]

Regardless of Josephus' assurances to the noncombatants, John and Simon would not alter their plans, but thousands of civilians decided to risk deserting the holy city. They jumped over the walls—fleeing from the insurgents—and ran into the arms of the Romans. Sadly, many of these refugees inadvertently died in the camps because, after starving for so long, they overate, and their stomachs ruptured—leading to their demise. Others were more careful when they finally indulged in food, but even if they exercised caution, the shock to their system meant that they needed to evacuate their bowels, which resulted in gruesome tragedy.[32]

Some auxiliary troops noticed a Jew plucking golden coins out of his excrement. At first, this seemed like a bizarre sight, but it was because many Jews had swallowed their savings to enable them to smuggle it out of Jerusalem. Rumors of this wealth circulated in the Syrian and Arab auxiliary camps, and these soldiers—along with some Roman legionaries—decided this was too tempting of an opportunity and resorted to savagery. They cruelly killed some 2,000 Jewish deserters in one night and ripped open their stomachs in search of loot. It was an unconscionable crime.[33]

It did not take long for news of this wanton barbarity to reach Titus. He undoubtedly exploded in anger and disgust. His first instinct was to call up the cavalry and have them summarily execute all of the wrongdoers. Eventually, he made a lamentable calculation. There were too many people involved in the crimes to punish in this form. They far exceeded the number of victims. Nevertheless, he convened the commanders of the accused and lambasted them for these evil deeds. As for the Arab and Syrian malefactors, he spared their lives but threatened them with death if they repeated their offenses. The Roman legionaries, on the other hand, probably did not get off so lightly. Titus ordered them to be brought before him, and he would deal with them then. Their ultimate fates are not apparent, but Titus may well have discharged, flogged or executed them. Regrettably, this did not end the crimes. Some auxiliaries continued the detestable practice when they believed that no Romans were paying attention, which deterred many deserters from seeking the safety of Rome's bivouacs.[34]

As this was underway, John and his accomplices were busily stripping the Temple of its gold and prized objects, drinking the sacred wine and using its oil for non-religious purposes. While John suggested that using the wine and oil to survive was acceptable, it is not clear how he tried to justify stealing the Temple's valuables. Clearly, this enriched himself and his men, but if they believed that they would be able to keep the precious objects after Titus conquered them, then they were sorely mistaken.[35]

With the Jews preoccupied in this manner, the Romans remained at work on the ramps, but the blockade's effect was taking a heavy toll. A Jewish deserter named Mannaeus reached one of the Roman camps and claimed that between April and June of 70 CE, he counted 115,880 corpses being transported out of the gate that he watched, although some modern historians doubt his testimony. As the Romans interrogated other refugees, they obtained a fuller picture of how terrible matters were in Jerusalem. At this point, supposedly over 600,000 dead Jews had been discarded out of the city's various gates—or so Josephus reported—and many more had perished. It was a death toll of apocalyptic proportions, but the war still was not over.[36]

XIV

ANTONIA

> *"I call the gods of my fathers to witness and any deity that once watched over this place—for now I believe that there is none—I call my army, the Jews within my lines, and you yourselves to witness that it is not I who force you to pollute these precincts. Exchange the arena of conflict for another and not a Roman shall approach or insult your holy places; nay, I will preserve the temple for you, even against your will."*
> —Titus[1]

IN THE DAYS THAT FOLLOWED, Jerusalem and its environs continued devolving into an unrecognizable scene. The Romans had toppled virtually all of the trees within a 10 mile radius of it, which gave the region the appearance of a barren desert. Starvation persisted among the Jews and even began to seriously affect the insurgents—leaving many emaciated or worse, dead. Corpses lined Jerusalem's perimeter, and they continued piling up in the streets within the city walls. Meanwhile, Titus and his legionaries had worked to erect four ramps, and after 21 days of arduous labor, the Romans completed them.[2]

John and Simon's men stared at the ramps with determination and understood that they must find a way to raze them before the siege engines punctured their wall. The Romans, on the other hand, feared losing their ramps to Jewish attacks again. Creating them required hard work and lumber that was no longer readily available. Following the Romans' prior failures, Titus refused to let the rebels set fire to the earthworks or their siege engines. So he placed a wall of legionaries around the ramps and arranged artillery to counter Jewish sorties, which inevitably came.[3]

Hoping to destroy the ramps before the Romans could breach the next line of defense, John's men charged toward them with torches and weapons drawn, but they met a determined Roman soldiery. The legionaries stood firm and unleashed their artillery on the exposed combatants—striking and killing a number of them from afar—and the wall of legionaries drew their *gladii* and made quick work of those who neared the earthworks. The revolutionaries were no match for Titus' men, and unlike before, the Jewish insurgents apparently had not managed to build new, effective mines under the ramps. After the most recent failed attempts, the Jews retreated back to their fortress, and the Romans proceeded with their plans.[4]

Now unimpeded by Jewish sallies, the legionaries began inching the siege engines up the ramps and toward the rebel-held wall. This was backbreaking and time-consuming work. It was also dangerous. From the wall's parapets, Jews hurled stones and firebrands at the Romans working on and around the ramps, but the Roman troops had prepared for this. When the bombardment nearly became too much, the soldiers formed the famed *testudo*, which translates to tortoise. It was a formation in which legionaries linked their shields together over their heads to form a protective barrier, like a tortoise shell. Upon doing so, their efforts resumed and their siege engines reached the walls.[5]

The battering rams then smashed into the wall in a regular rhythm and shook Jerusalem to its foundations. Throughout the city, nobody could escape the terrifying pounding. At the same time, legionaries scurried around the wall's base—searching for vulnerabilities and struggling to weaken the fortification's integrity. Before long, they scored a success. They pried four large stones out of the wall, while the battering rams kept ravaging it. This did not lead to any immediate advances, but they presumed it would pay off soon. As the sun began to set, the majority of the legionaries returned to their camps to rest for the night, but Titus stationed others to guard the structures from Jewish saboteurs.[6]

In the middle of the night, a loud crash startled the Jews and the Romans. Part of the wall had abruptly crumbled to the ground, but this was not entirely due to the legionaries' efforts. Prying stones out of the wall and battering it with rams was doubtless critical to the wall's downfall, but because John had previously mined under it, its foundation was unstable. The combination of the mines and the Romans' efforts spelled doom for the wall. It is easy to imagine cheers emanating from the Roman camps upon witnessing its collapse, but their joy was quickly spoiled. After they inspected the shattered section of the wall, they noticed that John and his Zealots had hastily built an inner wall. It was not particularly well-made, but crossing over the rubble from the collapsed wall to scale this new one would be a lethal undertaking—causing a pall to come over the legionaries.[7]

Titus sensed this apprehension and sought to encourage his soldiers who were close to seizing their prize: Jerusalem. Once he collected many of his troops, he exclaimed,

> Fellow soldiers, to deliver an oration inciting [you to pursue] enterprises involving no risk is to cast a direct slur on the persons addressed, while it assuredly convicts him who delivers it of unmanliness. Exhortation, in my opinion, is needed only for hazardous affairs, since in other circumstances men may be expected to act of their own accord. That the scaling of this wall is arduous I, therefore, myself grant you at the outset; but [contending] with difficulties best becomes those who aspire to heroism, that it is glorious to die with renown, and that the gallantry of those who lead the way will not go unrewarded—on those points I would now dwell. In the first place, then, let that be an incentive to you which to some might perhaps be a deterrent, I mean the long-suffering of the Jews and their fortitude in adversity.
>
> For [it would be] shameful [if] Romans, soldiers of mine, men who in peace are trained for war, and in war are accustomed to conquer, should be outdone, either in strength or courage, by Jews, and that when final victory is in sight and we are enjoying the cooperation of God. For our reverses are but the outcome of the Jews' desperation, while their sufferings are increased by your valiant exploits and the constant cooperation of [God]. For faction, famine,

siege, the fall of ramparts without impact of engines—what can these things mean but that God is [angry] with them and extending His aid to us? Surely, then, [allowing] ourselves not merely to be surpassed by inferiors but to betray a divine ally would be beneath our dignity. It would indeed be disgraceful that Jews, to whom defeat brings no serious discredit since they have [learned] to be slaves, should, in order to end their servitude, scorn death and constantly charge into our midst, not from any hope of victory, but for the sheer display of bravery; and yet [...] you, masters of [nearly] every land and sea, to whom not to conquer is disgrace, should never once venture into the enemy's ranks, but should wait for famine and fortune to bring them down, sitting idle with weapons such as these, and that though at a little hazard you have it in your power to achieve everything. Yes, Antonia once mounted [...] the city is ours; for, even if—and I do not expect it—any further battle awaits us with those within, your position over their heads commanding the very air your enemies breath would ensure a complete and speedy victory.

I refrain on this occasion from [a glowing speech] on the warrior's death and the immortality reserved for those who fall in the frenzy of battle, but for any who think otherwise the worst I could wish is that they may die in peace of disease, soul and body alike condemned to the tomb. For what brave man knows not that souls released from the flesh by the sword on the battlefield are hospitably welcomed by that purest of elements, the ether, and placed among the stars, and that as good *genii* and benignant heroes they manifest their presence to their posterity; while souls which pine away in bodies wasted by disease, however pure they may be from stain or pollution, are obliterated in subterranean night and pass into profound oblivion, their life, their bodies, [yes] and their memory, brought simultaneously to a close? But if men are doomed to an inevitable end and the sword is a gentler minister thereof than any disease, surely it was ignoble to deny to the public service what we must surrender to fate.

Thus far I have spoken on the assumption that any who may attempt this feat must necessarily perish. Yet the valiant may come safe through even the most hazardous of enterprises. For in the first place, the ruined wall will be easy to mount; again, all that has been built up will be easy to overthrow; [if you] summon courage for the task, with growing numbers stimulating and supporting one another, [then] your determination will soon break the enemy's spirit. [Perhaps] you may find the exploit bloodless, if you but begin; for, though they will in all probability endeavour to thwart your ascent, yet if unperceived you [...] force a way through, their resistance may well break down, though but a handful of you elude them. As for [whoever] leads the assault, I should blush were I not to make him an enviable man in the award of honours; and while the survivor shall command those who are now his equals, [posthumous honors] shall follow the fallen to the grave.[8]

Titus' troops did not receive his remarks well. Rather they recoiled at the obvious risks of being exposed and storming into portions of Jewish-held Jerusalem. While the legionaries timidly contemplated Titus' statement, a man serving in the auxiliary cohorts named Sabinus rose and shouted, "I readily surrender up myself to [you, Caesar]. I [shall] first ascend the wall. And I heartily wish that thy fortune may follow my courage, and my resolution. And if some ill fortune grudges me the success of my undertaking, take notice, that my ill success will not be unexpected; but that I choose death voluntarily for thy sake." Sabinus' words likely shamed the Roman legionaries who feared the task, especially when they compared themselves to him. He was a thin man of small stature, and contrasting with the Romans, he was apparently of sub-Saharan African descent. This man showed more mettle than nearly all others in Titus' army.[9]

Titus welcomed Sabinus' indomitable courage, and 11 others eventually agreed to follow him on the dangerous mission. While brandishing his sword and holding his shield over his head, Sabinus sprinted toward the enemy with his companions close behind him. The Jewish combatants threw everything they had at the men, including boulders, arrows and javelins. The stealthy Sabinus dodged all of these weapons, although some of 11 followers were not so lucky. Before long, Sabinus reached the makeshift wall, scaled it and routed its defenders who fled after facing his superhuman feat.[10]

Sabinus' heroics were sadly short-lived. While securing his footing on the wall, he tripped and fell. The insurgents saw this, quit their retreat, wheeled around and attacked him. He managed to defend himself for some time—giving and receiving blows—but a hailstorm of Jewish missiles battered his body until there was no more life within it. He fell dead. Three of his comrades also died, and the final eight suffered wounds but managed to withdraw to the Roman camp. The operation was a failure, but Sabinus' courage and sacrifice weighed on the soldiers.[11]

Two days later, sometime in July 70 CE, the Romans made another attempt to gain a foothold within the inner perimeter of the rebel-held portions of Jerusalem. Twenty-four Romans assembled at around 2 a.m. and quietly made their way to the Antonia Fortress' facade. Ensuring that they did not make the slightest noise, they carefully scaled the stronghold. Surprisingly, they climbed up the Antonia Fortress without being detected, and then they killed many of the fort's guards. Now in possession of the wall, one of the Romans blew his trumpet—loudly announcing to Titus that the first step of their mission had been a success—which terrified the Jews who believed a larger Roman company had seized the wall.[12]

Upon hearing the signal, Titus and a highly trained corps of men dashed to reinforce the brave 24 Romans, as others dug their way into one of John's previously built tunnels and used it to infiltrate the city. The Romans were overwhelming this section of the insurgents' defenses, and considering it a lost cause, the rebels abandoned their posts and sought refuge in the Temple complex. The Romans followed in quick pursuit—seeking to end the siege that night. Fighting side by side, John and Simon's men furiously defended the routes to the Temple to keep the Romans at bay. The Romans and the Jewish combatants clashed in a number of terrifying brawls as the battle ebbed and flowed for hours. It was not until 1 p.m. that the Romans withdrew from the Temple compound's entrances. The remaining Jewish revolutionaries had survived the onslaught, but they had lost the Antonia Fortress to the Romans. This was a critical reversal, and now John and Simon's gang, along with myriad civilians, was largely hemmed into the Temple complex and elsewhere within Jerusalem.[13]

At some point Titus ascended the Antonia Fortress, and while standing atop it, he witnessed another conspicuous example of bravery. A Roman centurion named Julianus decided to go on the offensive against the Jews single-handedly. He did so, which terrified the rebels who viewed him as more than a man. He even drove them to the inner court of the Temple compound, but like Sabinus, fate had other plans.

A section of the Temple Mount, Jerusalem, 2019.

Julianus fell, and the revolutionaries turned and assailed him. They received many wounds by Julianus' hands but ultimately overpowered and killed him. The scene was emotional. Titus no doubt yearned to come to Julianus' assistance, but he could not reach him in time.[14]

Following Julianus' death, Titus turned his attention elsewhere. He ordered his subordinates to prepare to raze the Antonia Fortress and clear an easy path for the legions and their siege equipment to reach the Temple and other parts of the city. With his army moving into position and preparing to seize the Temple complex, Titus decided to offer the insurgents an opportunity to save their holiest site and carry out their necessary religious obligations, which had laid in abeyance as of late. Titus had learned that the Jews had been unable to continue offering regular sacrifices because they supposedly no longer had officiants worthy and qualified to do so. This was causing great concern among the Jews. Hoping to allow the Jewish faithful to fulfill their religious duties, save the Temple and resolve the war, Titus charged Josephus with offering the revolutionaries an olive branch.[15]

Speaking on behalf of Titus, Josephus approached the enemy and said that the Romans were willing to offer terms: If the Jewish militants wished to continue waging their war on Rome, then they ought to leave the Temple complex under assurances that the Romans would not molest them as they departed; if they chose this path, then the city and Temple would be spared from the Romans' ire and would no longer be subject to the insurgents' profane use of it; and finally, Titus would allow the Jews to resume sacrifices using whatever priests they chose. However, Josephus hinted, failure to accept this deal could result in terrible destruction.[16]

As before, the revolutionaries rejected Josephus' pleas, derided him and claimed that the Romans would never capture the Temple because it belonged to God.

The sharp-tongued Josephus had a quick reply. "And of course you have kept it so immaculate for God, haven't you?" he retorted, and then delivered a stinging invective against the Jewish combatants who rejected his pleas and polluted some of Judaism's most holy places. Brought to tears, Josephus' speech moved the Romans—who greatly admired him—and the Jewish civilians. In fact, many of them continued to seek refuge with the Romans, including some notable priests, but the insurgents could not be swayed. They believed that they were fighting a just holy war against an oppressive, heretical regime.[17]

Hoping to stem the tide of refugees fleeing to the Romans, the rebels circulated accounts of the Romans murdering deserters, including a list of men that Titus had purportedly slaughtered. The truth was that Titus had spared these particular people and sent them to live in peace. Nevertheless, this slowed the flow of deserters toward the Romans because they feared what they presumed was certain death at their hands, but Titus wished to again establish his innocence. He somehow learned of the individual deserters whom he had allegedly killed, and he located them in the city of Gophna and brought them to Jerusalem. He subsequently marched them about the holy city as physical evidence that he was honest and merciful, unlike the insurgents. After observing this proof, a steady flood of Jewish civilians began to stream out the doomed city again, but not before begging the rebels to surrender, which proved to be a fatal mistake. They decided to respond by killing a large number of defenseless civilians and left their slain bodies strewn around the Temple complex.[18]

Titus witnessed the terrible carnage and gave the combatants one more opportunity to lay down their weapons and leave the Temple, which would ensure its survival. He cried out,

> Was it not you, most abominable wretches, who placed this balustrade before your sanctuary? Was it not you that ranged along it those slabs, engraved in Greek characters and in our own, proclaiming that none may pass the barrier? And did we not permit you to put to death any who passed it, even [if he was] a Roman? Why then, you miscreants, do you now actually trample corpses underfoot within it? Why do you defile your temple with the blood of foreigner[s] and native[s]?
> I call the gods of my fathers to witness and any deity that once watched over this place—for now I believe that there is none—I call my army, the Jews within my lines, and you yourselves to witness that it is not I who force you to pollute these precincts. Exchange the arena of conflict for another and not a Roman shall approach or insult your holy places; nay, I will preserve the Temple for you, even against your will.[19]

Josephus translated the message and relayed it to the revolutionaries, but they had no appetite for peace or leaving the Temple. This saddened Titus and likely also some Romans who—while not Jewish—apparently yearned to spare the beautiful Temple complex, at least according to Josephus. The insurgents disregarded Titus' offers, refused to cooperate with him and he realized that his regular overtures for peace or moving the battlefield elsewhere had all been futile. Titus consequently accepted the reality that the Romans would invariably raze Jerusalem and perhaps its grand Temple, and additional violence would ultimately resolve the war.[20]

XV

Temple

> *"The Temple hill, one huge mass of fire, seemed to be boiling over from its very roots, but you would also have seen rivers of blood outrunning |the flames and the killed outnumbering the killers. Nowhere could the ground be seen for the corpses covering it."*
> —*Josephus*[1]

DESPITE TITUS' REPEATED EFFORTS and Josephus' eloquent assistance, the Romans could not convince the insurgent leaders to seriously consider leaving Jerusalem to spare their holy city and its Temple. Given these realities, Titus begrudgingly decided to resume hostilities, and the results would be devastating for the Jews. After considering his options and realizing that his army was far too vast to participate in the siege of the Temple complex, Titus chose the 30 best warriors from each century and appointed a military tribune to lead each company of 1,000 such men. In total, this equaled several thousand legionaries, and he assigned his trusted officer, Sextus Vettulenus Cerialis, to lead the overall assault on the Temple grounds.[2]

Titus instructed them to launch their offensive before dawn on the Temple guards whom they hoped would be asleep. Then, if matters went to plan, the legionaries would infiltrate the Temple district and defeat the enemy—thus eliminating the last major obstacle to sacking Jerusalem. Everyone had their orders, but Titus did not intend on watching the battle from afar. He planned to enter the thick of the fighting and support his fellow Romans. He may have begun clothing himself in his battle garb and armor and ensuring that his weapons were battle-ready when his deputies challenged his plans.[3]

They claimed that the mission was far too hazardous for him and he would be better served by observing the battle from the Antonia Fortress, which the Romans had not dismantled yet. This would guarantee his well-being and invigorate the troops. Titus' lieutenants asserted that his men would fight even harder knowing that he was watching and judging their conduct from his lofty vantage point. Titus reluctantly acquiesced. He subsequently gave Cerialis orders to commence the operation, and the commander took position on the Antonia Fortress to witness what he hoped would be the final major victory needed to ensure the stubborn city's fall.[4]

Led by Cerialis, Rome's select troops approached the Temple district, but they found the Jews prepared and ready for action. The Jewish sentries were awake, and with loud cries and perhaps by sounding their horns, they alerted their comrades to the coming danger. This was a disappointing turn of events for the Romans, but they did not alter their plan. They assailed the Jewish guards at the Temple's different approaches anyway. The insurgents responded fiercely, and wave after wave of Jews smashed into the Roman shields. Facing this barrage, the Romans strove to push their enemies back without either side gaining a decisive edge in the struggle. It was an especially chaotic and dangerous affair, considering that it was still dark, but the sun soon rose.[5]

With sunlight appearing, the two factions withdrew to realign and readjust their battle strategies. Once prepared, they re-launched their ferocious attacks. They fought hand-to-hand, but neither side could gain and maintain notable progress. They fought over inches, and Romans and Jews fell dead in droves. Titus anxiously and helplessly watched the battle, and while he saw nothing but commendable martial behavior from his men, the battle ground to a deadly draw. Exhausted, at around 11 a.m., both parties quit the battle and returned to their respective camps to tend to the wounded, and Titus presumably hiked down the Antonia to meet with his soldiers.[6]

With this aforementioned battle concluded, Titus' legionaries could finalize the demolition of the Antonia Fortress. They may have enthusiastically completed the work, because it gave them an outlet for their rage and a response to the constant frustrations marking this siege. Within seven days of commencing the demolition project, they destroyed the once-proud Antonia Fortress, turned it into little more than rubble, removed much of the debris and created a wide pathway where it had stood. Now unimpeded by the hulking fortress, masses of troops could approach the Temple with ease, but the recent battle for the Temple taught Titus a lesson: The Romans could not seize it in short order without suffering massive casualties. So he wisely changed his strategy.[7]

In order to capture the Temple complex while risking as few Roman lives as possible, Titus needed to build more earthworks. This must have been the last thing he wanted to do in light of the time and resources needed and that they were not guaranteed to withstand the Jews' counterattacks. Nevertheless, ramps could enable him to batter the Temple compound walls and reach the heights needed to overwhelm the insurgents. After some thought, Titus instructed his men to build four ramps, and Josephus recorded their exact locations: "The one [ramp] was over against the northwest corner of the inner Temple. Another was at that northern edifice which was between the two gates. And of the other two, one was at the western cloister of the outer court of the Temple. The other against its northern cloister."[8]

After receiving orders to begin erecting ramps, Titus' legionaries started the laborious process. Parties of legionaries traveled up to 11 miles from Jerusalem in order to find lumber worth using, and they feverishly chopped down the trees and relocated them to the Roman camps. Day by day, the Roman ramps increased in size,

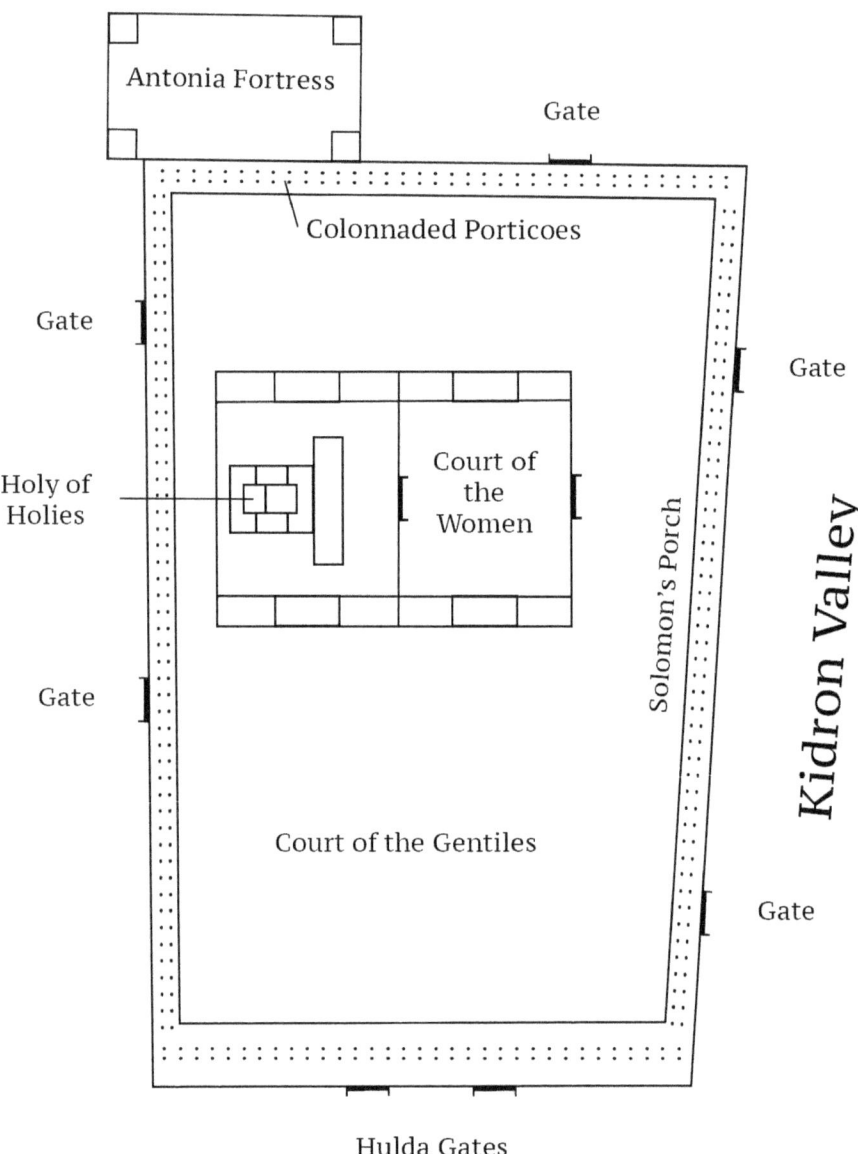

Jerusalem's Temple complex, circa 70 CE.

but the Jews did not watch the progress passively. They periodically harassed the Roman laborers, which slowed the process, but for the most part, the Romans considered the siege nearly over. This led to an erosion of discipline. Roman cavalrymen even let their horses loose to graze, and upon doing so, the Jews repeatedly captured the steeds, which they might have consumed. Eating horses is expressly forbidden in Judaism, but the conditions were dire enough for those in Jerusalem to violate the law in order to survive. Disappointed with the Romans' lackadaisical conduct, Titus made an example of a cavalryman whose horse the Jews stole. Titus ordered his execution. From then on, the Romans maintained much better military discipline.[9]

Driven by desperation and hunger, the insurgents continued their attacks, and a number of them somehow slipped out of Jerusalem just before sunset and sprinted toward the 10th Legion's camp on the Mount of Olives. How they were able to do this is not entirely clear. In whatever manner it was done, they had hoped to catch the Romans unawares and steal any provisions that they could find, but the Romans foiled their plans. The legionaries quickly detected them, and a battle erupted in which the legionaries easily routed the rebels. One particularly impressive vignette from this skirmish survives to the present day. A certain Roman cavalryman named Pedanius galloped directly for the retreating Jews. Riding alongside one armor-wearing combatant, Pedanius reached out his hand and snatched the man—demonstrating amazing dexterity and strength. Holding the Jew by the ankle with one arm, Pedanius turned his horse toward Titus and displayed his immobilized prisoner. This impressed Titus who presumably heaped praise on Pedanius. The captured man was not so lucky. Titus had him put to death.[10]

The insurgents watched in dread as the Roman earthworks moved closer and closer. In response, they burned some Temple complex colonnades in the north and west. These had once been connected to the Antonia Fortress and could have given the Romans easier access to the Temple compound, which reduced even more of Jerusalem to ruins. Two days later in July 70 CE, the Romans employed destructive fire for their uses too and set more of the colonnade ablaze, and it threatened to spread far and wide. To keep it contained, the Jews destroyed part of the colonnade's roof.

As the firing and ramp-building operations continued, a Jewish man named Jonathan boldly challenged any Roman to single combat. Most legionaries saw little need to accept his invitation, but Jonathan castigated and mocked the Romans as cowards until an auxiliary cavalryman answered the call. Jonathan ultimately bested him, and while hovering over the defeated dead man, Jonathan gloated and sneered at the Romans. Jonathan's disparaging taunts eventually became intolerable for one Roman, named Priscus, who fired an arrow that plunged into Jonathan. Writhing in extreme agony, Jonathan perished shortly thereafter, and his snipes fell silent.[11]

The Romans cheered Jonathan's demise, while it offended the rebels who yearned for revenge. In the succeeding days, they found opportunities to attempt to avenge his death. In fact, they encountered the Romans regularly as they strove to inhibit the Romans' slow advance toward the Temple complex, although they were not particularly successful. Looking for a novel way to counter the Romans, they settled on a new strategy. A roof lined much of the remaining western colonnade, and within it, they secretly stored dried timber smeared with combustible material. Once they filled the attics accordingly, they feigned retreat from the western colonnade as if they were exhausted from defending it.[12]

While numerous seasoned Roman legionaries were skeptical of the enemy's withdrawal, others believed they saw an opportunity to capture the Temple. They grabbed their ladders and dashed for the colonnade. After scaling it, the Romans scampered on the roof, likely surveyed the Temple complex and looked for signs of resistance. As they did and more soldiers crowded atop the colonnade, the insurgents set it ablaze, and the fire roared to life and spread across the roof with alarming speed. The Roman troops were almost instantly surrounded by flames and faced a horrific death. Some of them chose to fall on their swords and commit suicide. Others jumped toward their comrades, but the fall left many with broken bones. Some unfortunate Romans leaped from the colonnade and into the Temple complex where the enemy quickly and remorselessly dispatched them.[13]

Titus watched in anger and horror as his army suffered needless casualties because some men under his command had impetuously marched to certain death. Even so, he felt sadness for their loss and urged his lieutenants to find a way to rescue the doomed souls, but their efforts were largely futile. It was a massacre, and while it left a pall over the Roman soldiery, it served a valuable lesson: The legionaries should act more judiciously and not fall into the revolutionaries' traps. Nevertheless, the fire reduced part of the Jews' refuge, and the following day, Titus' soldiers burned the remaining northern colonnade. Very quickly, the outer portions of the Temple compound were becoming smoldering ruins.[14]

As the Romans continued their operations, the famine within the Jewish-held districts became largely inescapable. Thousands laid dead, and even the militants struggled to find anything to eat. They resorted to consuming belts, shoes, leather from their shields and decomposing hay, which demonstrates their desperation. However, some went to even greater lengths and the tales are haunting to this day.[15]

A wealthy woman called Mary and her child were lodged within Jerusalem and stricken with hunger, like the rest of her countrymen who were trapped there. Looking at the infant, she said, "Poor babe, amidst war, famine, and sedition, to what end should I preserve [you]? With the Romans slavery awaits us, should we live till they come; but famine is forestalling slavery, and [crueler] than both are the rebels. Come, be [...] food for me, to the rebels an avenging fury, and to the world a tale [that epitomizes] the calamities of the Jews." She heartlessly then killed her child, baked the body and consumed half it. She saved the rest for later.[16]

The smell of burning flesh quickly alerted the starving insurgents who excitedly forced their way into her quarters and demanded their portions of whatever she was cooking. She produced half of her child, and explained, "This is my own child, and this my handiwork. Eat, for I too have eaten. [Do not pretend to be] weaker than a woman, or more compassionate than a mother. But if you have pious scruples and shrink from my sacrifice, then let what I have eaten be your portion and the remainder also be left for me." This horrified the battle-hardened men who were no strangers to cruelty, but this monstrous act was too much even for them. In shock and disbelief, they fled from her presence, but news of her abominable deed could not be contained. It spread throughout Jerusalem and into the Roman camps.[17]

Accounts of Mary's crime reached Titus who was likewise appalled. Once again, he cried out to the gods that these tragedies were not of his making. Before the pantheon of deities, he defended himself, stating that he had repeatedly tried to negotiate a peace agreement with the Jews. They chose war, he asserted, and were even the first to destroy part of the Temple complex, which Titus had offered to safeguard for Jewish posterity. Titus did not wish for the gods to hold him accountable when he believed that the combatants were to blame.[18]

Titus and the rest of the Roman soldiery knew that matters were dire for the civilian Jews, but they now understood that it was so bad that unconscionable crimes were occurring. This was enough to spur Titus into action. While not all of the earthworks were complete, two ramps were ready for use, and Titus instructed his men to bring the battering rams up against the Temple compound's walls in August 70 CE. They began to besiege the Temple complex forthwith, but the rams hammered at the wall to little effect. The quality construction withstood the constant collisions. Meanwhile, the legionaries tried to pull the wall apart by prizing key stones out of place. After considerable effort, they pried some out, but the obstinate wall unbelievably still stood firm.[19]

Titus fully comprehended the depravity transpiring within the Jewish-held quarter and worked feverishly to end John and Simon's rule. So when the battering rams failed to produce the intended results, he ordered legionaries to conduct a full assault on the wall and rush toward it with ladders in hand. Without facing any opposition, they began to make their way up the wall. Then the Jews sprung their counterattack. They shoved the Romans down from the ladders' heights, stabbed some who made it near the top of the wall and numerous ladders slid onto others and off the wall—falling to the ground in what may have appeared like a deadly domino effect. After witnessing these disastrous attempts, successive lines of Roman soldiers opted against following their allies up the ladders.

While many Jews also lost their lives in the melee, the operation ended in failure for the legionaries as well as humiliation. That is because in the fighting the rebels managed to capture an unknown number of Roman standards. The Romans cared for them religiously, and losing any to the enemy was considered a colossal disgrace.[20]

Incensed, Titus decided to try another tactic: burning the barricaded entranceways to the Temple complex. He gave his lieutenants orders to fire the gates of the Temple's outer enclosure, and they hurried to fulfill his directive. As they neared the grand gates, they noticed that they were ornately lined with silver, but after sparking the fires, the precious metal melted away and exposed the dried wood. It caught fire, and the flames spread to the adjoining colonnade. Rather than attempting to extinguish the conflagration, the revolutionaries turned their ire on the Romans and brawled with them, which was a counterproductive choice. The flames raged throughout the day and night—destroying the gates and portions of the Temple's outer defenses.[21]

By the next morning, the once imposing gates had been reduced to smoldering ash, as had much of the adjoining colonnade's roof, and the fire was still burning. Titus commanded his troops to extinguish the flames and prepare a flat approach up to the gate for the legionaries to use. As this was underway, Titus convened a meeting with his top deputies, and he asked for their advice over what to do with the Jewish Temple. Some advocated for destroying it because, they claimed, so long as it stood, the Jews had a reason to unite against the Romans. Not everyone agreed. Some cooler-headed lieutenants stated that it should only be toppled if the insurgents used it as a fortress against the Romans. Upon mulling his options, Titus announced his decision: He planned to spare the Temple. This building had never offended him or any Roman, and it was a work of wonder and beauty and would continue to be after it fell into Rome's hands, he decided. Once he settled on this course of action, he ordered his deputies to share the message with their subordinates that the Temple should not be razed, and this command was presumably circulated among the troops. At least this is the account reported by the pro–Flavian propagandist Josephus.[22]

Notwithstanding Josephus' account, as other ancient narratives claim, it is very possible that Titus determined that the Temple must be destroyed to punish the Jews, eliminate the symbolic heart of their rebellion and halt future revolts. Other ancient writers strenuously disagreed with Josephus over Titus' decision on the Temple's fate. Early Christian writer Sulpicius Severus asserted, "Titus himself [held] the destruction of this temple to be a prime necessity of wiping out more completely the religion of the Jews and the Christians; for they urged that these religions, although hostile to each other, nevertheless sprang from the same sources; the Christians had grown out of the Jews: if the root were destroyed, the stock would easily perish." As modern scholars have suggested, Titus considered the Jews when determining the Temple's fate, but likely did not think of the Christians whatsoever. Instead, this is probably a later interpolation that Severus or one of his sources added. This aside, Orosius seemed to agree that Titus had identified the Temple as something that the Romans ought to consider toppling, "since its survival would encourage the enemy."[23]

Regardless of the differing accounts, the next day, the Jewish militants decided to risk assailing the Romans. They flooded out of the eastern gate and met a company of Romans who guarded this portion of the Temple complex's outer court. The Romans were not taken by surprise. As they saw the insurgents marching for their position, they linked their shields together and advanced toward the Jews. They quickly collided, and the Romans fought with distinction. Yet they were at the point of faltering before the revolutionaries' desperate gamble. At this moment, Titus realized their peril, and he and his cavalry galloped to their defense. They arrived in time and drove the Jews back, but the battle was not over. Each time the Romans would retire, the Jewish combatants would return to harry them again. This happened time and again, until the Romans finally overwhelmed them, and the rebels closed themselves up in the inner Temple court.[24]

After this battle, Titus resolved to invade the remainder of the Temple complex the next day and surround the Temple. Fate, however, had other plans. A host of legionaries were still attempting to extinguish the smoldering fire when the Jews ran out from their refuge and attacked them. While not ready for battle and still busy putting out the flames, these Romans defended themselves admirably and even managed to rout the insurgents. They then gave chase to the Jews who hid within the grand Temple, and one Roman legionary grabbed a piece of burning wood and hurled it toward the hallowed structure. It crashed through a gold encrusted window in a room adjacent to the sanctuary, and it did not take long for the flames to spread—causing the Jews to wail and bemoan the tragic turn of events.[25]

Titus was reclining in his tent and undoubtedly preparing for the battle he had planned for the following day when a message brought him news of the fire within the Temple. Aghast, he ran from his tent to the Temple to help extinguish the spreading fire. He gestured wildly and cried out to his fellow Romans to smother the flames, or so Josephus claimed, but his attempts were in vain. The conflagration had taken hold. Meanwhile, some soldiers were too busy fighting the Jews to notice his commands and others enjoyed the spectacle. They had an insatiable appetite for revenge, and destroying the sacred Temple served their purposes. So even when they heard Titus' earnest pleas to save the Temple, they ignored him and a number of them launched additional firebrands into the holy structure.[26]

Pandemonium ensued as insurgents and innocent civilians fled the flames, but were killed by grizzled Roman legionaries. Bodies fell to the ground and littered the pathways as the Roman legionaries showed no mercy whatsoever. With this underway, some Jews lamented the loss of their Temple to such a degree that they took turns killing each other—as all hope was lost—or simply jumped into the burning Temple to share its fate. Around the same time, Titus and some of his closest associates marched into the Temple, marveled at its interior and assessed whether it could be salvaged. As he noted at the time, only the outer rooms were ablaze. The holy of holies appeared untouched by fire, and Titus hoped that the stone structure could be saved. After concluding that it was not entirely lost yet, he ran out and again barked instructions at the legionaries to preserve the Temple and cease their assaults on it. He even empowered a centurion and lancers to keep away those seeking to do the Temple harm.[27]

Despite Titus' efforts, many of the legionaries' hatred for the Jews, irrational lust for killing and craving the valuables stored in the Temple overrode anything Titus could have done to stop them. The Romans fought in a frenzy and planned to strip the burning Temple of its wealth and destroy the holy site. As all of this was underway, another soldier marched into the Temple with a firebrand and torched the door's hinges. With the fires devouring everything and spreading out of control, the Temple was without a doubt lost. Its razing occurred on the anniversary of the Babylonian destruction of the Jewish Temple hundreds of years prior, according to Josephus, although there is some scholarly debate over this statement's veracity.

This was beyond tragic, and it has impacted Jews ever since then. In destroying the Temple, the Romans reduced the Jews' ability to offer appropriate sacrifices, and as they would eventually learn, the Romans never permitted the grand Temple's reconstruction.[28]

As fire consumed it, the Romans looted the Temple grounds and demonstrated their remorseless bloodlust. In addition to Jewish militants, they wantonly killed children, the elderly and priests. Amidst the widespread anguish, a terrible sound emanated from Jerusalem. Raging fires roared, Jews sobbed as they slowly died and the Romans belched out their victorious war cries. The scene was ghastly. "The Temple hill, one huge mass of fire, seemed to be boiling over from its very roots, but you would also have seen rivers of blood outrunning the flames and the killed outnumbering the killers," Josephus noted. "Nowhere could the ground be seen for the corpses covering it."[29]

During the tumult, some of the insurgents escaped from the Temple and into the city where they hoped to carry on their war with Rome. Some civilians who had quartered in the Temple remained behind to harass the legionaries, but even they saw that their efforts were pointless. A number of them retreated as the flames grew and a dense smoke obscured their view. Unfortunately, destroying the Temple was not enough for the vengeful Romans. They decided to raze more buildings in the Temple's vicinity, including the remaining colonnades, some of the gates, treasury storerooms and so forth. As they unrepentantly destroyed Judaism's holiest place, they noticed a number of civilians taking refuge under one of the surviving colonnades. Rather than waiting for orders, they set fire to the colonnade—resulting in the senseless deaths of around 6,000 Jews.[30]

Numerous portents had allegedly foretold of this doom, but the Jews had not properly heeded them. Now the city was in shambles, and the Romans were ruthlessly plundering it of its immense wealth. In an immeasurably profane insult, the Romans placed their standards on the Temple Mount, made sacrifices to them and cried out their support for Titus hailing him "Imperator!" Fires were still raging and terror pervaded Jerusalem, but the day was far from over; further terrors awaited the Jews.[31]

XVI

John and Simon

> *"Well, sirs, are you at length sated with your country's woes—you who, without bestowing a thought on our strength or your own weakness, have through inconsiderate fury and madness lost your people, your city, and your temple, and are yourselves justly doomed to perish."*
> —Titus[1]

As Titus and his legionaries secured the Temple complex, hope was largely lost for the Jewish rebels, although many continued to defy Rome. A host of surviving revolutionaries fled the Temple and took refuge throughout the city. Meanwhile, Titus' soldiers plundered it mercilessly and accumulated prodigious wealth from the gilded Temple. They gathered so much gold that it eventually disrupted the market, and the price of gold fell by half in Syria due to the influx of supply.[2]

While a host of insurgents had escaped the Temple compound, many other Jews had not. Numerous priests steadfastly remained there and refused to surrender, but they were running low on basic provisions, like water. One young man was among these priests, and he requested safe passage from the Romans in exchange for water. Believing that he would surrender afterward and pitying the boy, the legionaries agreed, but the youngster filled his water vessel and sprinted back to the priests. The boy's trickery angered the Romans, and his decision ultimately had dire consequences.[3]

Four days later, hunger pangs and mounting thirst became too much for the priests, and they decided to hand themselves over to Titus and his troops. They yearned for his mercy, but after the boy's apparent treachery—at least from the legionaries' perspective—the Romans were not in a forgiving mood. The priests implored Titus to act with restraint and spare their lives. Regrettably for them, he explained that the time for forgiveness had passed, and he subsequently ordered their executions—perhaps by crucifixion, strangulation or decapitation, depending on the Romans' preferences at the time.[4]

Myriad Jews had evaded the Romans and melted into Jerusalem where they hid and desperately sought an escape from the doomed city. However, this seemed unlikely. Titus had built a wall around Jerusalem, and his men were combing the city in search of loot and enemy combatants. Understanding their hopeless situation and praying that they could persuade Titus to show clemency, they invited him to parley, and Titus accepted. He sat in a prominent location on the western side of the outer Temple court and was flanked by his battle-hardened troops.[5]

Soon enough, John, Simon, their insurgents and even the broader Jewish populace converged on the area—hoping to avert their own massacre. Titus gave word to his armed soldiers—who took all of the strategic locations and were prepared to attack—to hold their fire and control their rage. Despite holding the upper hand, Titus planned to offer the revolutionaries a deal in good faith, and when the crowd quieted down, the Roman commander spoke to the Jews via an interpreter. He exclaimed,

> Well, sirs, are you at length sated with your country's woes—you who, without bestowing a thought on our strength or your own weakness, have through inconsiderate fury and madness lost your people, your city, and your temple, and are yourselves justly doomed to perish—you who from the first, ever since Pompey reduced you by force never ceased from revolution, and have now ended by declaring open war upon the Romans? Did you rely on numbers? [No], a mere fraction of the Roman soldiery has proved your match. On the fidelity of allies? Pray, what nation beyond the limits of our empire would prefer Jews to Romans? On physical strength, perhaps? Yet you are aware that the Germans are our slaves. On the solidity of your walls? But what wall could be a greater obstacle than the ocean, encompassed by which the Britons yet do homage to the Roman arms? On the determination of spirit and the astuteness of your generals? Yet you knew that even Carthaginians were defeated.
>
> No, assuredly you were incited against the Romans by Roman humanity. To begin with, we allowed you to occupy this land and set over you kings of your own blood; then we maintained the laws of your forefathers and permitted you, not only among yourselves but also in your dealings with others, to live as you willed; above all, we permitted you to exact tribute for God and to collect offerings, without either admonishing or hindering those who brought them—only that you might grow richer at our expense and make preparations with our money to attack us! And then, enjoying such privileges, you turned your superabundance against the donors, and like untamable reptiles spat your venom upon those who caressed you.
>
> You held, be it granted, Nero's indolence in contempt, and, like fractures or ruptures, remained for a time malignantly quiescent, only to show your true character on the outbreak of a more serious malady, when you let your ambitions soar unbounded to shameless expectations. My father came into the country, not to punish you for events under Cestius, but to admonish you. Had he come to extirpate the nation, his duty surely was to hasten to the root of your strength and to sack this city forthwith; whereas he proceeded to ravage Galilee and the surrounding district, thus affording you time for repentance. But by you his humanity was taken for weakness, and upon our clemency you nursed your audacity. On Nero's [death], you acted like the basest scoundrels. Emboldened by our intestine troubles, when I and my father had departed for Egypt, you abused your opportunities by preparing for hostilities, and were not ashamed to harass those, now made emperors, whose humanity as generals you had experienced. Thus, when the empire found refuge in us, when throughout its length was universal tranquility, and foreign nations were sending embassies of congratulation, once again the Jews were in arms.
>
> There were embassies from you to your friends beyond the Euphrates fostering revolt; fortifications being built up anew; seditions, contentions of tyrants, and civil war—the only things befitting men so base. I came to this city, the bearer of gloomy injunctions from my reluctant father. The news that the townsfolk were disposed to peace [made my heart rejoice]. As for you, before hostilities began I urged you to pause; for a long while after you had begun them

I spared you: I gave pledges of protection to deserters, I kept faith with them when they fled to me; many were the prisoners whom I compassionated, forbidding their oppressors to torture them; with reluctance I brought up my engines against your walls; my soldiers, thirsting for your blood, I invariably restrained; after every victory, as if defeated myself, I invited you to peace. On approaching the Temple, again in deliberate forgetfulness of the laws of war, I besought you to spare your own shrines and to preserve the Temple for yourselves, offering you unmolested egress and assurance of safety, or, if you so wished, an opportunity for battle on some other arena. All offers you scorned and with your own hands set fire to the Temple.

And after all this, most abominable wretches, do you now invite me to a parley? What [do you have] to save comparable to what is lost? What protection do you think you deserve after losing your Temple? Nay, even now you stand in arms and, at the last extremity, do not so much as pretend to be suppliants. Miserable men, on what do you rely? Is not your folk dead, your Temple gone, your city at my mercy, are not your very lives in my hands? And do you yet deem it glorious bravery to die in the last ditch? I, however, will not emulate your frenzy. Throw down your arms, surrender your persons, and I grant you your lives, like a lenient master of a household punishing the incorrigible and preserving the rest for myself.[6]

After Titus delivered his remarks, the rebels insolently refused his offer to spare their lives under his terms. They still believed that they could obtain a more favorable deal. They countered his proposal—asking that he allow the insurgents and their families safe passage to leave Jerusalem and settle in the desert without punishment. This was a stunning counter-offer. Titus felt as though he had already provided fair terms under the circumstances, but the revolutionaries now made demands as if they were in a position of strength. They were a broken fighting force; their city was partially in ruins; and their people were starving to death. Titus held all of the leverage, and the combatants had virtually none. Exasperated and incensed, Titus immediately rejected their proposal, and he announced in anger that he would not permit any Jewish desertions from Jerusalem or offer any further terms. Rather, the rebels needed to prepare for a final battle within the city where he promised they would all lose their lives. Then he handed down commands to his subordinates to begin razing the rest of Jerusalem to the ground beginning the following day.[7]

From the Jews' perspective, the interaction with Titus could not have gone worse, but the Roman rank and file was probably pretty pleased with the result. They would be able to plunder the rest of Jerusalem, exact their vengeance on the Jewish people and enjoy the revelry of brutally sacking a city. Sometime the next day, the legionaries began fulfilling their destructive orders. They set fire to Jerusalem's records office, citadel, council chamber and Jerusalem's Ophel district, which rests between the City of David and the Temple Mount. The flames quickly spread and engulfed a host of buildings—consuming them and their contents, including the decaying corpses of those who had previously died from hunger.[8]

Others within Jerusalem sued for peace, and despite his prior proclamations, Titus gave them an audience. Yet he would not relent to their countless counter-proposals even from noble petitioners. When leading Jews and relatives of King Izates—who had fought alongside the insurgents—of the nearby kingdom of Adiabene begged for Titus' forgiveness, he declined. Instead, he collected the members of the royal family and shipped them to Rome where they served as hostages to ensure Adiabene's good behavior.[9]

As this was underway, the revolutionaries sought a defensible refuge within Jerusalem to make another stand, and they quickly settled on one: Herod the Great's former palace. A number of them subsequently dashed for the opulent and fortified location. Once they arrived, they killed 8,400 innocent Jews who had huddled there, found some meager provisions and drove out the small number of Romans who were in or near the building. In the process, they seized two Romans—an infantryman and a cavalryman—and made them the targets of their frustration and rage. The rebels slew the infantryman and drug his dead body around the city in a vile display. The revolutionaries planned to behead the cavalryman in view of his comrades, but before they could sever his skull, the horseman slipped his restraints and dashed for the Roman lines where he arrived safely. However, his capture was considered shameful. As such, Titus stripped him of his rank and discharged him from the legions. His unforgiving point was clear: Romans do not suffer to be captured alive.[10]

On the next day, the Romans swept through a different portion of Jerusalem—the Lower City—forcing the combatants there to flee, but there was practically nothing for the legionaries to plunder after the insurgents left. This disappointed the soldiers who then torched much of the Lower City. John and Simon's remaining men sought to elude the Romans, but they were running out of places of refuge. They clashed with the legionaries who easily overpowered many of them—leading to their deaths or capture. Meanwhile, other rebels slaughtered their countrymen whom they believed were attempting to desert the city.[11]

Some other revolutionaries concocted a plan that they thought would guarantee their survival. They quietly slunk into Jerusalem's sewers—thinking that they could remain there undetected until the Romans left the soon-to-be ruined city. While there, they certainly grappled with the disgusting realities of ancient sewers as rats, feces and fungi surrounded them. Regardless of the health hazards, they continued defying Rome and engaged in theft and arson—just like the Romans—but their safety was fleeting. Titus and his soldiers would eventually locate them, but for the time being, the legionaries had larger prizes in mind—particularly capturing the Upper City, where Herod's Palace stood.[12]

The Upper City was still largely unsecured by the Romans, and approaching it was not especially easy. As a result, Titus reluctantly acknowledged that his troops needed to build ramps to seize the Upper City without unnecessarily risking many Roman lives. Given this reality, Titus gave orders in late August 70 CE to his legions to begin the process of building earthworks, which was exceedingly difficult. Nevertheless, they started the laborious endeavor as the ramps slowly inched higher and closer to their targets. Josephus provided their location: The legions worked to raise ramps on the city's western edge, near Herod's Palace, as auxiliary troops constructed ramps on the eastern side of the Upper City.[13]

Around this same time, one of the rebel factions—the Idumeans—pondered submitting to Titus, and their leader dispatched envoys to the Roman to secure their surrender. While Titus had vowed to slaughter all revolutionaries, he entertained the Idumeans' pleas. He agreed to spare their lives because he believed that it would further fracture and weaken the rebel forces, which might induce the remainder to capitulate too. Armed with Titus' assurances, the emissaries started their trek back, but Simon learned of their duplicity. Upon their return, he ordered their execution and imprisoned the remaining Idumean leadership. He would not permit them to abandon his foolhardy enterprise no matter how futile it was.[14]

Despite this setback and Titus' pledge to massacre those in Jerusalem, the commander was filled with compassion for the noncombatants and began accepting deserters. He pardoned and released around 40,000 innocent bystanders, but he had barbaric plans for the others. He maintained custody of the fleeing insurgents and their wives and children. Titus planned to sell many of them into slavery, execute others and use a host of them in his coming triumph through Rome.[15]

As Titus accepted refugees and combatants, he also received a bounty of wealth. A priest named Jesus and a Temple treasurer called Phineas received guarantees from Titus that they would be pardoned if they delivered some of Jerusalem's most prized possessions to the Romans. They stayed true to their agreement, and the two Jews handed over many sacred objects. Jesus surrendered "from the wall of the sanctuary two lampstands similar to those deposited in the sanctuary, along with tables, bowls, and platters, all of solid gold and very massive; he further delivered up the veils, the high-priests' vestments, including the precious stones, and many other articles used in public worship," according to Josephus. Meanwhile, Phineas produced "tunics and girdles worn by the priests, an abundance of purple and scarlet kept for necessary repairs to the veil of the Temple, along with a mass of cinnamon and cassia and a multitude of other spices, which they mixed and burnt daily as incense to God." He "also handed over many more of the treasures and a good number of temple ornaments," Josephus reported. This was an immense windfall, but it hardly represented the totality of the priceless goods seized from Jerusalem.[16]

Eighteen days after construction began—sometime in September of 70 CE—the Romans finished their ramps, and they began carting the siege engines up them. This spectacle caused many insurgents to concede their posts on the walls and seek cover elsewhere. Others, however, stood safely ensconced in the nearby towers—Phasael, Hippicus and Mariamme—that appeared impregnable. Very quickly, the legionaries started battering the walls in the weakest sections and toppled a portion protecting the western Upper City—causing further fear among the Jewish combatants. The remaining defenders on the walls retreated in disorder, and even those quartered in the imposing towers, which loomed over Herod's Palace, fled their posts. This was an imprudent decision; they were among the strongest defenses in Jerusalem. Nevertheless, without any bloodshed, the Romans took the wall, these towers and the palace as well.[17]

Shortly thereafter, these revolutionaries decided to try to escape through the Roman walls, but their fighting force and spirit was spent. With little effort, the Romans routed them and secured the Upper City and its environs. The Romans posted their standards in the district, congratulated one another for their victory and cheered in relief. Jerusalem was now practically theirs, and they flooded into the streets, put homes to the torch and methodically and unrepentantly killed every Jew they saw.[18]

The fires spread throughout the holy city, and Titus decided to enter the newly captured districts and inspect the fallen Jewish capital. He admired the three mighty towers that the Jews had deserted. "We have certainly had God [as] our assistant in this war: and it was no other than God who ejected the Jews out of these fortifications. For what could the hands of men, or any machines, do towards overthrowing these towers?" he rhetorically asked. Then he ordered the legionaries to preserve them as a testament of their strength and his victory, but he demanded that nearly all of Jerusalem's other walls, defenses and the city itself be reduced to rubble. Today, little remains other than the so-called Western Wall, which Jewish and Christian pilgrims visit en-mass every year. Titus' legionaries complied with his destructive directive and began to topple much of the city and burn the rest. They also entered the sewers to root out the remaining resistance, but what they found was part Jewish death trap and part tomb. The legionaries swept through the dank sewers and slaughtered their opposition, but many of the insurgents had already died of hunger, disease or suicide. The Romans found 2,000 bodies rotting below. During the course of the mopping up operations, the Romans captured Simon and John. Both were reserved for Titus' eventual triumph through Rome.[19]

While the legionaries destroyed Jerusalem, they also continued killing many

The Western Wall, Jerusalem, 2019.

Jews indiscriminately, but they—along with Titus—began growing weary of the massive slaughter. In time, the Roman commander gave orders to only kill those still under arms and actively resisting Rome. All others, he instructed, should be captured alive. At some point, Josephus conferred with Titus and begged him to spare his family from death and slavery, and the Roman commander accommodated his requests. Not only did he show them mercy, but he—on more than one occasion—offered Josephus a generous share of Jerusalem's spoils. Josephus claimed that he did not take anything of intrinsic value, but he asked for Titus to pardon more of his intimates—some 240 friends and acquaintances in total. Titus again acquiesced. Of course, a number of Romans continued murdering and enslaving many Jews, but a host of others were seized and restrained until one of Titus' trusted deputies—Fronto—could judge them.

Fronto investigated the captives and quickly passed judgment. Many of those found to be involved in terrorism or rebellion against Rome were quickly executed, except for the healthiest of them. They were reserved for Titus' triumph in Rome. Of the remaining noncombatants over the age of 17, the Romans shipped them to Egypt for hard labor—though some probably made it to Rome to live in servitude—or to serve as deadly entertainment in arenas across the empire. The legionaries sold those under the age of 17 into slavery. Some of these Jews—around 11,000—escaped this terrible fate because they died of starvation, thanks to exceptionally cruel Roman jailers who refused to feed them.[20]

After a nearly five-month-long siege, Titus was the undisputed master of Jerusalem, which he had mostly destroyed. Only part of a wall and the three towers—Phasael, Hippicus and Mariamme—remained standing. The Romans even razed the suburban regions of Jerusalem. In the end, there was little of Jerusalem's unrivaled beauty remaining. Ruins and death replaced it. The Romans captured nearly 100,000 prisoners and around 1.1 million Jews died in the siege, according to Josephus, although Tacitus placed the number of deaths to no more than 600,000. Whatever the astronomical number, the majority of them likely perished from disease or hunger and were innocent bystanders. They had traveled to Jerusalem for the Feast of Unleavened Bread only to find themselves trapped between insurgents and the Roman juggernaut.[21]

Due to Titus' efforts, the Jewish rebellion was largely quelled, but at a terrible cost. Now only relatively minor pockets of resistance remained, which could be handled by more junior officers. Soon enough, Titus would be able to depart for Caesarea Maritima to enjoy peace and the comfort of Berenice and look forward to a splendid triumph in Rome.[22]

XVII

Triumph

> *"It is impossible to give an adequate description of the wealth of spectacle on view in this procession, or of its magnificence in every conceivable display [which was] here on this day exhibited in profusion to demonstrate the reach of the Roman Empire."*
> —Josephus[1]

After concluding the siege of Jerusalem and sacking and razing the holy city, the Jewish War was practically over—save for a few notable holdouts. Mopping up operations were needed to eliminate these rebel enclaves, but they did not rise to the level of requiring Titus' direct involvement. As a result, Titus planned on returning to Rome to support his father with the empire's administration, but he needed to tend to other matters first.

Before departing from Jerusalem, Titus ordered his men to build a large platform in his camp. Once it was, he and his trusted deputies stood atop it, and the Roman general instructed his soldiers to huddle around him. When in place, Titus delivered a speech in which he congratulated his legionaries for their bravery, sacrifices and success. They deserved Rome's gratitude, but there were several Romans whose boundless courage and exploits were conspicuous and merited public recognition.[2]

One of Titus' officers called out these battle-tested troops' names, and one by one, they marched to the stage where Titus personally placed golden crowns upon their heads and gifted them golden necklaces and small symbolic trinkets. He also promoted them to higher ranks and awarded them a larger share of the war's spoils. In time, the ceremony concluded. Then Titus offered prayers for his legionaries and retreated from the platform—all to a thunderous applause—and Titus ordered the sacrifice of a massive number of oxen on various altars. The meat was subsequently distributed among the men who enjoyed days of celebratory festivities.[3]

Titus was still commander of four different legions, but with the Jewish War largely over, they needed new orders. To ensure peace reigned in the area and at Vespasian's direction, Titus ordered the 10th Legion to remain in Jerusalem and serve as a local garrison. He sent the 12th Legion to Melitene—modern-day Malatya, Türkiye—and he temporarily kept the 5th and 15th Legions attached to himself. With these matters settled, the 10th Legion began its garrison duty, and the 12th marched for Metilene. Meanwhile, Titus and his remaining soldiers headed to Caesarea Maritima to re-provision and rest.⁴

As much as Titus wished to return to Rome as soon as possible, he had to wait. It was fall by now, and it was simply too dangerous to risk a sea voyage on the tempestuous Mediterranean. Thankfully, Titus' assistance in Rome was not immediately needed. Around the same time, Vespasian departed from Alexandra, Egypt to Greece and then the Italian peninsula where the locals received him with great praise and excitement. Once he settled into Rome likely in September or October 70 CE, Vespasian consolidated his position of power, began issuing edicts, presided over the sprawling empire and gave orders to stamp out various smaller-scale conflicts. Fortunately, he had the steady and competent counsel of Mucianus on which to rely, but he probably needed someone in the East for a special purpose. As has been previously hypothesized, Vespasian may have ordered Titus to remain behind—at least in part—to ease the Parthians' concerns that Rome was preparing to clash with them. Vespasian and Titus wanted to secure the Roman/Parthian border but do not seem to have wanted war with the Parthians, which would have been a time-consuming and costly enterprise.⁵

With Rome in good hands, major operations in Jerusalem at a close and being given only one major diplomatic mission, Titus was left with substantial time on his hands. After depositing a vast amount of spoils and prisoners in Caesarea Maritima for their ultimate voyage to Rome for the coming triumph, Titus set out on a tour of nearby cities—exhibiting Rome's might and hosting games for the locals and his soldiers. His first stop after Caesarea Maritima was Caesarea Philippi where Titus likely planned to stay at Agrippa's ostentatious palace, spend more time with Berenice and host barbaric spectacles involving some of the Jewish prisoners of war.

In the local amphitheater, game organizers forced these Jews to spar with one another to the death or fight wild beasts that easily mauled the captives. While this rightly seems like a repugnant spectacle to modern eyes, the ancient Romans considered this blood-sport great leisurely fun to watch. In fact, the Jews' desperate fight for survival and painful cries echoing throughout the packed stadium must have elicited cheers from the spectators.⁶

Titus stayed in Caesarea Philippi for an extended period of time and he, his troops and the locals reveled in the macabre entertainment, but in time, Titus decided to return to Caesarea Maritima. Why he returned at this juncture is not entirely clear other than to oversee preparations for his eventual return to Rome and visit the rebel leader Simon who had been recently transported to Caesarea Maritima. Whatever Titus' justifications, more entertainment awaited him.⁷

Titus' arrival coincided with his brother Domitian's birthday—October 24—and Titus hosted lavish games and spectacles of death in his younger sibling's honor. In the local arena, a host of Jewish prisoners of war were fed to hungry carnivores as entertainment. The Romans forced others to engage in staged battles and fight to the death before a captivated audience. Meanwhile, the Romans simply burned other

Jews alive. All told, around 2,500 Jews needlessly perished in celebration of Domitian's birthday, but the Roman legionaries were filled with hate and demanded for more Jewish suffering.[8]

Not willing to remain in one location for long, Titus and his retinue set out for Berytus. Upon arriving, to celebrate his father's birthday—November 17—this time, Titus hosted additional games and contests. They left a terrible number of Jews dead and cost a considerable sum, which was doubtless bankrolled by the spoils captured at Jerusalem. After honoring his father in Berytus, Titus and his followers packed up their belongings and began a tour of various Syrian cities where he produced more spectacles for the locals as they watched countless Jews die.[9]

En route to Zeugma, which is in the modern-day Gaziantep Province, Türkiye, Titus passed through Antioch where throngs of adoring people watched his approach, waved at the emperor's son and congratulated him for his victories. They also had a request of him, which they evidently presumed he would approve. The local population bore animosity toward the Jews, and they asked Titus to expel all of them from Antioch. Interestingly for a man who had been treating Jewish captives as disposable objects of entertainment, Titus ignored the Antiochenes' requests and continued his trek. They were disappointed but had not resigned hope that he would eventually bow to their wills.[10]

From Antioch, Titus reached Zeugma where special guests awaited him. Ambassadors from King Vologases of the Parthian Empire requested an audience with Titus who granted it. In a respectful manner, the emissaries entered the meeting hall and congratulated the Roman. The Parthians and Romans had long maintained a bitter rivalry, which sometimes turned violent. This was most notable during triumvir Marcus Licinius Crassus' disastrous invasion of Parthia. In 53 BCE, they embarrassed him and the Romans at the Battle of Carrhae and killed or captured tens of thousands of Romans and allies. Spats between the superpowers continued, but Vologases might have had reason to show deference to Titus.

The Roman commander had thousands of battle-hardened men at his disposal and was the son of Rome's new emperor. Parthia was Rome's only serious challenger, and Vologases decided it wise to determine Rome's eastern intentions and ingratiate himself with Titus—something that the Roman evidently appreciated. Titus understood this and wanted to calm the Parthians' nerves. In fact, Titus held a banquet for the Parthians who gifted Titus a golden crown and probably treated them to games featuring condemned Jewish prisoners. This was not the only Parthian attempt to court the Flavians. Vologases had earlier offered Vespasian 40,000 Parthian cavalry—something Vespasian appreciated but declined since it was unnecessary. Perhaps after Titus assured the Parthians that the Romans had no desire to spark a conflict with them, they happily went on their way.[11]

Before long, Titus tired of Zeugma, and he and his cortege returned to Antioch, where the locals were eager to speak with Titus again. Upon his arrival, the city's leading men summoned Titus to the town theater where many of Antioch's citizens had congregated. It seems that Titus had little desire to entertain the Antiochenes' pending requests, but being a public servant, he acquiesced and marched into the theater.[12]

With Titus now before the city's citizens, they once more urged him to banish the Jews from Antioch—leaving only pagan gentiles to live there—but Titus flatly rejected the Antiochenes' petitions. The Jews in question were innocent first of all, Titus must have noted, and where would they go if he were to exile them? "But their own country to which, as Jews, they [would otherwise] be banished, has been destroyed, and no other place [will] now receive them," Titus explained to the Antiochenes.[13]

Titus demonstrated some compassion for the Jewish people who had played no part in the recent hostilities, and he seemed to welcome them to remain in the vast Roman Empire. The Antiochenes realized that they could not persuade Titus to reverse his decision. So they adopted a new tactic. They asked the commander to authorize the removal of bronze tablets from within the city that outlined the Jews' rights and liberties. With their removal, the Antiochenes averred that they could at least treat the Jews as second-class citizens, but to the Antiochenes' dismay, Titus again rebuffed them. The Jewish people would be permitted to remain in Antioch as long as they wished and enjoy the rights they held before the Jewish War.[14]

After his interaction with the Antiochenes, it seems that Titus was eager to leave Antioch, especially with winter winding down. Without demur, he quit Antioch and marched southward with his legions toward Egypt where he would eventually depart for Rome. On his way, he stopped by Jerusalem's ruins, visited with the 10th Legion that garrisoned the region and inspected the city's remains. He saw what appeared to be a cataclysmic scene, but it was not caused by a natural disaster. The legions had destroyed Jerusalem—leaving piles of fractured stone and charred wood where grand buildings, walls and homes once stood. The scars from the siege were ubiquitous and unmistakable, and the legionaries were still discovering riches among the ruins as they pilfered through the rubble. Rather than admiring the legions' handiwork in dismantling Jerusalem, he lamented the formerly magnificent holy city's fate. As he had done before, he lambasted the rebels for forcing his hand and repeatedly spurning his offers to spare Jerusalem.[15]

Regretful or not, the deed was done and Titus had been successful. For his endeavors and his father's, they would soon enjoy a triumph through Rome. With the winter nearly passed, Titus, his legions, Jerusalem's most impressive loot and hundreds of prisoners traveled through the desert toward their destination. They reached Egypt in rapid time. When in Memphis, Titus participated in a ritual dedicated to Apis, an Egyptian bull cult, and wore a diadem during it. This shocked some onlookers who believed that Titus was acting beyond his station. Be that as it may, afterward Titus journeyed to the port of Alexandra and made the final preparations to sail toward Rome with his spoils. First, he thanked the two legions for their dedication and service, and then he gave them orders to march to different parts of the empire to guard against revolts and barbarian incursions.[16]

He sent the 5th Legion to Moesia and the 15th Legion to Pannonia. After receiving their orders, the legions advanced to their respective destinations, and Titus focused his energies on journeying to Rome. He organized a flotilla to transport the immense riches he had obtained from Jerusalem and around 700 prisoners reserved for the triumph, including John and Simon. While he could have brought many more to Rome, the legionaries chose only the best looking and most physically fit, although they were still almost certainly emaciated from the extended siege. That aside, Titus, his guard, soldiers marked for the triumph, their spoils and even Titus' friend Josephus crowded onto warships to set sail for Rome and a celebratory triumph.[17]

Soon enough, Titus' flotilla reached port, and he made his way to the eternal city where—sometime around June 71 CE—its citizens greeted him and treated him as a conquering hero. Among those who rushed to welcome Titus back to Rome was his father—Emperor Vespasian. The two had not seen one another since they had parted ways in Egypt during the Year of Four Emperors, and while there are scarcely any details of their reunion, it must have been a joyous occasion. When Titus glimpsed Vespasian, he said, "I am here, father. I am here." Then they surely embraced one another and offered the other their congratulations. Titus' younger brother Domitian was likely also at Vespasian's side, and the scene of the trio together and safe elated the Roman audience.[18]

The Romans soon had something else to celebrate too. The Senate had approved two triumphs—one for Vespasian and another for Titus. The double-honor humbled the Flavians. While many men would have eagerly accepted the honor, a few days after Titus arrived in Rome, the imperial household decided that one shared triumph would be more than enough, especially considering the incredible cost of hosting a triumph. Thus Vespasian gave word to prepare for a single triumph shared between father and son. This may have been an early sign that Vespasian planned for Titus to succeed him, but the singular triumph doubtless disappointed some Romans who yearned for the carnival-like atmosphere of numerous triumphs. Nevertheless, the procession would not disappoint them, and after some discussion, the Flavians and the event's organizers settled on a date for the parade.[19]

The night before the triumph, Titus' soldiers who had been earmarked for the triumph congregated on the Campus Martius—or Field of Mars—just beyond the city's *pomerium*. They organized themselves into their respective companies and prepared their formal military uniforms. They polished their shields, swords, spears and breastplates, and for those lucky enough to ride their horse in the coming triumph, they ensured that their steeds were brushed and spotless.[20]

Similar to the army, Vespasian and Titus spent the night on the Campus Martius—as was tradition—with their troops, but their accommodations were much more luxurious. Just before dawn, the Flavians made their final preparations for the triumph. According to Josephus, they donned crowns of laurel leaves and purple robes known as the *toga picta*. However, if they were clothed in the rest of the traditional triumphal dress, then they also wore a flowered tunic called the *tunica palmata*. In addition to this, assistants might have painted the bodies—or at least the faces—of both Vespasian and Titus bright red as homage to the god Jupiter.[21]

Before the triumph began, Vespasian and Titus walked to a nearby platform topped with ivory thrones where they united with some of the city's chief officials, and they took their resplendent seats. As this was underway, the victorious legionaries advanced to their position and quickly reached their destination and awaited direction. Vespasian subsequently rose from his throne and offered prayers. Afterward, Titus did the same. Then Vespasian addressed the soldiers in a glowing speech, and the Flavians dismissed the horde of legionaries to enjoy breakfast and make sacrifices to the gods before they entered Rome in triumph.[22]

With these formalities complete, the Flavians and the other triumphal participants were ready for the celebratory procession to commence. Josephus recorded an extended narrative about the triumph, but many details are absent. Even so, enough is known from other triumphs and the relief found on the surviving Arch of Titus (completed in late 81 CE) to draw some likely conclusions. If Vespasian and Titus largely adhered to the triumphal script followed by many other Roman triumphants, then politicians, musicians, spoils and the troops were all organized meticulously so that they would enter Rome at a specific time and in a particular order.

Rome was gripped with excitement for the parade, and they flooded the procession route—ensuring that the normally large thoroughfare was nearly clogged with eager Romans hoping to see the wondrous events. Not a single seat was available; only standing room remained. To catch a better glimpse of the spectacle, some Romans lined the roofs of buildings, which rose numerous stories. Waiting in excited anticipation, the triumph began. Leading the celebratory cavalcade were Rome's magistrates and senators who entered the city wearing their finest attire and waved to the cheering Romans as they passed by.[23]

Next a troop of trumpeters followed and marched in unison, while blowing their instruments to announce the next sight: the war's spoils. Transported on carriages and floats, the Romans witnessed Jerusalem's true wealth. Gold, silver, ivory and bejeweled cups, bowls, crowns, tools and decorations adorned the wagons for all of Rome to see. They also viewed Jerusalem's artwork, fine fabrics, tapestries and some of the Jews' most sacred Temple objects. In fact, the Arch of Titus depicts Roman soldiers carrying the massive golden Menorah in the triumph. Josephus mentioned that within the spoils were also a golden table and lamp stand. It seems probable that the Temple's other hallowed possessions surrendered by Jesus and Phineas likewise made an appearance. If so, the Romans looked on at them as well. The entire scene demonstrated Jerusalem's once-prodigious wealth and must have elicited audible gasps and applause from the impressed audience. It is conceivable that this was exhibited to do more than impress. Since the Jewish religion did not center around a godly statue, nor were there images of their God in the Temple, the Romans seem to have presented these sacred objects as representatives of the

Jewish religion and to promote the Roman belief that the pagans had conquered the monotheistic religion.[24]

Within this section of the triumph were also artistic depictions of critical war scenes, and their presentations were awe-inspiring. These were housed on wheeled floats that reached up to four stories high. Some of them were decorated with gold-bordered curtains, and the carriages were overlaid with gold and had ivory affixed to them. Atop the floats were images of the Galilean and Judaean countrysides, climactic war scenes, cities falling to the Romans, the demolition of sacked cities and every terrible humiliation the Jews endured. Trailing the moving floats were ships being carted along, which may have represented the Roman navy's meager role in the war.[25]

As the carts full of riches, floats depicting the rebels' defeat and ships slowly lumbered by the Roman spectators, they witnessed a company of flute players loudly sounding their instruments as they marched past the Romans. Then they saw beasts specially prepared for triumphal sacrifices, and priests and their youthful assistants—known as *camilli*—accompanied them.[26]

Behind these participants were numerous groups of exotic animals that the Romans had captured during the Jewish War and possibly also in Syria and Egypt. Some were nudged along by their handlers who were dressed in uniforms with gold threading. Other animals were almost certainly too dangerous to be led around on a leash. They remained in cages and pulled on wagons. Josephus provided no detail over what beasts the Romans produced for the triumph, but lions, bears, camels, ostriches, antelope, leopards, cattle and perhaps even elephants could have conceivably made an appearance to the Romans' excitement.[27]

Next the Romans beheld examples of the Jewish combatants' weapons and insignia, and then the insurgents themselves. Dressed in fine garments, guards prodded Simon who had a noose around his neck and John along before the throngs of Romans who booed and sneered at the vanquished and restrained rebel leaders, but they were not alone. Some 700 defeated Jewish revolutionaries, likely in shackles, trailed them and received the audience's abuse. As the Jews marched onward, they understood that they were either approaching their doom or a life of torture.[28]

After the humbled Jews moped by, the Romans carried tokens of gratitude and appreciation for their allies, including client-kingdoms, who aided them in their quest to quell the Jewish revolt. Then the emperor's lictors marched forward while carrying laurel-adorned fasces, which were bundles of sticks denoting the emperor's authority. Finally, the Romans caught glimpses of the triumphants themselves. Standing proudly erect on a chariot drawn by four horses and grasping a scepter and a laurel bough, Vespasian rode by his adoring people. Likewise, Titus followed in his own chariot and received the people's admiration—although Orosius claimed Vespasian and Titus rode in the same chariot—and Domitian came next riding a horse.[29]

Behind Vespasian, Titus and Domitian were the bulk of the troops brought to

Rome for the triumph. Dressed in their finest armor, they advanced in unison while carrying their spears, which were decorated with laurel, and they sang songs praising the gods and poked fun at their commanders.[30]

The entire triumphal procession snaked along Rome's Via Sacra and concluded on the Capitoline Hill where the celebration paused momentarily. Roman public servants then escorted Simon to the nearby Mamertine Prison where executioners ingloriously strangled him to death. Cassius Dio asserted that the Romans executed no other prisoners in connection to this triumph. Vespasian and Titus spared John and the 700 captives for whatever reason, but they almost certainly ended up enslaved. Once Simon had met his demise, the Romans erupted into roaring cheers. Then they were free to finalize the triumphal sacrifices, and Vespasian and Titus surrendered their crowns of laurel to the god Jupiter. The entire city subsequently enjoyed a grand feast in which they engaged in gluttony and revelry. With this underway, the royal family and their deputies retired to a more secluded quarters to celebrate in private with their intimates.[31]

To commemorate the peace that mostly reigned in the empire—save for some remaining trouble spots—Vespasian ordered the construction of the *Templum Pacis*, or Temple of Peace. Flush with prodigious wealth from Jerusalem, Vespasian apparently spared no expense, and within a short period of time, engineers completed the opulent temple, which operated as a kind of art museum. Within it were some of the Mediterranean world's most renowned paintings and sculptures, which had been gathered from across the empire. Vespasian also displayed certain spoils from the Jewish War, including sacred gold ornaments and purple curtains from the holy Temple in Jerusalem. By 75 CE, the *Templum Pacis* became a world-class destination for art lovers across the empire, and the visitors had Vespasian and Titus to thank for it.[32]

Roman Forum, Rome, 2021.

Eventually, the festivities following Titus' victorious return subsided, and the Romans eased back into their normal routines. Even so, more celebratory events transpired. Orosius asserted that Vespasian and Titus ordered the closure of the Temple of Janus' gates, which was an important gesture. The temple was dedicated to a two-faced deity who was the god of various matters, including beginnings, transitions and endings, and his temple rested in the Roman Forum. Its gates provided symbolism that the Romans keenly understood. If the gates were open, then Rome was at war, and if they were closed, then Rome was at peace. To announce Rome's supposed universal peace, Vespasian and Titus reportedly barred the gates for only the sixth time in Rome's long history, and it must have been done to great excitement. As the celebrations and symbolic exercises died down, Titus gradually re-acclimated to a life outside of the army, which was all that he had known for some time. However, that likely suited him, but very quickly Vespasian charged his son with helping him manage the empire.[33]

XVIII

CAESAR

> "When Titus found fault with [his father] for contriving a tax upon public conveniences, [Vespasian] held a piece of money from the first payment to his son's nose, asking whether its odour was offensive to him. When Titus said 'No,' he replied, 'Yet it comes from urine.'"
> —Suetonius[1]

AFTER CELEBRATING AN EXTRAVAGANT TRIUMPH through Rome, Vespasian welcomed Titus to serve as his primary ruling partner, and as early as 69 CE, Titus received the title of Caesar—a glorious promotion for the man, which eventually led to increased responsibilities. The empire was enormous, filled with endless toils, and as the Year of the Four Emperors confirmed, potential rival claimants to the throne lurked in every corner. Put simply, Vespasian needed the help of a trusted ally, and there was no one better than his able and experienced son. Titus of course accepted Vespasian's offer and quickly shifted from military to civil duties. Thereupon, he worked as Vespasian's protector, proxy and right hand.[2]

Likely by no later than 71 CE, Vespasian began to bestow on Titus many of the same titles and powers that he enjoyed as emperor. Titus received *tribunicia potestas,* or tribunician powers. These permitted Titus to convene the Senate and provided him veto power over practically any senatorial, judicial or administrative decision. It seems that he additionally enjoyed proconsular imperium—giving him vast control over the empire's armies. These newfound powers and titles went far beyond sharing a triumph with Vespasian. It unmistakably marked Titus as Vespasian's chosen successor, but it is possible that Vespasian intended for Domitian to succeed Titus, given that the latter had no male offspring to serve as his heir. Regardless of this, while Vespasian and Titus shared some of the same formal authorities, Vespasian was clearly the one in charge. Nevertheless, this gave Titus the ability to assist in the empire's administration. Titus read Vespasian's speeches in the Senate, wrote and issued imperial edicts and probably served as Vespasian's secretary and chief of staff.[3]

Acting as his partner, Titus saw firsthand how Vespasian ruled. While he earned a reputation for being a laudable, even-tempered emperor, he was not without criticism. Vespasian openly accepted bribes. For the right price, he acquitted accused criminals and sold public offices to the highest bidder. He exploited his position to purchase goods at a discounted price, only to resell them for a significant profit. He also increased taxes—sometimes even doubling the tribute provinces were required to produce—but some of his revenue-raising efforts might have been necessary. Even after seizing Jerusalem's spoils, the Roman empire was in dire financial straits thanks to Nero's inept imperial tenure, the Year of Four Emperors and the Jewish War, and Vespasian knew this. Before the Senate, he disclosed that Rome needed a mind-blowing sum to meet all of its obligations that equaled many years' worth of tax revenue.

Perhaps to meet some of the state's commitments, Vespasian debased the denarius—to as low as about 80 percent silver to make the empire's wealth stretch a little further—according to some scholars. However, there is modern debate over whether Vespasian is to blame for this debasement or if he simply maintained an already diminished denarius standard that he inherited from Otho and Vitellius. Either way, ancient debasements generally weighed economies down, and it seems that Vespasian also ramped up minting—flooding the economy with *denarii*—until Rome's obligations were met.[4]

Despite being denounced for some of the aforementioned activities, Vespasian could be forgiving and generous, and he remained true to his simple roots. He rejected much of the indulgence associated with men like Nero and was a conscientious ruler. According to Suetonius, he never condemned an innocent person and loathed executions. He provided financial aid to impoverished ex-public-servants, provided a salary for numerous teachers and even funded artists. He also bankrolled the restoration of public works in cities across the empire that had fallen into disrepair or been destroyed, including Rome's Temple of Jupiter. He additionally began construction of the one structure that has become synonymous with ancient Rome.[5]

Sometime in the early 70s CE after Titus had returned to Rome, the Flavians settled on erecting the empire's largest amphitheater: the Colosseum, although it was not called that at the time. Ancient Romans likely referred to it as the *amphitheatrum*. It only became known as the Colosseum in the Middle Ages. Once completed, officials would be able to host riveting games there for the people's entertainment. While it would be a costly enterprise to complete, the Romans had ample resources to raise a massive structure. With a glut of slaves and wealth flowing in from Jerusalem and large, many un-redeveloped districts in Rome, Vespasian and Titus gave engineers and architects orders to build an amphitheater for the people. This would be an enduring monument to the Flavians' victories over the Jews, as well as a reminder of the countless gladiators, criminals and Christians who eventually died there.[6]

In order to create the Flavian amphitheater, it is probable that Vespasian and Titus recruited the best engineers and architects the empire had to offer. They asked them to produce meticulous plans to bring their concept to fruition: a stone amphitheater that would hold tens of thousands of cheering Romans and offer them the opportunity to witness various spectacles of death. The ancient authors did not record the name of the amphitheater's primary architect, but an ecclesiastical tradition states that it was a Christian—named Gaudentius who was ultimately executed in the arena. If there is any truth to this legend, then it represents a cruel irony—a Christian built a building that became the setting for an untold number of Christian executions, including his own, but the legend of Gaudentius is highly suspect and the evidence supporting this claim seems dubious at best.[7]

This aside, games and amphitheaters were not new concepts. Within Rome was the Circus Maximus, which was an ideal stadium for horse races, but the Romans also viewed gladiatorial bouts and exhibitions of animal hunts there too. The problem was that the Circus Maximus' shape was not conducive for these spectacles; the Circus was elongated, and a spina dividing the horse track blocked the audience's views.

Smaller, elliptical-shaped amphitheaters were better suited for spectacles that became associated with the Colosseum, but it was not the first such amphitheater. They had existed in one form or another for hundreds of years throughout Rome by this point, and the masses loved them. The advent of amphitheaters gave the Romans alternative places to watch various sporting events, but it came with danger. Early amphitheaters were built of wood, and they were prone to conflagrations and sudden collapse. In one terrible accident in Fidenae, an amphitheater caved in and killed tens of thousands of audience members. Eventually, the Romans began raising stone amphitheaters that spanned the Republic's realm.

Vespasian and Titus fully understood that the Romans loved blood sports but needed a safe, permanent venue to watch them. With this in mind, the Flavians surveyed locations within the city of Rome and found a nearly perfect spot. They settled on using part of the grounds that Nero had once annexed for his opulent estate following the Great Fire of Rome. There was a notable problem, though. They wanted to erect a stone amphitheater where Nero had created an artificial lake.

The decision to build here was an unmistakable public relations success. Not only were the Flavians planning on giving Rome an amphitheater, but they were building it on land Nero had appropriated from his people. So in a way, Vespasian and Titus were returning the Romans' property back to them, which was an incredibly popular decision. With this location in mind, the Flavians could begin their project in earnest, but nothing about this construction was easy.

Before laborers who were probably made up of thousands of slaves—presumably including many Jewish slaves—as well as skilled professionals could break ground, they needed to drain Nero's lake. There is no record of how they accomplished this feat, but sometime in the early 70s CE, they likely redirected the line that fed the body of water. Then they either let nature dry the area, created channels to direct the water elsewhere or they used an ancient siphon to remove it. In whatever manner they accomplished it, they dried Nero's lake in time, and could begin the next step in the process.

Slaves and construction workers then began digging into the ground so that they could lay the foundation in due time. Research at this location has shown that excavators removed alluvium as well as cut into tough bedrock to make way for the amphitheater's base. The work was backbreaking. In fact, a recent estimate suggests that digging into the would-be foundations may have taken a year to complete—even with thousands of slaves working in unison—and resulted in the removal of perhaps 30,000 tons of debris. After that time passed and they had concluded this phase of the project, they were able to install drainage channels and lay the amphitheater's sturdy foundations, which partly consisted of *opus caementicium* or Roman concrete.[8]

This is no ordinary concrete. Modern concrete can begin to crumble and disintegrate in a matter of decades, but Roman concrete has proven to be exceptionally durable even in challenging environmental conditions. Most surprising is that ancient Roman concrete can essentially repair itself. For years, this befuddled scientists who proffered different theories over why 2,000-year-old concrete is far superior to what modern construction workers use today. For some time, they believed it had to do with volcanic ash, which was one ingredient in the concrete mix, but recent studies have shown that it may be the lime clasts found in the mixture. How it works is fascinating and ingenious. When Roman concrete cracks and water seeps into the fissures, the water dissolves the lime clasts, which then recrystallizes and re-seals the cracks and pores—essentially healing the structures.[9]

While the foundations were dug and filled with concrete and stone, laborers and slaves were busy collecting the material needed to piece together the amphitheater, which was made primarily of volcanic tuff, marble, brick, concrete and travertine, which is a kind of limestone. Workers quarried it in the nearby city of Tivoli and then transported the stones—some weighing many tons—to Rome, which was around 20 miles away. Other building supplies were closer. Vespasian and Titus may have given construction managers permission to cannibalize much of the remains of Nero's *domus aurea* in order to build the amphitheater. With this authorization, workers picked it apart and moved the pieces near the construction project.

It seems that the Romans did not simply quarry stones haphazardly and pile them up without any order in Rome. Rather they were highly organized and exact. They marked the stones with inscriptions denoting where each one belonged in the construction plan and stored them accordingly. This demonstrates astoundingly meticulous planning, considering that an estimated 3.5 million cubic feet of travertine was used in the amphitheater's construction, and that does not include the other materials used.[10]

With the foundations dried and laid and materials prepared, laborers started piecing together the structure that modern tourists recognize today. Scaffolding and rudimentary cranes helped the workers move massive stones and put them into position. Some of the stones and bricks were subsequently bonded together using mortar, but others relied on dowels and clamps to hold them in place. It has been estimated that the Romans used around 300 tons of iron clamps in the amphitheater's construction, although all that remains of them today are pock marks where they once were before medieval Italians plundered them.[11]

Vespasian and Titus must have excitedly watched the *amphitheatrum's* construction progress, but they also kept a close eye on matters in the East. While they had pacified the overwhelming majority of Galilee and Judaea, there were still some who defied Rome. A handful of tenacious rebel bands obstinately opposed Rome and remained ensconced behind the fortresses of Machaerus, Herodium and Masada. Hoping to quickly stamp out the Jewish rebellion's embers, Vespasian—maybe along with Titus' approval—appointed Lucilius Bassus to serve in Judaea as a legate, and he quickly reached his posting, took over command of the troops stationed there and began the process of eliminating the remaining resistance.[12]

Sometime around 71 CE, Bassus turned his attention to Herodium—a fortress originally built by Herod the Great that stood around 10 miles south of Jerusalem. However, Josephus offered no details of Bassus' operations to take Herodium. This may imply that the Romans secured it painlessly and without the use of arms. Facing Rome's battle-hardened legionaries and after receiving favorable terms from Bassus, the rebels could have simply recognized their hopeless situation and handed the fortress over to the Romans, which left only two holdouts—Machaerus and Masada.[13]

Meanwhile, by 72 CE, Titus once again served as consul—sharing consular authority with his father for a second time. His first stint as consul was nominal since he was outside of Rome and engaged in serious military operations at the time. Now being in the empire's capital, Titus could relish his tenure as consul. While holding this position, he presumably convened and presided over the Senate, issued decrees of various kinds and ensured his father's business continued, including settling certain matters regarding the Jews. The Flavians issued orders for Bassus and the local Roman procurator Lucius Laberius Maximus to confiscate some Judaean land—possibly which had once belonged to the rebels—create new population centers and settle Roman veterans on parts of it, resulting in 800 legionaries relocating near Jerusalem

What's more, Vespasian and Titus proclaimed that all Jews—whether in Judaea or elsewhere—were responsible for paying a tax of two *denarii* (or two drachmas, according to some sources) annually per person to Rome. This Jewish tax was called the *fiscus judaicus*, and it particularly stung. Many male Jews between the ages of 20 and 50 had been accustomed to paying this amount each year to the Jewish Temple to ensure its upkeep. Now that there was no Jewish Temple, the Romans believed that the Jews did not need to fund its upkeep. So they mandated that the Jews, including women, very young children and the elderly as old as 62, pay this amount to the Roman state, and it would help fund the Temple of Jupiter—a pagan god—and whatever else the Romans saw fit.[14]

These edicts aside, Vespasian's policy toward the Jews who had remained loyal to Rome and continued to do so was largely one of toleration. Vespasian and Titus were particularly kind to Josephus whom they awarded land in Judaea, a salary and allowed him to live in an apartment in the emperor's home. Similar to their Jewish policy, Vespasian eschewed Christian persecutions and discrimination, and while Vespasian and Titus likely viewed Christianity as an oddity—if they understood it at all—they tolerated its adherents and permitted them to worship freely and unimpeded. As a result, this might have been a golden age of early Christianity. Without persecutions, it was permitted to take root and grow—albeit modestly.[15]

By this era, Christianity had been slowly spreading across the empire, and pagan gentiles were now converting to the nascent religion. There are no records of how many Christians existed in Rome by this period, but modern calculations suggest that there was anywhere from around 2,700–3,800—a paltry number compared to Rome's pagan population.[16]

Despite Vespasian's kindly approach to Christianity, its adherents may have been treated similarly to the Jews in some cases, including having to pay the *fiscus judaicus,* since many of the faithful had Jewish backgrounds. It is not clear how many Christians were subject to the tax. Certainly, many early Christians had converted from Judaism, but many of them were still Jewish in the Romans' eyes. Thanks to St. Paul's activities, gentiles also converted, which may have confused some Romans who tried to determine if Christianity was a Jewish offshoot or something entirely different.

Christians and Jews quickly observed their differences, though, and fractures between the two monotheistic religions were coming into focus by this era. Following prior persecutions, the Jews probably wanted to distance themselves from the largely unapproved religion of Christianity, while other Jewish leaders wanted to stamp it out for its perceived heresy. Meanwhile, numerous Christians did not want to be associated with the Jews whom the Romans were increasingly coming to loathe. Be that as it may, Christians and Jews would leave an indelible mark on the empire and play important roles in its future, but for now a select number of Jews were still in revolt.[17]

To this end, Bassus next turned his attention toward Machaerus—another Jewish rebel enclave—by no later than 72 CE, but it would not be nearly as easy to capture. It was a desert fortress on the eastern side of the Dead Sea, and was protected by deep ravines, walls and towers. The fortress itself loomed over the region—ensuring that it would be difficult to seize. Nevertheless, Bassus marched his legionaries toward his target. When they arrived and reconnoitered the fortress, Bassus ordered his troops to first fill part of the ravine with soil, stones and rubble to help them create a path to the fortress. Then they built ramps for their siege engines.[18]

The insurgents periodically harassed the Romans and tried to hinder their operations, and during these sorties, the Romans captured one of Machaerus' rebel leaders—a certain young man named Eleazar. Bassus now saw an opportunity to persuade the Jews to surrender the fort. So he instructed his subordinates to strip Eleazar nude and savagely beat him in view of Machaerus' defenders. This caused the Jews great sorrow, but not enough to lay down their arms, which Bassus sensed.

As such, the commander ordered his men to erect a cross in front of Machaerus as if they were going to crucify Eleazar on the spot. This spectacle combined with their hopeless situation induced many Jewish combatants to sue for peace, but they would only lay down their arms if Bassus promised to refrain from executing Eleazar. Bassus gladly accepted their offer to surrender, and as part of the deal, he agreed to spare Eleazar's life and provide Machaerus' defenders safe conduct to retire elsewhere.[19]

Unbeknownst to the Romans, not all of Machaerus' inhabitants agreed to Bassus' terms. Some opened the gates and escaped with plans to continue resisting Rome. Observing this, Bassus and his men charged through Machaerus' open gates to contain the situation in the face of perceived treachery, easily captured the fortress, slaughtered some 1,700 men and enslaved a host of women and children. However, Bassus kept his word and spared Eleazar and those who remained true to the peace agreement, even though some Jews slipped away to continue their doomed fight against Rome and opened a new front of resistance.[20]

Bassus learned that about 3,000 rebels from Jerusalem and the escapees from Machaerus had congregated in a forest called Jardes. Bassus marched his legionaries there with haste, surrounded the forest and destroyed many of the trees to remove their refuge and make it easier for the legionaries to overpower the insurgents. Without this shelter and with the Romans closing in, the revolutionaries attacked the Romans, but it was a massacre. Only 12 Romans allegedly died, while the legionaries slew all 3,000 Jews.[21]

This was to be celebrated in Rome, but Vespasian and Titus received troubling reports from Syria. The governor, known as Caesennius Paetus, claimed that the client-kingdom of Commagene was poised to revolt against Rome, join forces with the Parthian Empire and potentially wage a deadly and costly war against Rome. Yet it seems unlikely that Commagene's king, Antiochus, was seriously considering a revolt. Rumors of his alleged uprising might have simply been a pretext for Paetus to invade. Regardless of this, the Flavians had earlier witnessed what happened when Rome failed to act decisively to uprisings. Therefore they wasted little time in responding. They gave Paetus permission to pre-emptively invade Commagene. He did so and overran the client-kingdom and dethroned Antiochus. Instead of treating Commagene's deposed king as a vanquished foe, the Flavians provided him a generous allowance so that he could live as if he were still a wealthy monarch. Sometime later, the Flavians officially enrolled Commagene as a province in the growing empire.[22]

Meanwhile, with Herodium, Machaerus and the Jardes forest now neutralized, only the *Sicarii*-held Masada remained in rebel hands. Like Machaerus, it was a desert fortress near the Dead Sea, although Masada sat on the western end of it. The fortress itself rested atop a tall plateau, and is naturally protected by steep cliffs almost as high as 1,500 feet in some locations and 300 feet in others. On the plateau was an 18-foot-high and 12-foot-thick wall that was supplemented by 37 towers that each stood 75 feet high. While Masada had no natural spring—just cisterns—seizing it

The Masada plateau as two warplanes fly overhead, 2019.

still posed a daunting challenge, but Bassus would never capture Masada. Sometime in 72 CE, he died—presumably of natural causes—and Vespasian and Titus replaced him with an ally named Flavius Silva. Once in command, he and his legionaries marched toward Masada and intended on subjugating the war's final holdouts.[23]

Before long, Silva and his troops arrived, and he put them to work. After building camps to protect themselves, they began constructing a wall around Masada to prevent any rebels from escaping or importing provisions. The legionaries made quick work of the wall, and at Silva's direction, they took turns serving as sentries on the new construction. Silva next turned toward building a siege ramp, but there was only one suitable location for it—near the so-called White Cliff. Yet the Romans had to start building the earthworks some 450 feet below Masada's summit. Regardless of the challenges and being under constant fire, they began their drudgery and raised a ramp hundreds of feet high.[24]

Silva employed the use of a 90-foot-tall tower to provide a safe location for his soldiers to fire projectiles at the enemy and began battering the wall until part of it collapsed. To the legionaries' disappointment, the *Sicarii* had hastily built another, inner wall, but its construction was not as vulnerable to rams. Thus the Romans opted against battering it and simply set it ablaze, but the winds shifted and blew the fire toward their siege works. This caused great alarm among the legionaries, but before any serious damage was incurred, the winds turned again—this time toward the Jews, which left their wall utterly destroyed.[25]

The insurgents and their families realized that hope was lost. The Romans would easily gain admittance into the fortress and seize control of it. Upon doing so, they might massacre, rape or enslave the inhabitants. Rather than enduring this shame, in 73 or 74 CE, the *Sicarii* settled on one last act: They would kill each other— thereby spoiling the Romans' victory. First, they slew their wives and children,

Remains of the Roman mound at Masada, 2019.

and the men killed one another. The last surviving man burned Masada and then plunged a sword into himself.[26]

In the end, supposedly only two women and five children survived and 960 people in total died, although modern academics doubt the narrative of a mass murder-suicide of nearly 1,000 people. Whatever the case, not long after, the Romans entered Masada and expected fierce resistance from the *Sicarii*, but when they marched into the fortress, eerie silence and smoldering flames greeted them. Eventually, they learned what had transpired and saw lifeless bodies of men, women and children littering the site. The Romans were victorious, but what they witnessed was a tragedy. However, they admired an enemy so unified and determined to control their own destiny that they would choose this fate over capture. With this last act of defiance, all notable hostilities in the Jewish War ended, and Silva garrisoned Masada and dispatched a notice to Vespasian and Titus to let them know of the success.[27]

Josephus likened the Jews at Masada to little more than a grossly misguided band of terrorists and their families who fought against the inevitable. Yet Masada has taken on new prominence in the modern era. As the state of Israel formed, Masada became a national symbol of pride and defiance in the face of a seemingly irresistible force, and for years, Israeli Defense Forces inductees would ascend the plateau and conduct ceremonies in which they would shout "Masada shall not fall again!" While these rites are no longer regularly conducted, Masada remains one of the most popular tourist sites in Israel and an important part of Jewish history.[28]

Despite Masada's fall, this was not the last Jewish rebellion in the Roman empire that year. More than 600 members of the *Sicarii* had previously reached Alexandria, Egypt where there was a large Jewish population. While there, they incited many Jews to rise up against the Romans. Some were eager to join their cause, but many were not. When some influential Jews spoke out against the *Sicarii*'s activities, the insurgents murdered them. This was the final straw for the more moderate, pro–Roman Jewish population who joined together and captured the *Sicarii*. The restrained *Sicarii* then endured many forms of torture but refused to acknowledge the Roman emperor as their master and were ultimately executed.

News of the attempted uprising reached Titus, and he feared that another Jewish revolt might erupt and ensnare the empire. So he ordered the local Roman officials to destroy the Jewish Temple in the Onias District of Alexandria, which served as a warning against further disturbances and prevented it from becoming the new epicenter of Jewish worship. After all, this temple bore special symbolic and religious importance. It had long stood as a rival to Jerusalem, as Jews worshipped and offered sacrifices there, which may suggest a bald-faced Roman attempt at extinguishing Judaism—an endeavor that fortunately failed.[29]

This aside, the year 74 CE must have been a time for excitement for the Flavians. The Romans had eliminated all resistance in Judaea, and the *Sicarii* in Alexandria had been captured and killed. Moreover, Titus enjoyed double honors. In 74 CE, he shared the consulship with his father for the third time, and he and Vespasian both served as censors for terms that probably concluded in 74 CE. The censorship of the Roman Republic was an elected position of great prominence, which was normally held by former consuls, and it served as a crowning achievement after a long political career. By the imperial period, the censorship had evolved, but censuses were still vital to the empire and also quite complicated.[30]

Rome was an expanding empire that stretched from modern-day Great Britain to the Middle East. It required immense administrative planning to conduct a thorough empire-wide census, but unfortunately, little details remain about Vespasian and Titus' census. If it was similar to prior ones, then the Flavian rulers appointed a series of censitores to head to the provinces to make an account of the empire's population and wealth, or else they relied on other provincial officials to oversee them. Below the censitores were the censuales on the chain of command, and together they were tasked with carrying out much of the census.[31]

The censitores and censuales went to their respective city-centers and required the locals to make an account of their family and wealth. Then the administrators recorded the information and combined it with the findings throughout the empire—forming the census. Vespasian and Titus' roles in the process were more-or-less symbolic. They certainly were not involved in the day-to-day activities necessary to conduct a comprehensive census, but they knew how critically important it was. Without a census, emperors did not know how many subjects lived under their rule, how much they could reasonably tax them or gauge how many needed the state-provided welfare, like the grain dole.[32]

There is no record of Vespasian and Titus' findings, but estimates suggest that Rome was home to a minimum of 45.5 million people, including men, women, children and slaves, by 14 CE. Far more people likely lived under Rome's dominion by this era.[33] In fact, at Rome's peak years later, it may have comprised about 20 percent of the world's population.[34] Given the empire's size and success, there was immense wealth within it, but its incredible expanses meant that the costs of maintaining an empire were enormous. Immediately upon assuming control over Rome, Vespasian realized it was in dire financial straits. Civil wars, the Jewish War and a great fire siphoned the empire's wealth away—leaving the state dangerously short on cash. Perhaps after conducting the census, Vespasian decided that he needed to raise even more revenue to support the state.[35]

One new revenue-raising scheme Vespasian settled on was a urine tax, which may seem bizarre to modern readers, but urine was a critical part of Rome's industry because it was where they obtained ammonia. Romans collected urine from sewers and public urinals and then sold it to tanners and launderers for their use, and Vespasian decided that these buyers should pay a premium for the product.[36]

Vespasian viewed this as a fair tax and a viable method of raising revenue, and he put it into effect. For some reason, Titus objected to the new tax, although the ancient sources do not explain why. Regardless, Titus appears to have been less enthusiastic than his father about levying taxes in general. When the first urine tax collections arrived and Titus continued to show his disdain for it, Vespasian grabbed some of the coins, held them out to him and said, "See, my son, if they have any smell." Titus responded that they did not have any odor, and Vespasian replied, "Yet it comes from urine." Vespasian's point was clear: All money spends the same no matter its source.[37]

This example demonstrates that while Titus was a ruling partner with his father, Vespasian was clearly in charge, and despite periodic disagreements between the two, Vespasian was happy to humble and correct his son as only a father can do. These differences, however, did not draw a wedge between the two. Titus remained fiercely loyal to his father and carried out his directives to the letter, including matters related to the census. In due time, the censors—aided by an army of bureaucrats—completed it, but the census required more than just tallying up the empire's wealth and population.

Censors also investigated issues of immorality, removed unfit men from the Senate and refilled the senatorial ranks. Following years of civil strife, the Senate's numbers had dwindled, and Vespasian and Titus replenished it with staunchly pro-Flavian men of rank. This rewarded their allies and ensured that the Senate would be amenable to the Flavians' wishes. Once the census was complete, possibly in 74 CE, the duo completed the *lustrum*. It was a ritual cleansing of the Roman people conducted by the censors. Cleansed or not, like many prior emperors had observed, Vespasian and Titus learned that remaining in power—when surrounded by jealous subjects, spurned aristocrats and imperial court intrigue—was a delicate balancing act.[38]

XIX

Praetorian Prefect

"People not only thought, but openly declared, that [Titus] would be a second Nero."
—Suetonius[1]

As wildly popular as Titus was as a general, he was unpopular as a prince. Once he returned to Rome from dusty eastern battlefields, he seemed pleased to enjoy the luxuries provided by his family's success and took some egregious missteps, which offended the Romans. While everyone is flawed to some degree, he compounded his troubles by failing to competently manage his public perception once back in Rome. He may not have even particularly cared about how the people viewed him. Perhaps worst of all from Rome's point of view, he paraded his unrepentant zeal for protecting his father at all costs.[2]

Sometime during Vespasian's reign—probably as early as 71 CE but no later than 73 CE—the emperor made the astute decision to appoint Titus as praetorian prefect. This made the former Jewish War commander the head of the renown Praetorian Guard, which was an elite military unit that kept order in Rome, collected intelligence on plots against the emperor and served as his trusted bodyguard. This was not some small group of crack legionaries, but a sizable army. Vitellius had enlarged the Praetorian Guard to 16 cohorts, but Vespasian—likely looking to cut imperial spending and remove untrustworthy praetorians—reduced it to nine cohorts, each composed of as many as 1,000 men when at full strength. Thus Titus quickly found himself at the head of an army around the size of two legions interspersed around Rome.[3]

Vespasian's appointment of Titus was based on a shrewd calculation. The Praetorian Guard was incredibly influential and had previously served as kingmakers. It was praetorian guardsmen who assassinated Caligula and hailed Claudius as his successor. They even abandoned Nero when his luck had run out and played a role in Galba's death.[4] Vespasian recognized that if he wanted to retain power, then he needed the Praetorian Guard's undying loyalty, and one method of securing it was to appoint his son as one of its leaders, which was a novel idea. First of all, the role of praetorian prefect had long been largely reserved for equestrians, not senators, like Titus. What's more, never had an emperor's biological son assumed the role of praetorian prefect. Despite these long-standing precedents, Vespasian assigned his son to serve as his protector.[5]

While Titus gladly assumed the role, his tenure as praetorian prefect has understandably received ample criticism. As one of the Praetorian Guard's two chiefs, Titus essentially served as judge, jury and executioner. The ancient historians did not indicate who Titus' colleague was in the office, but modern theories and findings suggest that his former chief of staff, Tiberius Julius Alexander, may have been his partner. Regardless of who shared this office with Titus, as one of the praetorian prefects, he could now slay those suspected of conspiring against his father with little-to-no evidence, and he was pleased to wield this newfound authority. According to some sources, Titus exercised his extrajudicial powers as if he was an unforgiving tyrant—killing many suspected of conspiring against his father. Fair due process should have been afforded to his victims, but Titus may not deserve to be judged quite as harshly for his time as praetorian prefect nearly 2,000 years ago.[6]

To begin with, Titus viewed his role as praetorian prefect as one to safeguard his beloved father and his position as emperor. Furthermore, Titus understood that Vespasian—even as a popular emperor—was not safe. As history had shown, his grasp on power was tenuous at best. Of the eight prior emperors, most met grizzly ends. Caligula, Claudius, Galba and Vitellius had all been murdered. Meanwhile, Nero and Otho committed suicide once their fortunes had changed. Only two emperors in Rome's history to this point had died of natural causes. Titus wanted to ensure that his father joined the minority and lived a long life until its natural end, but that was easier said than done.[7]

As Suetonius pointed out, Vespasian faced nearly constant conspiracies. The ancient authors unfortunately did not record much about these plots, but as can be seen from prior imperial administrations, the conspiracies often came from aristocrats, senators and generals who wanted to seize power for themselves. Titus knew this and viewed himself as Vespasian's guardian in some respects. By using his network of spies and informers, Titus learned of numerous alleged conspiracies—whether real or unfounded. It is plausible that some of the intelligence was fraudulently created by politicians wishing to eliminate their competition, but the ancient historians never mentioned this. Nevertheless, after living through the Year of the Four Emperors, Titus understood what was at stake, and he was not willing to risk a plot against his father, regardless of how flimsy the evidence was.[8]

In the process, Titus proved himself to be a tyrannical enforcer, and it seems impossible that Vespasian was unaware of his activities. Indeed, he may have even been directing them behind the scenes, given that Vespasian sometimes refused to tolerate dissent or supposedly inappropriate behavior. Sometime in his reign, Vespasian banished a host of philosophers from Rome. He viewed them as a kind of threat to his imperial rule—presumably because they were hyper-critical of him and wanted to foment a revolution of sorts. Be that as it may, some philosophers eventually returned to Rome and continued to censure the Flavian household.[9]

Regardless of this, often when Titus suspected someone of conniving against Vespasian, he would quietly dispatch some of his praetorians to public locations, like theaters and camps, where the accused would be. Then they would publicly out them as traitors to the empire, turn the people against them and require their punishment. The guardsmen would subsequently haul the suspects away to a dungeon and torture and execute them. Depending on their status, they were most likely either strangled, beheaded, crucified or stabbed to death. Some might have been permitted to kill themselves, which was considered a more honorable death in ancient Rome.[10]

This heavy-handed approach aside, Titus' public reputation languished for other avoidable reasons too, including his behavior as a spoiled international playboy. Once back in Rome and away from Judaea's ruined cities and the strict discipline required on military campaigns, Titus seemed eager to indulge in Rome's many vices, and he earned a reputation for "riotous living" according to Suetonius. The Roman prince and his friends evidently spent myriad days and nights hosting debauched parties, drinking gluttonously and maybe even gambling.[11]

As the emperor's son, Titus had no shortage of Romans who eagerly accepted invitations to party with the prince. With Rome largely at peace, there was ample time to delight themselves with all of the empire's pleasures. Indeed, they were spendthrifts who piddled away small fortunes as they reclined on their couches, caroused and ate exotic foods, and they did so until late at night—all of which seemed unbecoming for the heir-apparent to the throne.[12]

Regardless of his profligate spending, Titus was immensely wealthy by this point, and he found new ways of generating additional wealth. Following his father's example, Titus accepted bribes from people who lobbied him to influence Vespasian to rule in manners beneficial to them. There is no detailed information regarding who provided these inducements or for what reason, but being the emperor's right-hand man meant that there were plenty of important decisions that he could influence. It is conceivable that aristocrats offered gifts in exchange for official government appointments; foreign delegations may have lavished wealth on Titus hoping to secure more favorable treaties; and those facing legal trouble likely also strove to persuade Titus to protect them. For the right price, he was happy to do so, which padded his coffers.[13]

The public could have ignored some of this behavior. After all, the pagans of old Rome loved being regaled with copious amounts of alcohol, food and sex, and accepting bribes was not uncommon among the elite. Rather it was business as usual, but after men like Nero and Vitellius had risen to power, the Romans must have cast a skeptical eye toward leaders with insatiable, hedonistic and greedy desires. Titus should have realized that engaging in such revelry could draw comparisons to these contemptible former emperors, and as the praetorian prefect with an intelligence apparatus at his disposal, he certainly knew that the Romans worried that he would become another Nero.[14]

Titus made another critical error in judgment, but in this case, love was to blame. Around 75 CE, following the Jewish War's conclusion, he summoned Berenice to Rome. While they had not seen each other in years, their bond remained incredibly strong. There is some scholarly debate over why Titus waited so long to invite his paramour to join him in the empire's capital. One theory states that Mucianus recognized that the relationship was far too scandalous for the public to accept, and he worked to block her arrival until he died. In fact, modern historians have suggested that Titus and Mucianus had a bitter rivalry, but the ancient authors show otherwise. Mucianus and Titus were close allies, and Mucianus could not overrule Vespasian on such matters, although he had access to the emperor's ear and could be persuasive. Moreover, historians do not know in which year Mucianus even died. What rather seems to be the case is that the Jewish War was over and the Flavians presumed that they had established themselves enough to survive any criticism over Titus' love interests. At any rate, after being summoned, Berenice excitedly made her way to Titus.[15]

In relatively short order, the queen arrived in Rome, and she moved into the imperial palace—even sharing a bed with Titus. While they were not married, she expected to wed him, and he may have even promised her his hand in marriage already. They evidently did not feel the need to formally marry in order for her to begin acting as a Roman princess and wielding official authority, which came as a great shock to the Roman people. She apparently flexed her newfound power too. The well-known educator and writer Quintilian even complained of pleading some sort of case before the eastern queen.[16]

To the Romans, this was unacceptable. To begin with, Romans in the imperial household—especially the heir to the purple—were expected to marry upstanding Roman women, not foreign queens. No shortage of racist claims circulated in Rome about the supposed dangers of letting Berenice infiltrate the imperial palace. These perhaps included that she would corrupt Titus with her eastern ways, anger the pantheon of gods with her monotheistic views and might induce the Flavians to adopt a more pro-Jewish policy following the Jewish War.[17]

The relationship between Titus and Berenice conjured up images of another unpopular non-Roman queen who had gained outsized influence in Rome: Cleopatra. She had begun a relationship with Julius Caesar and then Mark Antony, and wielded extraordinary influence in the Roman Republic. She even participated in a devastating Roman civil war. As such, the Roman people were highly suspicious of Berenice and openly spoke out against her, which was bold considering Titus' reputation as a praetorian prefect.[18]

Despite Berenice serving as a high-profile distraction, Titus continued assisting Vespasian in numerous ways—primarily including overseeing the Praetorian Guard and the empire's administration. Titus also shared the consulship with his father again in 75, 76, and 77 CE. During this time, the Flavians watched their greatest construction—the magnificent amphitheater—slowly rise from its foundations and monitored military developments.[19]

There was one in particular that dominated much of the latter portion of Vespasian's reign. Starting in 77 CE, war again erupted on the island of Britannia, but

Vespasian did not choose Titus to lead the campaign. He had already established his reputation as a military leader—helping assure his accession to the throne. Besides, Vespasian needed him in Rome to protect him and assist with imperial management. Rather Vespasian relied on Britannia's newly appointed provincial governor Gnaeus Julius Agricola. He demonstrated himself to be an able commander as he led Rome's legions into battle as they first pacified Wales and eyed the rest of the island, but this would become a prolonged affair that would take many years to resolve.[20]

At some point during Titus and Berenice's controversial liaison, two leading philosophers of the Cynic school snuck into Rome to denounce the relationship. First, the sophist Diogenes entered a packed Roman theater and delivered an incisive invective against the duo. His criticisms seem to have struck a chord with the audience members, but his campaign against Berenice was short-lived. Roman officials arrested and beat him severely, but that was not the last critique Titus and Berenice received. Not long after, another philosopher Heras denounced them in Rome, but Titus was less forgiving of Heras. Titus' associates seized and beheaded him for disparaging the couple.[21]

Despite trying to contain these objections to the relationship, it must have become clear to Vespasian and Titus that Berenice must return to her homeland. The Roman people had staunchly rejected her, and some felt so strongly about it that they were willing to risk violence and even death to make their disapproval heard. Vespasian did not need this distraction or wish to give his subjects and rivals a reason to challenge him or his son. So it appears that Vespasian—possibly with Titus' understanding—realized that it was best to part ways with Berenice. Upon coming to this realization sometime likely in 79 CE, Titus broke the news to the eastern queen, and full of sorrow, he bid her farewell. However, it is plausible that he told her that this was a temporary break until either he became emperor or the Roman people no longer felt so passionately about her presence.[22]

Either way, she departed in disappointment, and her absence weighed heavily on Titus. The man who was once renowned for his appetite for pleasure seemed to lose interest in much of it. Being Rome's leading bachelor, he had plenty of suitors, and since returning to Rome, he had sexual liaisons with many eunuchs and catamites. While carrying on relationships with the latter was not unusual in the Greco-Roman world, it does—and ought to—make modern readers recoil. It should be noted that only Suetonius mentioned Titus' involvement with pubescent boys, which means it is hardly strong evidence. This aside, Titus also bed numerous women and talented dancers who performed in the theater. After Berenice's departure, they brought him no joy, and he even refused to watch their onstage exhibitions.[23]

Titus mourned Berenice's loss, but he still had ample ways to refocus his troubled mind, particularly by eliminating rivals to the imperial purple. Only two specific instances were recorded for posterity, and they are light on details. In one case, a Gallic man named Julius Sabinus who styled himself like Julius Caesar and even claimed to be one of his descendants took up arms against the Romans years before but was defeated. He, his wife Peponila and children hid for some time, but the Romans—maybe at Titus' direction—discovered and captured them. They were then delivered to Rome to face their punishment in the late 70s CE. While Sabinus stood little chance of survival, Peponila pleaded before Vespasian for his mercy. Presenting her children, she exclaimed, "The little ones, Caesar, I bore and reared in the monument, that we might be a greater number to supplicate you." Her statements were moving and brought Vespasian to tears, but revolts could not be tolerated. Shortly thereafter, executioners slew Sabinus and Peponila. Cassius Dio—who related this event—did not record their children's fates, but it is possible that Vespasian spared their lives. However, they might have then sold into slavery or placed in an ancient orphanage.[24]

In 79 CE, Titus once again shared the consulship with Vespasian, while simultaneously serving as praetorian prefect. Perhaps during the course of the year, Titus received some ironclad evidence against two trusted and influential friends: a former suffect consul and military man named Aulus Caecina Alienus who had a history of corruption and disloyalty, and another former consul named Titus Clodius Eprius Marcellus. In the Year of the Four Emperors, Caecina had switched sides and joined with the Flavians, and he even had a long-standing relationship with Titus. In their youth, the two had sparred with one another in full armor. Regardless of this history, Caecina and Eprius apparently intended on leading a military coup against the Flavians, but Caecina made a critical error. He drafted and signed a speech he planned to deliver to Roman legionaries in which he laid out his intent to overthrow the Flavians and solicit the troops' support, which was a ridiculously foolish mistake.[25]

Somehow a Flavian partisan obtained Caecina's remarks and showed them to Titus, who must have been enraged. His close friends had planned to betray him. To forestall any successful uprising and without revealing that he knew of the conspiracy, Titus invited Caecina to dinner at the imperial palace. This was an offer he could not refuse, but it is not clear whether Caecina was concerned that his plans had been discovered. Either way, Caecina accepted the invitation, and the two men presumably exchanged pleasantries, ate and drank to excess and shared stories of their military exploits. Once the meal concluded, Caecina probably thanked Titus for his hospitality and eyed an exit. As Caecina made his way out, Titus directed his guardsmen to kill the traitor forthwith. Just as he was leaving the dining room, the prefect's subordinates leaped into action and brutally stabbed Caecina to death. It is not apparent why Eprius was not invited to attend the same dinner, but Titus' praetorians easily captured and arrested him. The humbled former consul then stood trial and was found guilty. Instead of enduring a public execution, he slit his own throat and perished.[26]

As a praetorian prefect, Titus adamantly refused to tolerate even the rumor of a conspiracy against his father. Rather, rumors were met with decisive violence. His heavy-handed approach was roundly criticized—at least quietly—but the results spoke for themselves. While serving as chief praetorian, there were a host of conspiracies against the Flavians, but not a single one was successful, which helped guarantee Vespasian's well-being and assured Titus of his ultimate succession to the imperial throne. In the process, Titus gained a terrible reputation, but he preferred that to risking his father's life, which is admirable in a cruel way.[27]

Sometime in 79 CE, Vespasian's health began to fade, although his wit did not. While visiting the Campania region of Italy, he contracted an unknown—but initially considered—mild illness. As he battled the ailment, he returned to Rome for a short time and then he left for Aquae Cutiliae in the Sabine countryside. It was near his family's provincial hometown, which is where he spent his summers. In time, his health continued to decline. The minor illness grew worse, and he also acquired a new symptom—a stomach disorder of some kind.[28]

For a man of 69 years, his worsening condition was becoming concerning, but he strove to continue serving the empire. Despite eventually being virtually bed-ridden, he entertained official embassies from Aquae Cutiliae as Titus and Domitian presumably managed matters from Rome, but it soon became clear that the disease would claim Vespasian's life. The standard protocol was to declare admirable emperors a deity upon their death, and sensing his own demise, he jokingly announced, "Woe's me. Methinks I'm turning into a god." He was right. Sometime later in June 79 CE, a bout of diarrhea and fever struck him. He knew the end was nigh, but tried to fulfill his imperial duties, even though his physicians instructed him to rest. When he sensed death approaching, he exclaimed, "An emperor ought to die standing," and the weathered old general and emperor struggled to his feet. Seconds later, he collapsed into the arms of his attendants and perished, supposedly from dysentery, according to Orosius.[29]

After a long military career and nearly a 10-year stint leading the empire, the popular old emperor died and left behind a laudable legacy to the Romans. He defied all odds to become emperor, he and his allies had ended the civil wars that gripped Rome during the Year of the Four Emperors and he and Titus had neutralized the Jewish uprisings. Beyond this, Vespasian's tightfisted and pro-tax rule had placed the empire on more stable financial footing, and he had begun the process of giving the Romans a monument that would survive the ages: the Roman Colosseum. He even formally expanded the empire's borders by adding the provinces of Achaia, Lycia, Rhodes, Byzantium, Samos, Trachian Cilicia and Commagene. In short, he left the empire in good standing and made it exceedingly clear who should succeed him: Titus.[30]

XX

Princeps

"He incurred such odium at the time that hardly anyone ever came to the throne with so evil a reputation or so much against the desires of all."
—Suetonius[1]

It is not evident if Titus was by Vespasian's side or in Rome when the emperor ultimately died, but one way or another, news of his father's passing reached Titus. While he knew that Vespasian's health had been declining for some time, word of the emperor's death still must have been stunning and sobering. Not only had the man who had raised him perished, but now the empire was at least nominally and momentarily leaderless, which was a dangerous time.

Perhaps the greatest flaw in the Roman imperial system Augustus instituted was that there was no clear guidance on imperial succession. Successors were generally related—at least by marriage or adoption—but the empire was not a hereditary monarchy. In fact, by Vespasian's time, no biological son had ever succeeded his father to the throne. Instead, emperors often made it clear who they would like to have replace them and even included that information in their wills. They also worked to position their preferred heirs to easily take the reins from them, by sharing imperial duties, appointing them to influential postings and so forth. After passing away, it was usually left up to the Senate to confirm the next emperor, but armies and the Praetorian Guard sometimes also played roles in these decisions.

Vespasian had long made it exceedingly obvious to the Senate that he planned for Titus to succeed him, and he worked to ensure that there was nobody else more prepared and influential than his son to obtain the Senate's confirmation. Titus had the backing of the Praetorian Guard thanks to his role as prefect, shared the consulship seven times and the censorship once with his father, led Rome's legions in successful battles and shared the burden of ruling with the now-deceased emperor. All told, Titus was an easy and obvious choice for the Senate, especially considering that the Senate was composed of pro–Flavian politicians. There was still some apprehension, given that people worried that Titus was a tyrant in the mold of Nero waiting in the wings.[2]

Despite any potential misgivings, the Senate needed to act quickly and saw Titus as the natural choice. While there are no records of the meeting, the Senate almost certainly convened—possibly at Titus' direction—and once in session, they read Vespasian's will, which endorsed Titus as his successor. At some point, a jealous Domitian claimed that the will was falsified because he contended that Vespasian wished for Titus and himself to rule as partners. Titus was known to be a talented forger, and Domitian knew this too. He might have hoped to use this information to buttress his assertions and curry enough support to achieve his imperial ambitions, but it was for naught. His protests aside, there is little evidence suggesting that Domitian was speaking the truth.

After hearing Vespasian's final wishes, the senators quickly confirmed the 39-year-old Titus as Rome's new emperor, and within a week of Vespasian's death, Rome began minting coins featuring Titus with the title of Augustus. Breaking with tradition, he became the first biological son of an emperor to replace his father, and during Titus' reign, coinage commemorated Titus' ascension by depicting Vespasian handing control of the empire over to his son. Titus' appointment aside, this was not necessarily the joyous occasion some envision. His beloved father had just died, there was a funeral to plan and he needed to rule a wide-stretching empire without Vespasian's guidance.[3]

The distraught Titus and his aides quickly began planning a public funeral and likely also an apotheosis ceremony for the revered emperor, although it is unclear when it occurred. For whatever reason, the Senate took considerable time before voting to deify Vespasian—perhaps because they needed to first create a Flavian cult with priests to serve the dead emperor. Regardless of when the official Senate vote was held, the imperial household may not have felt the need to wait on the senatorial approval in order to conduct the apotheosis ceremony. With the Senate full of pro-Flavian politicians and Titus leading the government, Vespasian's deification was assured. Even so, organizing an imperial funeral and apotheosis ceremony was an elaborate process and took considerable resources. Funerals for common people and aristocrats alike were already incredibly involved, but Vespasian's required much more effort and planning.[4]

Other than a single extant line from Suetonius, virtually nothing is known for certain about Vespasian's funeral, but ancient writers recorded enough about funerals for the rich and Emperor Augustus to draw some assumptions. After expiring, loved ones closed Vespasian's tired eyes, washed his body, anointed it with oils and perfumes and dressed him in clean, formal attire. Vespasian was probably then carried back to Rome and escorted by morose soldiers. When he arrived, servants placed Vespasian's body on a couch, and for days, mournful friends and relatives visited him and bade him farewell. Meanwhile, others made preparations for a funeral procession through Rome to the Campus Martius.[5]

Once the day of the funeral and apotheosis ceremony arrived, if it was anything like Augustus', Vespasian's decaying body was placed inside a special couch made for the occasion. It was resplendent, made of ivory and gold, and decorated with vibrant colors, like purple. Servants placed atop the coffin a wax effigy in Vespasian's likeness wearing triumphal garb similar to when he triumphed for the Jewish War. Then laborers lifted him up and carried him out, and they—along with a long cortege of sorrowful family members, friends, musicians, military officers and servants—began trudging through Rome.[6]

Among the many spectacles displayed during this procession were images of storied Romans, like Romulus, and Vespasian's deceased family members, presumably including his father, mother, brother, wife and daughter. Despite this being a solemn ceremony, it was not without some humor. An actor named Favor wore a mask resembling Vespasian, and poked fun at the dead, parsimonious emperor. He loudly asked how much the funeral cost. When someone responded, "Ten million sesterces," Favor replied, "Give me a hundred thousand and fling me [...] into the Tiber," as a way of mocking Vespasian for his miserly reputation.[7]

Eventually, the funerary cavalcade and the couch reached the city center, and flanked by onlookers, the procession halted. A speaker—very possibly Titus or one of Vespasian's close friends and confidants—approached the speaker's rostra and delivered a long, respectful and glowing eulogy whereupon he highlighted Vespasian's many successes, rise to power and tenure as emperor. The speech certainly brought tears to the eyes of a host of Romans in attendance, and after it concluded, Vespasian's couch was carried out of Rome through one of its gates and the cortege followed.[8]

Soon enough, they reached the Campus Martius where a grand funeral pyre had been constructed, and servants placed Vespasian's body upon it. Then in ceremonial fashion, the priests in attendance first marched around the pyre and others followed as they laid tokens of their love for and friendship with Vespasian on the pyre. With this matter completed, some centurions placed their torches below the pyre, and it erupted into flames—consuming Vespasian's body. Funeral participants subsequently released an eagle or a hawk, which ostensibly carried his soul to the heavens where he would live as a newly deified god.[9]

The pyre burned for some time, and when the flames died down, workers doused the ashes with wine, collected Vespasian's remains and placed them in an urn. A priest then purified these assistants, and the urn was probably handed to Titus who respectfully placed it in a mausoleum.[10] This largely reflects the ceremony provided for Augustus around 65 years earlier, but imperial funerals evolved over time. If Vespasian's more closely resembled that given to Pertinax, a later emperor, then there may have been two distinct ceremonies—a more public one only involving a wax effigy and another for the actual body. In whatever manner was used, Vespasian was laid to rest, but the mourning continued for days.[11]

In what must have been a challenging time for Titus, he was forced to juggle his duties as a newly installed emperor, while also grieving the loss of his father. Nevertheless, he assumed his new role, and the people of Rome braced themselves for a cruel emperor. Luckily for them, Titus turned out to be an even-handed, conscientious and judicious ruler—earning him the people's love and affection. In a way, he seemed to reinvent himself and did so successfully. As unpopular as he was as a prince, he was equally popular as an emperor.[12]

Cassius Dio attempted to determine why Titus went through this lauded metamorphosis, and he settled on two possibilities. He believed that Titus realized it was different to wield power as an assistant to the emperor as opposed to independently doing so as the emperor. Put simply, emperors are responsible for everything that happens during their reign. Now that the proverbial buck stopped with him, Titus resolved to rule fairly and as a forgiving father. While this was the correct course of action, he almost certainly understood that his legacy would benefit from this volte-face too. Dio's alternative reason was that Titus simply did not live long enough to act with cruelty.

The true reason could have also been because Titus surrounded himself with highly competent counselors who advised him on what actions to take. Many of them must have been the same ones Vespasian had relied on, but it is conceivable Titus added others. It seems probable that his relatives, Flavius Sabinus and Marcus Arrecinus Clemens, served him in this capacity as well as Marcus Ulpius Traianus and the future emperor Marcus Cocceius Nerva. Some of Titus' advisers were so capable that some of his successors relied on them too.[13]

That aside, Titus took concrete steps to become an emperor of great repute. While he must have largely followed his father's policies, he also charted a path of his own. To begin with, he assumed the title of pontifex maximus—the chief high priest in the Roman empire—as his predecessors did, but he differentiated himself in the role. He evidently embraced it, at least in part, to assuage the Romans' apprehensions over his leadership and demonstrate that he would rule with restraint. Not only did he act like a leader worthy of being chief priest, he governed with kindness and mercy.[14]

While he was the de facto leader of Roman religion and worshipped as a veritable god in the eastern portions of the empire, like his father, he apparently left the Jews and Christians largely to their own devices. The Jews continued to live within the empire and could do so freely so long as they paid the *fiscus judaicus*, and Christians likewise worshipped without any notable imperial persecutions or impediments. Local government officials may have taken it upon themselves to discriminate against them, but there is nothing to suggest Titus was involved in any such activity. In fact, some traditions suggest that a couple of his family members became early Christian converts, although the evidence for this is limited. It is largely based on them being accused of dabbling with atheism or Judaism and being punished accordingly after Titus' death.[15]

As Titus showed kindness to the Christians, aristocrats and much of Rome, numerous conspiracies formed against Titus. Yet he did not personally condemn and execute a single senator, nor any Roman for that matter. This was a stark departure from some prior emperors who notoriously purged the senatorial ranks of perceived political enemies and slew others without demur. Titus was unlike them, or even himself when he was praetorian prefect. He even announced that he would rather be slain than to slay another, and his tenure was evidence of that.[16]

Treason trials—known as *majestas*—had marred prior imperial reigns, and they gave emperors license to essentially conduct deadly witch-hunts and have them sanctioned by the justice system. These trials ensnared more than those accused of conspiring against the emperor. Romans could find themselves facing such a trial for simply making denigrating statements about the emperor. These proceedings apparently disgusted Titus. When people were charged with being overly critical of him or his predecessors, he refused to allow anyone to prosecute the accused. In justifying the abolition of these trials, he said, "It is impossible for me to be insulted or abused in any way. For I do naught that deserves censure, and I care not for what is reported falsely. As for the emperors who are dead and gone, they will avenge themselves in case anyone does them a wrong, if in very truth they are demigods and possess any power."[17]

In line with banning treason trials, Titus also cleansed Rome of the *delatores*. These were essentially members of a class of Romans who served as informers. They spied on the emperor's subjects and accused them of various crimes, and they shared their allegedly truthful information with emperors for a fee. Unfortunately, the informers formed a highly corrupt system. They targeted the rich or the emperor's rivals and falsely raised charges against them. In the process, they got rich, but ruined people's lives and caused chaos. Titus had witnessed enough of their treachery. Sometime later in his reign, in 80 or 81 CE, he ordered their arrest, and then officials brought them to the Forum where they beat them severely, sold some into slavery and banished the rest—all to great acclaim.[18]

Titus continued adopting other welcomed reforms as well. He empowered Roman legionaries to draft wills—something of a novel concept at the time. He outlawed double-jeopardy to guarantee that no Roman could be tried for the same crime under different laws. He also formed a kind of statute of limitations—unfortunately the length is unknown—on legal inquiries dealing with deceased Romans, presumably to prevent unfair meddling in wills and inheritances. In what was a more arcane reform, Titus reduced the number of praetors from 18 to 17 for an unknown reason.

In a measure that surely gratified much of the aristocracy, he summarily approved all prior imperial gifts wholesale, which was another departure from prior administrations. Emperors issued all kinds of incredibly valuable gifts during their reigns and in their wills, but succeeding emperors sometimes invalidated the favors or only approved them on a case-by-case basis. If the recipients wanted them, then they needed to petition the sitting emperor who had the power to reject their requests. Instead of pursuing this path, Titus showed his generosity and validated all prior gifts in a single edict—the first time this had ever been done.[19]

While he ensured previous imperial favors were considered valid, he personally stopped accepting gifts altogether, which was another stark deviation from his behavior as a prince. He had taken bribes of various kinds in exchange for his influence, and he was conspicuous in the manner of doing it. However, once he ascended to the throne, he would not even accept gifts that were considered legitimate and customary, maybe even including those from foreign delegations. This helped him remain objective and unbiased as an emperor, and he did not seek out choice property to seize from his subjects either. Rather he strove to respect people's private property and fortunes.[20]

Even though he did not pursue avenues to ill-gotten wealth, he was generous to the people, while remaining frugal in his own expenditures and pursuing a sound economic policy. He maintained a monetary policy similar to his father's. Surviving *denarii* from Titus' reign show that he largely kept the silver content at Vespasian's standard—around 80 percent or higher. Eastern coins—the Cistophoric tetradrachms and Alexandrian tetradrachms—likewise maintained silver fineness very similar to those under Vespasian's rule. This helped insulate the Roman economy from the shocks of major debasements.[21]

Moreover, he continued the construction of the great Flavian amphitheater, which slowly neared competition, but he wanted to provide Rome with another structure—one that was distinctly his own gift to Rome and likely hoped to finish it at the same time as the *amphitheatrum*. He settled on constructing a bath house. It should be noted that some modern scholars believe that construction may have actually begun under Vespasian, but there is not enough evidence to settle this matter. Nevertheless, after outlining this project, his workers began construction feverishly in order to erect it in time.[22]

Titus showed his munificence and loyalty in other ways too. Like his father, he remained steadfastly faithful to his friend Josephus, even defending him against wrongful accusations and permitting him to live a life of luxury. As emperor, he took pains to entertain various petitioners, and he instituted a personal policy to never allow any of his subjects to ask him a favor and leave without hope or satisfaction. So whenever they entered his presence and requested various forms of assistance, he always tried to provide it. He was so generous to petitioners that some of his deputies urged him to be more cautious because he was agreeing to do more than was possible. Regardless of their entreaties, he felt that it was his duty to serve the Romans and help them however he could, but one day initially passed unbeknownst to the emperor without him aiding anyone. After dinner with some associates, it dawned on him that he had not provided assistance to any single Roman that day. Disappointed, he looked at his companions and said, "Friends, I have lost a day."[23]

Titus strove to serve his subjects, but he certainly also found ways to enjoy his newfound position of power and wealth. As emperor, he hosted myriad banquets for politicians, family members, foreign embassies and holidays. Even so, he exercised temperance and eschewed the extravagance of men like Nero and Caligula, although he maintained exquisite artistic masterpieces within his palace, commissioned a golden statue of Britannicus, which he placed there, and enjoyed brilliant mosaics. This art aside, Titus was relatively frugal with his spending. He hosted cheaper—but still enjoyable—soirees, which was an admirable decision.

Mosaic, sunken city of Baiae, 2022.

Yet he became embroiled in one notable controversy. With him holding unchecked power and Vespasian no longer around to tell him otherwise, Titus either invited Berenice back to Rome or she came on her own accord. If Titus summoned her, then she eagerly accepted and arrived not long after. Nearly nothing is known about her time in Rome, but it seems safe to assume that the Roman populace once again rejected her and stirred up controversy in the process. Maybe upon sensing this, Titus again acquiesced to their will, and he sent her back to the East, while he wallowed in sadness after losing his lover again.[24]

The loss surely pained him, but managing the empire had a way of diverting his gaze. Besides, there was plenty of other business to consume his mind. At some point, a pretender named Terentius Maximus claimed to be the former Emperor Nero and that he escaped the patrols that had sought him in 68 CE and survived. There were often various kinds of such impostors in old Rome, but most of them did not gain much traction. Maximus was different. He bore a striking resemblance to Nero, sang similarly to him and even played the lyre like Nero. Given all of this and the compelling nature of his lies, he gained a modest following, and anyone claiming to be the living Nero and the last of the Julio-Claudian dynasty could create a headache for Titus.[25]

It is not evident what Maximus' aims were. He could have desired the imperial throne, but Titus was not about to surrender it to a pretender. Perhaps he simply enjoyed the attention and then realized his misbehavior could somehow be lucrative. Before any Roman official could put an end to his mischief, Maximus crossed over into the Parthian Empire, and its king known as Artabanus welcomed him with open arms. He saw this as a possible opportunity. Hoping to one day destabilize Rome and undermine Titus' claim to the throne, Artabanus thought that he might be able to support Maximus and help him claim the emperorship—something that never came to fruition.[26]

This probably created a mild annoyance for Titus, but a more important foreign entanglement dominated much of his imperial reign. Before he had replaced his father as the head of Rome, war broke out in Britannia. Led by Agricola, the conflict continued into Titus' tenure, and he likely monitored Agricola's progress and pored over his reports. By all accounts, Rome was winning the war. Agricola had conquered Wales and continued his efforts with plans to pacify much of the rest of the island and even push deep into Scotland.[27]

During the early days of his reign, Titus demonstrated himself to be a worthy successor to his popular father. While 79 CE was marked by Vespasian's sad passing, it must have also been punctuated by some excitement as Titus took control of Rome and managed it adeptly. However, he quickly learned that administering the empire was anything but easy, especially as natural calamities devastated his people.

XXI

Vesuvius

> *"You could hear the wailing of women, the screams of little children, and the shouts of men; some were trying to find their parents, others their children, others their wives, by calling for them and recognising them by their voices alone. Some were commiserating their own lot, others that of their relatives, while some again prayed for death in sheer terror of dying. Many were lifting up their hands to the gods, but more were declaring that now there were no more gods, and that this night would last forever, and the end of all the world."*
> —Pliny the Younger[1]

While Titus was exhibiting his strengths as a young emperor and presumably enjoying the honeymoon phase of his posting, a cataclysmic disaster rocked the empire. A little more than 130 miles southeast of Rome on the Bay of Naples, a calamity-in-the-making was quietly lurking. Cities throughout the region had felt the rumblings of increasingly frequent—but mostly minor—earthquakes. Physical proof of this comes from Pompeii where archaeologists discovered a home where workmen had been making repairs to a house with cosmetic damages due to an earthquake.

These rumblings and even the towering volcano—now known as Vesuvius—did not cause much concern. The Romans knew little about the science of seismotectonic activity and had only limited knowledge of volcanoes, but they were not entirely foreign to them. The Mediterranean had long been home to many active volcanoes, although the Romans' memory induced them to believe that they tended to be relatively tame. Furthermore, Campania often felt tremors due to the region's geologic attributes. They just seemed like a normal part of living there. Sadly for the locals, these quakes were harbingers and terrors to come.[2]

Thanks to two letters from Pliny the Younger to Tacitus, more recent archaeological discoveries and a better understanding of volcanic eruptions, modern scientists have been able to piece together what happened next. On an autumn or winter day in 79 CE (extant ancient accounts placed it in August, but this is almost certainly incorrect), both the youthful Pliny the Younger and his uncle Pliny the Elder—the famed writer and commander of the imperial fleet in Misenum—observed an unusual cloud. It was surging into the sky from across the Bay of Naples.[3]

The dark cloud soared higher in a column and mushroomed at its apex in a

Pompeii with Vesuvius in the background, 2022.

manner that resembled an umbrella pine, and it grew ever higher—reaching upward of 20 miles into the stratosphere. Little did the two *Plinii* know, but this was a plume billowing out of Mount Vesuvius and would soon wreak devastation on the land. The thick cloud was filled with rocks and debris from the Vesuvian volcanic pipe, white pumice—eventually replaced by gray-ish green pumice—and sizzling noxious gasses. Roughly 30 minutes or so after Vesuvius blew its top and vented this plume, the cloud's contents—primarily made up of pumice—began falling to the ground at a distance from Pliny the Elder.[4]

The sight of the plume piqued the interest of the curious Pliny the Elder who became renowned for his encyclopedia of natural history. With a fleet at his disposal, he decided that he should sail toward the phenomenon. He even invited the younger Pliny, who declined the invitation—choosing instead to remain in Misenum studying—but Pliny the Elder's plans quickly changed. As he prepared to embark, he received a message from a friend named Rectina, who lived near Vesuvius. She pleaded with him to rescue her—and perhaps her family and friends—because matters were becoming dire and she was unable to escape. Her specific location is not known, but she may have been close to the city of Oplontis—located south of Naples in the modern-day city of Torre Annunziata.[5]

Switching his mission from one of scientific curiosity to one of rescue, Pliny the Elder readied his ships and shoved off from Misenum and into the unknown. The skies quickly darkened as if it was night, and he made a lamentable realization as he neared Rectina: He could not save her and her companions in the current conditions. It was dark, the sea was full of pumice and presumably too choppy. In fact, the pumice rained down on the land and sea at an average of about 6 inches an hour in some areas—terrifying the locals, collapsing roofs and covering the landscape. As a result of his inability to reach his friend, the old naval commander changed course for Stabiae, where he and his seamen were able to dock and enter the town.[6]

Fear was doubtless rampant—even among the brave sailors—but Pliny the Elder wished to calm them and the people at Stabiae by exhibiting a courageous example. Yet he very greatly underestimated the danger facing them. When he reached Stabiae, he enjoyed a pleasant dinner, a leisurely bath and went to bed for the night. As he slumbered, earthquakes shook buildings to their foundation and pumice continued to pour across the region. It did so to such a degree that his aides worried that he would be sealed where he slept—turning his bedroom into his tomb. To prevent this, they awoke the commander, and they all fled from the buildings where they had taken refuge—choosing to risk exposing themselves outside instead. As a precaution, they placed pillows on their heads to protect them from the stones falling from the sky.[7]

Despite it being darker than night, the sun had risen, but Pliny the Elder and his men could not see but for their torches and lamps. Pumice poured over them, dust polluted the air and they desperately gasped to breathe, and then matters took an unusual turn: The sea shockingly retreated—stranding fish in the once verdant bay—but even worse terrors awaited the poor wretches still near the Bay of Naples. After roughly 18 to 22 hours of enduring a constant pumice barrage, this phase of the eruption ended, and a much more horrifying one began.[8]

A series of pyroclastic surges and flows began pouring out of Vesuvius at alarming speeds—reaching over 60 miles per hour. Within them were ash, rocks, volcanic glass, sand and superheated gasses that sizzled at several hundred degrees Fahrenheit. From a distance, it would have appeared as a dark cloud descending from the volcano and blanketing the region. As it rolled outward from Vesuvius, it smothered cities with even more debris in its path, like Pompeii, which was already buried in up to 9 feet of pumice at this point. Other cities were also entombed in this volcanic rock, and while the pumice fall was deadly—causing roof collapses and trapping frightened Romans—the pyroclastic surges and flows were even more devastating.[9]

Many of the locals could not outrun them. Rather, the superheated cloud of gas and rubble carbonized people, struck them with debris or asphyxiated them. In fact, Pliny the Elder and his associates watched as these clouds enveloped everything and the ground shook violently. The incessant volcanic barrage turned out to be too much for the old Pliny. He collapsed, and in fear, his friends deserted the corpulent man who died not long after. Meanwhile, Pliny the Younger and his mother made desperate attempts in Misenum to avoid danger. Unlike his uncle, Pliny the Younger survived.[10]

After two days of eruptions, Vesuvius' violence eased, and the skies gradually cleared. Only then could the Romans truly grasp the devastation's breadth. Vesuvius had destroyed or at least greatly damaged numerous cities, including Pompeii,

Street in Pompeii, 2022.

Herculaneum, Oplontis and Stabiae. The total number of casualties is unknown, but it seems as though a large number of Romans made their escape during the first phase of the eruption, when pumice was raining down on them. Pompeii was a city around the size of 20,000, and estimates suggest that roughly 2,000 died within Pompeii. Due to the nature of their deaths, today you can see plaster casts of those who perished as well as horses and dogs in their final disturbing moment frozen in time. While each of these deaths was tragic, some feel even more so. Archaeologists have discovered no shortage of harrowing finds, but the children and pregnant females—still cradling their beloved babies in their wombs—are particularly heart-wrenching.[11]

As survivors returned, many of them did not see ruined cities. Instead, large expanses of their towns had disappeared. The smaller, but more affluent, city of Herculaneum—about 5,000 in population—was buried under about 60 feet of volcanic deposits in some locations, and Pompeii was covered in 17 feet or more of ash and pumice. It was utter destruction, and the ash and clouds spread across the empire. Even in Rome, the sun's rays were weakened due to the eruption, and word reached Titus of the disaster very quickly. Needless to say, Titus and all of Rome was aghast by the events near Vesuvius. Never before had they witnessed such a disaster, but they presumably ordered emergency operations to rescue survivors and house the refugees.[12]

At some point after Vesuvius blew its top and wreaked mayhem on Campania, Titus and a retinue of assistants journeyed to the region to inspect the damage and perhaps observe the state's emergency response. When they arrived, the scene looked like a moonscape—an entirely foreign scene to Titus and his associates, who had likely visited the region numerous times. In many locations, gone were the fertile vineyards, decades-old trees, entire buildings and vibrant colors. Thick layers of gray and green pumice, ash and stones carpeted the region. The extent of the calamity was beyond anything they had ever seen or imagined. They were stricken with horror, disbelief and mourning.[13]

Plaster cast of the Crouching Man, Pompeii, 2022.

While Titus could not bring back the dead, he was confronted by the fact that thousands of people had lost their homes and nearly all of their possessions and needed aid. Hoping to help the homeless refugees, he appointed a commission composed of former consuls and tasked them with doling out aid to the displaced people, although there is a lack of details surrounding this emergency assistance.[14]

Much of it must have come from the imperial treasury because, at Titus' direction, the commissioners handed out financial assistance to help support Vesuvius' surviving victims. However, that did not provide them land on which to live, but Titus had a plan. He confiscated the property belonging to the dead who had no heirs, and he either awarded it to the survivors or sold it to fund the cities' reconstruction. This certainly took an inordinate amount of time, but the commissioners fulfilled their task and tried to satisfy every valid request.[15]

While Titus was away and touring the smoldering ruins of Campania, matters complicated the already challenging situation facing Titus. A fire erupted within the city of Rome sometime in 80 CE when Titus was serving in his eighth term as consul. Its cause is unknown, but with so many using fire for cooking, keeping warm and providing enough light to see in a city built with dried timber, it was only a matter of time. Thankfully, this did not prove as ruinous as the fire that destroyed much of

Herculaneum, 2022.

Rome during Nero's reign. Nevertheless, it was still devastating and reduced historical and holy sites to ruins.[16]

Cassius Dio wrote, "It consumed the Temple of Serapis, the Temple of Isis, the Saepta, the Temple of Neptune, the Baths of Agrippa, the Pantheon, the Diribitorium, the theatre of Balbus, the stage building of Pompey's theatre, the Octavian buildings together with their books, and the Temple of Jupiter Capitolinus with their surrounding temples. Hence the disaster seemed to be not of human but of divine origin; for anyone can estimate, from the list of buildings that I have given, how many others must have been destroyed." While each of these was a harrowing loss, the firing of the Temple of Jupiter was uniquely painful. It had only recently been rebuilt after having been destroyed during the Year of the Four Emperors. Now it was in ruins again.[17]

Titus' *vigiles* leapt into action and did what they could to contain the raging conflagration, but there was only so much they could do. Building after building was turned to ash, and officials alerted Titus to the destruction. Understanding the stress this placed on the people and the treasury after not one, but now two disasters, he simply said, "I am ruined." In order to rebuild many of the collapsed structures and aid the reconstruction effort, he donated personal property. He may have additionally been tempted to further debase Rome's currency to cover the costs of the disaster, which would have ultimately added economic troubles to the challenging situation, but he evidently did not. He maintained a consistent monetary policy, and he charged a group of equestrian men with seeing to Rome's reconstruction. Once the fires were out and they had raised enough funding, they began their daunting task.[18]

In what was a series of misfortunes, a deadly plague afflicted Rome sometime during Titus' rule. Pestilence was a common occurrence in old Rome, but this one was different in that it was particularly deadly. Suetonius wrote that it was so bad "the likes of which had hardly ever been known before." It's impossible to know if Suetonius was exaggerating the circumstances or not, but he is not the only ancient author to record the emergence of the unusually deadly pestilence.[19]

Titus once again wished to alleviate his people's plight. He and his lieutenants conducted sacrifices—attempting to expiate the Romans in case the epidemic was a manifestation of the gods' anger. They also relied on science and experimented with whatever medicines that were available. Unfortunately, it seems that nothing they did could tame the outbreak. Day by day, more Romans feel prey to it and perished until enough time passed, and the plague eventually lifted to the Romans' relief.[20]

The three-fold disasters striking Rome in such a short period of time surely seemed like a sign to the superstitious Romans. This could have led many to assume that they had somehow offended the pagan gods, but what did they do and how could they return to the gods' good graces? There was no answer available to them. Had Titus been less popular, then the Romans would have begun questioning whether Titus' accession had displeased the gods. After all, Vesuvius erupted, a great fire consumed much of the city and a plague ravaged Rome shortly following his ascension, but there is no record of the pagan Romans believing that Titus' coronation angered the pantheon of deities. In case there were any questions, Titus had coinage minted in 80 CE memorializing the sacrifices he conducted to assuage the gods' anger that may have led to the disasters. The Jews, on the other hand, were not swayed by his public relations attempts. They almost certainly believed that these calamities were a form of divine retribution sent to punish the Romans for razing Jerusalem and torching their Temple.[21]

Their beliefs aside, Titus' time as emperor from 79–80 CE was anything but peaceful. He grappled with the loss of his father, the eruption of Vesuvius, the outbreak of plague and a fire in Rome, and Agricola was still busy waging war. While Agricola was tasting further success as his troops continued fighting their northward, few—if any—Roman emperors before Titus had to deal with so many disasters in such a short span, but he responded with great aplomb. His people appreciated his munificence and loving demeanor, and as the year 80 CE continued, the greatest celebratory exhibition that the Romans had ever witnessed approached. It would ensure Titus' enduring fame and help guarantee the Romans' undying love for the emperor.

XXII

Amphitheatrum

> *"Let barbarian Memphis keep silence concerning the wonders of her pyramids, and let not Assyrian toil vaunt its Babylon. Let not the effeminate Ionians claim praise for their temple of the Trivian goddess; and let the altar, bristling with horns, speak modestly of the name of Delos. Their mausoleum too, hanging in empty air, let not the Carians with immoderate praise extol to the skies. Every work of toil yields to Caesar's amphitheatre; fame shall tell of one work for all."*
> —Martial[1]

BEFORE TITUS SUCCEEDED HIS FATHER, the duo had decided that they wanted to give the Romans a gift unmatched by anything in the empire, and they planned to use the proceeds from the Jewish War to fund the project. After considering their options, they settled on constructing a massive amphitheater in the heart of Rome where they could produce bloody spectacles to entertain the Romans.[2]

Early in Titus' tenure as emperor, the Romans could see the nearly completed fruits of Vespasian and Titus' labors. By no later than 80 CE, the Flavian amphitheater was largely functional and being prepared for a riveting inauguration that the Romans would never forget, and it was an awe-inspiring structure. It was architecturally different from any prior amphitheater, and it towered over nearby buildings. Today it stands at a height of nearly 160 feet. Once completed it was over 600 feet long and 500 feet wide and was divided into four main stories. However, the fourth story was likely finished following Titus' death, unless at this point it was simply made of wood. On the exterior, each story was adorned with 80 archways. On the ground level, which was decorated with Doric pillars, these archways were numbered so that they corresponded to spectators' tickets. They mostly served as entrances into the amphitheater, which provided quick and easy ingress and egress.[3]

The second and third stories were also decorated with 80 archways and Ionic and Corinthian columns, respectively. Instead of serving as entrances, construction workers placed either painted or gilded statues under these arches as ornaments. The fourth story was the tallest but was not as extravagantly designed. Rather it was essentially a plain wall with windows, bronze shields attached as decoration and pedestals and sockets to support an awning, which again, may have been completed after Titus' reign.[4]

In addition to its height, the Flavian amphitheater also covered an incredible space—almost six acres of land—and once it was finished, it could house around 50,000–55,000 cheering spectators on any given day. One ancient author asserted that 87,000 Romans could fit into it, but this was almost certainly an exaggeration.

Once inside, Romans could see a wide-open expanse at the ground level—measuring roughly 259 feet by 154 feet. This was the arena floor, which was covered with sand, in part, because it easily absorbed blood. There was a small number of primary entrances into the arena and some less assuming ones, which allowed game supervisors to rush in beasts, gladiators or anything that might be needed to entertain the masses. To ensure no animals exhibited during shows leaped into the crowd and mauled anyone, a 15-foot-tall wall wrapped around the arena floor.[5]

The section immediately above this wall was known as the podium, and this was where Rome's elite sat to view violent displays. Rome's emperor, his deputies, senators, the venerated Vestal Virgins and perhaps some women of distinction reclined on the podium. All other women were forbidden from sitting here—due to Rome's highly stratified society—because this was the most highly desired section where the privileged could enjoy luxury and comfort. After all, the seats on the podium level were far from simple bleachers. Rome's emperor, for instance, enjoyed a box suite that some have estimated could hold upward of 60 of his family members, friends and bodyguards. Its location has been the source of some debate. For years, experts assumed that it was located on the Colosseum's southern end, but a more recent theory relying on numismatic evidence suggests it was placed at the northern end of the short axis.

Colosseum, Rome, 2016.

Ascending from the podium were distinct sections, which separated different classes. The equestrians enjoyed the next section above the podium, and then the plebeians sat higher than them. Seated even further from the action were the freedmen, slaves and maybe foreign visitors. The top level was reserved for most of the

Colosseum interior, 2016.

female attendees. The higher the seat, the less desirable, and those atop the amphitheater strained their eyes to make out the games.[6]

To provide spectators with another layer of extravagance and comfort, builders installed drinking fountains and toilets, and at some point, workmen attached 240 long poles—or masts—at the top of the amphitheater that jutted upward. They attached colorful sails to these poles so that sailors could extend and retract them based on the weather and sun's location. This permitted them to shield attendees from the scorching Italian sun and rain. While this was not the Romans' first use of such awnings, it provided them a permanent stadium with a retractable roof, which was a novel solution that the Romans enjoyed for hundreds of years.[7]

Titus presumably watched the amphitheater's construction as it progressed, and he likewise monitored his other construction: the bath complex that he had hastily begun erecting upon his father's death. It was not nearly as grand as the amphitheater, but it still required a wealth of labor and supplies and demonstrated Roman ingenuity. Like the amphitheater, Titus' architects had already chosen a location—northeast of the amphitheater. Then laborers quarried stone and put the blocks into place. The structure came together very quickly and served as a gift to the Roman people, although not much of it exists today.[8]

By around 80 CE, it was nearly complete, and it would provide common and rich Romans alike with wonderful luxuries. Unfortunately, little is known about the Baths of Titus—other than its location—but enough other imperial bath complexes exist in some form today to draw some assumptions. While built quickly, it was sizable and may have been surrounded by fountains and gardens. It was made of stone and marble, and not only afforded the Romans an opportunity to take a bath, but to also enjoy an experience and many other amenities, possibly including a library, areas for lectures and exercise space.[9]

Within Titus' bath house were a series of chambers with different functions. At the primary entrance, prospective bathers could check-in with the administrator and depending on Titus' policy, they either paid a trifling sum to use the complex or else it was free. From there, they could walk to the *apodyterium*, the room where they would disrobe, perhaps put on a pair of wooden bath clogs to protect their feet in the hot bath rooms, and meet the slaves who would guide the nude bathers through a labyrinth of baths. Contingent upon how individual bathers wished to proceed, they likely would have next entered the *frigidarium*, which was a cold-water bath.[10]

After relaxing for some time, their attendants subsequently delivered them to another room—this one called the *tepidarium,* which was considerably warmer thanks to the furnaces bath houses employed. The *tepidarium* probably served a couple purposes: It helped slowly warm up bathers so they would not be shocked by the hot water bath and would help cool them down after lingering in the hot baths.[11]

With this completed, slaves escorted the Romans into the *caldarium*, which was a room with a hot bath, a vapor bath and possibly space to exercise so that bathers could generate a healthy sweat. Once the Romans had perspired enough, they returned to the *tepidarium* and cooled down and then passed through the *frigidarium* again to lower their body temperature further. During the process, slaves anointed the bathers with oils and perfumes, and either the bathers or assistants used *strigiles*—a straight-edged tool—to scrape the excess sweat from their bodies.[12]

Under the *caldarium* were the inner workings of the bath. Furnaces and boilers heated water piped in from aqueducts and turned some water into steam, which filled underfloor cavities that warmed rooms to the desired temperature. The bath was a technological marvel, but it was also artfully designed. Just as the exterior of the bath house was designed to impress, so was the interior. Roman architects and interior designers made use of vaulted ceilings, pillars and adorned it all with marble, statues and beautifully painted frescoes.[13]

The amphitheater and the bath house were not Titus' only architectural works. They are his most well-known, but he focused on more utilitarian structures too. By 80 CE, it appears that some of Rome's famed aqueducts had been falling into disrepair. Despite this, they were architectural wonders in and of themselves. Rome and many cities in the empire did not have ample access to clean or pressurized water. To address this deficiency, the Romans relied on man-made channels to redirect water to the desired locations and used gravity to do much of the work.[14]

Many aqueducts are tall arched water highways, but they also cut through mountains as engineers meticulously designed them to have a slight decreasing gradient as they approached Rome or whatever their destination was. This ingenious

First century aqueduct known as Pont Du Gard, 2019.

use of gravity and various water pipe sizes ushered water in from many miles away with enough pressure to power fountains, but their most important use was providing safer drinking and bathing water. Without aqueducts at this time, many cities would rapidly shrink in population. Titus understood their importance, and upon taking office, he ordered the restoration of aging aqueducts. In addition to these constructions, he bankrolled the creation of roads, temples and entertainment venues across the empire.[15]

Beyond this, builders began erecting a triumphal arch dedicated to Titus, and it stood on the Circus Maximus' eastern side and boasted about Titus' victory over the Jewish revolutionaries. Estimates suggest that it was nearly 50 feet tall and 56 feet wide. While barely any of it remains today, it still existed in the Middle Ages, and a dutiful monk thankfully recorded the arch's alleged inscription:

> The Roman Senate and people [dedicate this] to the Emperor Titus Caesar Vespasian Augustus, son of the deified Vespasian, pontifex maximus, holding the tribunician power for the tenth year, acclaimed imperator seventeen times, consul eight times, father of his country, their princeps, because with the guidance and plans of his father, and under his auspices, he subdued the Jewish people and destroyed the city of Jerusalem, which all generals, kings, and peoples before him had either attacked without success or left entirely unassailed.

While the inscription is undeniably false—prior armies had captured Jerusalem—it nonetheless celebrated Titus' victory over the Jewish rebels. This aside, the arch's completion date has been the source of scholarly debate. Various researchers have argued that it happened under Titus' successor, but it seems as though it occurred during Titus reign, probably in early to mid–81 CE.[16]

Before this came to fruition, Titus' primary construction projects were nearing completion by some point in 80 CE, and he planned to produce games the likes of which had never before been seen. They would celebrate *amphitheatrum*'s grand opening and possibly also Vespasian's apotheosis. Through heralds and public notices, Titus announced that he would host a hundred days of spectacles for the Romans to enjoy, and he imported many thousands of beasts, myriad gladiators and maybe condemned prisoners to ensure that it was exceptionally bloody and exhilarating, which was exactly what the Romans wanted.[17]

Cassius Dio and Suetonius recorded some details regarding the hundred days of games, as did Martial. While historians have traditionally considered Martial's *Liber de Spectaculis* to exclusively describe the hundred days of games, some modern historians now believe that it contains a mixture of references to the games of Titus and another set produced by his brother Domitian. Regardless of how much of it describes those held under Domitian's reign or Titus', when combined with Cassius Dio and Suetonius' accounts, they broadly describe the kind of events the Romans would have enjoyed.[18]

As opening day for the games arrived, throngs of Romans eagerly gathered to behold the spectacles, but according to Cassius Dio, the first days of spectacles did not occur in the newly built amphitheater. Rather there was a nearby man-made basin, which had been flooded with the Tiber River's waters, and it was surrounded by wooden seating and covered by a platform that Titus had bankrolled. The festivities began here. On the appropriate day, the Romans excitedly took their seats, and Rome's emperor—flanked by musicians, officials, priests and others—marched into the staging area. Then Titus presumably delivered some remarks and conducted a sacrifice to begin the games.[19]

While Dio is short on many details, he wrote that on the first day of the hundred days of games, the Romans enjoyed gladiatorial bouts between professionally trained fighters and staged animal hunts, which allowed the Romans to watch skilled hunters vanquish various beasts. On the second day, Titus hosted chariot races, likely in the Circus Maximus, which could easily hold 150,000 screaming Romans or more, and they watched a series of races in which charioteers hurtled down the long thoroughfares of the Circus and made tight turns—leading to tragic accidents for some participants and victory for others. The people saw this and much more in the Circus. In memory of his childhood friend, Titus commissioned the creation of an ivory statue of Britannicus riding a horse, and it became a permanent fixture in processions in the Circus Maximus. On the third day, Titus produced a naval battle, involving 3,000 participants. During the dramatic spectacle, ships violently collided into one another, sailors boarded other ships and fought in hand-to-hand combat, and then they ultimately staged an infantry battle on a small island.[20]

Eventually, it was time to inaugurate the resplendent amphitheater, and the Romans filed into it through the appropriate entrances, excitedly took their seats and prepared for events that would overwhelm their senses—even their sense of smell. That is because amphitheater workers may have piped in incense and various fragrances, including expensive saffron, to the delight of the crowd. Titus and his retinue also entered the grand structure to the sound of music in a procession that could have looked like a small Roman triumph. However, Titus was not there to celebrate a military victory but to preside over the games. Yet it seems more than likely that before any events took place, Titus once again delivered some remarks to the Roman people in the opening ceremony, and the audience would have been amazed at how well sound traveled in the arena. Even today, Rome's amphitheaters boast amazing acoustics. This fact aside, Titus or a priest probably then made a sacrifice to the gods and dedicated the structure to them. With these matters finished, the much-anticipated games could finally begin.[21]

Over the course of the succeeding days, Titus organized a host of hunts, gladiatorial bouts and battle scenes. If they adhered to the sequence of events followed in later games in the amphitheater, then the mornings were dominated by various kinds of animal exhibitions and hunts, which were costly and deadly. The Romans were treated to the deaths of 9,000 beasts throughout the hundred days of games, according to Cassius Dio. At first, this sounds like an exaggeration. Such a staggering death roll would have been incredibly expensive and plausibly led to extirpations, but Suetonius seems to confirm the widespread killing. He stated that the Romans exhibited 5,000 animals in a single day.[22]

During these hunts, the amphitheater's arena might have been designed to appear like a forest or a jungle of some kind. Then beast masters would release their animals to the Romans' excitement, but this did not always end well for the hired help. Martial mentioned a lion injuring its keeper. Despite this, the show had to go on. What happened next depended on what kind of show Titus had produced that day. In many cases, a skilled huntsman stalked the animals and killed them with a spear blow, but it was not only men who slew various creatures in the arena. Armed women also slaughtered beasts before an impressed crowd. During these exhibitions, the Romans viewed domesticated and wild animals alike, presumably including elephants, bears, boars, lions, leopards, wolves and so forth—the bigger and more exotic the beast, the better.[23]

Martial speaks of several hunts and beast fights that merit retelling. In one bout, a hunter speared a female boar. From the deep laceration, little boarlets escaped unharmed, but their mother died. While this seems like an excessively sullen spectacle today, the ancient Romans found it riveting, and they wanted more and were not disappointed. Martial recorded an account of a female huntress slaying a lion. As Dio and Suetonius claim, the combination of these spectacles left myriad animals dead, but their deaths were not entirely in vain. Much of this meat was given to the Romans to consume, but man against beast hunts were not the only action. Sometimes the Romans pit animals against each other. They enjoyed watching dogs hunt rabbits and deer but preferred more exotic matchups. Martial wrote in *Liber de Spectaculis* about a lion fighting a tiger and a bull taking on an elephant, but the animal trainers also provided some nonviolent spectacles, including inducing an elephant to kneel before the emperor—ostensibly demonstrating the immense power and authority that he even wielded over nature.[24]

Once the animal shows concluded, some attendees may have left to have lunch, but those who lingered in the amphitheater witnessed firsthand just how brutal the Romans truly were. Midday was often reserved for public executions. With so many condemned people and prisoners of war, the Romans apparently felt that it was wasteful to slay them without making it an entertaining spectacle. So they found barbaric ways of disposing of the criminals. Sometimes they forced them to re-enact mythological events, which invariably ended violently. Meanwhile, the Romans fed some criminals to hungry wild beasts and crucified and set alight others.[25]

Martial wrote about a criminal who was evidently dressed as Daedalus—a mythological man known for crafting wings for himself and his son Icarus. The condemned individual was covered with feathers and perhaps makeshift wings, but instead of being able to fly away from the amphitheater, animal keepers released a bear that mauled the man to death. In another incident recorded by Martial, the Romans crucified a man in the amphitheater, but that was a slow method of dying. To give the crowd a more exciting death, they released a bear transported from Scotland that slowly devoured the poor wretch as he writhed in pain.[26]

When the bloody executions concluded, the bulk of the Romans re-entered the amphitheater and prepared to watch gladiatorial bouts. Most gladiators were professionally trained slaves—men and women—who specialized in one particular mode of combat. Armed with their approved weaponry and armor, they sprinted into the arena and fought relentlessly against their foes. It was a bloody mode of entertainment, but it did not always end in death. While there is no way of being certain, one modern estimate suggests that a professional gladiator in the first century CE had about an 80 percent chance of surviving any fight in the arena. It was incredibly costly to train and maintain gladiators. As such, there was an incentive to keep them alive, although they certainly received many wounds and some ultimately succumbed to them.

Even though gladiators were slaves, they were not only great entertainment for their fighting abilities, but they were also sex symbols, which women fawned over. Their sweat was even sold as a sex potion. This aside, gladiatorial matches were a wildly popular form of entertainment in Rome. As the gladiators fought, the audience watched them brandish their weapons, dodge blows and go on the offensive with great anticipation. The tens of thousands of Romans filling the amphitheater went from silence to roaring cheers depending on how the fight was proceeding.[27]

Martial tells of one particularly epic gladiatorial fight between two trained fighters named Priscus and Verus. The two men fought valiantly against each other for an inordinate amount of time, but according to the rules, the fight must continue until one of the fighters yielded by raising his thumb, is incapacitated or dies. The two gladiators steadfastly refused to yield to their opponent until they were both exhausted and possibly wounded. Unable to continue fighting, they yielded simultaneously, which put the emperor in an unusual position. How could he declare one the winner over the other? Faced with this conundrum, he declared them both victors and even awarded them their freedom—to the audience's delight.[28]

The gladiators, beasts and executions thrilled the people, but they likely were not the most impressive spectacles. Titus had a real surprise for the Romans. One day as the Romans returned to the amphitheater, they noticed that the arena had been flooded—making it a shallow lake—and boats were floating on the water. When the time was right and the spectators were anxiously sitting in their seats, a faux sea battle commenced for the audience members. While modern historians and archaeologists have cast doubt over whether the Romans actually flooded the amphitheater, it is attested in the ancient records.[29]

Titus organized an additional treat for the Romans who watched the spectacles. He instructed his men to fashion wooden balls and inscribe on them something of value, like food, clothing and even silver and gold. Then amphitheater workers tossed the balls from atop the structure, and whoever caught them could return their ball to vendors in exchange for the prize carved on the sphere, which only added to the excited, carnival-like atmosphere.[30]

It appears that sometime around the opening of the amphitheater, Titus' Praetorian Guard uncovered a plot to assassinate him. Upon bringing this to Titus' attention, the young emperor chose to meet with the two conspirators who hailed from patrician families. Rather than executing them, Titus explained that the emperorship had come to him by fate, and while he would not relinquish that gift to them, he would fulfill any other request that they had. They were stunned by his forgiving response. Being caught red-handed, they must have been happy to live and requested nothing else.[31]

The mother of one of the men evidently knew that they had been plotting against the emperor and had been discovered. She naturally worried for her son, but being a patient and merciful ruler, Titus dispatched messengers to inform her of her son's well-being. In fact, Titus even invited the two conspirators to a banquet, which was attended by the emperor's friends. Probably fearing that they did not have a choice and assuming that they would be poisoned, they anxiously arrived but enjoyed a pleasant dinner. Then to show that he bore absolutely no ill-will against them, Titus invited them to attend games at the amphitheater the next day and sit with him in the choicest seats—the imperial box. Again, they accepted his invitation, and as was usual, the gladiators' swords were ceremonially offered to Titus to inspect and ensure that they were sharp. In an act of overt trust, he handed them to the patricians who had plotted his death and told them that he posed no danger to them.[32]

This was not the only dangerous conspiracy that formed against Titus, despite being a popular emperor. He faced others, but he apparently ignored some of the threats or dispatched others mercilessly and without bloodshed—earning him great acclaim. Some ancient accounts claim that one of his primary agitators was his brother Domitian who connived against him and encouraged the legions to rebel, but this may be little more than ancient writers attempting to disparage Domitian's memory. Whether or not there is truth to Domitian's scheming, Titus treated his brother with love and respect. He entreated Domitian to marry his daughter Julia on more than one occasion. He even openly declared Domitian as a ruling partner—at least nominally—and his successor, since Titus had not borne any male heirs. His lack of biological sons was not necessarily considered a problem. Titus was young enough that he could have expected to sire more children, but Rome was not a hereditary monarchy passed from father to son. Appointing a viable male family member, like Domitian, as his successor was sufficient. Unfortunately, Domitian did not respond with the same loyalty and gratitude, and Titus privately implored his sibling to return his kindness and even minted coins depicting the two brothers existing in harmony and holding hands.[33]

In spite of these threats, the hundred days of games continued, and following each day, spectators—along with Titus—were tired, dirty and even smelled of foul death. Fortunately for them, Titus' new bath house was presumably open to the public, and even though he was head of the known world's preeminent superpower, he chose to bathe with the commoners in the bath house. Probably in the evenings, he and some of his guardsmen made their way to the nearby bath and enjoyed all of the luxuries it provided alongside commoners who were surprised to see the nude, pot-bellied emperor bathing next to them. They may have had ample opportunities to see Titus too, given his love for bathing and apparent preference to do so before eating. Lingering at his eponymous bath house likely resulted in some awkward conversations as the Romans peppered the emperor with questions and requests, but he responded affably and with great aplomb.[34]

While Titus' games were wildly popular, they could not go on in perpetuity. They were incredibly costly, and Titus had slated them to only last a hundred days. Soon enough, they drew to a close. On the final day of the games, the Romans witnessed Titus weeping in public. The reason for his emotional outburst is not clear. Perhaps he mourned the end of the games or knew that something else was amiss. What followed is a veritable mystery. There is a months-long gap in the record following the hundred days of games in which practically nothing is known about Titus' activities. This might not have been a particularly exciting time in and around Rome—other than Titus studiously managing the empire—which may explain why the ancient authors mentioned nothing during this period.

This omission aside, Suetonius noted that some other issues eventually caused Titus grief. The young emperor slipped into a kind of depression at some point because a sacrificial beast had escaped as he attempted to slay it and the Romans observed a loud thunderclap. Both occurrences were portentous to the highly superstitious Romans and worried them, especially Titus. Nevertheless, months after the games concluded, he decided to leave for the countryside, and he would soon learn what calamity awaited him.[35]

XXIII

Domitian

> *"Titus, on the other hand, ruled with mildness and died at the height of his glory, whereas, if he had lived a long time, it might have been shown that he owes his present fame more to good fortune than to merit."*
> —Cassius Dio[1]

SOMETIME FOLLOWING THE HUNDRED DAYS OF GAMES, Titus decided to withdraw to the countryside where the Flavian family originally hailed. He probably wanted to enjoy some privacy and peace after presiding over raucous games, issuing edicts, poring over financial and military reports and entertaining delegations of various kinds. Being Rome's emperor could be a time-consuming and mentally and physically draining job. Faced with these realities, Titus simply wanted a respite, and the quaint, quiet life of Reate and its surroundings seemed attractive.[2]

In mid-September 81 CE, Titus, his attendants and some praetorian guardsmen quit Rome and headed toward Sabine country, but he and his comrades very quickly realized something was wrong. At the first rest stop, Titus was stricken with fever, but this was no mild illness. While few details exist of the malady, it appears to have come on quickly and strongly. Perhaps after quenching his thirst, his assistants helped him onto his litter, and as swiftly as they safely could, they rushed toward their destination—a farmhouse near Reate.[3]

They hurried along, but the fever worsened to such a degree that Titus concluded that he was dying. He threw open the litter's curtains, and he looked up to the sky and bemoaned his looming fate. He rhetorically asked the gods why he would receive this dreadful punishment—losing his life at the height of his power and at a relatively young age—when he had led a supposedly virtuous life. After all, he claimed, "I have made but one mistake." He received no answers to his question to the gods.[4]

The ailing Titus never disclosed what his solitary sin was, although ancient writers offered their opinions. Some apparently hypothesized that he had carried on an affair with Domitian's wife Domitia, which caused him remorse, but even Suetonius, who salivated over sharing ribald stories and was quick to repeat rumors, rejected these reports. Cassius Dio likewise did not believe that this was Titus' alleged "one mistake," but rather he theorized that Titus regretted not executing his scheming brother because Domitian might have organized his assassination. Again, this is more than likely an attempt to undermine Domitian's memory. There may be simpler explanations than these. It is quite possible that as Titus slowly began to succumb to the illness, he rued rejecting Berenice and sending her back to Judaea, wished that he had sired a male successor of his own or regretted executing his friends, Caecina and Eprius.[5]

Regardless of his ambiguous declaration, the fever took hold, and Titus died shortly thereafter on September 13, 81 CE—in the same farmhouse where his father had died. Titus had reigned for two years, two months and 20 days and was only 41 years old. His rapid death caused rumors to abound with some suggesting that foul play was involved, while others asserted that Titus had died naturally. Considering that there was no shortage of deadly pathogens in old Rome, he may very well have died from natural causes and nothing more. Yet one account claims that Domitian deviously ordered the still-ailing Titus to be placed in a chest packed with ice—presented as a way to bring down the fever—but it worsened his condition and hastened his demise, according to Domitian's plan. Other ancient historians wrote that he poisoned Titus with an unknown toxin. Flavius Philostratus more specifically claimed that Domitian tainted Titus' food or drink with a sea-hare.[6]

While the ancient authors were quick to impugn Domitian's dedication to Titus and suggest that he somehow caused his brother's death, there is nothing to suggest that he truly was behind it. Roman historians were hostile to Domitian's memory, and given his lack of popularity, thought him an easy target to further denigrate.

A Jewish tradition provides a different cause of Titus' death. It asserts that—as punishment from God—a gnat flew up Titus' nose and lodged in his brain where it tortured the Roman and grew to the size of a small bird, which ultimately led to his demise. Plutarch, on the other hand, vaguely implied that Titus' love of bathing may have contributed to his death. One modern theory, however, claims that Titus died naturally by contracting a form of malignant malaria, which is more convincing than some other hypotheses. Malignant malaria was a relatively common ailment in Titus' day, it surged during particular seasons (from late summer to early fall) and it struck its victims down quickly.[7]

Regardless of whether Domitian played a role in Titus' death, the surviving sibling did not do much to dispel any suspicions at first. Before Titus had even died, Domitian galloped posthaste back to Rome and entered the Praetorian Guard's camp where Domitian either told them that Titus was seriously ill or had already perished. Thereupon they hailed him emperor, and because he abandoned his brother on his deathbed and pursued his appointment as emperor, Cassius Dio rebuked him. While Domitian's actions may seem heartless *prime facie*, in Rome's flawed imperial system of succession, they were entirely understandable. If he knew that Titus was going to die, he needed to do whatever he could to act decisively and secure his path to power. If he did not, he risked having the Senate, the army or the praetorians appoint someone else—thereby ending the Flavian dynasty, which could have resulted in Domitian's assassination.[8]

Not long after Domitian left Titus' side, he passed away, and in addition to the praetorian guardsmen hailing Domitian emperor, the Senate soon did as well. The rapid turn of events must have surprised and saddened the Roman populace. They had lost their popular emperor whom they had seen in public only months ago as he presided over lavish games. Nevertheless, Rome needed a leader, and prepared or not, Domitian assumed the role.[9]

Meanwhile, the Romans were left to deal with more solemn issues, like organizing Titus' funeral, but much like Vespasian's, virtually no details of it have survived. If it was like Augustus' funeral, then upon his expiration, loved ones or servants closed Titus' eyes and cleaned and prepared his body for the upcoming funeral—dressing him in proud, dignified attire. Then, flanked by guards and close associates, Titus and a funerary train made their way to Rome where his remains were displayed for loved ones to view and even kiss goodbye.[10]

When the day came for the funeral and perhaps also the apotheosis ceremony, Titus' corpse was placed into a splendidly designed and decorated litter or carriage of some form, while his wax effigy rested atop. Mourners, relatives, officials, musicians and servants carrying images of Titus' deceased family members surrounded his coffin. Together, they escorted it to the Forum where Domitian delivered a heartfelt, tear-filled eulogy in Titus' honor, although Cassius Dio claimed that it was insincere.[11]

With this completed, the group—along with Titus' body—marched to the Campus Martius where they placed the deceased emperor atop a funeral pyre. After conducting some ceremonies and depositing mementos with his body, it was set ablaze. Then an eagle or a hawk was released, which carried his soul to be with his deified father where the two would live as gods together. Once the fire died, priests collected Titus' remains, and they were presumably stored alongside his father's ashes as Rome remained in mourning.[12]

Despite the funeral occurring shortly after Titus' death, it does not appear that the Senate deified him until October 1, 81 CE or sometime later. It is not clear whether this represents the official act of his deification or the ceremony. It is certainly plausible that the ceremony occurred before the Senate officially approved the apotheosis. Nevertheless, Domitian saw that his brother was officially deified, and Titus formally joined his father as a god among the pantheon of deities.[13]

After Titus' death and funeral, Domitian started to settle into his new role as Rome's emperor, but the early days of his reign were marked by a strange habit. According to Suetonius, Domitian would close himself off from others in a room where he would catch flies and then stab them with his stylus. This apparently was not a one-off incident. The emperor reportedly engaged in this bizarre activity over the course of many days. Eventually, he turned his gaze toward more actively managing the empire and honoring his brother's memory.[14]

Suetonius claimed that Domitian's disdain for his brother continued following Titus' death. The Roman historian asserted that Domitian did nothing to remember and honor Titus save for deifying him. He even asserted that he disparaged his memory in various forms of official correspondence, but this does not comport with reality. Domitian not only deified Titus and gave his eulogy, but also left behind monuments in remembrance of his popular brother.[15]

Domitian built or at least completed temples honoring the Flavian family, including the Temple of Vespasian and Titus in the Roman Forum. The most widely known monument to Titus is his other eponymous arch, which stands prominently to this day on the Via Sacra near the Roman Forum and celebrates Titus' victory over the Jews and his deification. This was built in addition to the Titus' arch near the Circus Maximus. There is some debate over when construction began. It is possible that Titus started the project to further advertise his exploits in Galilee and Judaea—as well as his father's—but he died prematurely, which left Domitian to finish it and show his brother's ascent into the heavens. This scholarly debate aside, Domitian ensured that it was completed and incredibly impressive. It featured panels depicting Titus' triumph through Rome, the spoils of Jerusalem and his apotheosis. An inscription on the arch exclaims, "The Roman Senate and people [dedicate this] to the deified Emperor Titus Caesar Vespasian Augustus, son of the deified Vespasian, pontifex maximus."[16] This is particularly notable since this appears to be the first and only time in Roman history that a commander received two triumphal arches within Rome for the same victory.[17]

To outsiders, Domitian at first seemed like a worthy successor to Titus. He eschewed avarice, demonstrated his generosity, lavished his people with games and served as a conscientious judge. He was also a bit of a reformer—altering Rome's monetary policy as he increased the silver content of the denarius to about 98.5 percent fine. It is not clear if he took these paths of his own accord or because Titus' remaining advisers guided the young emperor. Regardless of this, he repaired civic and religious buildings, and he apparently even finished the fourth floor of the Roman Colosseum and added the hypogeum to it, which was an underground system of tunnels, chambers, winches and trap doors. With its completion, wild beasts and gladiators could lurk below the arena floor and appear through passages—making the amphitheater even more exciting.[18]

Once seeming benevolent and magnanimous, Domitian eventually reversed his ways, and his rule turned greedy, violent and tyrannical. He executed numerous senators on conspiracy charges. While much of the evidence appears scant and suggests only minor offenses, some of them were likely involved in legitimate coup attempts. After one poorly executed uprising against him, he ordered his trusted associates to carry out a ruthless campaign of locating and torturing those who opposed him. His preferred method was apparently cutting the hands off his enemies or, as Suetonius put it, "inserting fire into their privates." He crucified other perceived enemies, but in a manner that seemed manic. He would act as their dedicated friend and then instantly turn against them and order their deaths.[19]

Even his relatives were not safe from his violence. He had his cousin Titus

Arch of Titus, Rome, 2016.

Flavius Clemens put to death and Domitilla—who was married to Clemens—banished, and he executed another cousin, Titus Flavius Sabinus who was married to Julia, Titus' daughter. She subsequently moved into the imperial palace, and the two apparently began a romantic relationship. However, she died, according to Juvenal, during an abortion Domitian forced upon her, but modern historians believe this to be baseless slander. Nevertheless, she perished somehow during Domitian's reign.[20]

Unlike Vespasian and Titus, Domitian is accused of launching a persecution against the Christians. If this is based in truth, then it was probably a short-lived affair of narrow scope, but it may have hit close to home since some have assumed that a few of Domitian's family members and others in his orbit were followers of Jesus Christ. Domitilla and Titus Flavius Clemens have even been considered possible Christians, but it is difficult to parse through these assertions to determine the truth.[21]

Be that as it may, Domitian certainly lost sight of himself. He adopted the title *Dominus et Deus*, or "Lord and God," which must have stunned and offended some of his subjects. He additionally renamed the months of September and October for himself—calling them Germanicus and Domitianus, respectively. What's more, he forbade statues to be built in his honor in the Capitol unless they were made of gold or silver.[22]

Domitian also found himself mired in different military campaigns. While hostile writers suggest that he sparked unjust, unprovoked wars, the evidence is not so clear. During his reign, the Romans waged war with numerous barbarian tribes, and under Domitian's rule Agricola settled matters in Northern England and even pushed into Scotland.[23] These wars were costly, but Domitian spent frivolously and seriously strained the imperial budget in other ways. The state purse was so stressed that Domitian debased the denarius to 93 percent silver and resorted to reducing the size of Rome's armies until they reached a number considered dangerously low. In order to recoup some money, Domitian and his aides confiscated the property of the dead and living, often without any justification. Before too long, Domitian roused the hatred of the nobility, and some of the commoners might have also grown wary of him too. The army, on the other hand, remained steadfastly loyal, in large part because he increased their pay by one quarter and treated them with deference, which was a smart move. Domitian understood that his position and power greatly depended upon the legions.[24]

While Domitian became a cruel and paranoid emperor, the latter trait is understandable. Roman emperors were regularly subjected to plots against their lives and rule, and a soothsayer had even predicted Domitian's assassination and provided him the day and time of the deed. This naturally terrified Domitian who had polished, reflective stone installed on certain corridors that he frequented so that he could see potential assassins from all angles. However, his attempts to ward off death were futile. A conspiracy formed against him, and its ringleaders knew of the prediction given to him about his murder. As the day and the hour approached, he asked for the time, and a servant lied—stating that it was one hour past the dreaded time. Thrilled, Domitian's anxiety melted, and he retired to his bedroom where he was stabbed to death.[25]

After ruling for 15 years, the 44-year-old Domitian's oppressive rule was over, and the Senate wished to blot him from the history books. Its members approved a *damnatio memoriae*, which was intended to destroy Domitian's memory and remove him from official accounts. Yet it appears to have been narrowly executed since his coinage and statues have survived to this day. This limited approach aside, it seems that Rome was happy to let the Flavian dynasty die with Domitian. Earlier in his reign, Domitian had named the children of his cousin Flavius Clemens, whom he had put to death, his successors. Instead of perpetuating the Flavian dynasty, the Senate appointed an elderly member from their ranks to the throne. His name was Nerva, and he had previously served Titus. Highly experienced, Nerva was the first of the so-called "five good emperors." Trajan succeeded Nerva and then Hadrian, Antoninus Pius and Marcus Aurelius. While Aurelius managed an empire in transition and faced dire barbarian, economic and epidemiological threats, the first four "good emperors" oversaw a period marked by more prosperous times. Even with this relative calm, revolts and attacks of various kinds cropped up periodically, including continued Jewish uprisings.[26]

Around the time that Emperor Trajan invaded Parthia, Jews from around the Roman empire rebelled—causing instability from within Rome and reportedly resulted in the deaths of many thousands of Greeks and Jews. It also diverted Trajan's focus from his Parthian adventure to quelling domestic disturbances among the Jewish diaspora. Not long after, Trajan died—likely from a stroke—and Hadrian replaced him.[27]

Under Emperor Hadrian's rule, another Jewish uprising in Judaea shook Rome, during the bar Kokhba revolt. Jerusalem had laid in ruins since Titus razed it, but Hadrian decided to rebuild it. However, he did it in his image, not the Jews'. First, he renamed Jerusalem Aelia Capitolina—after his family *nomen*—and built over the destroyed holy city—even erecting a temple to Jupiter on the Temple Mount. This outrage could not be ignored.[28]

If this were not enough, the Romans continued their heavy-handed rule over the Jewish people and found myriad ways to offend them. None of this sat well with the Jews, and understandably. A Jewish rebellion—led in large part by Simon bar Kokhba—subsequently took root in Judaea around 132 CE and gained support. Some even believed that Simon was a messianic leader, and if ancient accounts are true, hundreds of thousands of revolutionaries flocked to his standard. Yet it was not enough. Hadrian and his generals organized a crushing response. While it took a few years, they managed to subdue the revolt and were ruthless in the process.[29]

During the conflict, the Romans killed as many as 580,000 Jews, many others died from famine and pestilence, and the Romans destroyed city-after-city—leaving Judaea a wasteland. Hadrian was not pleased with this result, but went steps further. He forbade Jews from living in Aelia Capitolina, limited their ability to even enter the city, enslaved tens of thousands of Jews and enacted a policy of Jewish persecution. Likely around this time, the Romans also renamed the province of Judaea to Palestinian Syria—with the word Palestine at least partially being a reference to the Biblical Philistines who were historically the Jews' mortal enemies. The results of this war were incredibly disastrous for the Jews, and it is easy to see how Roman involvement in the region has contributed to conflict in the holy land even to this day. Titus' role was central to this development too.[30]

Because of this and Titus' many exploits and misbehavior, his legacy is complex and controversial. In ancient times, the pagan Romans lauded him for his achievements as a military man. He sacked Jerusalem and mostly brought the Jewish War to an end—save for some pockets of resistance that he delegated to others. Unlike some generals who watched battles from a safe distance, he was willing to get his hands dirty. During the war—whether he was serving as a legate or the overall commander—he willfully rushed headlong into danger in order to achieve victory or save his comrades. The ancient Romans loved him for all of this even though he was nothing short of brutal and sometimes demonstrated himself to be a headstrong, immature commander.

Many of Titus' Jewish contemporaries understandably loathed him for destroying Jerusalem and its hallowed Temple, but later rabbis took an interesting perspective. They believed that God had ordained this destruction in response to Jewish sins, and Titus had acted as an agent—fulfilling God's will. While many Jews still detested Titus—and also detested Vespasian—they increasingly held the leaders of the Jewish revolt responsible for the Temple's destruction.[31] Early Christians, on the other hand, took a different view of Jerusalem's razing. They believed that it was God's will and a kind of announcement of the emergence of their religion, Christianity, replacing Judaism.[32]

There is more to Titus' legacy than just his participation in the Jewish Revolt, including his tenure as a Roman prince in the eternal city, which was nearly disastrous for Titus. He was too zealous as a Praetorian Guard prefect—leading him to quickly order the deaths of anyone suspected of conspiring against the Flavian family. He also did not act virtuously as a prince. He preferred to drink wine with his friends late into the night and conspicuously paraded Berenice around Rome. None of this pleased the Romans who worried that he was a Nero in the making.

Somehow Titus managed to correct his behavior upon becoming emperor, and he proved to be a conscientious ruler from the Roman perspective. He funded grand construction, hosted lavish games, eschewed killing senators and helped bankroll emergency responses to major disasters. He died long before anyone could gather what kind of emperor he would have been later in life. Perhaps he would have evolved into the person Domitian became or remained an upstanding Roman. Whatever the case, the Romans considered him an exemplary emperor virtually without fault, and overall, he served as a model for Romans for hundreds of years. Some of this might be due to the great press ancient writers provided him because the Flavians were their benefactors.

Modern examinations of his legacy are not quite so glowing. Yes, he was incredibly accomplished, but he led ruthless campaigns—leaving an untold number of Jews dead. He enslaved a host of others, flattened Jerusalem, including the Temple, ethnically cleansed part of Judaea, used Jewish prisoners of war as entertainment and killed any Roman who threatened his father without trial. From the modern perspective, these are not the traits of a hero but a villain. Taken within the ancient Roman context, however, Titus' exploits during the Jewish War were considered appropriate methods of dealing with rebellions, and his actions as a praetorian prefect might have been expected of someone who faced regular plots and witnessed the Year of the Four Emperors.

While Titus' name and victories are not as widely known as those of, say, Julius Caesar, he has received some attention in modern times. In 2020, an opinion article called for the dismantling of the Arch of Titus. "Most famously, one of its panels depicts a triumphal procession of Roman soldiers proudly parading their spoils from the capture of Jerusalem," wrote the article's author. "These include the vessels they stole from the Jerusalem Temple, and perhaps most famously, the golden menorah. Titus, the man that this arch honors, led the Roman siege of Jerusalem in 68–70 CE that culminated in the destruction of the Temple, the enslavement and murder of hundreds of thousands of Jews, and the gradual end of communal Jewish life in the land of Israel, our indigenous home. It's time it came down."[33]

This is unlikely to happen anytime in the near future, but it is an interesting response to pursue a modern *damnatio memoriae* for Titus and his arch. It is a vital link to the past and tells an important story, but this demonstrates Titus' legacy is not easy to untangle nor has it emerged unscathed over the centuries.

In the end, the Romans remembered Titus as an emperor to be celebrated and deity to be worshipped. Regardless of his copious transgressions, his victories are still impressive, and he was inextricably linked to more decisive events and calamities in Roman history than most others. He survived imperial turnover and even the assassination attempt against Britannicus; served in Britannia after the Boudica rebellion; lived through the great fire of Rome; played a contributing role in the Year of the Four Emperors that led to Vespasian's coronation; sacked Jerusalem and mostly brought the Jewish War to a close; presided over the empire as Vesuvius destroyed numerous cities; helped build Rome's greatest construction, the Colosseum; witnessed early Christianity's early spread; and hosted the vaunted hundred days of games.

Hero or villain, there are few pivotal historical figures like Titus who straddled more momentous history and whose effects are felt even to this day.

Chapter Notes

Abbreviations:

App. BC—Appian, *The Civil Wars*
CAH X—Bowman, Alan K., et. al., *The Cambridge Ancient History Volume X*
CAH XI—Bowman, Alan K., et. al., *The Cambridge Ancient History Volume XI*
CIL—*Corpus Inscriptionum Latinarum*
Dio—Cassius Dio, *Roman History*
Diod.—Diodorus Siculus, *The Library of History*
Dion. Hal.—Dionysius of Halicarnassus, *The Roman Antiquities*
Eus. H.E.—Eusebius, *Ecclesiastical History*
Gittin—Gittin, *Babylonian Talmud*
Jos.—Josephus, *The Jewish War*
Jos. AJ—Josephus, *Antiquities of the Jews*
Jos. Life—Josephus, *Life of Josephus*
Lact. Mort.—Lactantius, *De Mortibus Persecutorum*
Livy—Livy, *History of Rome*
Mart. Spect.—Martial, *Liber de Spectaculis*
Matt.—*The Gospel According to Matthew*
Neh.—*The Book of Nehemiah*
Oros.—Orosius, *The Seven Books of History Against the Pagans*
Philostr. VA: Flavius—Philostratus, *Life of Apollonius of Tyana*
Plin. Ep.—Pliny the Younger, *The Epistulae*
Plin. Nat.—Pliny the Elder, *The Natural History*
Plut. De Tuenda—Plutarch, *De tuenda sanitate praecepta*
Plut. Pomp.—*Plutarch, Life of Pompey*
Suet. Aug.—Suetonius, *Life of Augustus*
Suet. Calig.—Suetonius, *Life of Caligula*
Suet. Claud.—Suetonius, *Life of Claudius*
Suet. Dom.—Suetonius, *Life of Domitian*
Suet. Galb.—Suetonius, *Life of Galba*
Suet. Jul.—Suetonius, *Life of Julius Caesar*
Suet. Ner.—Suetonius, *Life of Nero*
Suet. Otho—Suetonius, *Life of Otho*
Suet. Tib.—Suetonius, *Life of Tiberius*
Suet. Tit.—Suetonius, *Life of Titus*
Suet. Vesp.—Suetonius, *Life of Vespasian*
Suet. Vit.—Suetonius, *Life of Vitellius*
Sulp. Sev. H.E.—Sulpicius Severus, *Sacred History*
Tac. Ann.—Tacitus, *The Annals*
Tac. Hist.—Tacitus, *The Histories*
Tert. Apol.—Tertullian, *Apologeticum*

Chapter I

1. Suet. Vesp. 1.1 (Translated by J.C. Rolfe).
2. Suet. Vesp. 1.2-4.
3. Suet. Vesp. 2.1; Jones, Brian W., *The Emperor Titus*, St. Martin's Press, New York, 1984, pg. 1.
4. Suet. Vesp. 22.1.
5. Suet. Vesp. 1.1-2.
6. Suet. Vesp. 1.2 and 1.4.
7. Livy 1.60.1-3.
8. Abbott, Frank Frost, *A History and Description of Roman Political Institutions*, Third Edition, Ginn and Company, Boston, 1911, pg. 24-40 and 175-181.
9. Long, George, *Nobiles*, A Dictionary of Greek and Roman Antiquities, John Murry, London, 1875, https://penelope.uchicago.edu/Thayer/E/Roman/Texts/secondary/SMIGRA*/Nobiles.html; Everett, Anthony, *The Rise of Rome*, Random House Trade Paperbacks, New York, 2013, pg. 61, 286-287, 296, 310, 402.
10. Suet. Jul. 77.1 (Translated by J.C. Rolfe).
11. Suet. Vesp. 1.2; Suet. Jul. 25.1 and 30.1-4; App. BC 2.30-35 (Translated by Horace White).
12. Suet. Vesp. 1.2; Fields, Nic, *Boudicca's Rebellion AD 60-61: The Britons rise up against Rome*, Osprey Publishing, Oxford, 2011, pg. 33.
13. Plut. Pomp. 77.1-4, 79.1-3, 80.1, and 80.5.
14. Suet. Vesp. 1.2 and 2.1; Jones, Brian W., *The Emperor Titus*, St. Martin's Press, New York, 1984, pg. 1.
15. Suet. Jul. 76.1.
16. Suet. Jul. 82.1-3.
17. Suet. Aug. 13.1.
18. Suet. Aug. 17.1-2.
19. Dio 53.1-12; Suet. Aug. 17.4 and 28.1-2.
20. Suet. Vesp. 1.2 (Translated by J.C. Rolfe).
21. Suet. Vesp. 1.2 (Translated by J.C. Rolfe); Jones, Brian W., *The Emperor Titus*, St. Martin's Press, New York, 1984, pg. 1.
22. Suet. Vesp. 1.2; Jones, Brian W., *The Emperor Titus*, St. Martin's Press, New York, 1984, pg. 1; Levick, Barbara, *Vespasian*, Routledge, New York, 1999, pg. 5.
23. Matt. 9.10-12.
24. Suet. Vesp. 1.2-3 (Translated by J.C. Rolfe); Jones, Brian W., *The Emperor Titus*, St. Martin's Press, New York, 1984, pg. 4.

25. Suet. Vesp. 1.3
26. Suet. Vesp. 2.1.
27. Suet. Tib. 9.1–2, 10.1, 36.1, 43.1–2, 44.1–2, 45.1, 46.1; Tac. Ann. 2.85 and 6.19; Dio 57.18.5a; Suet. Vit. 3.2.
28. Suet. Vesp. 2.2 (Translated by J.C. Rolfe).
29. Abbott, Frank Frost, *A History and Description of Roman Political Institutions*, Third Edition, Ginn and Company, Boston, 1911, pg. 291–292 and 374–375.
30. Smith, William, "Clavus Latus," *A Dictionary of Greek and Roman Antiquities*, John Murray, London, 1890, https://www.perseus.tufts.edu/hopper/text?doc=Perseus:text:1999.04.0063:entry=clavus-latus-cn.
31. Suet. Vesp. 1.3 and 2.3. Abbott, Frank Frost, *A History and Description of Roman Political Institutions*, Third Edition, Ginn and Company, Boston, 1911, pg. 374–5, 378–9, and 381; Levick, Barbara, *Vespasian*, Routledge, New York, 1999, pg. 8; Jones believes Vespasian's tenure as military tribune started as late as AD 30: Jones, Brian W., *The Emperor Titus*, St. Martin's Press, New York, 1984, pg. 6.
32. Levick, Barbara, *Vespasian*, Routledge, New York, 1999, pg. 8.
33. Abbott, Frank Frost, *A History and Description of Roman Political Institutions*, Third Edition, Ginn and Company, Boston, 1911, pg. 374 and 379–380; Levick, Barbara, *Vespasian*, Routledge, New York, 1999, pg. 8–9.
34. Suet. Vesp. 2.3; Jones, Brian W., *The Emperor Titus*, St. Martin's Press, New York, 1984, pg. 6. Abbott, Frank Frost, *A History and Description of Roman Political Institutions*, Third Edition, Ginn and Company, Boston, 1911, pg. 374–5, 378–9; Levick, Barbara, *Vespasian*, Routledge, New York, 1999, pg. 9.
35. Suet. Vesp. 2.3 and 5.3. Levick, Barbara, *Vespasian*, Routledge, New York, 1999, pg. 10; Abbott, Frank Frost, *A History and Description of Roman Political Institutions*, Third Edition, Ginn and Company, Boston, 1911, pg. 378.
36. Suet. Calig. 9.1, 22.1–2, 24.1, 25.1, 27.1, 30.1–2, and 36.2; Dio 59.14.7.
37. Tac. Hist. 5.9.1; Philo Legat. 186–190 and 352–353 (Translated by F.H. Colson); Jos. Ant. 18.261–268.
38. Suet. Vesp. 5.3.
39. Suet. Vesp. 3.1; Levick, Barbara, *Vespasian*, Routledge, New York, 1999, pg. 12.

Chapter II

1. Suet. Tit. 1.1 (Translated by J.C. Rolfe).
2. Suet. Vesp. 2.3; Abbott, Frank Frost, *A History and Description of Roman Political Institutions*, Third Edition, Ginn and Company, Boston, 1911, pg. 374–7; George, Long, "Praetor," *A Dictionary of Greek and Roman Antiquities*, John Murray, London, 1875, https://penelope.uchicago.edu/Thayer/E/Roman/Texts/secondary/SMIGRA*/Praetor.html; Levick, Barbara, *Vespasian*, Routledge, New York, 1999, pg. 10–11.
3. Suet. Vesp. 3.1; Suet. Tit. 1.1; Zissos, Andrew, *A Companion to the Flavian Age of Imperial Rome*, John Wiley and Sons, Inc., January 2016, pg. 77; Jones, Brian W., *The Emperor Titus*, St. Martin's Press, New York, 1984, pg. 1.
*Suet. Tit. offers contradicting dates for Titus' birth—39 or 41 CE—but most have accepted 39 CE as his birth year.
4. Roser, Max, "Mortality in the past—around half died as children," *Our World in Data*, July 11, 2019. https://ourworldindata.org/child-mortality-in-the-past.
5. Dion. Hal. 2.15.2; Cohen, Ada, Rutter, Jeremy B., *Constructions of Childhood in Ancient Greece and Italy* (American School of Classical Studies at Athens; Volume XLI edition, 2007), pg. 283.
6. Harrill, J. Albert. "Coming of Age and Putting on Christ: The Toga Virilis Ceremony, Its Paraenesis, and Paul's Interpretation of Baptism in Galatians." *Novum Testamentum*, vol. 44, no. 3, 2002, pp. 252–277; Rawson, Beryl, *Children and Childhood in Roman Italy* (Oxford University Press, 2003), pg. 144; Diod. 5.30.1.
7. Suet. Vesp. 2.3; Suet. Calig. 58.2–3; Suet. Claud. 10.2–4.
8. Suet. Claud. 3.2, 25.4, 30.1, 40.1, and 41.1; Oros. 7.6.15–16; Mellowes, Marilyn, "The Gospel of Mark," PBS, April 1998, https://www.pbs.org/wgbh/pages/frontline/shows/religion/story/mmmark.html.
9. Suet. Claud. 25.4 (Translated by J.C. Rolfe); Oros. 7.6.15–16 (Translated by I.W. Raymond); Rutgers, Leonard Victor. "Roman Policy towards the Jews: Expulsions from the City of Rome during the First Century C.E." *Classical Antiquity*, vol. 13, no. 1, 1994, pp. 56–74.
10. Suet. Aug. 28.3 (Translated by J.C. Rolfe).
11. Storey, Glenn R., "The population of ancient Rome," Cambridge University Press, Last Accessed April 4, 2024, https://www.cambridge.org/core/services/aop-cambridge-core/content/view/BACD7DF32B0B77609CD6713B8AF88882/S0003598X00085859a.pdf/the-population-of-ancient-rome.pdf.
12. Lanciani, Rodolfo, "The Sky Scrapers of Rome," The North American Review 162.475 (1896), pg. 705–15; Suet. Aug. 25.2.
13. Leigh, Lex, "Nine Absolutely Disgusting Ancient Foods Our Ancestors Enjoyed," Ancient Origins, December 30, 2022, https://www.ancient-origins.net/history-ancient-traditions/disgusting-ancient-food-0017727.
14. "Stone Phalluses of Pompeii," Atlas Obscura, Last Accessed July 31, 2024, https://www.atlasobscura.com/places/stone-phalluses-of-pompeii.
15. Eyre, J.J. "Roman Education in the Late Republic and Early Empire." Greece & Rome, vol. 10, no. 1, 1963, pp. 47–59; Poynton, J.B. "Roman Education." Greece & Rome, vol. 4, no. 10, 1934, pp. 1–12.

16. Suet. Vesp. 3.1 and 4.1; Jones, Brian W., *The Emperor Titus*, St. Martin's Press, New York, 1984, pg. 5; Southern, Pat, Domitian, *Tragic Tyrant*, Routledge, New York, 1997, pg. 4; Smith, William, "Libertus," A Dictionary of Greek and Roman Antiquities, John Murray, London, 1875, https://penelope.uchicago.edu/Thayer/E/Roman/Texts/secondary/SMIGRA*/Libertus.html.
17. Suet. Aug. 23.1–2 (Translated by J.C. Rolfe).
18. Tac. Ann. 1.62.1.
19. Suet. Vesp. 4.1; Dio 39.50.1 and 40.1.2.
20. Suet. Calig. 46.1; Barrett, Anthony, *Caligula, The Corruption of Power*, Yale University Press, New Haven, 1989, pg. 135.
21. Suet. Vesp. 4.1.
22. Eyre, J.J. "Roman Education in the Late Republic and Early Empire." Greece & Rome, vol. 10, no. 1, 1963, pp. 47–59; Poynton, J.B. "Roman Education." Greece & Rome, vol. 4, no. 10, 1934, pp. 1–12.
23. Eyre, J.J. "Roman Education in the Late Republic and Early Empire." Greece & Rome, vol. 10, no. 1, 1963, pp. 47–59; Poynton, J.B. "Roman Education." Greece & Rome, vol. 4, no. 10, 1934, pp. 1–12.
24. Eyre, J.J. "Roman Education in the Late Republic and Early Empire." Greece & Rome, vol. 10, no. 1, 1963, pp. 47–59; Poynton, J.B. "Roman Education." Greece & Rome, vol. 4, no. 10, 1934, pp. 1–12.
25. Eyre, J.J. "Roman Education in the Late Republic and Early Empire." Greece & Rome, vol. 10, no. 1, 1963, pp. 47–59; Madden, John. "Slavery in the Roman Empire Numbers and Origins." *Classics Ireland*, vol. 3, 1996, pp. 109–28.
26. Suet. Vesp. 3.1 and 4.1–2. Jones, Brian W., *The Emperor Titus*, St. Martin's Press, New York, 1984, pg. 10–11; Abbott, Frank Frost, *A History and Description of Roman Political Institutions*, Third Edition, Ginn and Company, Boston, 1911, pg. 376; Southern, Pat, Domitian, *Tragic Tyrant*, Routledge, New York, 1997, pg. 7.
27. Eyre, J.J. "Roman Education in the Late Republic and Early Empire." Greece & Rome, vol. 10, no. 1, 1963, pp. 47–59; Poynton, J.B. "Roman Education." Greece & Rome, vol. 4, no. 10, 1934, pp. 1–12.
28. Suet. Tit. 2.1; Jones, Brian W., *The Emperor Titus*, St. Martin's Press, New York, 1984, pg. 7 and 11.
29. Suet. Vesp. 4.2.
30. Suet. Tit. 2.1.
31. Eyre, J.J. "Roman Education in the Late Republic and Early Empire." Greece & Rome, vol. 10, no. 1, 1963, pp. 47–59; Poynton, J.B. "Roman Education." Greece & Rome, vol. 4, no. 10, 1934, pp. 1–12; Suet. Tit. 2.1; Suet. Claud. 44.2.
32. Suet. Tit. 2.1; Tac. Ann. 13.16; Suet. Ner. 33.2–3; Retief, Francois P., Cilliers, Louise, "Poisons, Poisoning, and Poisoners in Rome," Medicina Antiqua, Last Accessed April 4, 2024, https://www.ucl.ac.uk/~ucgajpd/medicina%20antiqua/sa_poisons.html.
33. Suet. Vesp. 4.2; Jones, Brian W., *The Emperor Titus*, St. Martin's Press, New York, 1984, pg. 11.
34. Eyre, J.J. "Roman Education in the Late Republic and Early Empire." Greece & Rome, vol. 10, no. 1, 1963, pp. 47–59; Poynton, J.B. "Roman Education." Greece & Rome, vol. 4, no. 10, 1934, pp. 1–12.
35. Harrill, J. Albert. "Coming of Age and Putting on Christ: The Toga Virilis Ceremony, Its Paraenesis, and Paul's Interpretation of Baptism in Galatians." *Novum Testamentum*, vol. 44, no. 3, 2002, pp. 252–277; Rawson, Beryl, *Children and Childhood in Roman Italy* (Oxford University Press, 2003), pg. 144; Smith, William, "Toga," A Dictionary of Greek and Roman Antiquities, 1875, Lacus Curtius. https://penelope.uchicago.edu/Thayer/e/roman/texts/secondary/smigra*/toga.html; Jones, Brian W., *The Emperor Titus*, St. Martin's Press, New York, 1984, pg. 13.
36. Suet. Tit. 3.1–2.

Chapter III

1. Dio 62.2 (Translated by Earnest Cary)
2. Suet. Tit. 4.1.
3. Tac. Ann. 14.3–9, Dio 61.11–14; Suet. Nero 34.1–4.
4. Jones, Brian W., *The Emperor Titus*, St. Martin's Press, New York, 1984, pg. 14–15.
5. Goldsworthy, Adrian, *The Complete Roman Army*, Thames and Hudson, New York, 2003, pg. 50 and 60.
6. Suet. Tit. 4.1; Jones, Brian W., *The Emperor Titus*, St. Martin's Press, New York, 1984, pg. 14.
7. Dio 62.2.1.
8. Tac. Ann. 14.31.1.
9. Tac. Ann. 14.31.1.
10. Dio 62.2.3–4 (Translated by Earnest Cary).
11. Tac. Ann. 14.31.1; Dio 62.2.2–3 and 62.8.2.
12. Tac. Ann. 14.32.1 and 14.33.1; Dio 62.1.1 and 62.7.1–2 (Translated by Earnest Cary).
13. Tac. Ann. 14.32.1 and 14.33.1; Dio 62.1.1; Fields, Nic, *Boudicca's Rebellion AD 60–61: The Britons rise up against Rome*, Osprey Publishing, Oxford, 2011, pg. 57.
14. Suet. Ner. 18.1.
15. Tac. Ann. 14.34.1; Dio 62.8.1; Fields, Nic, *Boudicca's Rebellion AD 60–61: The Britons rise up against Rome*, Osprey Publishing, Oxford, 2011, pg. 21.
16. Tac. Ann. 14.34.1, 14.35.1, and 14.36.1 (Translated by Alfred John Church, William Jackson Brodribb); Dio 62.8.2; Fields, Nic, *Boudicca's Rebellion AD 60–61: The Britons rise up against Rome*, Osprey Publishing, Oxford, 2011, pg. 25–30 and 67.
17. Tac. Ann. 14.37.1; Dio 62.8.2–3 and 62.12.5–6.
18. Tac. Ann. 14.38.1; Suet. Tit. 4.1; Fields, Nic, *Boudicca's Rebellion AD 60–61: The Britons rise up against Rome*, Osprey Publishing, Oxford, 2011, pg. 83; Jones, Brian W., *The Emperor Titus*, St. Martin's Press, New York, 1984, pg. 16.

19. Tac. Hist. 2.77; Jones, Brian W., *The Emperor Titus*, St. Martin's Press, New York, 1984, pg. 15–17.
20. Tac. Ann. 14.38.1 and 14.39.1; Suet. Tit. 4.1; Dio 62.12.6.
21. Suet. Tit. 4.1.
22. Suet. Tit. 4.2; Jones, Brian W., *The Emperor Titus*, St. Martin's Press, New York, 1984, pg. 16–17.
23. Suet. Tit. 4.2; Jones, Brian W., *The Emperor Titus*, St. Martin's Press, New York, 1984, pg. 18; Southern, Pat, Domitian, Tragic Tyrant, Routledge, New York, 1997, pg. 5; Levick, Barbara, *Vespasian*, Routledge, New York, 1999, pg. 23.
24. Plut. Rom. 15.5; Jones, Brian W., *The Emperor Titus*, St. Martin's Press, New York, 1984, pg. 18; Smith, William, "Matrimonium," *A Dictionary of Greek and Roman Antiquities*, 1875, Lacus Curtius; https://penelope.uchicago.edu/Thayer/E/Roman/Texts/secondary/SMIGRA*/Matrimonium.html.
25. Smith, William, "Matrimonium," *A Dictionary of Greek and Roman Antiquities*, 1875, Lacus Curtius; https://penelope.uchicago.edu/Thayer/E/Roman/Texts/secondary/SMIGRA*/Matrimonium.html.
26. Plut. Rom. 15.1–2; Smith, William, "Matrimonium," *A Dictionary of Greek and Roman Antiquities*, 1875, Lacus Curtius, https://penelope.uchicago.edu/Thayer/E/Roman/Texts/secondary/SMIGRA*/Matrimonium.html; Smith, William, "Thala'ssius," *A Dictionary of Greek and Roman Antiquities*, 1875, Perseus Digital Library, https://www.perseus.tufts.edu/hopper/text?doc=Perseus:text:1999.04.0104:entry=thalassius-talassius-bio-1.
27. Smith, William, "Matrimonium," *A Dictionary of Greek and Roman Antiquities*, 1875, Lacus Curtius; https://penelope.uchicago.edu/Thayer/E/Roman/Texts/secondary/SMIGRA*/Matrimonium.html.l
28. Smith, William, "Matrimonium," *A Dictionary of Greek and Roman Antiquities*, 1875, Lacus Curtius; https://penelope.uchicago.edu/Thayer/E/Roman/Texts/secondary/SMIGRA*/Matrimonium.html.
29. Suet. Tit. 4.2; Philostr. VA 7.7; Jones, Brian W., *The Emperor Titus*, St. Martin's Press, New York, 1984, pg. 19.
30. Todman D. Childbirth in ancient Rome: from traditional folklore to obstetrics. Aust N Z J Obstet Gynaecol. 2007 Apr;47(2):82–5. doi: 10.1111/j.1479-828X.2007.00691.x. PMID: 17355293.
31. Smith, William, "Funus," A Dictionary of Greek and Roman Antiquities, John Murray, London, 1875, Lacus Curtius, https://penelope.uchicago.edu/Thayer/E/Roman/Texts/secondary/SMIGRA*/Funus.html.
32. Suet. Vesp. 4.3; Jones, Brian W., *The Emperor Titus*, St. Martin's Press, New York, 1984, pg. 10; Levick, Barbara, *Vespasian*, Routledge, New York, 1999, pg. 23; Long, George, "Provincia," A Dictionary of Greek and Roman Antiquities, John Murray, London, 1875, Lacus Curtius, https://penelope.uchicago.edu/Thayer/E/Roman/Texts/secondary/SMIGRA*/Provincia.html.
33. Suet. Vesp. 4.3; Tac. Hist. 3.65.1; Levick, Barbara, *Vespasian*, Routledge, New York, 1999, pg. 23–24.
34. Suet. Tit. 4.2.
35. Smith, William, *Abaeus-Dysponteus*, John Murray, 1890, pg. 539.
36. Suet. Tit. 4.2; Tac. Ann. 16.30; Jones, Brian W., *The Emperor Titus*, St. Martin's Press, New York, 1984, pg. 19.
37. Suet. Vesp. 3.1; Suet. Tit. 4.2; Philostr. VA 7.7; Southern, Pat, Domitian, *Tragic Tyrant*, Routledge, New York, 1997, pg. 9; Smith, William, "Divortium," A Dictionary of Greek and Roman Antiquities, John Murray, London, 1875, Lacus Curtius, https://penelope.uchicago.edu/Thayer/E/Roman/Texts/secondary/SMIGRA*/Divortium.html.

Chapter IV

1. Quote: Jos. 2.356–357 (Translated by Martin Hammond); Josephus, Flavius and Hammond, Martin, *The Jewish War*, Oxford University Press, Oxford, 2017, pg. 127–128.
2. Suet. Ner. 20–25.
3. Suet. Ner. 23.2.
4. Suet. Vesp. 4.4.
5. Suet. Ner. 24.2.
6. Tac. Ann. 15.37.1.
7. Suet. Ner. 28.1 and 35.3.
8. Dio 62.16–18; Tac. Ann. 15.38–43; Suet. Ner. 38.1–3; Dando-Collins, Stephen, *The Great Fire of Rome*, Da Capo Press, Philadelphia, 2010, pg. 57, 87–88, 90, 94–95, 97–98.
9. Dio 62.16.1–3 and 62.18.1; Suet. Ner. 38.1–3; Tac. Ann. 15.39 and 15.43; Dando-Collins, Stephen, *The Great Fire of Rome*, Da Capo Press, Philadelphia, 2010, pg. 84, 100, and 104.
10. Suet. Nero 31.1–2; Dando-Collins, Stephen, *The Great Fire of Rome*, Da Capo Press, Philadelphia, 2010, pg. 111–112; Harl, Kenneth W., *Coinage in the Roman Economy 300 B.C. to A.D. 700*, The Johns Hopkins University Press, Baltimore, 1996, pg. 91.
11. Suet. Tit. 4.3; Jones, Brian W., *The Emperor Titus*, St. Martin's Press, New York, 1984, pg. 20; Levick, Barbara, *Vespasian*, Routledge, New York, 1999, pg. 23.
12. Tac. Ann. 15.44.
13. Tac. Hist. 5.4–6 and 5.8; Asiedu, F.B.A., *Josephus, Paul, and the Fate of Early Christianity*, Lexington Books, New York, 2019, pg. 130–131; Schnelle, Udo, *The First One Hundred Years of Christianity: An Introduction to Its History, Literature, and Development*, Baker Academic, 2020, pg. 59, 429, 433, 437–438.
14. Tac. Ann. 15.44 (Translated by Alfred John Church and William Jackson Brodribb).
15. Schnelle, Udo, *The First One Hundred Years*

of Christianity: An Introduction to Its History, Literature, and Development*, Baker Academic, 2020, pg. 299; SHAW, BRENT D. "The Myth of the Neronian Persecution." *The Journal of Roman Studies*, vol. 105, 2015, pp. 73–100; Dando-Collins, Stephen, *The Great Fire of Rome*, Da Capo Press, Philadelphia, 2010, pg. 106–7.

16. Dio 63.22; Oros. 7.9.2; Jones, Brian W., *The Emperor Titus*, St. Martin's Press, New York, 1984, pg. 22.

17. Ben-Sasson, H.H., *A History of the Jewish People*, Harvard University Press, Cambridge, 1976, pg. 110–112, 159–186, and 201–222.

18. Tac. Hist. 5.9; Jos. Ant. 14.4.4; Jos. 1.133–155; Goodman, Martin, *Rome and Jerusalem*, Vintage Books, New York 2008, pg. 51–53.

19. Tac. Hit. 5.4–10; Dio 63.22; Berlin, Andrea M., Overman, Andrew J., *The First Jewish Revolt*, Routledge, New York, 2002, pg. 27–39; Bloom, James, *The Jewish Revolts Against Rome, A.D. 66-135*, McFarland, Jefferson, NC, 2010, pg. 62.

20. Berlin, Andrea M., Overman, Andrew J., *The First Jewish Revolt*, Routledge, New York, 2002, pg. 43–55, 98–99.

21. Jos. 2.289–308.

22. Jos. 2.309–311 and 2.333–334.

23. Jos. 2.351–354 (Translated by John Thackeray); Josephus, Flavius, and Thackeray, John, *Josephus Volume II, The Jewish War Books I–III*, Harvard University Press, Cambridge, 1927, pg. 461.

24. Jos. 2.400 (Translated by John Thackeray); Josephus, Flavius, and Thackeray, John, *Josephus Volume II, The Jewish War Books I–III*, Harvard University Press, Cambridge, 1927, pg. 479–481.

25. Jos. 2.356–357 (Translated by Martin Hammond); Josephus, Flavius and Hammond, Martin, *The Jewish War*, Oxford University Press, Oxford, 2017, pg. 127–128.

26. Tac. Hist. 5.10; Jos. 2.406–410, 2.422–427, 2.430–432.

27. Jos. 2.433–435 and 2.441–442.

28. Jos. 2.457–460, 2.466, 2.477–478, 2.484–485, 2.496–497 and 2.561.

29. Jos. 2.499–501, 2.506, 2.509, 2.512, 2.521, 2.527–529, 2.550–555, and 2.564–565; Oros. 7.9.2; Levick, Barbara, *Vespasian*, Routledge, New York, 1999, pg. 28.

30. Jos. AJ 20.9; Jos. 2.562–571.

31. Jos. 2.562–571; Jos. Life 1–5 and 7; Bloom, James, *The Jewish Revolts Against Rome, A.D. 66-135*, McFarland, Jefferson, NC, 2010, pg. 80–81; Berlin, Andrea M., Overman, Andrew J., *The First Jewish Revolt*, Routledge, New York, 2002, pg. 87–106.

32. Jos. 2.556, 2.572–577, 2.583, 2.598–599, 2.608–610 2.615, 2.621–624, 2.627–628; Eus. HE 3.5.3; Jos. Life 7; Bloom, James, *The Jewish Revolts Against Rome, A.D. 66-135*, McFarland, Jefferson, NC, 2010, pg. 95; Levick, Barbara, *Vespasian*, Routledge, New York, 1999, pg. 150.

33. Jos. 3.1.

34. Jos. 3.1–3.

35. Vesp. 4.4–6; Jos. 3.6–7; Jones, Brian W., *The Emperor Titus*, St. Martin's Press, New York, 1984, pg. 34.

36. Vesp. 4.4–6; Jos. 3.6–7; Dio 63.22; Oros. 7.9.3.

Chapter V

1. Jos. 3.265 (Translated by Martin Hammond); Josephus, Flavius and Hammond, Martin, *The Jewish War*, Oxford University Press, Oxford, 2017, pg. 180.

2. Jos. 3.7–8 and 3.64; Jones, Brian W., *The Emperor Titus*, St. Martin's Press, New York, 1984, pg. 35–36; Jones, Brian W. "Titus in Judaea, A.D. 67." *Latomus*, vol. 48, no. 1, 1989, pp. 127–34.

3. Jos. 3.64.

4. Jos. 3.8, 3.29–30, 3.65 and 3.68; Jones, Brian W., *The Emperor Titus*, St. Martin's Press, New York, 1984, pg. 36; Schoenfeld, Andrew J. "Sons of Israel in Caesar's Service: Jewish Soldiers in the Roman Military." *Shofar: An Interdisciplinary Journal of Jewish Studies*, vol. 24 no. 3, 2006, pp. 115–126.

5. Jos. 3.11–12, 3.19–20 and 3.25.

6. Jos. 3.30–34 and 3.59; Berlin, Andrea M., Overman, Andrew J., *The First Jewish Revolt*, Routledge, New York, 2002, pg. 110–113.

7. Jos. 3.59–63 and 3.110.

8. Jos. 3.64–69, 3.110 and 3.115; Jones, Brian W., *The Emperor Titus*, St. Martin's Press, New York, 1984, pg. 60–63; Bloom, James, *The Jewish Revolts Against Rome, A.D. 66-135*, McFarland, Jefferson, NC, 2010, pg. 117; Crook, John A. "Titus and Berenice." *The American Journal of Philology*, vol. 72, no. 2, 1951, pp. 162–75.

9. Jos. 3.132–134.

10. Jos. 3.141.

11. Jos. 3.141–145 and 3.158–160; Berlin, Andrea M., Overman, Andrew J., *The First Jewish Revolt*, Routledge, New York, 2002, pg. 121–133.

12. Jos. 3.146–149.

13. Jos. 3.150–157; Berlin, Andrea M., Overman, Andrew J., *The First Jewish Revolt*, Routledge, New York, 2002, pg. 121–133.

14. Jos. 3.161–170; Campbell, Duncan B., *Siege Warfare in the Roman World*, Oxford, Osprey Publishing, 2005, pg. 32–45.

15. Jos. 3.171–180; Campbell, Duncan B., *Siege Warfare in the Roman World*, Oxford, Osprey Publishing, 2005, pg. 32–45.

16. Jos. 3.181–188.

17. Jos. 3.188–192, 3.197–200 and 3.213.

18. Jos. 3.204–212 (Translated by Martin Hammond); Josephus, Flavius and Hammond, Martin, *The Jewish War*, Oxford University Press, Oxford, 2017, pg. 175–176.

19. Jos. 3.213–230.

20. Jos. 3.235–243.

21. Jos. 3.251–254 and 3.265–270.

22. Jos. 3.271–288.

23. Jos. 3.289–298.

24. Jos. 3.298–306; Jones, Brian W., *The Emperor Titus*, St. Martin's Press, New York, 1984, pg. 36.
25. Jos. 3.307–315; Bloom, James, *The Jewish Revolts Against Rome, A.D. 66–135*, McFarland, Jefferson, NC, 2010, pg. 126.
26. Jos. 3.316–322.
27. Zias, Joe, "THE ANTHROPOLOGICAL EVIDENCE," Joezias.com, Last Accessed April 6, 2024, https://web.archive.org/web/20120212185552/http://www.joezias.com/CrucifixionAntiquity.html; Zugibe, Frederick T., "FORENSIC AND CLINICAL KNOWLEDGE OF THE PRACTICE OF CRUCIFIXION," E-Forensic Medicine, Last Accessed April 6, 2024, https://web.archive.org/web/20040402184621/http://www.e-forensicmedicine.net/Turin2000.htm; Edwards WD, Gabel WJ, Hosmer FE. "On the physical death of Jesus Christ," JAMA, 1986 Mar 21;255(11):1455–63. PMID: 3512867, https://pubmed.ncbi.nlm.nih.gov/3512867/; Kyle, Donald, *Spectacles of Death in Ancient Rome*; Routledge, New York, 1998, pg. 168–169.
28. Jos. 3.323–328.
29. Jos. 3.316 and 3.328–339; Jones, Brian W., *The Emperor Titus*, St. Martin's Press, New York, 1984, pg. 38; Berlin, Andrea M., Overman, Andrew J., *The First Jewish Revolt*, Routledge, New York, 2002, pg. 121–133.
30. Jos. 3.341–391.
31. Jos. 3.392–398 and 3.408; Jos. Life 74–75.
32. Jos. 3.399–402 (Translated by Martin Hammond); Josephus, Flavius and Hammond, Martin, *The Jewish War*, Oxford University Press, Oxford, 2017, pg. 490.
33. Jos. 3.403–408; Jos. Life 74–75; Oros. 7.9.3.
34. Jos. 3.409–413; Bloom, James, *The Jewish Revolts Against Rome, A.D. 66–135*, McFarland, Jefferson, NC, 2010, pg. 128.

Chapter VI

1. Jos. 3.484 (Translated by Martin Hammond); Josephus, Flavius and Hammond, Martin, *The Jewish War*, Oxford University Press, Oxford, 2017, pg. 196.
2. Jos. 3.414–417; Jones, Brian W., *The Emperor Titus*, St. Martin's Press, New York, 1984, pg. 38; Bloom, James, *The Jewish Revolts Against Rome, A.D. 66–135*, McFarland, Jefferson, NC, 2010, pg. 129–130.
3. Jos. 3.417–423.
4. Jos. 3.422–427.
5. Jos. 3.427–431.
6. Jos. 3.443–445.
7. Jos. 3.445–447.
8. Jos. 3.447–456.
9. Jos. 3.457–462.
10. Jos. 3.462–466; Bloom, James, *The Jewish Revolts Against Rome, A.D. 66–135*, McFarland, Jefferson, NC, 2010, pg. 133.
11. Jos. 3.467–471.
12. Jos. 3.472–484 (Translated by E. Mary Smallwood); Josephus, Flavius and Smallwood, Mary, *The Jewish War: Revised Edition*, Penguin Classics, Kindle Edition, London 1984, pg. 227–229.
13. Jos. 3.485–487.
14. Jos. 3.487–491; Suet. Tit. 4.3.
15. Jos. 3.492–496 (Translated by John Thackeray); Josephus, Flavius, and Thackeray, John, *Josephus Volume II, The Jewish War Books I–III*, Harvard University Press, Cambridge, 1927, pg. 513–515.
16. Jos. 3.497–502; Suet. Tit. 4.3.
17. Jos. 3.503–505 and 522; Suet. Tit. 4.3.
18. Jos. 3.522–529.
19. Jos. 3.529–532; Jones, Brian W., *The Emperor Titus*, St. Martin's Press, New York, 1984, pg. 39.
20. Jos. 3.532–542.
21. Jos. 3.542 and 4.1–2.
22. Jos. 4.4–10; Bloom, James, *The Jewish Revolts Against Rome, A.D. 66–135*, McFarland, Jefferson, NC, 2010, pg. 135; Berlin, Andrea M., Overman, Andrew J., *The First Jewish Revolt*, Routledge, New York, 2002, pg. 134–152.
23. Jos. 4.11 and 4.32–33; Tac. Hist. 2.5 and 2.74.1; Jones, Brian W., The Emperor Titus, St. Martin's Press, New York, 1984, pg. 43; de Kleijn, Gerda. "C. Licinius Mucianus, Leader in Time of Crisis." *Historia: Zeitschrift Für Alte Geschichte*, vol. 58, no. 3, 2009, pp. 311–24; Jones, Brian W. "Titus in Judaea, A.D. 67." *Latomus*, vol. 48, no. 1, 1989, pp. 127–34.
24. Jos. 4.11–13 and 4.17–20.
25. Jos. 4.20–36 and 4.51–53; Bloom, James, *The Jewish Revolts Against Rome, A.D. 66–135*, McFarland, Jefferson, NC, 2010, pg. 138; Berlin, Andrea M., Overman, Andrew J., *The First Jewish Revolt*, Routledge, New York, 2002, pg. 134–152.
26. Jos. 4.54–61.
27. Jos. 4.62–70.
28. Jos. 4.69–72 (Translated by William Whiston).
29. Jos. 4.73–83; Suet. Tit. 4.3; Jones, Brian W., *The Emperor Titus*, St. Martin's Press, New York, 1984, pg. 39; Berlin, Andrea M., Overman, Andrew J., *The First Jewish Revolt*, Routledge, New York, 2002, pg. 149 and 151.

Chapter VII

1. Jos. 4.92 (Translated by Martin Hammond); Josephus, Flavius and Hammond, Martin, *The Jewish War*, Oxford University Press, Oxford, 2017, pg. 210.
2. Jos. 4.84 and 4.87–91; Jones, Brian W. "Titus in Judaea, A.D. 67." *Latomus*, vol. 48, no. 1, 1989, pp. 127–34.
3. Jos. 4.84–88; Jos. Life 10, 13, and 15.
4. Jos. 4.92–96.
5. Jos. 4.97–105; Bloom, James, *The Jewish Revolts Against Rome, A.D. 66–135*, McFarland, Jefferson, NC, 2010, pg. 142.
6. Jos. 4.106–114.

7. Jos. 4.112–116.
8. Jos. 4.117–120 and 4.130.
9. Jos. 4.130–136; Bloom, James, *The Jewish Revolts Against Rome, A.D. 66–135*, McFarland, Jefferson, NC, 2010, pg. 143.
10. Jos. 4.121–128; Bloom, James, *The Jewish Revolts Against Rome, A.D. 66–135*, McFarland, Jefferson, NC, 2010, pg. 144.
11. Jos. 4.138–157 and 4.208–216.
12. Jos. 4.151–193 (Translated by Martin Hammond and John Thackeray): Josephus, Flavius, and Thackeray, John, *Josephus Volume III, The Jewish War Books IV-VII*, Harvard University Press, Cambridge, 1928, pg. 45–59; Josephus, Flavius and Hammond, Martin, *The Jewish War*, Oxford University Press, Oxford, 2017, pg. 214–218.
13. Jos. 4.194–301.
14. Jos. 4.305–333 and 4.345–353; Bloom, James, *The Jewish Revolts Against Rome, A.D. 66–135*, McFarland, Jefferson, NC, 2010, pg. 144–145.
15. Jos. 4.375–381 and 4.389–396 (Translated by John Thackeray); Josephus, Flavius, and Thackeray, John, *Josephus Volume III, The Jewish War Books IV-VII*, Harvard University Press, Cambridge, 1928, pg. 111–116.
16. Jos. 4.398–409 and 2.254–255 (Translated by William Whiston).
17. Jos. 4.412.
18. Jos. 4.413–416.
19. Jos. 4.417–420.
20. Jos. 4.419–436; Joshua 6:1–27.
21. Jos. 4.437–438.
22. Jos. 4.438–439.
23. Jos. 4.440.

Chapter VIII

1. Dio. 63.29.2 (Translated by Earnest Cary).
2. Jos. 4.440; Plut. Galb. 4.2–3 and 5.2; Suet. Ner. 40.1 and 40.4; Dio 63.22.1–6 (Translated by Earnest Cary); Morgan, Gwyn, *69 A.D. The Year of Four Emperors*, Oxford University Press, Oxford, 2006, pg. 20.
3. Jos. 4.440; Plut. Galb. 4.2–3; Suet. Ner. 40.1, 40.4, and 42.1; Dio 63.22.2 and 63.23.1.
4. Plut. Galb. 3.1–2, 4.1–3 and 5.2; Suet. Ner. 40.4, and 42.1; Dio 63.23.1, 63.26.1–2, and 63.27.1; Suet. Galb. 2.1, 6.3, 7.1, 8.1, 9.2, and 10.1; Tact. Hist. 1.5–6 and 1.49.
5. Plut. Galb. 6.3; Suet. Galb. 11.1; Tac. Hist. 1.51; CAH X, pg. 259.
6. Jos. 4.440–441.
7. Jos. 4.442–444.
8. Jos. 4.444–448; Jones, Brian W., *The Emperor Titus*, St. Martin's Press, New York, 1984, pg. 41.
9. Jos. 4.450–452.
10. Jos. 4.486–491.
11. Plut. Galb. 5.4; Dio 63.25.1–3, 63.27.1–3, and 63.28.3; Suet. Ner. 47.1–3; Tac. Hist. 1.8.
12. Plut. Galb. 7.1–3; Suet. Ner. 49.1–4; Dio. 63.28.1–5 and 63.29.1–3 (Translated by Earnest Cary); Suet. Galb. 11.1; Jones, Brian W., *The Emperor Titus*, St. Martin's Press, New York, 1984, pg. 41; Morgan, Gwyn, *69 A.D. The Year of Four Emperors*, Oxford University Press, Oxford, 2006, pg. 31.
13. Jos. 4.491 and 4.497–498; Suet. Tit. 5.1; Tac. Hist. 1.10 and 2.1.
14. Jos. 4.498–502; Suet. Tit. 5.1; Tac. Hist. 2.1.
15. Plut. Galb. 22.1–8, 23.1; Dio. 63.2.1, 63.3.3–4, 63.4.1–2, 63.5.1–2 and 63.6.1–5 (Translated by Earnest Cary); Jos. 4.494; Suet. Vit. 4.1, 7.1–3, 8.1–2, 13.1–3 and 14.1; Suet. Galb. 12.1–2, 13.1, 14.1, and 16.1–2 (Translated by J.C. Rolfe); Tac. Hist. 1.5, 1.9, 1.18, 1.57, and 2.62.1.
16. Plut. Galb. 22.1–8, 23.1–4 and 27.1–4 (Translated by Bernadotte Perrin); Dio. 63.5.1–2 and 63.6.1–5 (Translated by Earnest Cary); Jos. 4.494; Suet. Galb. 17.1, 19.1–2, and 20.1–2; Suet. Oth. 3.2, 4.1, 5.1, 6.3 and 12.1; Tac. Hist. 1.9, 1.21, 1.41, and 1.49; CAH X, pg. 264 and 268; Syme, Ronald. "Partisans of Galba." *Historia: Zeitschrift Für Alte Geschichte*, vol. 31, no. 4, 1982, pp. 460–83.
17. Plut. Galb. 28.1; Dio 63.8.1–2 and 64.9.3; Jos. 4.494; Suet. Vit. 9.1; Tac. Hist. 1.47.
18. Suet. Oth. 8.1 and 9.2–3; Dio 63.10.1. and 63.12.1.
19. Jos. 4.501–502; Tac. Hist. 2.1–6; Jones, Brian W., *The Emperor Titus*, St. Martin's Press, New York, 1984, pg. 45.
20. Jos. 4.503–508.
21. Jos. 4.514–537.
22. Jos. 4.538–544.
23. Jos. 4.545–549; Suet. Vit. 10.1 and 11.1; Suet. Oth. 9.1–3 and 11.2 (Translated by J.C. Rolfe); Dio 63.10.3, 63.11.2, and 63.15; Tac. Hist. 2.43.1, 2.44.1, 2.49.1, and 2.55.1; Morgan, Gwyn, *69 A.D. The Year of Four Emperors*, Oxford University Press, Oxford, 2006, pg. 145.
24. Jos. 4.550–555 and 4.588.
25. Jos. 4.556–563.
26. Jos. 4.566–584.

Chapter IX

1. Jos. 4.597–598 (Translated by John Thackeray); Josephus, Flavius, and Thackeray, John, *Josephus Volume III, The Jewish War Books IV-VII*, Harvard University Press, Cambridge, 1928, pg. 175–176.
2. Jos. 4.586–591; Suet. Vit. 11.2, 12.1, 14.1 and 14.4; Dio 64.1–7; Tac. Hist. 2.56.1, 2.60.1, 2.68.1 and 2.93.1.
3. Jos. 4.592–600 (Translated by John Thackeray); Josephus, Flavius, and Thackeray, John, *Josephus Volume III, The Jewish War Books IV-VII*, Harvard University Press, Cambridge, 1928, pg. 175–176; Dio 64.8.3–4.
4. Jos. 4.601.
5. Jos. 4.601–602; Suet. Vesp. 6.3; Dio 64.8.3–4.
6. Jos. 4.602–603.
7. Jos. 4.603–604; Suet. Vesp. 6.3; Oros. 7.9.3; Morgan, Gwyn, *69 A.D. The Year of Four Emperors*,

Oxford University Press, Oxford, 2006, pg. 184–185; Berlin, Andrea M., Overman, Andrew J., *The First Jewish Revolt*, Routledge, New York, 2002, pg. 213.

   8. Jos. 4.605–607; Tac. Hist. 2.76.1 and 2.78.1.

   9. Jos. 4.606–607 and 4.616–617; Suet. Vesp. 6.3; Tac. Hist. 2.74.1 and 2.81.1; Jones, Brian W., *The Emperor Titus*, St. Martin's Press, New York, 1984, pg. 44; Morgan, Gwyn, *69 A.D. The Year of Four Emperors*, Oxford University Press, Oxford, 2006, pg. 184–185; Schoenfeld, Andrew J. "Sons of Israel in Caesar's Service: Jewish Soldiers in the Roman Military." *Shofar: An Interdisciplinary Journal of Jewish Studies*, vol. 24 no. 3, 2006, pp. 115–126.

   10. Jos. 4.618–620; Suet. Vesp. 6.1–2; Suet. Vit. 15.1; Tac. Hist. 2.6.1, 2.11.1, 2.80.1, and 2.81.1; Bloom, James, *The Jewish Revolts Against Rome, A.D. 66–135*, McFarland, Jefferson, NC, 2010, pg. 150.

   11. Jos. 4.618–620; Suet. Vesp. 6.1–2; Suet. Vit. 15.1–2; Bloom, James, *The Jewish Revolts Against Rome, A.D. 66–135*, McFarland, Jefferson, NC, 2010, pg. 150.

   12. Jos. 4.620–627 (Translated by John Thackeray); Josephus, Flavius, and Thackeray, John, *Josephus Volume III, The Jewish War Books IV–VII*, Harvard University Press, Cambridge, 1928, pg. 185–187; CAH X, pg. 276.

   13. Jos. 4.627–629 (Translated by John Thackeray); Josephus, Flavius, and Thackeray, John, *Josephus Volume III, The Jewish War Books IV–VII*, Harvard University Press, Cambridge, 1928, pg. 187.

   14. Jos. 4.630–632; Suet. Vesp. 7.1; Dio 64.9.2 and 65.9.2; Tac. Hist. 3.48.1.

   *Dio 65.9.2 suggests Titus never traveled to Alexandria but stayed in the East.

   15. Jos. 4.633–641; Dio 64.9.3–4, 64.10.1–4, and 64.11.2; Tac. Hist. 3.8.1 and 3.9.1.

   16. Jos. 4.641–644; Dio 64.11.3–5, 64.12.1–4, 64.13.2–5, 64.14.1–4, and 64.15.1–2; Tac. Hist. 3.33.1; Morgan, Gwyn, *69 A.D. The Year of Four Emperors*, Oxford University Press, Oxford, 2006, pg. 201.

   17. Jos. 4.645–649; Dio. 64.17.1–4; Tac. Hist. 3.65.1–3.66.1 and 3.69.1–3.74.1; Suet. Vit. 15.1–3; CAH X, pg. 278.

   18. Jos. 4.650–651; Tac. Hist. 3.79.1–3.82.1; Levick, Barbara, *Vespasian*, Routledge, New York, 1999, pg. 52.

   19. Jos. 4.651–654; Suet. Vit. 17.1–2 and 18.1; Suet. Vesp. 7.1; Dio 64.19.3, 64.20.1–3, 64.21.1–2; Tac. Hist. 3.55.1–3.56.1, 3.84.1–3.86.1, 4.1.1–4.2.1, and 4.47.1.

   20. Jos. 4.654–655; Dio 64.22.2; Tac. Hist. 4.2.1, 4.3.1, 4.11.1, and 4.39.1; Southern, Pat, *Domitian, Tragic Tyrant*, Routledge, New York, 1997, pg. 20.

   21. Jos. 4.656–657; Suet. Vesp. 7.1; Dio 65.9.2; Levick, Barbara, *Vespasian*, Routledge, New York, 1999, pg. 53.

   22. Suet. Vesp. 7.1–3; Tac. Hist. 4.81.1–4.83.1.

   23. Jos. 4.656–658; Suet. Tit. 5.2; Tac. Hist. 2.82.1, 4.3.1, 4.38.1, 4.47.1, 4.51.1–4.52.1 (Translated by C.H. Moore); Oros. 7.9.3; Jones, Brian W., *The Emperor Titus*, St. Martin's Press, New York, 1984, pg. 47; Zissos, Andrew, *A Companion to the Flavian Age of Imperial Rome*, John Wiley and Sons, Inc., January 2016, pg. 80; Levick, Barbara, *Vespasian*, Routledge, New York, 1999, pg. 66, 79, and 184.

Chapter X

   1. Jos. 5.97 (Translated by Martin Hammond); Josephus, Flavius and Hammond, Martin, *The Jewish War*, Oxford University Press, Oxford, 2017, pg. 263.

   2. Jos. 5.5–6.

   3. Jos. 5.6–9.

   4. Jos. 5.9–10.

   5. Jos. 5.10–14.

   6. Jos. 5.21–26 (Translated by John Thackeray); Josephus, Flavius, and Thackeray, John, *Josephus Volume III, The Jewish War Books IV–VII*, Harvard University Press, Cambridge, 1928, pg. 207–209.

   7. Jos. 5.27–38.

   8. Jos. 4.659–660 and 5.43–45.

   9. Jos. 4.660–663.

   10. Jos. 5.40–44; Bloom, James, *The Jewish Revolts Against Rome, A.D. 66–135*, McFarland, Jefferson, NC, 2010, pg. 158.

   11. Jos. 4.556–557 and 6.420; Tac. Hist. 5.13; Oros. 7.9.3.

   12. Jos. 5.47–48.

   13. Jos. 5.48–49.

   14. Jos. 5.50–55.

   15. Jos. 5.54–58.

   16. Jos. 5.59–64.

   17. Jos. 5.63–66.

   18. Jos. 5.67–71.

   19. Jos. 5.71–74 (Translated by William Whiston).

   20. Jos. 5.75–76.

   21. Jos. 5.76–80.

   22. Jos. 5.81–82.

   23. Jos. 5.82–84.

   24. Jos. 5.85–87.

   25. Jos. 5.87–89.

   26. Jos. 5.89–90.

   27. Jos. 5.91–94.

   28. Jos. 5.94–97.

   29. Jos. 5.97 (Translated by Martin Hammond); Josephus, Flavius and Hammond, Martin, *The Jewish War*, Oxford University Press, Oxford, 2017, pg. 263.

Chapter XI

   1. Jos. 5.19–20 (Translated by Martin Hammond); Josephus, Flavius and Hammond, Martin, *The Jewish War*, Oxford University Press, Oxford, 2017, pg. 256.

   2. Jos. 5.98; Dio 65.4.5.

   3. Jos. 5.99–100.

   4. Jos. 5.100–105 and 5.250; Tac. Hist. 5.12.

5. Jos. 5.106–108; Bloom, James, *The Jewish Revolts Against Rome, A.D. 66–135*, McFarland, Jefferson, NC, 2010, pg. 161.
6. Jos. 5.109–114; Dio 65.4.1–2.
7. Jos. 5.109–120.
8. Jos. 5.120–129.
9. Jos. 5.129–133.
10. Jos. 5.133–135.
11. Jos. 5.136, 5.142–145, 5.159, 5.161–183; 6.400–401; Neh. 6.15; Dio 65.4.1.
12. Jos. 5.146, 5.158, 5.238–243; Dio 65.4.1.
13. Jos. 5.147–158 and 5.160; Dio 64.4.1.
14. Jos. 5.248–254.
15. Jos. 5.255–257.
16. Jos. 5.258–259.
17. Jos. 5.259–260.
18. Jos. 5.261–262.
19. Jos. 5.262–264.
20. Jos. 5.262–265; Dio 65.4.2.
21. Jos. 5.266–268.
22. Jos. 5.268–274.
23. Jos. 5.268–277 and 5.291–297.
24. Jos. 5.291–297; Bloom, James, *The Jewish Revolts Against Rome, A.D. 66–135*, McFarland, Jefferson, NC, 2010, pg. 164–165.
25. Jos. 5.275–277.
26. Jos. 5.278–280; Dio 65.4.4.
27. Jos. 5.281–284.
28. Jos. 5.284–287; Dio 65.4.4.
29. Jos. 5.287–290; Suet. Tit. 5.2; Dio 65.5.1.
30. Dio 65.4.5 and 65.5.3.
31. Jos. 5.289–290.

Chapter XII

1. Jos. 5.299 (Translated by Martin Hammond); Josephus, Flavius and Hammond, Martin, *The Jewish War*, Oxford University Press, Oxford, 2017, pg. 279.
2. Jos. 5.291–293.
3. Jos. 5.292–295.
4. Jos. 5.296–301.
5. Jos. 5.301–302; Dio 65.5.2.
6. Jos. 5.303–308; Dio 65.5.2.
7. Jos. 5.314–316.
8. Jos. 5.317.
9. Jos. 5.317–320.
10. Jos. 5.320–329.
11. Jos. 5.329–330 (Translated by William Whiston).
12. Jos. 5.331 and 5.336–338; Dio 65.5.2.
13. Jos. 5.331–334; Dio 65.5.2.
14. Jos. 5.333–336; Dio 65.5.3.
15. Jos. 5.335–338.
16. Jos. 5.338–341.
17. Jos. 5.342–345.
18. Jos. 5.346–347.
19. Jos. 5.347.
20. Jos. 5.348–356.
21. Jos. 5.356–357.
22. Jos. 5.357–359.
23. Jos. 5.361–368.
24. Jos. 5.369–414 (Translated by Martin Hammond); Josephus, Flavius and Hammond, Martin, *The Jewish War*, Oxford University Press, Oxford, 2017, pg. 286–290.
25. Jos. 5.415–419 (Translated by William Whiston and John Thackeray); Josephus, Flavius, and Thackeray, John, *Josephus Volume III, The Jewish War Books IV–VII*, Harvard University Press, Cambridge, 1928, pg. 331–333.
26. Jos. 5.420–423.
27. Jos. 5.424–445 (Translated by John Thackeray); Josephus, Flavius, and Thackeray, John, *Josephus Volume III, The Jewish War Books IV–VII*, Harvard University Press, Cambridge, 1928, pg. 333–339; Dio 65.5.4.

Chapter XIII

1. Jos. 5.566 (Translated by Martin Hammond); Josephus, Flavius and Hammond, Martin, *The Jewish War*, Oxford University Press, Oxford, 2017, pg. 303.
2. Jos. 5.446–449.
3. Jos. 5.446–450.
4. Jos. 5.450.
5. Jos. 5.449–451.
6. Jos. Life 75.
7. Keys, David, "Crucifixion was practised in Roman Britain, new evidence reveals," Independent, December 8, 2021, https://www.independent.co.uk/news/science/archaeology/crucifixion-roman-britain-fenstanton-cambridgeshire-b1971956.html; Lewis, Stephen, "Some Notes on Crucifixion, Open Repository, Last Accessed April 6, 2024, https://web.archive.org/web/2011071817 1841/http://chesterrep.openrepository.com/cdr/bitstream/10034/40813/1/Some%20Notes%20 on%20Crucifixion.pdf.
8. App. BC 1.120; Kyle, Donald, *Spectacles of Death in Ancient Rome*; Routledge, New York, 1998, pg. 168–169.
9. Jos. 5.452–454.
10. Jos. Jos. 5.455–456.
11. Jos. 5.446, 5.460–463 (Translated by Martin Hammond); Josephus, Flavius and Hammond, Martin, *The Jewish War*, Oxford University Press, Oxford, 2017, pg. 293, 294–295.
12. Jos. 5.464–465.
13. Jos. 5.466–469.
14. Jos. 5.469.
15. Jos. 5.469–472.
16. Jos. 5.473–480.
17. Jos. 5.480–486.
18. Jos. 5.486–490.
19. Jos. 5.491.
20. Jos. 5.491–492.
21. Jos. 5.493–498.
22. Jos. 5.498–501.
23. Jos. 5.502–511.
24. Jos. 5.512–515.
25. Jos. 5.513–517.
26. Jos. 5.517–519 (Translated by William Whiston).

27. Jos. 5.520–522.
28. Jos. 5.522–524.
29. Jos. 5.527–540.
30. Jos. 5.541–542.
31. Jos. 5.542–547.
32. Jos. 5.548–550.
33. Jos. 5.550–552.
34. Jos. 5.553–561.
35. Jos. 5.562–565.
36. Jos. 5.567–571.

Chapter XIV

1. Jos. 6.126–127 (Translated by John Thackeray); Josephus, Flavius, and Thackeray, John, *Josephus Volume III, The Jewish War Books IV–VII*, Harvard University Press, Cambridge, 1928, pg. 413.
2. Jos. 6.1–8.
3. Jos. 6.9–22.
4. Jos. 6.15–22.
5. Jos. 6.23–27.
6. Jos. 6.27–28.
7. Jos. 6.28–32; Dio 65.6.1.
8. Jos. 6.33–53 (Translated by William Whiston).
9. Jos. 6.54–57 (Translated by William Whiston).
10. Jos. 6.58–62.
11. Jos. 6.63–67.
12. Jos. 6.68–69.
13. Jos. 6.70–80.
14. Jos. 6.81–90.
15. Jos. 6.93–95; Bloom, James, *The Jewish Revolts Against Rome, A.D. 66–135*, McFarland, Jefferson, NC, 2010, pg. 170; Jones, Brian W., *The Emperor Titus*, St. Martin's Press, New York, 1984, pg. 52.
16. Jos. 6.95–99.
17. Jos. 6.98–114 (Translated by John Thackeray); Josephus, Flavius, and Thackeray, John, *Josephus Volume III, The Jewish War Books IV–VII*, Harvard University Press, Cambridge, 1928, pg. 405–409.
18. Jos. 6.114–123.
19. Jos. 6.124–128 (Translated by John Thackeray); Josephus, Flavius, and Thackeray, John, *Josephus Volume III, The Jewish War Books IV–VII*, Harvard University Press, Cambridge, 1928, pg. 413.
20. Jos. 6.123, 6.129–130 (Translated by John Thackeray); Josephus, Flavius, and Thackeray, John, *Josephus Volume III, The Jewish War Books IV–VII*, Harvard University Press, Cambridge, 1928, pg. 413.

Chapter XV

1. Jos. 6.275–276 (Translated by Martin Hammond); Josephus, Flavius and Hammond, Martin, *The Jewish War*, Oxford University Press, Oxford, 2017, pg. 327.
2. Jos. 6.129–131.
3. Jos. 6.131–133.
4. Jos. 6.133–135.
5. Jos. 6.136–141.
6. Jos. 6.141–148.
7. Jos. 6.93 and 6.149–150.
8. Jos. 6.150–151 (Translated by William Whiston).
9. Jos. 6.151–156.
10. Jos. 6.157–163.
11. Jos. 6.164–176; Dio 65.6.1.
12. Jos. 6.177–179.
13. Jos. 6.179–182.
14. Jos. 6.182–185, 6.190–192.
15. Jos. 6.193–198.
16. Jos. 6.201–208 (Translated by John Thackeray); Josephus, Flavius, and Thackeray, John, *Josephus Volume III, The Jewish War Books IV–VII*, Harvard University Press, Cambridge, 1928, pg. 435–437.
17. Jos. 6.209–215 (Translated by John Thackeray); Josephus, Flavius, and Thackeray, John, *Josephus Volume III, The Jewish War Books IV–VII*, Harvard University Press, Cambridge, 1928, pg. 437–439.
18. Jos. 6.214–219.
19. Jos. 6.220–222.
20. Jos. 6.222–228.
21. Jos. 6.228, 6.232–235; Dio 65.6.1–2.
22. Jos. 6.236–243; Jones, Brian W., *The Emperor Titus*, St. Martin's Press, New York, 1984, pg. 54–55.
23. Chronica 2.30.6–7; Oros. 7.9.4–6 (Translated by I.W. Raymond); Bloch, Rene, *Ancient Jewish Diaspora*, Brill, Sept. 2022, pg. 128–129, https://brill.com/display/book/9789004521896/BP000008.xml; Levick, Barbara, *Vespasian*, Routledge, New York, 1999, pg. 118.
24. Jos. 6.244–248; Dio 65.6.2.
25. Jos. 6.249–253; Dio 65.6.3.
26. Jos. 6.254–259; Dio 65.6.3.
27. Jos. 6.260–263; Dio 65.6.3.
28. Jos. 6.263–270; Oros. 7.9.6; Barron, Caroline. "The (lost) Arch of Titus: The Visibility and Prominence of Victory in Flavian Rome." *Reconsidering Roman Power*, edited by Katell Berthelot, Publications de l'École française de Rome, 2020; Shahar, Meir Ben. "When Was the Second Temple Destroyed? Chronology and Ideology in Josephus and in Rabbinic Literature." *Journal for the Study of Judaism in the Persian, Hellenistic, and Roman Period*, vol. 46, no. 4/5, 2015, pp. 547–73.
29. Jos. 6.271–276 (Translated by Martin Hammond); Josephus, Flavius and Hammond, Martin, *The Jewish War*, Oxford University Press, Oxford, 2017, pg. 327; Oros. 7.9.6.
30. Jos. 6.277–287.
31. Jos. 6.288–317.

*Oros. 7.9.6 claims that Titus burned the Temple after being hailed Imperator.

Chapter XVI

1. Jos. 6.328–329 (Translated by John Thackeray); Josephus, Flavius, and Thackeray, John,

Josephus Volume III, The Jewish War Books IV–VII, Harvard University Press, Cambridge, 1928, pg. 471–477.
    2. Jos. 6.316–318.
    3. Jos. 6.318–320; Oros. 7.9.4.
    4. Jos. 6.320–322.
    5. Jos. 6.323–325.
    6. Jos. 6.326–350 (Translated by John Thackeray); Josephus, Flavius, and Thackeray, John, *Josephus Volume III, The Jewish War Books IV–VII*, Harvard University Press, Cambridge, 1928, pg. 471–477.
    7. Jos. 6.351–354.
    8. Jos. 6.354–355.
    9. Jos. 6.356–357.
    10. Jos. 6.358–362.
    11. Jos. 6.363–369.
    12. Jos. 6.370–373.
    13. Jos. 6.374–377.
    14. Jos. 6.378–382.
    15. Jos. 6.382–386.
    16. Jos. 6.387–391 (Translated by John Thackeray and Martin Hammond); Josephus, Flavius, and Thackeray, John, *Josephus Volume III, The Jewish War Books IV–VII*, Harvard University Press, Cambridge, 1928, pg. 487–489; Josephus, Flavius and Hammond, Martin, *The Jewish War*, Oxford University Press, Oxford, 2017, pg. 336.
    17. Jos. 6.392–401.
    18. Jos. 6.402–408; Suet. Tit. 5.2; Oros. 7.9.4–7.
    19. Jos. 6.409–413, 6.428–434 (Translated by William Whiston); Dio 65.7.1–2.
    20. Jos. 6.414–419; Jos. Life 75.
    21. Jos. 6.420–421, 6.434, 7.1–2; Tac. Hist. 5.13; Oros. 7.9.4–7.
    22. Jos. 7.5 and 7.23–24.

Chapter XVII

    1. Jos. 7.132–134 (Translated by Martin Hammond); Josephus, Flavius and Hammond, Martin, *The Jewish War*, Oxford University Press, Oxford, 2017, pg. 351.
    2. Jos. 7.5–11.
    3. Jos. 7.11–17.
    4. Jos. 7.17–20.
    5. Jos. 7.20–22, 7.63–65, 7.75–76, 7.89–90; Jones, Brian W. "TITUS IN THE EAST, A.D. 70–71." *Rheinisches Museum Für Philologie*, vol. 128, no. 3/4, 1985, pp. 346–52; CAH XI, pg. 4; Levick, Barbara, *Vespasian*, Routledge, New York, 1999, pg. 107.
    6. Jos. 7.23–24; Jones, Brian W., *The Emperor Titus*, St. Martin's Press, New York, 1984, pg. 56; Jones, Brian W. "TITUS IN THE EAST, A.D. 70–71." *Rheinisches Museum Für Philologie*, vol. 128, no. 3/4, 1985, pp. 346–52.
    7. Jos. 7.36.
    8. Jos. 7.36–38.
    9. Jos. 7.39–40 and 7.96.
    10. Jos. 7.100–105.
    11. Jos. 7.105–107; Tac. Hist. 4.51; Jones, Brian W. "TITUS IN THE EAST, A.D. 70–71." *Rheinisches Museum Für Philologie*, vol. 128, no. 3/4, 1985, pp. 346–52.
    12. Jos. 7.106–108.
    13. Jos. 7.108–110 (Translated by William Whiston).
    14. Jos. 7.110–111.
    15. Jos. 7.111–115.
    16. Jos. 7.116–118; Suet. Tit. 5.3; Oros. 7.9.8; Jones, Brian W., *The Emperor Titus*, St. Martin's Press, New York, 1984, pg. 57.
    17. Jos. 7.117–118; Jos. Life 76; Dio 65.7.1.
    18. Jos. 7.119–121; Suet. Tit. 5.3 (Translated by J.C. Rolfe); Jones, Brian W., *The Emperor Titus*, St. Martin's Press, New York, 1984, pg. 78.
    19. Jos. 7.121–122; Oros. 7.9.8; Jones, Brian W., *The Emperor Titus*, St. Martin's Press, New York, 1984, pg. 78.
    20. Jos. 7.123.
    21. Jos. 7.123–124; Ramsay, William, "Triumphus," A Dictionary of Greek and Roman Antiquities, John Murray, London, 1875, Lacus Curtius, https://penelope.uchicago.edu/Thayer/E/Roman/Texts/secondary/SMIGRA*/Triumphus.html.
    22. Jos. 7.125–131.
    23. Jos. 7.122; Ramsay, William, "Triumphus," A Dictionary of Greek and Roman Antiquities, John Murray, London, 1875, Lacus Curtius, https://penelope.uchicago.edu/Thayer/E/Roman/Texts/secondary/SMIGRA*/Triumphus.html.
    24. Jos. 6.387–391, 7.132–136 and 7.148–152; "Arch of Titus," University of Chicago, Last Accessed May 12, 2024, https://penelope.uchicago.edu/~grout/encyclopaedia_romana/romanurbs/archtitus.html; Ramsay, William, "Triumphus," A Dictionary of Greek and Roman Antiquities, John Murray, London, 1875, Lacus Curtius, https://penelope.uchicago.edu/Thayer/E/Roman/Texts/secondary/SMIGRA*/Triumphus.html; Barron, Caroline. "The (lost) Arch of Titus: The Visibility and Prominence of Victory in Flavian Rome." *Reconsidering Roman Power*, edited by Katell Berthelot, Publications de l'École française de Rome, 2020.
    25. Jos. 7.139–147; Ramsay, William, "Triumphus," A Dictionary of Greek and Roman Antiquities, John Murray, London, 1875, Lacus Curtius, https://penelope.uchicago.edu/Thayer/E/Roman/Texts/secondary/SMIGRA*/Triumphus.html.
    26. Ramsay, William, "Triumphus," A Dictionary of Greek and Roman Antiquities, John Murray, London, 1875, Lacus Curtius, https://penelope.uchicago.edu/Thayer/E/Roman/Texts/secondary/SMIGRA*/Triumphus.html.
    27. Jos. 7.136–138; Ramsay, William, "Triumphus," A Dictionary of Greek and Roman Antiquities, John Murray, London, 1875, Lacus Curtius, https://penelope.uchicago.edu/Thayer/E/Roman/Texts/secondary/SMIGRA*/Triumphus.html.
    28. Jos. 7.138 and 7.154; Dio 65.7.1; Ramsay, William, "Triumphus," A Dictionary of Greek and Roman Antiquities, John Murray, London, 1875, Lacus Curtius, https://penelope.uchicago.edu/

Thayer/E/Roman/Texts/secondary/SMIGRA*/Triumphus.html.
29. Jos. 7.152; Oros. 7.9.8; Ramsay, William, "Triumphus," A Dictionary of Greek and Roman Antiquities, John Murray, London, 1875, Lacus Curtius, https://penelope.uchicago.edu/Thayer/E/Roman/Texts/secondary/SMIGRA*/Triumphus.html.
30. Ramsay, William, "Triumphus," A Dictionary of Greek and Roman Antiquities, John Murray, London, 1875, Lacus Curtius, https://penelope.uchicago.edu/Thayer/E/Roman/Texts/secondary/SMIGRA*/Triumphus.html.
31. Jos. 7.153–157; Dio 65.7.1; Ramsay, William, "Triumphus," A Dictionary of Greek and Roman Antiquities, John Murray, London, 1875, Lacus Curtius, https://penelope.uchicago.edu/Thayer/E/Roman/Texts/secondary/SMIGRA*/Triumphus.html.
32. Jos. 7.158–162; Levick, Barbara, *Vespasian*, Routledge, New York, 1999, pg. 126–127.
33. Oros. 7.9.9.

Chapter XVIII

1. Suet. Vesp. 23.3 (Translated by J.C. Rolfe).
2. Suet. Tit. 6.1; Perry M. Rogers. "Titus, Berenice and Mucianus." *Historia: Zeitschrift Für Alte Geschichte*, vol. 29, no. 1, 1980, pp. 86–95; Zissos, Andrew, *A Companion to the Flavian Age of Imperial Rome*, John Wiley and Sons, Inc., January 2016, pg. 82; Levick, Barbara, *Vespasian*, Routledge, New York, 1999, pg. 66, 79, and 184.
3. Suet. Tit. 6.1; Jones, Brian W., *The Emperor Titus*, St. Martin's Press, New York, 1984, pg. 78–81 and 86; Southern, Pat, Domitian, *Tragic Tyrant*, Routledge, New York, 1997, pg. 25 and 27.
4. Suet. Vesp. 16.1–3; Harl, Kenneth W., *Coinage in the Roman Economy 300 B.C. to A.D. 700*, The Johns Hopkins University Press, Baltimore, 1996, pg. 92; SCHWEI, DAVID. "Exchange Rates, Neronian Silver Standards, and a Long-Term Plan to Unify the Empire's Mints." *The Numismatic Chronicle (1966–)*, vol. 177, 2017, pp. 107–34; Butcher, Kevin and Matthew Ponting. "The denarius in the first century." University of Warwick, 2011; Levick, Barbara, *Vespasian*, Routledge, New York, 1999, pg. 95; Levick, Barbara, *Vespasian*, Routledge, New York, 1999, pg. 104.
5. Suet. Vesp. 17.1, 18.1, and 19.1; Tac. Hist. 4.53.1.
6. "The Colosseum," National Geographic, Last Accessed April 6, 2024, https://education.nationalgeographic.org/resource/colosseum/.
7. Smith, Philip, *A Dictionary of Greek and Roman Antiquities*, John Murray, London, 1875, https://penelope.uchicago.edu/Thayer/E/Roman/Texts/secondary/SMIGRA*/Amphitheatrum.html; "Colosseum," Archeoroma, Last Accessed July 26, 2024, https://www.archeoroma.org/sites/colosseum/; "Holy Martyr Gaudentius," Orthodox Christianity then and Now, December 31, 2018, https://www.johnsanidopoulos.com/2018/12/holy-martyr-gaudentius.html.

8. Elkins, Nathan T., *A Monument to Dynasty and Death*, Johns Hopkins University Press, 2009, pg. 22–24; Lancaster, Lynne C. "The Process of Building the Colosseum: The Site, Materials, and Construction Techniques." *Journal of Roman Archaeology* 18 (2005): 57–82; Smith, Philip, "Amphitheatrum," *A Dictionary of Greek and Roman Antiquities*, 1875, The University of Chicago, https://penelope.uchicago.edu/Thayer/E/Roman/Texts/secondary/SMIGRA*/Amphitheatrum.html; Welch, Katherine E., *The Roman Amphitheater*, Cambridge University Press, Cambridge, 2007, pg. 71, 82, and 128–129.
9. Chandler, David, "Riddle solved: Why was Roman concrete so durable?," MIT News, January 6, 2023, https://news.mit.edu/2023/roman-concrete-durability-lime-casts-0106; Dunham, Will, "Scientists chip away at how ancient Roman concrete stood test of time," Reuters, January 9, 2023, https://www.reuters.com/lifestyle/science/scientists-chip-away-how-ancient-roman-concrete-stood-test-time-2023-01-09/; Kwan, Jacklin, "Scientists may have found magic ingredient behind ancient Rome's self-healing concrete," Science.org, https://www.science.org/content/article/scientists-may-have-found-magic-ingredient-behind-ancient-romes-self-healing-concrete.
10. "Interesting Facts," Colosseum.info, Accessed February 10, 2024, https://colosseum.info/colosseum1/#:~:text=Over%20100%2C000%20cubic%20metres%20of,Tivoli%20and%20back%20(33km); Elkins, Nathan T., *A Monument to Dynasty and Death*, Johns Hopkins University Press, 2009, pg. 16–17 and 22–24; Lancaster, Lynne C. "The Process of Building the Colosseum: The Site, Materials, and Construction Techniques." *Journal of Roman Archaeology* 18 (2005): 57–82.
11. "Architecture of the Colosseum," The Colosseum, Last Accessed May 12, 2024, https://www.thecolosseum.org/architecture/.
12. Jos. 7.163–164.
13. Jos. 7.163–164.
14. Jos. 7.216–218; Dio 65.7.2; Donfried, Karl P., Richardson, Peter, *Judaism and Christianity in First-Century Rome*, William B. Eerdmans Publishing Company, Grand Rapids, Michigan, 1998, pg. 183–189; Bloom, James, *The Jewish Revolts Against Rome, A.D. 66-135*, McFarland, Jefferson, NC, 2010, pg. 180–183; *The Bar Kokhba Revolt*, Captivating History, Columbia, 2021, pg. 48; Levick, Barbara, *Vespasian*, Routledge, New York, 1999, pg. 101.
15. Jos. Life 76; Lact. Mort. 3; Tert. Apol. 5; Eus. H.E. 3.17; Sulp. Sev. H.E. 2.30.
16. Sim, David C., "How many Jews became Christians in the first century? The failure of the Christian mission to the Jews," Australian Catholic University, Semantic Scholar, 2005, https://pdfs.semanticscholar.org/7906/bd37ed9d9d34bd408b01121ab653423752f8.pdf.
17. Donfried, Karl P., Richardson, Peter, *Judaism and Christianity in First-Century Rome*,

William B. Eerdmans Publishing Company, Grand Rapids, Michigan, 1998, pg. 183–189; Bloom, James, *The Jewish Revolts Against Rome, A.D. 66–135*, McFarland, Jefferson, NC, 2010, pg. 180–183; Lact. Mort. 3; Tert. Apol. 5; Eus. H.E. 3.17; Sulp. Sev. H.E. 2.30.

18. Jos. 7.164–177 and 7.190–191.
19. Jos. 7.196–206.
20. Jos. 7.206–209.
21. Jos. 7.210–215.
22. Jos. 7.219–251.
23. Jos. 7.252, 7.286–287; "Masada," Jewish Virtual Library, Last Accessed May 12, 2024, https://www.jewishvirtuallibrary.org/vie-masada; "Masada National Park," National Parks, Last Accessed May 12, 2024, https://national-parks.org/israel/masada.
24. Jos. 7.252–253, 7.275–279, 7.304–308.
25. Jos. 7.308–319.
26. Jos. 7.389–398; David, Ariel, "Roman Siege of Masada Was Much Quicker Than Assumed, Israeli Archaeologists Say," Haaretz, Sept. 3, 2024, https://www.haaretz.com/archaeology/2024-09-03/ty-article-magazine/roman-siege-of-masada-was-much-quicker-than-assumed-israeli-archaeologists-say/00000191-b7ca-d13c-a39b-bfcf76ed0000.
27. Jos. 7.399–408; Bloom, James, *The Jewish Revolts Against Rome, A.D. 66–135*, McFarland, Jefferson, NC, 2010, pg. 173.
28. Magness, Jodi, "The fall of Masada," The Princeton Press, Jun. 24, 2021, https://press.princeton.edu/ideas/the-fall-of-masada; Linde, Steve, "The symbol of Masada," The Jerusalem Post, Dec. 14, 2009, https://www.jpost.com/israel-news/the-symbol-of-masada-610479; Sherwood, Harietta, "This article is more than 10 years old Israel's Masada myth: doubts cast over ancient symbol of heroism and sacrifice," The Guardian, Sept. 22, 2013, https://www.theguardian.com/world/2013/sep/22/israel-masada-myth-doubts.
29. Jos. 7.409–432; Barron, Caroline. "The (lost) Arch of Titus: The Visibility and Prominence of Victory in Flavian Rome." *Reconsidering Roman Power*, edited by Katell Berthelot, Publications de l'École française de Rome, 2020; Levick, Barbara, *Vespasian*, Routledge, New York, 1999, pg. 121.
30. Suet. Tit. 6.1; Jones, Brian W., *The Emperor Titus*, St. Martin's Press, New York, 1984, pg. 82.

*CAH X, pg. 281 states that the censorship could have begun as early as 72 CE.

31. Smith, William, Censor, A Dictionary of Greek and Roman Antiquities, John Murray, London, 1875, https://penelope.uchicago.edu/Thayer/E/Roman/Texts/secondary/SMIGRA*/Censor.html.
32. Smith, William, Censor, A Dictionary of Greek and Roman Antiquities, John Murray, London, 1875, https://penelope.uchicago.edu/Thayer/E/Roman/Texts/secondary/SMIGRA*/Censor.html.
33. Potter, David. "Measuring the Power of the Roman Empire." *East and West in the Roman Empire of the Fourth Century: An End to Unity?*, edited by Roald Dijkstra et al., Brill, 2015, pp. 26–48.
34. Roman Empire Population, UNRV Roman History, Last Accessed August 8, 2024, https://www.unrv.com/empire/roman-population.php.
35. Suet. Vesp. 23.3; Dio 65.14.5; Jones, Brian W., *The Emperor Titus*, St. Martin's Press, New York, 1984, pg. 77.
36. Suet. Vesp. 23.3; Dio 65.14.5; Milani, Maria, "Urine Trouble: Taxes in Ancient Rome," National Geographic, April 15, 2016, https://blog.education.nationalgeographic.org/2016/04/15/urine-trouble-taxes-in-ancient-rome/; Hill, Bryan, "Money Does Not Stink: The Urine Tax of Ancient Rome," Ancient Origins, July 12, 2015, https://www.ancient-origins.net/history-ancient-traditions/money-does-not-stink-urine-tax-ancient-rome-003408.
37. Suet. Vesp. 23.3 (Translated by J.C. Rolfe); Dio 65.14.5.
38. Jones, Brian W., *The Emperor Titus*, St. Martin's Press, New York, 1984, pg. 82–83; Schmidtz, Leonard, "Lustrum," A Dictionary of Greek and Roman Antiquities, John Murray, London, 1875, https://penelope.uchicago.edu/Thayer/E/Roman/Texts/secondary/SMIGRA*/Lustrum.html.

Chapter XIX

1. Suet. Tit. 7.1 (Translated by J.C. Rolfe).
2. Suet. Tit. 1.1 and 7.1.
3. Suet. Tit. 6.1; Jones, Brian W., *The Emperor Titus*, St. Martin's Press, New York, 1984, pg. 84; Smith, William, "Praetoriani," A Dictionary of Greek and Roman Antiquities, John Murray, London, 1875, Lacus Curtius, https://penelope.uchicago.edu/Thayer/E/Roman/Texts/secondary/SMIGRA*/Praetoriani.html; Tac. 2.93.1; CIL 16.21; ILS 1993; Hermann, Dessau, *Inscriptiones latinae selectae*, Berolini Apud Weidmannos, 1982, pg. 396–397 https://archive.org/details/inscriptioneslat01dessuoft/page/n11/mode/2up.

Bingham, Sandra, "The Praetorian Guard in the Political and Social Life of Julio-Claudian Rome," The University of British Columbia, 1997, pg. 122, https://open.library.ubc.ca/media/stream/pdf/831/1.0099480/2; Perry M. Rogers. "Titus, Berenice and Mucianus." *Historia: Zeitschrift Für Alte Geschichte*, vol. 29, no. 1, 1980, pp. 86–95; Zissos, Andrew, *A Companion to the Flavian Age of Imperial Rome*, John Wiley and Sons, Inc., January 2016, pg. 85.

4. Suet. Calig. 56.1–2; Suet. Ner. 47.3; Suet. Galb. 25.3.
5. Suet. Tit. 6.1; Jones, Brian W., *The Emperor Titus*, St. Martin's Press, New York, 1984, pg. 84; Bingham, Sandra, "The Praetorian Guard in the Political and Social Life of Julio-Claudian Rome," The University of British Columbia, 1997, pg. 122, https://open.library.ubc.ca/media/stream/pdf/831/1.0099480/2.

6. Suet. Tit. 1.1 and 6.1; Jones, Brian W. "TITUS IN THE EAST, A.D. 70–71." *Rheinisches Museum Für Philologie*, vol. 128, no. 3/4, 1985, pp. 346–52; Perry M. Rogers. "Titus, Berenice and Mucianus." *Historia: Zeitschrift Für Alte Geschichte*, vol. 29, no. 1, 1980, pp. 86–95; Schoenfeld, Andrew J. "Sons of Israel in Caesar's Service: Jewish Soldiers in the Roman Military." *Shofar: An Interdisciplinary Journal of Jewish Studies*, vol. 24 no. 3, 2006, pp. 115–126.

7. Retief, Francois Peiter and Cilliers, Louise, "Causes of death among the Caesars (27 BC–AD 476)," Acta Theologica, March 2010, https://www.researchgate.net/publication/272124974_Causes_of_death_among_the_Caesars_27_BC-AD_476.

8. Suet. Vesp. 25.1.
9. Suet. Tit. 6.1; Dio 65.12–13.
10. Suet. Tit. 6.1.
11. Suet. Tit. 7.1.
12. Suet. Tit. 7.1.
13. Suet. Tit. 7.1.
14. Suet. Tit. 7.1.
15. Suet. Tit. 7.1; Dio 65.15.3; Tac. Hist. 2.2.1; Jones, Brian W., *The Emperor Titus*, St. Martin's Press, New York, 1984, pg. 87–91 and 94; Braund, D.C. "Berenice in Rome." *Historia: Zeitschrift Für Alte Geschichte*, vol. 33, no. 1, 1984, pp. 120–23; Crook, John A. "Titus and Berenice." *The American Journal of Philology*, vol. 72, no. 2, 1951, pp. 162–75; Perry M. Rogers. "Titus, Berenice and Mucianus." *Historia: Zeitschrift Für Alte Geschichte*, vol. 29, no. 1, 1980, pp. 86–95.

16. Suet. Tit. 7.1; Dio 65.15.3–4; Quint. Inst. 4.1.19.
17. Dio 65.15.4.
18. Dio 65.15.4.
19. Hydatius, "HYDATII EPISCOPI DESCRIPTIO CONSULUM EX QUO PRIMUM ORDINATI SUNT," Date Accessed April 6, 2024, http://thelatinlibrary.com/hydatiusfasti.html.
20. Jones, Brian W., *The Emperor Titus*, St. Martin's Press, New York, 1984, pg. 149–150; "Agricola," The Persians, Last Accessed April 6, 2024, https://www.the-persians.co.uk/theromans/timelines/agricola.htm.
21. Dio 65.15.5.
22. Suet. Tit. 7.2; Braund, D.C. "Berenice in Rome." *Historia: Zeitschrift Für Alte Geschichte*, vol. 33, no. 1, 1984, pp. 120–23; Crook, John A. "Titus and Berenice." *The American Journal of Philology*, vol. 72, no. 2, 1951, pp. 162–75; Perry M. Rogers. "Titus, Berenice and Mucianus." *Historia: Zeitschrift Für Alte Geschichte*, vol. 29, no. 1, 1980, pp. 86–95; Jones, Brian W., *The Emperor Titus*, St. Martin's Press, New York, 1984, pg. 93.
23. Suet. Tit. 7.1–2.
24. Dio 65.16.1–2 (Translated by Earnest Cary); Jones, Brian W., *The Emperor Titus*, St. Martin's Press, New York, 1984, pg. 91.
25. Suet. Tit. 6.2; Dio 65.15.2 and 65.16.3–4; Tac. Dial. 8; Southern, Pat, *Domitian, Tragic Tyrant*, Routledge, New York, 1997, pg. 30; Jones, Brian W., *The Emperor Titus*, St. Martin's Press, New York, 1984, pg. 89–90.
26. Suet. Tit. 6.2; Dio 65.16.3–4.
27. Suet. Tit. 6.2.
28. Suet. Vesp. 24.1; Hydatius, "HYDATII EPISCOPI DESCRIPTIO CONSULUM EX QUO PRIMUM ORDINATI SUNT," Date Accessed April 6, 2024, http://thelatinlibrary.com/hydatiusfasti.html.
29. Suet. Vesp. 23.4 and 24.1 (Translated by J.C. Rolfe); Dio 66.17.1–3; Oros. 7.9.12; Jones, Brian W., *The Emperor Titus*, St. Martin's Press, New York, 1984, pg. 114.
30. Dio 66.17.3; Suet. Vesp. 8.4.

Chapter XX

1. Suet. Tit. 6.1 (Translated by J.C. Rolfe).
2. Suet. Tit. 7.1.
3. Dio 66.18.1; Suet. Dom. 2.3; Oros. 7.9.13; CAH XI, pg. 46; Jones, Brian W., *The Emperor Titus*, St. Martin's Press, New York, 1984, pg. 115; Zissos, Andrew, *A Companion to the Flavian Age of Imperial Rome*, John Wiley and Sons, Inc., January 2016, pg. 76.
4. Levick, Barbara, *Vespasian*, Routledge, New York, 1999, pg. 197–198; Jones, Brian W., *The Emperor Titus*, St. Martin's Press, New York, 1984, pg. 152–153.
5. Dio 56.31.2; Smith, William, "Funus," A Dictionary of Greek and Roman Antiquities, John Murray, London, 1875, Lacus Curtius, https://penelope.uchicago.edu/Thayer/E/Roman/Texts/secondary/SMIGRA*/Funus.html.
6. Dio 56.34.1–2; Smith, William, "Funus," A Dictionary of Greek and Roman Antiquities, John Murray, London, 1875, Lacus Curtius, https://penelope.uchicago.edu/Thayer/E/Roman/Texts/secondary/SMIGRA*/Funus.html.
7. Dio 56.34.1–3; Suet. Vesp. 19.2 (Translated by J.C. Rolfe); Smith, William, "Funus," A Dictionary of Greek and Roman Antiquities, John Murray, London, 1875, Lacus Curtius, https://penelope.uchicago.edu/Thayer/E/Roman/Texts/secondary/SMIGRA*/Funus.html.
8. Dio 56.34.4 and 56.42.1; Smith, William, "Funus," A Dictionary of Greek and Roman Antiquities, John Murray, London, 1875, Lacus Curtius, https://penelope.uchicago.edu/Thayer/E/Roman/Texts/secondary/SMIGRA*/Funus.html.
9. Dio 56.42.2–3; Smith, William, "Funus," A Dictionary of Greek and Roman Antiquities, John Murray, London, 1875, Lacus Curtius, https://penelope.uchicago.edu/Thayer/E/Roman/Texts/secondary/SMIGRA*/Funus.html.
10. Dio 56.42.4; Smith, William, "Funus," A Dictionary of Greek and Roman Antiquities, John Murray, London, 1875, Lacus Curtius, https://penelope.uchicago.edu/Thayer/E/Roman/Texts/secondary/SMIGRA*/Funus.html.
11. Dio 56.43.1; Smith, William, "Spectacle in the Roman Imperial Funeral Procession," Theses, Dissertations, and Student Creative Activity, School of Art, Art History and Design, 2023,

https://digitalcommons.unl.edu/cgi/viewcontent.cgi?article=1180&context=artstudents; Erasmo, Mario, *Reading Death in Ancient Rome*, Ohio State University Press, Columbus, 2008, pg. 69, https://kb.osu.edu/server/api/core/bitstreams/dd09c276-ebfd-51a1-a7fe-7822317c9ee4/content.

12. Suet. Tit. 7.1; Dio 66.18.1.
13. Dio 66.18.1–3; Suet. Tit. 7.2; Jones, Brian W., *The Emperor Titus*, St. Martin's Press, New York, 1984, pg. 135 and 138.
14. Suet. Tit. 9.1; Jones, Brian W., *The Emperor Titus*, St. Martin's Press, New York, 1984, pg. 140.
15. Lact. Mort. 3; Tert. Apol. 5; Eus. H.E. 3.17; Sulp. Sev. H.E. 2.30; Dio 67.14.1–3.
16. Dio 66.18.1, 66.19.1 and 66.26.4; Suet. Tit. 9.1–3; Oros. 7.9.13.
17. Dio 66.19.1–2 (Translated by Earnest Cary); Long, George, Majestas, A Dictionary of Greek and Roman Antiquities, John Murray, London, 1875, Lacus Curtius, https://penelope.uchicago.edu/Thayer/E/Roman/Texts/secondary/SMIGRA*/Majestas.html.
18. Dio 66.19.3; Suet. Tit. 8.5; Smith, William, "Delator," A Dictionary of Greek and Roman Antiquities, John Murray, London, 1875, Lacus Curtius, https://penelope.uchicago.edu/Thayer/E/Roman/Texts/secondary/SMIGRA*/Delator.html.
19. Suet. Tit. 8.1 and 8.5; Dio 66.19.3; Digest 1.2.2.32 and 29.1.1; Jones, Brian W., *The Emperor Titus*, St. Martin's Press, New York, 1984, pg. 147–148; Long, George, "Praetor," A Dictionary of Greek and Roman Antiquities, John Murray, London, 1875, https://penelope.uchicago.edu/Thayer/E/Roman/Texts/secondary/SMIGRA*/Praetor.html.
20. Suet. Tit. 7.3.
21. Harl, Kenneth W., *Coinage in the Roman Economy 300 B.C. to A.D. 700*, The Johns Hopkins University Press, Baltimore, 1996, pg. 92 and 99; SCHWEI, DAVID. "Exchange Rates, Neronian Silver Standards, and a Long-Term Plan to Unify the Empire's Mints." *The Numismatic Chronicle (1966–)*, vol. 177, 2017, pp. 107–34; CAH XI, pg. 51.
22. Suet. Tit. 7.3 and 8.2; Dio 66.19.3 and 66.25.1; Elkins, Nathan T., *A Monument to Dynasty and Death*, Johns Hopkins University Press, Baltimore, 2009, pg. 65.
23. Suet. Tit. 8.1 (Translated by J.C. Rolfe); Jos. Life 76.
24. Suet. Tit. 2.1 and 7.2; Dio 66.18.1; Plin. Nat. 34.19 and 36.4; Crook, John A. "Titus and Berenice." *The American Journal of Philology*, vol. 72, no. 2, 1951, pp. 162–75.
25. Dio 66.19.3b.
26. Dio 66.19.3b and 66.19.3c.
27. Dio 66.20.1; "Agricola," The Persians, Last Accessed April 6, 2024, https://www.the-persians.co.uk/theromans/timelines/agricola.htm.

Chapter XXI

1. Plin. Ep. 6.20 (Translated by J.B. Firth).
2. Plin. Ep. 6.20; Beard, Mary, *The Fires of Vesuvius Pompeii Lost and Found*, The Belknap Press of Harvard University, Cambridge, 2008, pg. 10; Giacomelli L, Perrotta A, Scandone R, Scarpati C. The eruption of Vesuvius of 79 AD and its impact on human environment in Pompeii. Episodes. 2003; 26: 234–237.
3. Plin. Ep. 6.16 and 6.20; Sigurdsson, Haraldur, et al. "The Eruption of Vesuvius in A.D. 79: Reconstruction from Historical and Volcanological Evidence." American Journal of Archaeology, vol. 86, no. 1, 1982, pp. 39–51. Accessed 15 Jan. 2024; Giacomelli L, Perrotta A, Scandone R, Scarpati C. The eruption of Vesuvius of AD 79 and its impact on human environment in Pompeii. Episodes. 2003; 26: 234–237; Beard, Mary, *The Fires of Vesuvius Pompeii Lost and Found*, The Belknap Press of Harvard University, Cambridge, 2008, pg. 17; "Pompeii: Vesuvius eruption may have been later than thought," BBC, October 16, 2018, https://www.bbc.com/news/world-europe-45874858.
4. Plin. Ep. 6.16 and 6.20; Oros. 7.9.14; Sigurdsson, Haraldur, et al. "The Eruption of Vesuvius in A.D. 79: Reconstruction from Historical and Volcanological Evidence." American Journal of Archaeology, vol. 86, no. 1, 1982, pp. 39–51. Accessed 15 Jan. 2024; Giacomelli L, Perrotta A, Scandone R, Scarpati C. The eruption of Vesuvius of 79 A.D. and its impact on human environment in Pompeii. Episodes. 2003; 26: 234–237.
5. Plin. Ep. 6.16 and 6.20; Sigurdsson, Haraldur, et al. "The Eruption of Vesuvius in A.D. 79: Reconstruction from Historical and Volcanological Evidence." American Journal of Archaeology, vol. 86, no. 1, 1982, pp. 39–51. Accessed 15 Jan. 2024; Giacomelli L, Perrotta A, Scandone R, Scarpati C. The eruption of Vesuvius of 79 AD and its impact on human environment in Pompeii. Episodes. 2003; 26: 234–237.
6. Plin. Ep. 6.16 and 6.20; Sigurdsson, Haraldur, et al. "The Eruption of Vesuvius in A.D. 79: Reconstruction from Historical and Volcanological Evidence." American Journal of Archaeology, vol. 86, no. 1, 1982, pp. 39–51. Accessed 15 Jan. 2024; Giacomelli L, Perrotta A, Scandone R, Scarpati C. The eruption of Vesuvius of 79 AD and its impact on human environment in Pompeii. Episodes. 2003; 26: 234–237.
7. Plin. Ep. 6.16 and 6.20.
8. Plin. Ep. 6.16 and 6.20; Sigurdsson, Haraldur, et al. "The Eruption of Vesuvius in A.D. 79: Reconstruction from Historical and Volcanological Evidence." American Journal of Archaeology, vol. 86, no. 1, 1982, pp. 39–51. Accessed 15 Jan. 2024; Giacomelli L, Perrotta A, Scandone R, Scarpati C. The eruption of Vesuvius of 79 AD and its impact on human environment in Pompeii. Episodes. 2003; 26: 234–237.
9. Plin. Ep. 6.16 and 6.20; Sigurdsson, Haraldur, et al. "The Eruption of Vesuvius in A.D. 79: Reconstruction from Historical and Volcanological Evidence." American Journal of Archaeology, vol. 86, no. 1, 1982, pp. 39–51. Accessed 15 Jan. 2024; Giacomelli L, Perrotta A, Scandone R,

Scarpati C. The eruption of Vesuvius of 79 AD and its impact on human environment in Pompeii. Episodes. 2003; 26: 234–237; Cioni, R., L. Gurioli, R. Lanza, and E. Zanella (2004), Temperatures of the A.D. 79 pyroclastic density current deposits (Vesuvius, Italy), *J. Geophys. Res.*, 109, B02207, doi:10.1029/2002JB002251; Pensa, A., Giordano, G., Corrado, S. *et al*. A new hazard scenario at Vesuvius: deadly thermal impact of detached ash cloud surges in 79CE at Herculaneum. *Sci Rep* 13, 5622 (2023). https://doi.org/10.1038/s41598-023-32623-3.

10. Plin. Ep. 6.16 and 6.20; Sigurdsson, Haraldur, et al. "The Eruption of Vesuvius in A.D. 79: Reconstruction from Historical and Volcanological Evidence." American Journal of Archaeology, vol. 86, no. 1, 1982, pp. 39–51. Accessed 15 Jan. 2024; Giacomelli L, Perrotta A, Scandone R, Scarpati C. The eruption of Vesuvius of 79 AD and its impact on human environment in Pompeii. Episodes. 2003; 26: 234–237.

11. Plin. Ep. 6.16 and 6.20; Oros. 7.9.14; Sigurdsson, Haraldur, et al. "The Eruption of Vesuvius in A.D. 79: Reconstruction from Historical and Volcanological Evidence." American Journal of Archaeology, vol. 86, no. 1, 1982, pp. 39–51. Accessed 15 Jan. 2024; Giacomelli L, Perrotta A, Scandone R, Scarpati C. The eruption of Vesuvius of 79 AD and its impact on human environment in Pompeii. Episodes. 2003; 26: 234–237; Killgrove, Kristina, "Pregnant Women and Fetuses Among Vesuvius' Victims, Archaeologists Reveal," Forbes, August 24, 2017, https://www.forbes.com/sites/kristinakillgrove/2017/08/24/pregnant-women-and-fetuses-among-vesuvius-victims-archaeologists-reveal/?sh=101e7313cc33; Beard, Mary, *The Fires of Vesuvius Pompeii Lost and Found*, The Belknap Press of Harvard University, Cambridge, 2008, pg. 8–9.

12. Plin. Ep. 6.16 and 6.20; Dio 66.23.3–4; Sigurdsson, Haraldur, et al. "The Eruption of Vesuvius in A.D. 79: Reconstruction from Historical and Volcanological Evidence." American Journal of Archaeology, vol. 86, no. 1, 1982, pp. 39–51. Accessed 15 Jan. 2024; Giacomelli L, Perrotta A, Scandone R, Scarpati C. The eruption of Vesuvius of 79 AD and its impact on human environment in Pompeii. Episodes. 2003; 26: 234–237.

13. Dio 66.24.1.
14. Dio 66.24.3; Suet. Tit. 8.3–4.
15. Dio 66.24.3; Suet. Tit. 8.3–4.
16. Dio 66.24.1–3; Suet. Tit. 8.4; Oros. 7.9.14.
17. Dio 66.24.2–3 (Translated by Earnest Cary); Oros. 7.9.14; CAH XI, pg. 49.
18. Suet. Tit. 8.4.
19. Suet. Tit. 8.3 (Translated by J.C. Rolfe); Dio 66.23.5.
20. Suet. Tit. 8.4.
21. CAH XI, pg. 49–50; Levick, Barbara, *Vespasian*, Routledge, New York, 1999, pg. 125.

Chapter XXII

1. Mart. Spect. 1 (Anonymous translator; Bohn's Classical Library).
2. Elkins, Nathan T., *A Monument to Dynasty and Death*, Johns Hopkins University Press, 2009, pg. 22.
3. Elkins, Nathan T., *A Monument to Dynasty and Death*, Johns Hopkins University Press, 2009, pg. 3, 21, 24–25 and 29; Lancaster, Lynne C. "The Process of Building the Colosseum: The Site, Materials, and Construction Techniques." *Journal of Roman Archaeology* 18 (2005): 57–82; Smith, Philip, "Amphitheatrum," *A Dictionary of Greek and Roman Antiquities*, 1875, The University of Chicago, https://penelope.uchicago.edu/Thayer/E/Roman/Texts/secondary/SMIGRA*/Amphitheatrum.html; Welch, Katherine E., *The Roman Amphitheater*, Cambridge University Press, Cambridge, 2007, pg. 128–129 and 135–137.
4. Elkins, Nathan T., *A Monument to Dynasty and Death*, Johns Hopkins University Press, 2009, pg. 26–27, 43 and 61; Lancaster, Lynne C. "The Process of Building the Colosseum: The Site, Materials, and Construction Techniques." *Journal of Roman Archaeology* 18 (2005): 57–82; Smith, Philip, "Amphitheatrum," *A Dictionary of Greek and Roman Antiquities*, 1875, The University of Chicago, https://penelope.uchicago.edu/Thayer/E/Roman/Texts/secondary/SMIGRA*/Amphitheatrum.html; Welch, Katherine E., *The Roman Amphitheater*, Cambridge University Press, Cambridge, 2007, pg. 135–137.
5. Elkins, Nathan T., *A Monument to Dynasty and Death*, Johns Hopkins University Press, 2009, pg. 3 and 58; Lancaster, Lynne C. "The Process of Building the Colosseum: The Site, Materials, and Construction Techniques." *Journal of Roman Archaeology* 18 (2005): 57–82; Smith, Philip, "Amphitheatrum," *A Dictionary of Greek and Roman Antiquities*, 1875, The University of Chicago, https://penelope.uchicago.edu/Thayer/E/Roman/Texts/secondary/SMIGRA*/Amphitheatrum.html.
6. Elkins, Nathan T., *A Monument to Dynasty and Death*, Johns Hopkins University Press, 2009, pg. 51–53, 55 and 57; Lancaster, Lynne C. "The Process of Building the Colosseum: The Site, Materials, and Construction Techniques." *Journal of Roman Archaeology* 18 (2005): 57–82; Smith, Philip, "Amphitheatrum," *A Dictionary of Greek and Roman Antiquities*, 1875, The University of Chicago, https://penelope.uchicago.edu/Thayer/E/Roman/Texts/secondary/SMIGRA*/Amphitheatrum.html; ELKINS, NATHAN T. "Locating the Imperial Box in the Flavian Amphitheatre: The Numismatic Evidence." *The Numismatic Chronicle (1966–)*, vol. 164, 2004, pp. 147–57.
7. Elkins, Nathan T., *A Monument to Dynasty and Death*, Johns Hopkins University Press, 2009, pg. 31–32, and 60.
8. Elkins, Nathan T., *A Monument to Dynasty*

and Death, Johns Hopkins University Press, 2009, pg. 67.

9. Elkins, Nathan T., *A Monument to Dynasty and Death*, Johns Hopkins University Press, 2009, pg. 67; Rich, Anthony, "Balneae," *A Dictionary of Greek and Roman Antiquities*, 1875, The University of Chicago, https://penelope.uchicago.edu/Thayer/E/Roman/Texts/secondary/SMIGRA*/Balneae.html.

10. Rich, Anthony, "Balneae," *A Dictionary of Greek and Roman Antiquities*, 1875, The University of Chicago, https://penelope.uchicago.edu/Thayer/E/Roman/Texts/secondary/SMIGRA*/Balneae.html; "Bath Clog," Vindolanda Charitable Trust, Last Accessed May 27, 2024, https://www.vindolanda.com/bath-clogs.

11. Rich, Anthony, "Balneae," *A Dictionary of Greek and Roman Antiquities*, 1875, The University of Chicago, https://penelope.uchicago.edu/Thayer/E/Roman/Texts/secondary/SMIGRA*/Balneae.html; Elkins, Nathan T., *A Monument to Dynasty and Death*, Johns Hopkins University Press, 2009, pg. 68.

12. Rich, Anthony, "Balneae," *A Dictionary of Greek and Roman Antiquities*, 1875, The University of Chicago, https://penelope.uchicago.edu/Thayer/E/Roman/Texts/secondary/SMIGRA*/Balneae.html.

13. Rich, Anthony, "Balneae," *A Dictionary of Greek and Roman Antiquities*, 1875, The University of Chicago, https://penelope.uchicago.edu/Thayer/E/Roman/Texts/secondary/SMIGRA*/Balneae.html.

14. Smith, Philip, "Aquaeductus," *A Dictionary of Greek and Roman Antiquities*, 1875, The University of Chicago, https://penelope.uchicago.edu/Thayer/E/Roman/Texts/secondary/SMIGRA*/Aquaeductus.html; CAH XI, pg. 48–49; Jones, Brian W., *The Emperor Titus*, St. Martin's Press, New York, 1984, pg. 144–145.

15. Smith, Philip, "Aquaeductus," *A Dictionary of Greek and Roman Antiquities*, 1875, The University of Chicago, https://penelope.uchicago.edu/Thayer/E/Roman/Texts/secondary/SMIGRA*/Aquaeductus.html; CAH XI, pg. 48–49; Jones, Brian W., *The Emperor Titus*, St. Martin's Press, New York, 1984, pg. 144–145.

16. CAH XI, pg. 47; Tommaso, Leoni, "Urbem Hierusolymam delevit: The Arch of Titus in the Circus Maximus in Antiquity and the Middle Ages," York University, April 2018, pg. 280 and 394, https://yorkspace.library.yorku.ca/home; Ariel, David, "Second Monumental Arch of Titus Celebrating Victory Over Jews Found in Rome," Haaretz, March 21, 2017, https://www.haaretz.com/archaeology/2017-03-21/ty-article-magazine/second-arch-of-titus-celebrating-victory-over-jews-found/0000017f-df31-df9c-a17f-ff3987260000; Elkins, Nathan T., *A Monument to Dynasty and Death*, Johns Hopkins University Press, Baltimore, 2009, pg. 70–71; Barron, Caroline. "The (lost) Arch of Titus: The Visibility and Prominence of Victory in Flavian Rome." *Reconsidering Roman Power*, edited by Katell Berthelot, Publications de l'École française de Rome, 2020.

17. Dio 66.25.3–4; Suet. Tit. 7.3; Elkins, Nathan T., *A Monument to Dynasty and Death*, Johns Hopkins University Press, 2009, pg. 86; Zissos, Andrew, *A Companion to the Flavian Age of Imperial Rome*, Wiley-Blackwell, Hoboken, New Jersey, 2016, pg. 87–88.

18. Buttrey, T.V. "Domitian, the Rhinoceros, and the Date of Martial's 'Liber De Spectaculis.'" *The Journal of Roman Studies*, vol. 97, 2007, pp. 101–12.

19. Dio 66.25.3

20. Dio 66.25.3–4; Suet. Tit. 2.1. Dio 66.25.3–4 is muddled. It is unclear whether the faux sea-fight was held in the man-made basin or the amphitheater.

21. Elkins, Nathan T., *A Monument to Dynasty and Death*, Johns Hopkins University Press, 2009, pg. 1–2.

22. Elkins, Nathan T., *A Monument to Dynasty and Death*, Johns Hopkins University Press, 2009, pg. 87 and 93; Dio 66.25.1; Suet. Tit. 7.3.

23. Elkins, Nathan T., *A Monument to Dynasty and Death*, Johns Hopkins University Press, 2009, pg. 88–94; Mart. Spect. 6 and 10; Lancaster, Lynne C. "The Process of Building the Colosseum: The Site, Materials, and Construction Techniques." *Journal of Roman Archaeology* 18 (2005): 57–82; Smith, Philip, "Amphitheatrum," *A Dictionary of Greek and Roman Antiquities*, 1875, https://penelope.uchicago.edu/Thayer/E/Roman/Texts/secondary/SMIGRA*/Amphitheatrum.html.

24. Mart. Spect. 6, 10, 12, 17, 18 and 19; Elkins, Nathan T., *A Monument to Dynasty and Death*, Johns Hopkins University Press, 2009, pg. 88–94.

25. Elkins, Nathan T., *A Monument to Dynasty and Death*, Johns Hopkins University Press, 2009, pg. 95–100.

26. Mart. Spect. 7 and 8.

27. Elkins, Nathan T., *A Monument to Dynasty and Death*, Johns Hopkins University Press, 2009, pg. 100–110; Dio 66.25.2; Suet. 7.3 and 9.2; Kyle, Donald, *Spectacles of Death in Ancient Rome*; Routledge, New York, 1998, pg. 86.

28. Mart. Spect. 39.

29. Dio 66.25.3–4; Mart. Spect. 24 and 28; Elkins, Nathan T., *A Monument to Dynasty and Death*, Johns Hopkins University Press, 2009, pg. 110–112.

30. Dio 66.25.4–5.

31. Suet. Tit. 9.1.

32. Suet. Tit. 9.2.

33. Suet. Tit. 9.3; Dio 66.18.1; Suet. Dom. 22.1; CAH XI, pg. 53.

34. Suet. Tit. 8.2; Plut. De Tuenda 3.

35. Suet. Tit. 10.1; Dio 66.26.1.

Chapter XXIII

1. Dio 66.18.5 (Translated by Earnest Cary).
2. Suet. Tit. 10.1.

3. Suet. Tit. 10.1 and 11.1.

*Dio 66.26.1 makes no mention of reaching a farmhouse. He called it a "watering-place."

4. Suet. Tit. 10.1–2; Dio 66.26.3 (Translated by J.C. Rolfe).

*Dio 66.26.3 states that Titus uttered his declaration "as he expired."

5. Suet. Tit. 10.2; Dio 66.26.3–4

6. Suet. Tit. 11.1; Dio 66.26.1–2 and 66.26.4; Oros. 7.9.15; Philostr. VA 6.32; Bastomsky, S.J. "The Death of the Emperor Titus—A Tentative Suggestion." *Apeiron*, vol. 1, no. 2, 1967, pp. 22–23.

*Dio 66.26.1 calls it a "watering-place" rather than a farmhouse

7. Gittin 56b; Plut. De Tuenda 3; Jones, Brian W., *The Emperor Titus*, St. Martin's Press, New York, 1984, pg. 154–155; Bastomsky, S.J. "The Death of the Emperor Titus—A Tentative Suggestion." *Apeiron*, vol. 1, no. 2, 1967, pp. 22–23.

8. Dio 66.26.3.

9. Dio 66.26.3; Oros. 7.9.15 and 7.10.1.

10. Suet. Dom. 2.3; Dio 56.31.2; Smith, William, "Funus," A Dictionary of Greek and Roman Antiquities, John Murray, London, 1875, Lacus Curtius, https://penelope.uchicago.edu/Thayer/E/Roman/Texts/secondary/SMIGRA*/Funus.html.

11. Dio 56.34.1–3 and 67.2.6; https://penelope.uchicago.edu/Thayer/E/Roman/Texts/secondary/SMIGRA*/Funus.html

12. Dio 56.42.1–4; Smith, William, "Funus," A Dictionary of Greek and Roman Antiquities, John Murray, London, 1875, Lacus Curtius, https://penelope.uchicago.edu/Thayer/E/Roman/Texts/secondary/SMIGRA*/Funus.html.

13. Southern, Pat, *Domitian, Tragic Tyrant*, Routledge, New York, 1997, pg. 37–38; Jones, Brian W., *The Emperor Titus*, St. Martin's Press, New York, 1984, pg. 155.

14. Suet. Dom. 3.1.

15. Suet. Dom. 2.3.

16. Elkins, Nathan T., *A Monument to Dynasty and Death*, Johns Hopkins University Press, Baltimore, 2009, pg. 70–71; Southern, Pat, *Domitian, Tragic Tyrant*, Routledge, New York, 1997, pg. 37–38 and 126; Jones, Brian W., *The Emperor Titus*, St. Martin's Press, New York, 1984, pg. 155–156; Berlin, Andrea M., Overman, Andrew J., *The First Jewish Revolt*, Routledge, New York, 2002, pg. 217.

17. Ariel, David, "Second Monumental Arch of Titus Celebrating Victory Over Jews Found in Rome," Haaretz, March 21, 2017, https://www.haaretz.com/archaeology/2017-03-21/ty-article-magazine/second-arch-of-titus-celebrating-victory-over-jews-found/0000017f-df31-df9c-a17f-ff3987260000.

18. Suet. Dom. 4.1, 4.5, 5.1, 7.3, and 8.1; Harl, Kenneth W., *Coinage in the Roman Economy 300 B.C. to A.D. 700*, The Johns Hopkins University Press, Baltimore, 1996, pg. 92; Elkins, Nathan T., *A Monument to Dynasty and Death*, Johns Hopkins University Press, Baltimore, 2009, pg. 29 and 59.

19. Suet. Dom. 6.2, 10.1–5, 11.1, and 15.1 (Translated by J.C. Rolfe).

20. Suet. Dom. 10.4, 15.1; Dio 67.3.2 and 67.14.1–3; Juv. Sat. 2.32; Southern, Pat, *Domitian, Tragic Tyrant*, Routledge, New York, 1997, pg. 41, 43, 87–90, 109, and 115.

21. Southern, Pat, *Domitian, Tragic Tyrant*, Routledge, New York, 1997, pg. 115.

22. Suet. Dom. 13.2–3, Dio 67.4.7.

23. Suet. Dom. 6.1, Dio 67.10.1–4; Tac. Ag. 29 and 37.

24. Suet. Dom. 7.3, 12.1–2; Harl, Kenneth W., *Coinage in the Roman Economy 300 B.C. to A.D. 700*, The Johns Hopkins University Press, Baltimore, 1996, pg. 92; Southern, Pat, *Domitian, Tragic Tyrant*, Routledge, New York, 1997, pg. 64 and 67.

25. Suet. Dom. 14.1, 14.4, 16.1–2, 17.1–3.

26. Suet. Dom. 15.1, 17.3 and 23.1.

27. Bloom, James, *The Jewish Revolts Against Rome, A.D. 66–135*, McFarland, Jefferson, NC, 2010, pg. 191–200; Goodman, Martin, *Rome and Jerusalem*, Vintage Books, New York, 2008, pg. 453–459; *The Bar Kokhba Revolt*, Captivating History, Columbia, 2021, pg. 54–55.

28. Bloom, James, *The Jewish Revolts Against Rome, A.D. 66–135*, McFarland, Jefferson, NC, 2010, pg. 201–216; Goodman, Martin, *Rome and Jerusalem*, Vintage Books, New York, 2008, pg. 464–469; GEIGER, JOSEPH. "The Bar-Kokhba Revolt: The Greek Point of View." *Historia: Zeitschrift Für Alte Geschichte*, vol. 65, no. 4, 2016, pp. 497–519; *The Bar Kokhba Revolt*, Captivating History, Columbia, 2021, pg. 59–62.

29. Bloom, James, *The Jewish Revolts Against Rome, A.D. 66–135*, McFarland, Jefferson, NC, 2010, pg. 201–216; Goodman, Martin, *Rome and Jerusalem*, Vintage Books, New York, 2008, pg. 464–469; GEIGER, JOSEPH. "The Bar-Kokhba Revolt: The Greek Point of View." *Historia: Zeitschrift Für Alte Geschichte*, vol. 65, no. 4, 2016, pp. 497–519; *The Bar Kokhba Revolt*, Captivating History, Columbia, 2021, pg. 59–62, 65–71, and 78–95.

30. Bloom, James, *The Jewish Revolts Against Rome, A.D. 66–135*, McFarland, Jefferson, NC, 2010, pg. 201–216; Goodman, Martin, *Rome and Jerusalem*, Vintage Books, New York, 2008, pg. 464–469; GEIGER, JOSEPH. "The Bar-Kokhba Revolt: The Greek Point of View." *Historia: Zeitschrift Für Alte Geschichte*, vol. 65, no. 4, 2016, pp. 497–519; *The Bar Kokhba Revolt*, Captivating History, Columbia, 2021, pg. 109–119.

31. Berlin, Andrea M., Overman, Andrew J., *The First Jewish Revolt*, Routledge, New York, 2002, pg. 221–233.

32. Berlin, Andrea M., Overman, Andrew J., *The First Jewish Revolt*, Routledge, New York, 2002, pg. 237–250.

33. Weiner, Michael, "The Arch of Titus must come down," Forward, July 8, 2020, https://forward.com/opinion/450377/the-arch-of-titus-must-come-down/.

Bibliography

Abbott, Frank Frost, *A History and Description of Roman Political Institutions*, Third Edition, Ginn and Company, Boston, 1911.

Asiedu, F.B.A., *Josephus, Paul, and the Fate of Early Christianity*, Lexington Books, New York, 2019.

Barrett, Anthony, *Caligula, The Corruption of Power*, Yale University Press, New Haven, 1989.

Beard, Mary, *The Fires of Vesuvius, Pompeii Lost and Found*, Belknap Press of Harvard University, Cambridge, 2008.

Ben-Sasson, H.H., *A History of the Jewish People*, Harvard University Press, Cambridge, 1976.

Berlin, Andrea M., Overman, Andrew J., *The First Jewish Revolt*, Routledge, New York, 2002.

Bloom, James, *The Jewish Revolts Against Rome, A.D. 66-135*, McFarland, Jefferson, NC, 2010.

Campbell, Duncan B., *Siege Warfare in the Roman World*, Osprey Publishing, Oxford, 2005.

Dando-Collins, Stephen, *The Great Fire of Rome*, Da Capo Press, Philadelphia, 2010.

Donfried, Karl P., Richardson, Peter, *Judaism and Christianity in First-Century Rome*, William B. Eerdmans Publishing Company, Grand Rapids, Michigan, 1998.

Elkins, Nathan T., *A Monument to Dynasty and Death*, Johns Hopkins University Press, Baltimore, 2009.

Everett, Anthony, *The Rise of Rome*, Random House Trade Paperbacks, New York, 2013.

Fields, Nic, *Boudicca's Rebellion AD 60-61: The Britons Rise Up Against Rome*, Osprey Publishing, Oxford, 2011.

Freeman, Philip, *Julius Caesar*, JR Books, London, 2008.

Goldsworthy, Adrian, *The Complete Roman Army*, Thames and Hudson, New York, 2003.

Goodman, Martin, *Rome and Jerusalem*, Vintage Books, New York, 2008.

Griffin, Miriam, "The Flavians," *The Cambridge Ancient History*, Ed. Bowman, Alan K., et. al., Cambridge: Cambridge University Press, 2000.

Harl, Kenneth W., *Coinage in the Roman Economy 300 B.C. to A.D. 700*, The Johns Hopkins University Press, Baltimore, 1996.

Jones, Brian W., *The Emperor Titus*, St. Martin's Press, New York, 1984.

Kyle, Donald, *Spectacles of Death in Ancient Rome*; Routledge, New York, 1998.

Levick, Barbara, *Vespasian*, Routledge, New York, 1999.

Morgan, Gwyn, *69 A.D. The Year of Four Emperors*, Oxford University Press, Oxford, 2006.

Schnelle, Udo, *The First One Hundred Years of Christianity: An Introduction to Its History, Literature, and Development*, Baker Academic, 2020.

Southern, Pat, *Domitian, Tragic Tyrant*, Routledge, New York, 1997.

The Bar Kokhba Revolt, Captivating History, Columbia, 2021.

Welch, Katherine E., *The Roman Amphitheater*, Cambridge University Press, Cambridge, 2007.

Wells, Peter S., *The Battle That Stopped Rome*, W.W. Norton & Company, New York, 2003.

Zissos, Andrew, *A Companion to the Flavian Age of Imperial Rome*, Wiley-Blackwell, Hoboken, New Jersey, 2016.

INDEX

Abila 69
Achabari 39
Achaia 171
Actium 7
Adiabene 139–140
Adida 72
Aedile 10–12, 35
Aelia Capitolina 203
Aeneas 107
Africa 29–30, 34, 86, 124
Agricola, Gnaeus Julius 169, 179, 186, 202
Agrippa I 99
Agrippa II 32, 36–38, 44–45, 55, 59, 62, 74, 99, 145
Agrippina 19–20, 22–23, 27, 29
Alexandria 38, 42–43, 82–84, 86, 89, 162, 177
Amphitheatrum 157, 177, 192
Amygdalon Pool 116
Ananus ben Ananus 38, 65–66, 77
Annius Pollio, Gaius 30
Antioch 44, 84, 146–147
Antiochus Epiphanes 115–116
Antiochus IV of Commagene 44, 159
Antipatris 72
Antium 33
Antonia Fortress 37, 99, 101, 110, 116–117, 119, 122, 125–126, 128–129, 131
Antoninus Pius 203
Antony, Mark 6–7, 37, 168
Apis 147
Apodyterium 190
aqueduct 14, 190–191
Aquitania 70
Arch of Titus (extant) 200–201, 205
Arch of Titus (located at the Circus Maximus) 191
Aristobulus 35
Arrecinus Clemens, Marcus (Titus' brother-in-law) 175
Arrecinus Clemens, Marcus (Titus' father-in-law) 27
Artabanus 179

Ascalon 38, 44, 90
Asia 7–8
Augustus (Octavian) 1, 6–8, 10, 14, 17, 41, 71, 172, 174, 199
Aurelius, Marcus 203
Azotus 64

Babylonians 35, 44, 135, 187
Bassus, Lucilius 157–160
Baths of Titus 189–190
Bephleptenpha 72
Berenice 36, 45, 53, 62, 76, 83, 90, 143, 145, 168–169, 178, 198, 204
Bersabe 39
Berytus 83, 146
Besimoth 69
Bethennabris 68–69
Bezetha 99
Boudica 1, 22, 24–26, 205
Britannia 1, 17–18, 23, 25–26, 34, 42, 168, 179, 205
Britannicus 1, 19–20, 177, 192, 205
Brutus, Marcus Junius 6
Bulla 13, 20
Byzantium 171

Caecina Alienus, Aulus 84–85, 170, 198
Caenis 16
Caesar, Gaius Julius 1, 5–6, 14, 17, 41, 168–169, 205
Caesarea Maritima 36, 38, 52–53, 55, 62, 64, 68, 73, 76, 78, 83, 90, 143, 145
Caesarea Philippi 55, 145
Caldarium 190
Caligula 10–13, 16–17, 27, 75, 81, 165–166, 177
Camulodunum 24
Canaanites 35
Caphareccho 39
Caphartoba 72
Capitol 85, 151, 185, 202
Capitoline Hill 151
Carrhae 146
Casian Zeus Temple 90

Cassius Longinus, Gaius 6
Castor 107
Censitores 162
censor 3, 162–164, 172
Censuales 162
census 162–163
Cerialis, Sextus Vettulenus 50, 128
Cestius Gallus, Gaius 36, 38, 138
Charabis 78
Chrestus 13
Christianity 1, 13, 34, 158, 205
Circus Maximus 14–15, 33, 155, 191–192, 200
Cisapline Gaul 77
Claudius 1, 13–19, 23, 70–71, 81, 99, 165–166
Cleopatra 7, 168
Colosseum 1, 154–155, 171, 188–189, 200
Commagene 44, 115, 159, 171
Consul 3–4, 11, 18, 87, 153, 157, 162, 168, 170, 172, 184, 191
Corinth 74, 82
Cosa 8
Crassus, Marcus Licinius 115, 146
Cremona 84
Crete 10
crucifixion 50–52, 104, 114–115, 137, 159, 167, 194, 200
Cursus honorum 8, 10, 12, 23
Cypros 38
Cyprus 76
Cyrene 10

Dalmatia 76, 83
Damascus 38
damnatio memoriae 202, 205
Dead Sea 38, 66, 69, 158–159
Delatores 176
Denarii 34, 154, 157, 177, 200, 202
Dio, Cassius 2, 22, 24, 26, 103, 151, 170, 175, 185, 192–193, 197–199
Domitia 197

227

Index

Domitian 19, 85, 86–87, 145, 148, 150, 153, 171, 173, 192, 196–204
Domitilla, Flavia (Titus' mother) 11–12, 16–18, 31
Domitilla, Flavia (Titus' sister) 19, 31
domus aurea 34, 156
Drachmas 157

Egypt 6–7, 34–35, 42–43, 82–83, 86, 89, 138, 143, 145, 147–148, 150, 162
Eleazar (Leader at Machaerus) 158–159
Eleazar ben Simon 65–67, 77–78, 88–89, 92, 96–97, 99
Emmaus 72
Eprius, Titus Clodius 170, 198
equestrians 4–7, 9, 27, 41, 165, 186, 188

Falacrina 8
favor 174
Fidenae 155
fiscus judaicus 157–158, 175
Flavia, Julia (Titus' first daughter) 28, 31, 196, 201
Flavius Clemens, Titus 200–201
Flavius Sabinus, Titus (Titus' cousin) 175, 201
Flavius Sabinus, Titus (Titus' grandfather) 6–8
Flavius Sabinus, Titus (Titus' uncle) 8, 83, 85–86
Florus, Gessius 36
Frigidarium 190
Fronto 143
Furnilla, Marcia 30–31

Gadara 68
Galba, Servius Sulpicius 71–76, 80–81, 165–166
Galilee 34, 39, 44–46, 55–56, 58, 61–62, 69, 138, 157, 200
Gallia Lugdunensis 70
Gamala 39, 59–61
Gaudentius 155
Gaul 5, 8, 70, 77, 84
Gaza 90
Gerasa 73, 77
Germanicus 10, 17
Germany 16–18, 23, 26–27, 34, 71, 74
Gischala 39, 59, 61–65
Gophna 91, 127
Grammaticus 19

Hadrian (Emperor) 1, 203
Hadrumetum 29–30
Hasmonean dynasty 35
Heracleopolis 90
Herculaneum 183, 185

Herod the Great 37, 98, 140, 157
Herodium 78, 157, 159
Herod's palace 140–141
Hippicus Tower 98, 103, 141, 143
Hispania Tarraconensis 71
Horace 19
Hyrcanus 35

Iceni 23–24
Idumea 66–67, 72, 77–78, 99, 103, 141
Isis 8, 34, 185
Izates 139

James (brother of Jesus Christ) 38
Jamnia 64, 72, 90
Japha 39, 49–50
Jardes 159
Jericho 38, 68, 72
Jerusalem 1, 3, 36–39, 42, 44, 61–68, 72–74, 77–78, 80, 88–132, 136–137, 139–149, 151, 154, 157, 159, 162, 186, 191, 200, 203–205
Jesus 141, 149
Jesus Christ 8, 13, 38, 202
John of Gischala 62–67, 77–78, 80, 88–89, 92, 96–97, 99, 101, 103, 106, 110–113, 115–116, 120–123, 125, 133, 138, 140, 142, 148, 150–151
Jonathan 131
Joppa 54–55, 72, 90
Joseph ben Gurion 38, 65
Josephus, Flavius 2, 38–39, 43–46, 48–52, 58–62, 64–65, 67–68, 82–84, 88, 90, 94, 96–97, 101, 105–107, 110–111, 113–114, 119–121, 126–129, 134–136, 140–141, 143–144, 148–150, 157, 161, 177
Jotapata 2, 39, 46–55
Judaea 1–2, 34–36, 38–41, 43–44, 64, 67, 69, 74, 78, 80, 83, 87, 90, 101, 103, 150, 157, 162, 167, 198, 200, 203–204
Julianus 125–126
Julias 69
Jupiter 85, 149, 151, 154, 157, 185, 203
Juventus 21

Kadasa 63
Kidron 93–94, 99

Laberius Maximus, Lucius 157
Liberalia 21
Litterator 18
Locusta 20, 73–74
Londinium 24
Lusitania 75
Lustrum 163

Lycia 171
Lydda 72

Machaerus 38, 78, 157–159
Majestas 176
Malchus of Nabatea 44
Mannaeus 121
Mare Nostrum 43
Mariamme Tower 98, 141, 143
Martial 187, 192–194
Mary 132–133
Masada 37, 67, 77–78, 157, 159–162
Maximus, Terentius 178–179
Melitene 144
Memphis 147, 187
Misenum 180–182
Moesia 76, 83, 148
mos maiorum 5, 15
Mount Gerizim 50
Mount of Olives 92–94, 98, 131
Mount Tabor 39, 59–61
Mucianus, Gaius Licinius 26, 59–60, 62, 82–84, 86, 145, 168

Naples 71, 180–182
Narcissus 16, 19
Nero 1, 10, 14, 19–20, 22–23, 25–26, 29–36, 39, 41–42, 52, 55, 59, 63, 70–75, 80–81, 83, 87, 138, 143, 154–156, 159, 165–167, 172, 176–178, 185, 200, 204
Nerva, Marcus Cocceius 175, 203
Nicanor 101
Niger of Perea 44
Nikon 106

Onias 162
Ophel 139
Oplontis 181, 183
Optimates 6
opus caementicium 156
Orosius, Paulus 13, 134, 150, 152, 171
Ostracine 90
Otho 75–78, 80–81, 83, 109, 125, 154, 166
Ovid 19

Paetus 159
Pannonia 76, 83–84, 148
Parthia 41, 145–146, 159, 179, 203
Passover 90, 96
patricians 5, 195
Paulinus, Gaius Suetonius 25
Pax Romana 4, 12, 14, 71
Pedanius 131
Pella 39
Pelusium 90
Peponila 170
Perea 44, 68

Pertinax 174
Petro, Titus Flavius 4–6, 8
Petronius Turpilianus, Publius 73
Pharsulus 6
Phasael Tower 98, 141, 143
Philistines 35, 203
Philostratus, Flavius 198
Phineas 141, 149
Piso Licinianus, Lucius Calpurnius 75
Placidus 44–45, 60, 68–69
Plebeians 4–6, 188
Pliny the Elder 180–182
Pliny the Younger 180–182
Plutarch 198
Polla, Vespasia 8
Pompeii 16, 180–184
Pompey the Great 6, 32, 35, 37, 138, 185
Pontifex Maximus 175, 191, 200
Populares 5
Praetor 12–13, 43
Praetorian Guard 3, 13, 19, 27, 73, 75, 165–168, 170–172, 176, 197–199, 204–205
Prasutagus 23–24
Primus, Antonius 84–86
Princeps 7, 86, 191
Priscus (Gladiator) 194
Priscus (Roman archer during the Jewish Revolt) 131
Psephinus Tower 98–99
Ptolemais 38, 44–45
Ptolemy XIII 6
Pythagoras 32, 70

Quaestor 9–12, 34
Quinctilius Varus, Publius 16–17
Quintilian 168

Raphia 90
Reate 6, 8, 197
Rectina 181
Rhetor 19–20
Rhinocorura 90
Rhodes 76, 171

Sabina, Poppaea 33
Sabinus (auxiliaryman) 124–125
Sabinus, Julius 169–170
Samos 171
Scopus 92–93
Scythopolis 52, 55, 62
Sea of Galilee 39, 55–56, 58–59
Seleucia 39
Senate 5–6, 9–10, 12–13, 18, 22, 34, 70–71, 73–76, 81, 86, 148, 153–154, 157, 163, 172–173, 191, 198–200, 202–203
Sepphoris 39, 44–45, 55

Serapis 86, 185
Servilia Sorana, Marcia 30
Sesterces 174
Severus, Sulpicius 134
Sicarii 67, 77, 159–162
Sigo 39
Silva, Flavius 160–161
Simeon, son of Gamaliel 65
Simon bar Kokhba 203
Simon, son of Gioras 77–80, 88–89, 92, 97, 99, 101, 103, 106–107, 110–113, 115–117, 120, 122, 125, 133, 138, 140–142, 145, 148, 150–151
Sinai Peninsula 90
Soaemus of Emesa 44
Sogane 39
Soranus, Barea 30
Sporus 33, 70, 73
Stabiae 182–183
Strigiles 190
Struthion Pool 116
Suetonius (author) 2–3, 8, 12–13, 18, 23, 26, 57, 71, 74, 77, 86, 153–154, 165–167, 169, 172–173, 186, 192–193, 196, 199
Syria 38, 42, 44, 59, 61, 83, 87, 106, 119, 121, 137, 146, 150, 159, 187, 203

Tacitus 2, 25–26, 33–34, 86, 90, 97, 143, 180
Talassius 28
Tanis 90
Tarichaea 39, 55–59
Tarquinius Superbus 4
temple, Jewish 2, 11, 35, 37–38, 65–66, 76, 78, 88, 96–99, 111, 121–122, 125–139, 141, 149, 151–152, 154, 157, 186, 204
Templum Pacis 151
Tepidarium 190
Tertulla 8
Tertulla, Arrecina 27–29
Testudo 123
Thamna 72
Tiber River 86, 174, 192
Tiberias 39, 55–56, 59
Tiberius (Emperor) 10, 41
Titus (Emperor): Aedileship 35; Amphitheatrum/Colosseum 1, 154–157, 171, 177, 187–189, 192, 200; Antioch, trips to 146–147; Apis, sacrifice to 147; Apotheosis 199; aqueducts, repaired 190–191; Baths of Titus 177, 189–190; Berenice 36, 45, 53, 62, 76, 83, 90, 143, 145, 168–169, 178, 198, 204; Berytus, trip to 146; Boudica revolt 1, 24–27; Britannicus, friends with 1, 19–20, 177, 192, 205; Caecina, execution of 170, 198; censorship 3, 162–164, 172; childhood 12–21; Christians, attitudes toward the 175; commander, Jewish War 87–143; consulship, first 87; consulship, second 157; consulship, third 162; consulship, fourth 168; consulship, fifth 168; consulship, sixth 168; consulship, seventh 170; consulship, eighth 184; death 197–198; Domitian, relations with 87, 145, 148, 150, 173, 192, 196–200; education 17–21; emperor, tenure as 173–198; Eprius, execution of 170, 198; Fire of Rome, response to the 84–86; funeral 199; Gabara, sacking of 45–46; Galba, trip to visit 74, 76; Gamala, siege of 59–61; Gischala, sacking of 62–65; Imperium 153; Japha, sacking of 49–50; Jerusalem, siege of 1, 91–143, 204–205; Josephus, relations with 52, 84, 97, 114, 120, 143, 148, 177; Jotapata, siege of 46–53; Kidron, battle of 93–94; Legate, Jewish War 42–64, 67–69, 72–79; marriage to Arrecina Tertulla 27–29; marriage to Marcia Furnilla 30–31; monetary policy 177; Mucianus, friendship with 59–62, 83, 168; 100-days of games 1, 4, 192–197, 205; Paphian Venus, sacrifice to 76; Parthians, interaction with the 145–146; Plague, response to the 1, 186; Praetorian Guard Prefect 165–169; Quaestorship 34; reforms 175–177; Tarichaea 39, 55–59; temple, destruction of 134–136; *Tribunicia potestas* 153; *tribunus laticlavius* 23; Triumph 148–150; Vesuvius eruption, response to the 184–185; Vigintivirate 23; Year of the Four Emperors, Titus' role in the 74, 76, 82–87; Zeugma, trip to 146
Tivoli 156
Toga picta 148
Toga praetexta 13
tomb of John Hyrcanus 101, 110, 116
Trachian Cilicia 171
Traianus, Marcus Ulpius 49–50, 57, 72, 175
Trajan (Emperor) 1, 49, 203

Tribune 9–10, 12, 23, 27, 34, 44, 91, 128
Tribunicia potestas 153
Tribunus laticlavius 23
triumph 3–4, 26, 141–143, 145–151, 153, 200, 205
Tunica palmata 149

urine tax 153, 163

Valerianus 55
Verginius Rufus, Lucius 71–73
Verulamium 24
Verus 194
Vespasian (Emperor) 1–4, 8–13, 16–20, 23, 27, 29–30, 32–35, 41–62, 64, 67–74, 76–78, 80–87, 89, 92, 101, 145–146, 148–166, 168–175, 177–179, 187, 191–192, 199–201, 205
Vesuvius 1, 4, 180–184, 186, 205
Vigiles 15, 33, 185
Vigintivirate 9–10, 23
Vindex, Gaius Julius 70–73

Virgil 19
Vitellius 8, 74–78, 80–87, 89, 154, 165–167
Vologases 146

Western Wall 142

zealots 65–67, 77, 96, 103, 110, 123
Zeugma 146

www.ingramcontent.com/pod-product-compliance
Lightning Source LLC
Chambersburg PA
CBHW060341010526

44117CB00017B/2917